ECCLESIASTES, SONG OF SONGS

THE NIV
APPLICATION
COMMENTARY

From biblical text . . . to contemporary life

THE NIV APPLICATION COMMENTARY SERIES

EDITORIAL BOARD

General Editor
Terry Muck

Consulting Editors
Old Testament

Tremper Longman III   *Robert Hubbard*
John H. Walton   *Andrew Dearman*

Zondervan Editorial Advisors

Stanley N. Gundry
Vice President and Editor-in-Chief

Jack Kuhatschek   *Verlyn Verbrugge*
Senior Acquisitions Editor   Senior Editor

THE NIV
APPLICATION
COMMENTARY

From biblical text . . . to contemporary life

IAIN PROVAN

ZONDERVAN.com/
AUTHORTRACKER
follow your favorite authors

The NIV Application Commentary: Ecclesiastes, Song of Songs
Copyright © 2001 by Iain Provan

Requests for information should be addressed to:

Zondervan, *Grand Rapids, Michigan 49530*

Library of Congress Cataloging-in-Publication Data

Provan, Iain W.(Iain William)
     Ecclesiastes, Song of Songs / Iain Provan.
        p. cm.—(NIV application commentary)
     Includes bibliographical references and indexes.
     ISBN-10: 0-310-21372-x
     ISBN-13: 978-0-310-21372-7
     1. Bible. O.T. Ecclesiastes—Commentaries. 2. Bible. O.T. Song of Songs—
Commentaries. I. Title. II. Series.
     BS 1475.53 .P76 2001
     223'.8077—dc21

                                                00–051293
                                              CIP

This edition printed on acid-free paper.

Printed in the United States of America

07 08 09 10 11 12 13 14 • 16 15 14 13 12 11 10 9 8 7

For Lynette, Andrew, Kirsty, Duncan, and Catherine

Contents

The NIV Application Commentary Series

When complete, the NIV Application Commentary
will include the following volumes:

Old Testament Volumes

Genesis, John H. Walton

Exodus, Peter Enns

Leviticus/Numbers, Roy Gane

Deuteronomy, Daniel I. Block

Joshua, Robert L. Hubbard Jr.

Judges/Ruth, K. Lawson Younger

1-2 Samuel, Bill T. Arnold

1-2 Kings, Gus Konkel

1-2 Chronicles, Andrew E. Hill

Ezra/Nehemiah, Douglas J. Green

Esther, Karen H. Jobes

Job, Dennis R. Magary

Psalms Volume 1, Gerald H. Wilson

Psalms Volume 2, Jamie A. Grant

Proverbs, Paul Koptak

Ecclesiastes/Song of Songs, Iain Provan

Isaiah, John N. Oswalt

Jeremiah/Lamentations, J. Andrew Dearman

Ezekiel, Iain M. Duguid

Daniel, Tremper Longman III

Hosea/Amos/Micah, Gary V. Smith

Jonah/Nahum/Habakkuk/Zephaniah,
   James Bruckner

Joel/Obadiah/Malachi, David W. Baker

Haggai/Zechariah, Mark J. Boda

New Testament Volumes

Matthew, Michael J. Wilkins

Mark, David E. Garland

Luke, Darrell L. Bock

John, Gary M. Burge

Acts, Ajith Fernando

Romans, Douglas J. Moo

1 Corinthians, Craig Blomberg

2 Corinthians, Scott Hafemann

Galatians, Scot McKnight

Ephesians, Klyne Snodgrass

Philippians, Frank Thielman

Colossians/Philemon, David E. Garland

1-2 Thessalonians, Michael W. Holmes

1-2 Timothy/Titus, Walter L. Liefeld

Hebrews, George H. Guthrie

James, David P. Nystrom

1 Peter, Scot McKnight

2 Peter/Jude, Douglas J. Moo

Letters of John, Gary M. Burge

Revelation, Craig S. Keener

To see which titles are available,
visit our web site at www.zondervan.com

NIV Application Commentary
Series Introduction

THE NIV APPLICATION COMMENTARY SERIES is unique. Most commentaries help us make the journey from our world back to the world of the Bible. They enable us to cross the barriers of time, culture, language, and geography that separate us from the biblical world. Yet they only offer a one-way ticket to the past and assume that we can somehow make the return journey on our own. Once they have explained the *original meaning* of a book or passage, these commentaries give us little or no help in exploring its *contemporary significance*. The information they offer is valuable, but the job is only half done.

Recently, a few commentaries have included some contemporary application as *one* of their goals. Yet that application is often sketchy or moralistic, and some volumes sound more like printed sermons than commentaries.

The primary goal of the NIV Application Commentary Series is to help you with the difficult but vital task of bringing an ancient message into a modern context. The series not only focuses on application as a finished product but also helps you think through the *process* of moving from the original meaning of a passage to its contemporary significance. These are commentaries, not popular expositions. They are works of reference, not devotional literature.

The format of the series is designed to achieve the goals of the series. Each passage is treated in three sections: *Original Meaning, Bridging Contexts,* and *Contemporary Significance.*

THIS SECTION HELPS you understand the meaning of the biblical text in its original context. All of the elements of traditional exegesis—in concise form—are discussed here. These include the historical, literary, and cultural context of the passage. The authors discuss matters related to grammar and syntax and the meaning of biblical words.[1] They also seek to explore the main ideas of the passage and how the biblical author develops those ideas.

---

1. Please note that in general, when the authors discuss words in the original biblical languages, the series uses a general rather than a scholarly method of transliteration.

After reading this section, you will understand the problems, questions, and concerns of the *original audience* and how the biblical author addressed those issues. This understanding is foundational to any legitimate application of the text today.

THIS SECTION BUILDS a bridge between the world of the Bible and the world of today, between the original context and the contemporary context, by focusing on both the timely and timeless aspects of the text.

God's Word is *timely*. The authors of Scripture spoke to specific situations, problems, and questions. The author of Joshua encouraged the faith of his original readers by narrating the destruction of Jericho, a seemingly impregnable city, at the hands of an angry warrior God (Josh. 6). Paul warned the Galatians about the consequences of circumcision and the dangers of trying to be justified by law (Gal. 5:2–5). The author of Hebrews tried to convince his readers that Christ is superior to Moses, the Aaronic priests, and the Old Testament sacrifices. John urged his readers to "test the spirits" of those who taught a form of incipient Gnosticism (1 John 4:1–6). In each of these cases, the timely nature of Scripture enables us to hear God's Word in situations that were *concrete* rather than abstract.

Yet the timely nature of Scripture also creates problems. Our situations, difficulties, and questions are not always directly related to those faced by the people in the Bible. Therefore, God's word to them does not always seem relevant to us. For example, when was the last time someone urged you to be circumcised, claiming that it was a necessary part of justification? How many people today care whether Christ is superior to the Aaronic priests? And how can a "test" designed to expose incipient Gnosticism be of any value in a modern culture?

Fortunately, Scripture is not only timely but *timeless*. Just as God spoke to the original audience, so he still speaks to us through the pages of Scripture. Because we share a common humanity with the people of the Bible, we discover a *universal dimension* in the problems they faced and the solutions God gave them. The timeless nature of Scripture enables it to speak with power in every time and in every culture.

Those who fail to recognize that Scripture is both timely and timeless run into a host of problems. For example, those who are intimidated by timely books such as Hebrews, Galatians, or Deuteronomy might avoid reading them because they seem meaningless today. At the other extreme, those who are convinced of the timeless nature of Scripture, but who fail to discern its timely element, may "wax eloquent" about the Melchizedekian priesthood to a sleeping congregation, or worse still, try to apply the holy wars of the Old Testament in a physical way to God's enemies today.

The purpose of this section, therefore, is to help you discern what is timeless in the timely pages of the Bible—and what is not. For example, how do the holy wars of the Old Testament relate to the spiritual warfare of the New? If Paul's primary concern is not circumcision (as he tells us in Gal. 5:6), what *is* he concerned about? If discussions about the Aaronic priesthood or Melchizedek seem irrelevant today, what is of abiding value in these passages? If people try to "test the spirits" today with a test designed for a specific first-century heresy, what other biblical test might be more appropriate?

Yet this section does not merely uncover that which is timeless in a passage but also helps you to see *how* it is uncovered. The authors of the commentaries seek to take what is implicit in the text and make it explicit, to take a process that normally is intuitive and explain it in a logical, orderly fashion. How do we know that circumcision is not Paul's primary concern? What clues in the text or its context help us realize that Paul's real concern is at a deeper level?

Of course, those passages in which the historical distance between us and the original readers is greatest require a longer treatment. Conversely, those passages in which the historical distance is smaller or seemingly nonexistent require less attention.

One final clarification. Because this section prepares the way for discussing the contemporary significance of the passage, there is not always a sharp distinction or a clear break between this section and the one that follows. Yet when both sections are read together, you should have a strong sense of moving from the world of the Bible to the world of today.

THIS SECTION ALLOWS the biblical message to speak with as much power today as it did when it was first written. How can you apply what you learned about Jerusalem, Ephesus, or Corinth to our present-day needs in Chicago, Los Angeles, or London? How can you take a message originally spoken in Greek, Hebrew, and Aramaic and communicate it clearly in our own language? How can you take the eternal truths originally spoken in a different time and culture and apply them to the similar-yet-different needs of our culture?

In order to achieve these goals, this section gives you help in several key areas.

(1) It helps you identify contemporary situations, problems, or questions that are truly comparable to those faced by the original audience. Because

contemporary situations are seldom identical to those faced by the original audience, you must seek situations that are analogous if your applications are to be relevant.

(2) This section explores a variety of contexts in which the passage might be applied today. You will look at personal applications, but you will also be encouraged to think beyond private concerns to the society and culture at large.

(3) This section will alert you to any problems or difficulties you might encounter in seeking to apply the passage. And if there are several legitimate ways to apply a passage (areas in which Christians disagree), the author will bring these to your attention and help you think through the issues involved.

In seeking to achieve these goals, the contributors to this series attempt to avoid two extremes. They avoid making such specific applications that the commentary might quickly become dated. They also avoid discussing the significance of the passage in such a general way that it fails to engage contemporary life and culture.

Above all, contributors to this series have made a diligent effort not to sound moralistic or preachy. The NIV Application Commentary Series does not seek to provide ready-made sermon materials but rather tools, ideas, and insights that will help you communicate God's Word with power. If we help you to achieve that goal, then we have fulfilled the purpose for this series.

The Editors

General Editor's Preface

HERMAN MELVILLE, in *Moby Dick*, said that "the truest of all books is Solomon's and Ecclesiastes is the fine hammered steel of woe." The Song of Songs has garnered similar "critical" acclaim. Iain Provan, the author of this fine commentary, agrees, although he doesn't sugarcoat the exegetical task: "Ecclesiastes is a difficult book."

Why is Ecclesiastes so difficult? The language is difficult, the book is filled with word plays, the argument is complex, it doesn't mention other major biblical figures like Abraham, Isaac, and Jacob, and it doesn't refer to any of God's dealings with Israel. Its themes, other commentators have said, border on contradictions, heresies, and licentiousness. It is a difficult book because when compared with the rest of the Old Testament books, it is different.

So too with the Song of Songs. An erotic love song, even if its ultimate meaning is an extended metaphor of God's love for Israel and/or the church and vice versa, does not lend itself easily to division into pericopes and word studies. On a human level, it seems almost too explicit for our sensitivities.

So what can we learn from these unusual pieces of writing? According to Iain Provan, these two book are in fact *not* filled with contradictions, heresies, and licentiousness. Rather, as he so ably points out, they reveal truth in ways different from historical and prophetic literature.

Consider the authorship of Ecclesiastes. In truth, we do not know who the author is. The book effectively veils the writer's identity so that we are forced to focus on the content. This pattern was typical of ancient Near Eastern literature, where it was commonplace to write anonymously. Conversely, in the Greek pattern, the author usually proudly proclaimed his or her identity—a pattern still evident today. We therefore have difficulty digesting or paying attention to an idea unless it is personified in a personality. Perhaps one lesson we need to learn is that ideas don't always need personality.

Consider another example: The text of Ecclesiastes is filled with what appear to be contradictions. In one place pleasure is condemned ("What does pleasure accomplish?" 2:2) and in another place endorsed ("I commend the enjoyment of life," 8:15). Two theories have regularly been put forth to try to explain these contradictions. According to the quotation theory, the author of Ecclesiastes quotes people he does not agree with in order to highlight his own view. The addition theory, by contrast, maintains that a later editor added material in order to "correct" the author's view. But an even better explanation is that by the juxtapositioning of these simple though contrasting statements, the author reveals a deeper truth on the subject—revelation through comparison and paradox.

Or consider a third example: The tone of Ecclesiastes is often seen as gloomy. Perhaps the most well-known and oft-quoted verse in the whole text is 1:2 ("Everything is meaningless"), although 12:7 ("The dust will return to the ground it came from") will win no happy-face awards. Note what Professor Provan says: "The emphasis [in 1:2] lies on the passing nature of existence and on its elusiveness and resistance to human and physical control." It is true that death is a frequent topic in Ecclesiastes. Yet one does not come away from reading this book seeing death as victor. On the contrary,. it is obvious that life is the theme—more specifically, the life we have in God. Such life, Qohelet seems to say, can only be fully enjoyed in the context of human death and futility.

Finally, a fourth example: What better way to gain an appreciation for the inexhaustible love of God than by comparing it to human love? By telling a love story with explicit imagery of love, the author of the Song of Songs points us beyond human love to God's love. This can be dangerous because human love, like everything else human, is tainted by the Fall, and as such is open to abuse. Yet one cannot come away from reading the Song of Songs without a deepened appreciation for God's passionate providence for us.

We live in a paradoxical age. It is a time of unparalleled discovery and knowledge. Science has made it possible for us to approach the distant stars and the microscopic atom. We know more than our ancestors could have ever dreamed. Yet somehow we don't seem to understand the many facts of our existence with any more alacrity than our ancestors understood the far fewer number of facts they had at their fingertips. Nevertheless, when all is said and done, these two books encourage us to fall at the feet of God and find out meaning in life through him.

Author's Preface

I AGREED TO WRITE this book in 1996, when my life was relatively uncomplicated. The invitation to write a commentary focused on the application of Scripture, yet dealing with two Old Testament books that in many ways are among the more challenging of the Scriptures as they address the modern church, was simply too tempting. I have since moved halfway across the world to a new country, and I have changed the context in which I am teaching Bible.

This disruption has proved both helpful and unhelpful to the project. On the one hand, I have had less time than I would have liked to complete the work. The deficiencies of the book that have arisen from this fact will be obvious at least to some. On the other hand, I have had my thinking helpfully unsettled and challenged—part of a long process that has lasted many years and has affected my understanding of myself, the Christian faith and life, and the world around me. One result is that I believe (rightly or wrongly!) that I understand both Ecclesiastes and Song of Songs better than before, and I see more clearly what they have to say as Christian Scripture to both church and world. We shall see . . .

I need to thank some people for their input and support. The exercise of leading a men's Bible study on these two books in 1998–1999 in Surrey, British Columbia, was valuable as preparation for the task of writing. I therefore want to express my appreciation to Dieter Glups and his circle for their part in the process (and also for the front-row seats to the Grizzlies/Lakers game!). The Board of Regent College granted me research leave, and Ivan Gaetz and Charles Bellinger of the Regent College library gave great research support and bibliographical help. My teaching assistant Sungmin Min Chun did an outstanding job in offering all kinds of help, especially in his thorough and careful proofreading of the final drafts and his preparation of the Scripture index. He operated well above and beyond the call of duty throughout, and I am deeply grateful to him and to Rick Reed, who offered valuable help with the subject index.

Above all I want to thank my family, with whom I have learned, often painfully, what it means to be a Christian and a human being at the same time. If Ecclesiastes and Song of Songs are about anything, as Christian Scripture, they are about this, and my ability to write coherently about these books (if I have succeeded in doing so) arises in the first instance from my pilgrimage with this small band of travelers. The commentary is therefore dedicated to them, with deep love and affection.

Iain Provan
December 1999

17

Abbreviations

AB	Anchor Bible
AnBib	Analecta biblica
ANET	*Ancient Near Eastern Texts Relating to the Old Testament* (J. B. Pritchard, ed., 3d ed. [Princeton: Princeton Univ. Press, 1969])
AUSS	*Andrews University Seminary Studies*
b. Šab.	Babylonian Talmud *Shabbat*
BDB	F. Brown, S. R. Driver, and C. A. Briggs, *A Hebrew and English Lexicon of the Old Testament* (Oxford: Clarendon, 1959)
BETL	Bibliotheca ephemeridum theologicarum lovaniensium
Bib	*Biblica*
BibInt	*Biblical Interpretation*
BibIntS	Biblical Interpretation Series
BJL	The Bible of Judaism Library
BL	Bible and Literature Series
BSac	*Bibliotheca Sacra*
BSem	Biblical Seminar
BST	The Bible Speaks Today
BT	*The Bible Translator*
BTB	*Biblical Theology Bulletin*
CBC	Cambridge Bible Commentary
CBQ	*Catholic Biblical Quarterly*
CBS	Classic Bible Series
CDRSQ	Geoffrey Parrinder, ed., *Collins Dictionary of Religious and Spiritual Quotations*
CFS	Cistercian Fathers Series
CR:BS	*Currents in Research: Biblical Studies*
CSS	Cistercian Studies Series
CT	*Christianity Today*
CTR	*Criswell Theological Review*
DSBOT	The Daily Study Bible—Old Testament
esp.	especially
EvQ	*Evangelical Quarterly*
ExpTim	*Expository Times*
FS	Festschrift
Gk.	Greek

Abbreviations

GKC	W. Gesenius, *Gesenius' Hebrew Grammar*, E. Kautzsch, ed., A. E. Cowley, ed. and trans. (Oxford: Clarendon, 1910)
HAR	*Hebrew Annual Review*
Heb.	Hebrew
HTR	*Harvard Theological Review*
ICC	International Critical Commentary
ITC	International Theological Commentary
JBL	*Journal of Biblical Literature*
JETS	*Journal of the Evangelical Theological Society*
JQR	*Jewish Quarterly Review*
JSOT	*Journal for the Study of the Old Testament*
JSOTSup	JSOT Supplement Series
JSS	*Journal of Semitic Studies*
KJV	King James Version
KPG	Knox Preaching Guides
lit.	literally
LQ	*Lutheran Quarterly*
LXX	Septuagint
m. ʿEd.	Mishnah *ʿEduyyot*
m. Qidd	Mishnah *Qiddushin*
m. Yad.	Mishnah *Yadaim*
MBPS	Mellen Biblical Press Series
ms(s)	manuscript(s)
MT	Masoretic text
NAC	New American Commentary
NASB	New American Standard Bible
NCB	New Century Bible
NE	Near East
NEB	New English Bible
NIBC	New International Biblical Commentary
NICOT	New International Commentary on the Old Testament
NIV	New International Version
NRSV	New Revised Standard Version
OBT	Overtures to Biblical Theology
OTG	Old Testament Guides
OTL	Old Testament Library
OTM	Old Testament Message
PCC	Pilgrim Classic Commentaries
PSB	*Princeton Seminary Bulletin*
RA	*Revue d'assyriologie et d'archéologie orientale*
RNBC	Readings, a New Biblical Commentary

RTR	*Reformed Theological Review*
SJOT	*Scandinavian Journal of the Old Testament*
SR	*Studies in Religion*
StudBL	Studies in Biblical Literature
Syr.	Syriac
t. Sanh.	Talmud *Sanhedrin*
TBC	Torch Bible Commentaries
TOTC	Tyndale Old Testament Commentaries
TSJTSA	Texts and Studies of the Jewish Theological Seminary of America
TynBul	*Tyndale Bulletin*
VT	*Vetus Testamentum*
VTS	Vetus Testamentum Supplements
Vulg.	Vulgate
WBC	Word Biblical Commentary
ZAW	*Zeitschrift für die Alttestamentliche Wissenschaft*

Introduction to Ecclesiastes

IS BEST TO BE FRANK from the outset: Ecclesiastes is a difficult book. It is written in a form of Hebrew different from much of the remainder of the Old Testament, and it regularly challenges the reader of the original as to grammar and syntax. The interpretation even of words that occur frequently in the book is often unclear and a matter of dispute, partly because there is frequent wordplay in the course of the argument. The argument is itself complex and sometimes puzzling and has often provoked the charge of inconsistency or outright self-contradiction.

When considered in the larger context of the Old Testament, Ecclesiastes stands out as an unusual book whose connection with the main stream of biblical tradition seems tenuous. There is nothing here of Abraham, Isaac, and Jacob; of the Exodus; of God's special dealings with Israel in the Promised Land; or of prophetic hope in a great future. Instead we find ourselves apparently reading about the meaninglessness of life and the certainty of death, in a universe in which God is certainly present, but is distant and somewhat uninvolved. When considered in the context of the New Testament, the dissonance between Ecclesiastes and its scriptural context seems even greater, for if there is one thing that we do not find in this book, it is the joy of resurrection. Perhaps this is one reason why Ecclesiastes is seldom read or preached in modern churches.

The discomfort of the community of biblical faith with Ecclesiastes is not, however, a new phenomenon. From the very beginning it is evident that the nature of the book itself as authoritative Scripture was doubted by significant numbers of Jews. Two famous passages in the Mishnah,[1] echoed in the Talmud and in later Jewish writings, refer to disputes among the rabbis on precisely this point—whether or not Ecclesiastes "defiles the hands." They make clear that this issue divided the famous rabbinic schools of Hillel (which thought it did defile the hands) and Shammai (which thought it did not).

One of the main grounds of rabbinic difficulty clearly lay in the contradictions perceived in the book, which were felt to be unusually difficult to harmonize (e.g., 2:2 and 8:15, respectively questioning and commending Heb. śimḥa, "pleasure, joy"; 7:3 and 9, respectively commending and criticizing Heb. kaʿas, "anger, frustration").[2] This led to ongoing attempts throughout

---

1. m. Yad. 3:5; m. ʿEd. 5:3.

2. Thus b. Šab. 30b claims that "the sages sought to withdraw the book . . . because its words are mutually contradictory."

the succeeding centuries to offer readings of the book that satisfactorily and coherently accounted for all of its content.

Another concern was its perceived hedonistic tone, found in the frequent advice to "eat and drink and find satisfaction" (e.g., 2:24; 3:13). Connected with this is an alleged heretical tendency, insofar as the book questions, for example, whether there is any real profit to be made from life God has created (e.g., 1:3), and claims that there is nothing better than a life of eating, drinking, and enjoyment (e.g., 2:24; 8:15). The author particularly commends a licentious way of life to the young (11:9).[3] Our earliest commentaries on Ecclesiastes, whether Jewish or Christian, indicate just how uncomfortable such sentiments made many religious readers of the book feel, for they often avoided interpreting the text according to its plain sense when dealing with such troublesome passages, attempting to make it more "spiritual" than it otherwise appeared to them.

We are dealing here, then, with an unsettling book. Ecclesiastes has a long history of perturbation behind it. What is to be done with it? We might organize a campaign to remove it from the canon of Scripture, perhaps; but such a campaign would be unlikely to succeed, given the long-standing acceptance of the book by the church universal, and we ourselves with our new, slightly slimmer canon would stand in questionable relationship to this larger church. We should also require to ask ourselves questions about our view of its Founder and his first apostles, all of whom regarded the Old Testament Scriptures as foundational to Christian faith and life, and none of whom ever intended their sayings and writings to be understood outside the context of the Old Testament Scriptures.

A more popular alternative, adopted by many modern Christians, is to continue to accept Ecclesiastes in principle as part of the canon but to ignore it in practice. Whole areas of the modern church, indeed, seem to have adopted this strategy in respect of almost the entire Old Testament, in the mistaken belief that there exists something called "New Testament Christianity." To claim that Scriptures are authoritative, however, while in reality ignoring them, is to provoke serious questions about one's integrity.

A third possible response to our problematic book might be to find ways of reinterpreting what it has to say—perhaps by resorting to the kind of allegorical, spiritualizing approach to biblical interpretation that was so popular among ancient and medieval Christian commentators. As the long history of biblical interpretation has itself shown, however, this approach makes it simply too easy to force the text to say what one wishes it to say and thus

---

3. See R. Beckwith, *The Old Testament Canon of the New Testament Church, and Its Background in Early Judaism* (Grand Rapids: Eerdmans, 1985), 283–91, for some discussion.

simply to subvert its authority in a different way. Such an interpretative method may increase the reader's comfort level, but it can do great violence to the text.

When, for example, Jerome interprets Ecclesiastes as a treatise aiming "to show the utter vanity of *every* [my italics] sublunary enjoyment, and hence the necessity of betaking one's self to an *ascetic life* [my italics] devoted entirely to the service of God,"[4] it seems obvious to us (although presumably not to Jerome) that the text is not in control of Jerome, but Jerome of the text. His method of reading enabled him too easily to shape the text in his own image and disabled him from hearing anything in it that might challenge his own assumptions and beliefs.

What is to be done, instead, with Ecclesiastes? It is to be struggled with as an intrinsic part of the Scriptures. It is to be wrestled with in terms of its original meaning, with all its unusual grammar and syntax and with all its clever wordplays, as we seek to understand its parts in terms of the whole and to come to some understanding of its "contradictions" and "heresies" and "licentiousness." It is to be grappled with in its connectedness (or not) with the remainder of the Old Testament and in its advocacy of a joy that is not yet a fully biblical resurrection joy. This struggle with the text is to be engaged in with determination (which will be necessary), but not with fear or trepidation, for whatever the truth is that Ecclesiastes has to tell us in the context of biblical truth overall, Christian readers know that it will be truth that sets us free (John 8:32). Cherished beliefs that are found not to be true, by contrast, when examined by the searchlight of biblical truth, are not worth retaining and can do us no good if we insist on doing so.

Above all, then, Ecclesiastes is to be encountered with openness—openness to God and openness to change. For we must always consider the possibility, when we encounter a difficult biblical book, that the problem lies not with the book but with ourselves. The "difficulty" may be that the book speaks truly about reality while we are devoted to illusions. The "difficulty" may be that we are not too keen to embrace the truth, but prefer to embrace half-truths or lies.

There is, of course, no substitute for the verse-by-verse reading of the text, if one is truly to wrestle with it. There is some value, however, in attempting to summarize in advance some of the conclusions arising from this reading so that the reader of this commentary may possess something of a map for the journey. To this summarizing task we now turn.

---

4. Cited in G. A. Barton, *A Critical and Exegetical Commentary on the Book of Ecclesiastes* (ICC; Edinburgh: T. & T. Clark, 1908), 20.

Ecclesiastes in Historical Context

The Author and the Speaker

WHO WROTE THE book of Ecclesiastes, when did (s)he do it, and what did the author want to say? Ancient tradition held that Solomon, "son of David, king in Jerusalem" (1:1), was the author, writing in his weary old age. Although Solomon himself is never explicitly mentioned in the book (unlike the case in Prov. 1:1; 10:1; 25:1; Song 1:1), it is certainly true that his reign is evoked in numerous ways throughout its opening chapters (cf. Eccl. 1:12–2:11 especially with the account in 1 Kings 3–11).

Yet there are good reasons to believe that Solomon was not himself the author. Even in the "Solomonic" sections of the book, it seems evident from verses like 1:16 and 2:7, 9 that the "real" historical location of the speaker who refers to himself as "I" is at some distance from the era of Solomon. These verses imply numerous predecessors in Jerusalem, whereas Solomon had only one (David). It is not likely, moreover, that Solomon himself would tell us that he *was* king over Israel in Jerusalem (1:12), referring to his kingship in the past tense (as if there were a period in his life when he was functioning as a thinker but no longer as a king). Equally striking is that many of the later passages in Ecclesiastes appear to be written from a non-Solomonic point of view (i.e., from the perspective of the subject rather than the ruler, e.g., 5:8–9; 8:1–9).

We may add to all of this that the language of the book, taken as a whole, gives every indication of being later rather than earlier Hebrew—the language of the postexilic rather than the preexilic period.[5] Finally, a fairly obvious point should be made, namely, that the speaker in passages like 1:12–18 (the "I" who was king) should not be confused with the author of the book who reports the speaker's words and who refers to him in the third person as "he" (12:9–14; probably also at least 1:1; 7:27). Even if the speaker were Solomon (which he is probably not), the speaker is assuredly not the author of the book as it has been passed on to us. To claim otherwise would be a little like claiming that Jesus (the central and dominant "I"-speaker), and not John (who refers to Jesus as "he"), wrote John's Gospel.

Further examination of both author and speaker is thus in order. Little can be mooted about the anonymous author other than that he was probably a postexilic writer[6] who stood within the wisdom tradition of ancient Israel. The

---

5. See, e.g., M. V. Fox, *Qohelet and His Contradictions* (JSOTS 71; Sheffield: Almond, 1989), 154–55, for a brief discussion.

6. Scholarly debate continues as to the era that the language in particular points to. Most believe that we are dealing with a fourth to third century B.C. book, but an earlier dat-

balance of historical probability favors the view that he was male, although nothing explicitly said in 12:9–14 necessitates this view. He reports the words of the speaker because he values them as some of the "words of the wise" (12:11), addressing them (and his own final advice) to his "son" (12:12), whether literal or metaphorical (cf., e.g., 1 Kings 20:35; 2 Kings 2:3, 5, for Heb. *ben*, son, in the sense of disciple, follower).

We find a similar concern in the book of Proverbs (e.g., Prov. 1:8, 10; 2:1) that wisdom should be passed on (whether by father or mother) to the "son" and understood and lived out by him. Like Ecclesiastes (e.g., Eccl. 12:13), Proverbs is anxious to remind its readers that "the fear of the LORD" is the foundation of true wisdom and knowledge (e.g., Prov. 1:7, 29; 2:5; 3:7; 8:13; 9:10).

If little that is specific can be said about the author, what of the speaker? We learn from the author that he, too, stands within the same wisdom tradition, gathering and reflecting on proverbial wisdom and seeking to arrive at its proper interpretation (Eccl. 12:9–10). Beyond this it is difficult to proceed with any certainty. Part of the reason is that the speaker himself is evidently capable of taking on personae other than his own in reflecting on the nature of the universe and of mortal life. He explores reality "as if" he were Solomon in 1:12–2:26, for example, imaginatively reenacting Solomon's reign ("I . . . was king over Israel in Jerusalem") in order to facilitate those aspects of his exploration of "life under the sun" that require the experience of great wealth and power and wisdom. He "becomes" a king within the world of the text (takes on "the Solomonic guise"[7]), in order to persuade his hearers of truths about the world as it is confronted by the wealthy, the powerful, and the wise— among whose ranks certainly number kings like Solomon.

In due course in the book, the speaker ceases to act out this royal character from his script and moves on to explore dimensions of human life that do not require him to speak "as if" he were a king. Commentators have for some reason often imagined that in these later parts we may more certainly assume that the "real" speaker is to be found and that we may use the text in these places to reconstruct his actual social and historical context. It is far from clear, however, that simply because passages like 4:13–16; 9:13–16; and 10:16–17 describe situations in which kings are involved, our speaker must himself have lived in a time of kings (sayings about kings are common in wisdom literature) or indeed himself have experienced the situations he

---

ing retains adherents (e.g., C. L. Seow, *Ecclesiastes* (AB; New York: Doubleday, 1997), 11–21, who dates the book to the late fifth or early fourth century; and the doubtful response in a review by T. Longman III in *Bib* 80 (1999): 420–24, who wonders "whether the language of the book can prove to be a reliable guide to the date of the book."

7. The phrase is E. S. Christianson's, *A Time to Tell: Narrative Strategies in Ecclesiastes* (JSOTS 280; Sheffield: Sheffield Academic Press, 1998), 128–72.

describes. If he can imaginatively place himself in Solomon's time for the purposes of communicating his message, he can assuredly place himself imaginatively in other times as well, drawing in "cases" from here and there that contribute to his overall scheme.

Yet this obvious fact has apparently eluded those many who have written so confidently about the political, social, and economic context out of which the speaker's words arose, sometimes even mentioning specific historical events as the likely background to particular passages. The imagination of the commentator has not come near to reckoning with the imagination of the speaker.

Even the name or title that the speaker takes to himself conceals as much as it reveals. It is *qohelet* (1:12)—a feminine Qal participle from the verb *qhl*, which means "to assemble (as a group of people),"[8] and the word that gives the book of Ecclesiastes its Hebrew name *Qohelet*. The associated common noun *qahal* refers to a group of assembled people, most frequently to the people of Israel gathered together for war (e.g., Judg. 20:2) or for a specifically religious purpose such as listening to God's Word (e.g., Deut. 5:22) or worshiping (e.g., 2 Chron. 30:25). A *qohelet* was probably in origin a person who participated in—played an (unspecified) role in—an assembly (*qahal*). The Greek rendering of *qohelet* as *ekklesiastes* (from which we derive our English title for the book) captures this sense, for an *ekklesiastes* was a person who sat or spoke in an *ekklesia* (an assembly of local citizens).

The question is this: Is *qohelet* in 1:12, as well as in 1:1–2; 7:27; 12:9–10 (where it is either certainly or probably used by the author, referring to the speaker in the third person), likewise intended simply to be understood as referring to the role of the speaker in addressing the readers—most likely, in the biblical context, to be understood as all Israel gathered together in assembly? Or is it intended to be understood as a proper name (as *soperet*, originally "scribe," has apparently become in Neh. 7:57; and as roles throughout history have characteristically in due course become names, as in the case of the common English name "Smith," which originally refers to an occupation)? The term *qohelet* is entirely ambiguous. Despite what may at first be thought, the author does not help us to resolve the ambiguity in his usage of *qohelet* with the definite article in 12:8 (*haqqohelet*), for the proper name *soperet* itself appears in variant form as *hassoperet* in Ezra 2:55.

The author is indeed complicit in the veiling of the speaker behind the words in the main part of the book. He himself affirms in 1:1 the fiction of

---

8. The verb is always used in the Old Testament with reference to people, not things. It is therefore difficult to defend another popular line of interpretation throughout the centuries, which understands *qohelet* primarily to refer to the assembling or collecting of tradition, experience, or wisdom.

the opening chapters—that Qohelet (whoever or whatever this is) was "son of David, king in Jerusalem"—and in 12:9–14 he clarifies only what Qohelet did, not who he was.

In one respect, indeed, the author may be said to add to the veiling. The book as a whole claims or implies throughout, from 1:1 onwards, that the speaker is male. The world that provides the illustrations for the message of the book is indeed predominantly the male world (e.g., 4:13–16; 8:1–9; 9:13–18), and it is a book that envisages men as its primary audience (e.g., 9:9; 12:12). Consistent with this, the word *qohelet*, although a feminine participle, appears in virtually every place it is used alongside masculine verbs. The curiosity of this mixture of masculine and feminine forms is usually explained in terms of an occasional preference for the feminine gender in Hebrew when referring to someone's role, even where the subject is masculine.[9]

What is more difficult convincingly to explain is the occurrence in 7:26–27, at precisely a point where women are explicitly the focus of attention (albeit from a resolutely male point of view), of *qohelet* with a feminine verb (*ʾamᵉrah qohelet*). It is generally claimed that this curiosity is the result of erroneous word division by the scribes who passed the text on to us and that the original text read *ʾamar haqqohelet* (as in 12:8). Yet there is not a jot of actual evidence that this most convenient of explanations is correct, and it is not even plausible as a hypothesis: Are we really to believe that a scribe, presumably knowing that *qohelet* occurs elsewhere in Ecclesiastes with masculine verbs and that the variant *haqqohelet* appears in 12:8, would have made such an error, creating a wise woman where in context there had only previously been a loose one? It is much more likely that the Masoretic word division is the original one, which has survived in spite of the difficulties it has caused many readers.

Taken seriously as such, the authorial insertion in 7:27 introduces an element of doubt into our minds about the gender of the speaker, for it makes us ask just how far our firm conviction that he is male arises from the same source as the firm convictions held by others that he is Solomon or that he finished his book around 198 B.C.[10]—namely, a failure to distinguish the speaker as he appears (in different guises) in the text from the speaker as he may truly and historically have been in reality.

The fact of the matter is that Qohelet is all but completely veiled behind the text of Ecclesiastes, subsumed by "his" words. (The) *qohelet* addresses the gathered readers/listeners, the Israelites, but all the emphasis falls on the words, not the speaker. There is no good reason to doubt that he existed and

---

9. See GKC, §122 p-r.
10. This is the view, e.g., of Barton, *Ecclesiastes*, 58–65.

worked just as the author who quotes his words asserts to us (12:9–10); it would be curious to receive the speaker's words from this author and yet reject his rather clear testimony about their originator.

It is clearly what the speaker *said*, however, not who he was or even when he said it, that this author wants us to understand. For this reason it is difficult to agree with the assertion that Ecclesiastes occupies the literary middle ground somewhere between ancient Near Eastern literature (including earlier biblical literature), whose canons required that the personality as well as the name of an author should remain concealed, and Greek literature, whose authors tended to proclaim their identity.[11] The words dominate in Ecclesiastes even as the "I" speaks them, and in that sense Ecclesiastes is much like other books in the Old Testament, whose originators have taken great pains to retreat behind the words and to erase their footsteps.

It is one of the great ironies of modern biblical scholarship (of whatever theological and confessional complexion) that what the originators of Old Testament tradition have thus themselves pronounced unimportant about the text, its modern readers have pronounced crucial for its understanding, expending enormous and futile effort in an attempt to trace the erased footsteps across the sands of time and exhume their alleged owners' corpses from their self-sealed tombs.

It is important, nonetheless, if only so that we can get on with writing about Ecclesiastes without endless qualifications and parentheses, that we refer to the producers of the words in the book by some agreed conventions. Following recent custom, therefore, we will refer in what follows to Qohelet (with a capital Q, yet not necessarily indicating a proper name) when referring to the speaker of most of the words. As we have already done in this Introduction, however, we will refer to the person who has passed on Qohelet's words to us as the "author," rather than as the "editor" or the "epilogist" (two common alternatives). The latter might give the impression that the role of the writer visible to us in 12:9–14 is limited to peripheral tinkering with an already preexisting book that passed, somehow, across his or her editorial desk.

This is, in fact, what many modern commentators have thought (albeit arguing among themselves about the extent of the tinkering). The fact of the matter is, however, that we know of no book of Ecclesiastes other than the one we have received from the hand of the writer of 12:9–14, and we possess no evidence that such a book ever existed. We possess only this writer's version of what Qohelet had to say, in which his own and Qohelet's words flow seamlessly together (as in 1:1–12, e.g., where we move gently from

---

11. R. N. Whybray, *Ecclesiastes* (NCB; London: Marshall, Morgan and Scott, 1989), 6.

third person to first without quite being sure of where the "join" is; or 7:26–27, where we are suddenly reminded that Qohelet's words are indeed being quoted to us by someone else). The term "author" is used to keep us mindful of such things.

The Message

WHAT WAS THE author of the book intent on saying? Was he saying much the same as Qohelet? From the earliest times, as we have seen, readers of Ecclesiastes were aware of the complex nature of the book, indeed of the "contradictions" in it, which for some of them (in combination with other perplexing aspects of the book) raised questions about its scriptural authority. Those who accepted its scriptural nature often tended to resort to a spiritualizing or allegorizing approach in addressing the problem. The perceived lack of a coherent message was, to all, religiously problematic in a book inspired by God.

In modern times marked by impatience with spiritualizing and allegorizing, on the one hand, and a more literal and historical mindset, on the other, this same perception of incoherence has issued in various attempts to account for the complexity of the book in terms of the alleged stages by which it was composed. The two broad theories that have attracted most support may be referred to as the "quotation theory" and the "addition theory."

(1) The *quotation theory* holds that in the course of his argument Qohelet often quotes material with whose opinions he does not himself agree. He reproduces what is termed "traditional wisdom" only in order then to refute it. Verses like 2:16 and 9:10 were already regarded as quotations—what the "people" say—in earlier times (by the Targum and Ibn Ezra respectively). The quotation approach simply builds on these early beginnings, identifying greater or lesser numbers of citations in the text, sometimes to the extent of viewing the overall genre of the book as a dialogue between a master and his students or between two schools of thought. In this way Qohelet's own thoughts can be distinguished from other, earlier material in the book and a coherent picture of his own philosophy attained.

The difficulty with this method of approaching the text, however, is to identify satisfactory criteria for identifying the proverbial wisdom with which Qohelet is thought to disagree. That he is interacting with such wisdom is clear enough—the epilogue to the book itself tells us this (12:9–10)—and we frequently find in its main part sayings lacking the truly distinctive marks of Qohelet's writing, which could comfortably be accommodated within a book like Proverbs and which may well therefore be preexisting proverbs that Qohelet picks up and uses (e.g., 2:14; 4:5). That he often offers further comment on such proverbial wisdom, exploring how far it is true and where its limitations lie, is also implied in the epilogue (12:9, where Qohelet is said to have examined the proverbs thoroughly and have arrived at just the right interpretation) and evidenced in the main text (e.g., 2:14a, followed by 2:14b–16).

Yet there is no obvious reason even in these cases why we should believe that Qohelet completely disagrees with the wisdom he is citing, rather than embracing it while offering a qualification of it, nor indeed that this wisdom itself was ever intended *by its original authors* to be accepted without any kind of qualification. There is even less reason to believe these things in cases where Qohelet himself does not offer any explicit comment on a proverbial saying but simply juxtaposes material so that we may reflect on the totality together (e.g., 4:5 followed by 4:6). We are indeed justified in expecting that if disagreement were intended, Qohelet would have used recognized formulae to indicate this clearly in the text.[12]

The complexity of Ecclesiastes may well be diminished, then, by the ungrounded assumption that Qohelet rejects many of the ideas to which he gives expression, and the comfort level of the reader may perhaps be correspondingly and dramatically increased. Whether the "Qohelet" we are left with is anyone other than the product of our own limited imagination is, however, an important question.

(2) The *addition theory* holds that the explanation for the complexity of the book of Ecclesiastes lies in whole or in part, not in Qohelet's utilization of earlier wisdom material with which he does not agree, but in interpolation into Qohelet's text by a later editor or editors who were alarmed by the unorthodox nature of Qohelet's thinking and wished to neutralize its most troubling aspects. Verses like 4:5; 5:3; and whole sections of chapters 7 and 10 are often said on this view so to interrupt the argument of the book that they cannot have been put there by Qohelet himself, but must have been added by an editor interested in wisdom literature. In the same way verses like 2:26; 3:17; and 8:2b, 3a, 5, 6a, 11–13 interrupt or contradict the main teachings of the book and must derive (it is said) from the hand of a Jewish orthodox glossator whose worldview was similar to the Pharisees and who wished to find support in a work of Solomon for orthodox religion.

Despite its popularity among modern commentators, however, the addition theory is implausible. We are apparently to believe that editors who fundamentally disagreed with the book's sentiments nevertheless copied it, only lightly editing it as they went, and passed it on to later generations, rather than simply suppressing or ignoring it. We are to believe this in the

---

12. M. V. Fox, "The Identification of Quotations in Biblical Literature," *ZAW* 92 (1980): 416–31.

complete absence of any convincing demonstration, across the whole breadth of the book, of the grounds for the belief—other than alleged inconsistency with Qohelet's "real" thought (which is arbitrarily determined by focusing on some parts of Ecclesiastes rather than others)—and in the knowledge that the allegedly "secondary" material is often so closely linked syntactically to its context as to defy removal.

We are to believe it, further, even though the putative additions make little sense as additions designed to correct Qohelet, being in placement and content poorly designed for the task, and even though their removal does not in any case result in the completely "consistent" argument for which the theorists are searching. We are to believe it, finally, even though the only early character whom we actually know to have transmitted Qohelet's words, and who speaks about them in 12:9–10, makes clear to us that he did so because he *valued* them—and this indeed is the obvious reason that someone would transmit them.[13]

It is, frankly, difficult in all the circumstances to believe in these hypothetical editors, although many commentators have done so. These commentators too have managed by such means to arrive at a less complex Qohelet than the one presented to us in the text; but he is not likely to be a Qohelet who ever existed, even in the mind of the author of Ecclesiastes. It is one of the ironies of modern interpretation of Ecclesiastes, indeed, that while quotation and addition theorists have often looked critically and condescendingly on earlier exegetes whom they have characterized as "precritical" in their allegorizing and spiritualizing of the text and have accused them of fantasy in their reading of it, these theorists too have by means of their theorizing managed no less than their predecessors to make the text say just what they wanted it to say.

One of the intriguing questions about this whole discussion of contradiction, quotation, and addition is why, in the first place, we should expect Qohelet or the book of Ecclesiastes as a whole to be less than complex. It is a book that grapples with reality, and reality is complex. Should the words of a wise man about reality not be difficult to simplify? After all,

---

13. I cannot myself see that 12:8–12 offers an evaluation of Qohelet's teaching "which begins with praise and then moves to doubt and finally to criticism" (so T. Longman III, *The Book of Ecclesiastes* [NICOT; Grand Rapids: Eerdmans, 1998], 38), nor do I find it generally plausible that Qohelet's voluminous words would be cited in full just so that the author of 12:8–12 could append a few comments allegedly doubting and criticizing them (and even then not managing to do so clearly). The wisdom of a wise man who thus so spectacularly shot himself in the foot would surely be in doubt. If the genre of the book may rightly be described as a "framed wisdom autobiography" (ibid., 15–20), then I cannot agree that the "frame" intends somehow to correct or relativize the message of the autobiography. See further A. G. Shead, "Reading Ecclesiastes 'Epilogically,'" *TynBul* 48 (1997): 67–91.

The well-bred contradict other people. The wise contradict themselves.[14]

Yet commentator after commentator has agonized over the book as if it,
rather than they, had a problem, because it is resistant to linear, systematic
treatment. This has particularly been the case in the last two centuries, as
commentators influenced by positivistic science in general and by Darwin-
ian social evolutionary theory in particular have come to share a narrow view
of reality in general and of Israel's past in particular. This is a world of logical black and white and of linear progress or regress in ideas. It is a world of
hermetically sealed entities like "traditional wisdom teaching" or "deutero-
nomic schools," whose adherents apparently only and always hold fully and
consistently to their own stated beliefs and views, and who are constantly
looking to subvert, undermine, and suppress those who disagree with them
and to win the argument.

Complexity in such a world is a sure sign that things that should be separate have become confused, probably deliberately and with ideological purpose—a sign that one idea is in truth earlier or later than another, or at least
from a different intellectual stable than another. Thus is the (apparently)
ideal world of the modern scholar superimposed not only on the real and
messy world of the present, but also on the equally real and likely just as
messy world of the past. Wildly implausible constructs result.

In the present context the most important of these implausible constructs
is "traditional wisdom teaching," which is alleged by many to have been either
the entity that Qohelet was reacting against or the entity that set out to (help)
devour this skeptical heretic after the fact. It is allegedly the proponents of traditional wisdom teaching as is found in books like Proverbs, to whose narrow
dogma about the way in which the world works Qohelet is objecting (e.g.,
the claim that righteous people are blessed and wicked people suffer); and it
is their dogma that is essentially reimposed by Qohelet's editors.

Yet it is far from clear why we should assume such a dichotomy between
Qohelet and the broader wisdom context and on that basis go searching for
their allegedly straightforward worldviews. That there have been throughout the ages numerous Israelites, and later Jews, of dogmatic and narrow
outlook need not be questioned; Job's comforters stand as the most famous
literary examples of what we may assume was a wider historical phenomenon (and one by no means restricted to this one religious grouping, as any
cursory review of *Christian* history will reveal). It is also reasonable to believe
that Qohelet may have had some of these compatriots in mind as he wrote.

---

14. O. Wilde, "Phrases and Philosophies for the Use of the Young," *Chameleon,* December 1894.

These assumptions, however, do not permit us to make any generalized assertion about the nature of "traditional wisdom," as if "traditional wisdom" were all the same kind of thing until some imagined day in Israel's history when enlightenment dawned and writers like Qohelet came to the fore. One might well think from the way in which this issue has sometimes been discussed that no Israelite ever noticed in earlier times, for example, that righteous people are not always blessed and wicked people are far from always suffering, and that every early Israelite thinker considered the world a perfectly ordered and comprehensible place, capable of comprehensive description in pithy proverbs. Unlike the assumptions mentioned above, however, this is certainly not a reasonable one. It stretches credulity, in fact, and there is no evidence to justify us in making it.

The book of Proverbs certainly cannot be cited in support of it. Proverbs for the most part does not tell us anything about what the earliest users of proverbs thought about them and how they used them; rather, it simply records some of the proverbs that formed the basis of their reflection and use. It does not for the most part enable us, for example, to form any sure impression of how far these early Israelites thought the proverbs absolutely or only situationally true, or of how far they believed the truth of an individual proverb stretched, and which limitations (if any) they believed to apply in each individual case.

It would again be a reasonable assumption that individual readers of the proverbs might well disagree with each other on this kind of point, given the variety of individual experience and wisdom they would be bringing to the task of interpretation. Proverbs, by their very nature brief and usually self-standing entities (with no true literary context to help the reader with their meaning), demand this kind of individual engagement with them in order to ascertain what they mean. They demand reflection. Occasionally the book of Proverbs itself forcibly underlines the point, as in Proverbs 26:4–5:

> Do not answer a fool according to his folly,
>   or you will be like him yourself.
> Answer a fool according to his folly,
>   or he will be wise in his own eyes.

It is particularly clear from this juxtaposition that the authors of the book of Proverbs were not of the opinion that proverbs could provide ethical guidance at no cost to the intellect. The two proverbs together demand that the reader think carefully about the question of "answering the fool" before acting, taking into consideration such things as the circumstances and the inner motivation for responding. The reader must, in other words, examine the proverbs carefully and "set them in order" (understand their relationship to each other and to the larger empirical reality), if the correct conclusions are to be drawn from them.

It is, of course, this task of examining and "ordering" proverbs that the author of Ecclesiastes attributes to Qohelet himself (12:9–10), setting him firmly within the wisdom tradition. That is what Qohelet observably does in the course of his speaking. He considers what proverbial wisdom has to say about the world, and he presses on to see how far it is true and which qualifications exist in respect of its individual statements. If, for example, there are proverbs that speak of the "profit" that comes from hard work (Heb. *motar*, Prov. 14:23; 21:5), Qohelet still wishes to press the question whether in the end human beings have any "advantage" over the animals (Heb. *motar*, Eccl. 3:19). In what sense do mortal beings know "profit" in life? Of what kind of profit are we speaking?

In this endeavor of examining and ordering, Qohelet contrasts with Job's friends. These "comforters" present to us a rather different picture of how to handle "wisdom"—a less critical, less thoughtful, and in the end much less helpful treatment. There is no reason to think, however, that Qohelet is reacting to some hypothetical, monolithic "wisdom tradition" in what he says, nor is there any reason to imagine that his affirmations (as well as his qualifications) of "traditional wisdom" are not seriously and sincerely meant. He is responding to a messy universe. That is why, in the end, his book is somewhat messy, nonlinear, and nonsystematic. Its form mirrors its content and its focus of interest. It is difficult to see how any author of intelligence and integrity could approach a complicated universe in a markedly different way.

This commentary does not, in sum, regard the message of the book of Ecclesiastes as explicable in terms of a reconstructed "traditional wisdom" rejected by or rejecting of a reconstructed Qohelet, whose views are somehow known to us apart from the reading of the book that gives us access to his words. It approaches this book, rather, by taking its own closing statements about its nature seriously and expecting to find throughout its pages the unified though complex whole that these statements imply. Qohelet had something to say that is knowledge and truth (12:9–10), which the author has passed on to his readers because it is valuable. This being clear, we are now in a position to go on and sketch the broad outlines of what this knowledge and truth consist in.

The author himself, in concluding the book, sets the whole of Qohelet's teaching in the context of reverence for and obedience to God, who has created a moral universe in which there is accountability for actions (12:13–14). He does so with ample justification in terms of Qohelet's teaching itself, quite apart from the wider scriptural context. It is not simply that Qohelet himself refers explicitly to this foundation of his own thinking and teaching, although he does do this. His reflection on the "times" of human existence in 3:1–17, for example, refers both to reverence for God as something appropriate for human beings (3:14; cf. also 5:7, where he exhorts the worshiper to reverence, and 7:18; 8:12) and to the "time of judgment" that awaits all when the moral corruption of the world is confronted by God (3:16–17).

Qohelet returns to the theme of judgment in 8:1–9, advising the wise man at court who is faced with a foolish ruler to remember that there is a time for everything, including divine judgment on foolishness and wickedness (8:5–6). In 11:9 the young man is urged to live his life in the certain knowledge of divine judgment. More broadly than this, however, it is also apparent that everywhere (although often implicitly rather than explicitly) the "two ways" through life as described throughout Proverbs and in a psalm like Psalm 1 lie in the background of Ecclesiastes.

The categories of sinner and righteous appear in 2:26 as well as 3:17, for example (note also the conjunction of the wicked and the God-fearing in 8:12–13), and the categories of wise and foolish are frequently to be found throughout (correlated with "righteous" and "wicked/sinner," e.g., in 9:1–2). If Qohelet has some qualifications to offer concerning wisdom, he has no doubt that "wisdom is better than folly" (2:13), and he therefore also offers voluminous wisdom to his readers, expecting that they will be the better for it (e.g., in 7:1–22; 10:1–20). This advice is offered, as in Proverbs, in the context of belief in a Creator God who loves what is right and hates what is wrong.

It is this overarching backdrop to Qohelet's thought that makes it so inexplicable that commentators have sometimes characterized him as a hedonist. They have done so on the basis of passages like 2:24–26; 3:12–13, 22; 5:18–20; 9:7–10; and 11:9–10, which commend such things as eating, drinking wine, and enjoyment of wife, work, wealth, and possessions. Yet it is patently obvious that God himself is prominently present in all the passages just mentioned. God is the One who enables the eating, drinking, and enjoyment of work (2:24–25); who gives mortals as a gift both the days in which joy can be found and enjoyment and contentment (3:12–13; 5:18–20); who smiles on these human activities (9:7–10); and who sets their moral boundaries (11:9–10). There is pleasure here, to be sure, and enjoyment of the good things of life, but it is pleasure received from God's hand and joy expressed in his presence.

This way of being is by no means antithetical to faith in God as far as Qohelet is concerned, and it is certainly not antithetical to the morally good life (note esp. the reference to "doing good" in 3:12). That both aspirant orthodox Christian commentators and those neither orthodox nor Christian have seen antitheses here tells us much more about them and their fractured thinking and living than about Qohelet. It reminds us that all sorts of people would prefer, for their own personal and cultural purposes, that God and creation should not be so closely identified as they are in the Bible. Qohelet, however, understands what the confession that *God* created the *world* and made it *good* (Gen. 1) truly means. We cannot have God without embracing his world, and we cannot in the end have the world without embracing God.

This brings us neatly to consider next the more troubled and gloomy tone in Ecclesiastes, which marks out significant sections of the book and has so often grasped the attention of readers to the exclusion of the other material we have considered to this point. The parts of Qohelet's discourse that have this tone are best understood, in my opinion, only in relation to the obviously hortatory passages, which he directs at his hearers in the hope of leading them to think and live in a certain way. They are designed to gain a hearing for Qohelet's more positive advice by dispelling false consciousness about the world and by undermining false dreams and hopes.

The general heading under which all of this gloomier material is presented is found in 1:2 and 12:8, which enclose all of Qohelet's other words: "Everything is meaningless," according to the NIV, but better translated as "Everything is a breath" (see the comments on 1:1–11). As a consideration of the whole book reveals, the emphasis lies on the passing nature of existence and on its elusiveness and resistance to intellectual and physical human control. The main obstacle to living well in the world is that mortal beings consistently refuse to accept their mortality and finitude. Qohelet sets out to convince them of these. It is not insignificant in this context that his positive advice to his hearers (esp. in 9:7–10) is similar to the advice given in the Babylonian Epic of Gilgamesh to the hero Gilgamesh, in the context of his search for immortality:

> When the gods created mankind, they set aside death for mankind,
>   retaining life in their own hand.
> You, Gilgamesh, let your stomach be full; make merry by day
>   and by night.
> Of each day make a feast of rejoicing; day and night dance and play.
> Let your garments be sparkling fresh, and your head be washed;
>   bathe in water.
> Pay heed to the little one that holds on to your hand.
> Let your spouse delight in your bosom.
> For this is the task (of mankind).[15]

---

15. The text is found in *ANET*, 90.

Gilgamesh is thus dissuaded from his quest and encouraged to accept the limitations of human existence. The Bible as a whole sets the *entirety* of human existence as we know it within the context of such a failed human attempt to become "like God" (Gen. 3), deriving from a refusal to accept divinely ordained boundaries. It is against this background that Qohelet speaks, seeking to persuade his hearers of the futility of this ongoing human quest and thus to save them from a life that is itself characterized by futility.

Qohelet's two favorite targets, as we will see, are the pursuit of knowledge and the pursuit of wealth. The universe, he argues, is beyond human comprehension and cannot be fathomed. Wisdom may indeed be better than folly, but wisdom does not enable us to give a comprehensive account of reality and thus provide us with the means somehow to control it (e.g., 1:1–18; 2:12–16; 3:11; 7:23–29). The pursuit of wealth is likewise a futile chase, for one cannot guarantee even if one attains it that one will be able to keep it, use it, or pass it on to one's descendants. The possession of wealth does not in any case inevitably lead to the possession of fulfillment and of joy (e.g., 2:1–11, 17–23; 4:7–8; 5:10–17; 6:1–6).

Overshadowing all such human attempts to overcome the limitations set to life is the ultimate empirical reality that demonstrates they cannot: death. It is above all death that mocks human attempts at godlikeness, and to this subject Qohelet constantly returns. Death brings the wise man and the fool in the end to the same place (2:12–16), and it renders futile a life devoted to the accumulation of wealth (2:17–23). Death, which lies in the future, should persuade the young man to embrace life in the present (11:7–12:8). It is the reality of death that makes rational the way of life that Qohelet commends to all his readers, with its focus on living each moment of life joyfully before God rather than on the pursuit of wisdom, wealth, or any other human end that comes under the heading "chasing after the wind" (1:14, 17, and throughout the book).

Death, after all, comes to everyone, whether wise or foolish, rich or poor, good or bad (e.g., 9:1–6); there is no way in which human beings can avoid it. It is best therefore to give up any attempt to control destiny and simply to live life out before God. This "simple living" involves human activities like work and wealth-creation; it also involves the employment of wisdom. These activities will be undertaken in the fear of God, however, and with no illusions about the nature of the universe or about what can be humanly achieved within it. Undertaken in this way, we can find joy whether in work or in wealth and find in wisdom valuable help for living.

Ecclesiastes in the Modern Context

OUR ATTEMPTS TO understand the text of Ecclesiastes in its own terms, as outlined above and developed in the commentary, come under the heading of

Original Meaning. It is, of course, already the case as we consider this original meaning that we are already doing so in the context of some broader, fundamental assumptions about how Ecclesiastes fits into the Bible as a whole—this is already apparent in our discussion above. It is impossible to seal off the original meaning of a text entirely from all other meanings, as if it could be grasped completely objectively by the reader before anything else were considered. It is nevertheless a useful exercise to consider Ecclesiastes somewhat in isolation from the remainder of the Bible in the first instance, lest we are tempted too quickly to merge it into the rest of the Bible and in so doing miss its distinctive contribution to the Scriptures.

The Original Meaning sections in this commentary (as in the entire commentary series) are thus separated from others headed Bridging Contexts and Contemporary Significance, in which we wrestle in a more focused way with questions such as these:

> What difference does it make to our Christian reading of Ecclesiastes that we now read it as part of the whole Christian Bible that is centered on the gospel story?
> What does Ecclesiastes mean for today?

Although we cannot be sure about the precise historical background of the book of Ecclesiastes, it seems clear from the content of the book that the world into which Qohelet is speaking is not entirely dissimilar from our own world. We, too, live in a world in which there is much "toiling after gain," as people strive to get ahead of the game of life and exercise control over their lives. The oppression and injustice that such a pursuit of gain and advancement all too often produces is as much a feature of our own world as it is of Qohelet's (e.g., 4:1–3), and it is as obvious in our world as in Qohelet's that joy and fulfillment do not automatically flow from this pursuit.

In extensive parts of the Western world, indeed, the ever-more-frantic pursuit of such things is evidently accompanied by spiritual emptiness and world-weariness, as people strive to achieve what they can never possess by the means they have chosen for the attempt. One important aspect of the pursuit is the part played by knowledge and technique. At the heart of the chase lies a conviction that the universe is ultimately comprehensible and therefore malleable; it can be fashioned to our own ends. Accumulating human wisdom can be brought to bear upon it, enabling the constant march of progress towards a universal, or at least a personal, utopia.

At the same time, however, the weakness of empirical inquiry as a foundation for human life has never been so evident. The information explosion has resulted in individual human beings knowing more and more about less and less, since no one can possibly process all the "facts" that exist in order to arrive at overarching truths about the universe in which we live. It may be true, as the popular TV show *The X-Files* has it, that "the truth is out there," but what that truth is, how it may be known, and what it means for living are to many people unclear.

Overshadowing everything in our world, as in Qohelet's, is the reality of death. It is a reality that in part drives the insane rush after gain, as people try to protect themselves from death and seize everything from life that can be seized before it is taken away. At the same time it is a reality denied and dismissed from public discourse—the Christian thinker Francis Schaeffer once called death "the 20th century's pornography"—since it is common knowledge that it is coming and that it renders much of life futile; yet there is no common knowledge about how to handle it. Death is, in our world as in Qohelet's, the ultimate reality of life that demonstrates the universe cannot be "handled" by human beings at all.

Qohelet's world is not so different from our world; this means it is not a difficult task on the whole to apply his message to ourselves. (1) It is first of all a message for those who cling still to the world of illusion, which is daily and powerfully presented to us as substantial reality by our various media. Qohelet dispels our illusions. The universe is not comprehensible and malleable. We cannot make any lasting mark on it. We cannot by pursuing wisdom or wealth find fulfillment and joy. Death, in particular, mocks all attempts at elevation to divinity and the refusal to be mortal and human.

(2) It is also a message for those who understand all this and are looking for a different way of thinking and living—who are seeking to replace illusion with truth. Qohelet says to such people: Understand that God exists. The universe we inhabit comes from his hand and comes to us as a gift. Our lives are a gift, offered for a short period and then taken back once again. Embrace life for what it is, rather than what you would like it to be. Live it out before God, reverencing and obeying him. This is the pathway on which joy lies, even though puzzlement and pain will also be found there, and there are never guarantees about how things will turn out.

Christian readers of Ecclesiastes, of course, know more than Qohelet did about God and about God's plans for the world and for individual human beings. We know, for example, about resurrection and new life. We are therefore able, among other things, to solve a puzzle that Qohelet himself does not solve: how divine justice is ultimately delivered in the universe and how in the end it goes better with God-fearers than with the wicked (8:12–13).

Qohelet holds on firmly to belief in the moral coherence of the universe; yet what he sees is that every living creature dies without any apparent distinction among them (2:15–16; 3:18–21), that the wicked can live longer and more fully than the righteous (7:15), and that in general righteous people can get what the wicked deserve and vice versa (8:14; 9:1–2). He is agnostic about what happens after death (3:21). *That* justice will be done is therefore clear in Ecclesiastes; *how* it will be done is unclear. We require the remainder of the Bible, both Old Testament and (especially) New Testament, to arrive at a fuller picture.

Nevertheless, the more extensive truth that Christians have on this topic and on others, although it expands on Qohelet's message, does not undermine it or make it less important that we listen to it. That Christians have even greater reason for faith and obedience and an even deeper foundation for joy than Qohelet does not mean we must heed less his warnings about illusions and his advocacy of a better way. For Christians are still called to live in this world that God has created and loves, even while anticipating a world to come. We are no less in need, therefore, of advice about living (as well as about waiting), about the pitfalls of wealth and wisdom, about the folly of attempting to control our destinies, about the importance of living life fully and daily in the certain knowledge of death, about the centrality of God to the good life, and about our response to puzzlement and pain.

Ecclesiastes, as part of the Scripture that is given us for shaping faith and life, offers us such advice, correlating as it does so with extensive sections of the New Testament that also touch on such themes. In focusing our attention on this life rather than the next, indeed, this book contributes to the correction of an all-too-frequent imbalance throughout the ages in Christian thinking, which has sometimes presented Christianity as if it were more a matter of waiting for something than a matter of living.

Outline of Ecclesiastes

Select Bibliography
on Ecclesiastes

READERS WHO WISH to pursue the study of Ecclesiastes further than this limited bibliography allows are invited to peruse the recent and fuller bibliographies in the commentaries by Longman and Seow (see below).

Allender, D. B., and T. Longman III. *Bold Purpose: Exchanging Counterfeit Happiness for the Real Meaning of Life*. Wheaton, Ill.: Tyndale, 1998.

Anderson, W. H. U. *Qoheleth and Its Pessimistic Theology: Hermeneutical Struggles in Wisdom Literature*. MBPS 54. Lewiston, N.Y.: Mellen Biblical Press, 1997.

_____. "Philosophical Considerations in a Genre Analysis of Qoheleth." *VT* 48 (1998): 289–300.

_____. "The Curse of Work in Qoheleth: An Exposé of Genesis 3:17–19 in Ecclesiastes." *EvQ* 70 (1998): 99–113.

Baltzer, K. "Women and War in Qohelet 7:23–8:1a." *HTR* 80 (1987): 127–32.

Bartholomew, C. G. *Reading Ecclesiastes: Old Testament Exegesis and Hermeneutical Theory*. AnBib 139. Rome: Pontificio Istituto Biblico, 1998.

Barton, G. A. *A Critical and Exegetical Commentary on the Book of Ecclesiastes*. ICC. New York: Scribner, 1908.

Beal, T. K. "C(ha)osmoplis: Qohelet's Last Words." Pp. 279–89 in *God in the Fray: A Tribute to Walter Brueggemann*. Ed. T. Linafelt and T. K. Beal. Minneapolis: Augsburg Fortress, 1998.

Bergant, D. *Job, Ecclesiastes*. OTM 18. Collegeville, Minn.: Liturgical, 1990.

Bickerman, E. J. *Four Strange Books of the Bible: Jonah, Daniel, Koheleth, Esther*. New York: Schocken, 1967.

Blenkinsopp, J. "Ecclesiastes 3.1–15: Another Interpretation." *JSOT* 66 (1995): 55–64.

Boadt, L. *Sayings of the Wise: The Legacy of King Solomon*. CBS. New York: St. Martin's, 1999.

Bottoms, L. *Ecclesiastes Speaks to Us Today*. Atlanta: John Knox, 1979.

Brenner, A., and F. van Dijk-Hemmes. *On Gendering Texts: Female and Male Voices in the Hebrew Bible*. BibIntS 1. Leiden: Brill, 1993.

Broyde, M. J. "Defilement of the Hands, Canonization of the Bible, and the Special Status of Esther, Ecclesiastes, and Song of Songs." *Judaism* 44 (1995): 65–79.

Chia, P. P. "Wisdom, Yahwism, Creation: In Quest of Qoheleth's Theological Thought." *Jian Dao* 3 (1995): 1–32.

Chittister, J., and J. A. Swanson. *There Is a Season*. Maryknoll, N.Y: Orbis, 1995.

Christianson, E. S. *A Time to Tell: Narrative Strategies in Ecclesiastes*. JSOTS 280. Sheffield: Sheffield Academic Press, 1998.

Clemens, D. M. "The Law of Sin and Death: Ecclesiastes and Genesis 1–3." *Themelios* 19 (1994): 5–8.

Collins, J. J. *Proverbs, Ecclesiastes*. KPG. Atlanta: John Knox, 1980.

Cooke, G. A. *A Critical and Exegetical Commentary on the Book of Ecclesiastes*. ICC. Edinburgh: T. & T. Clark, 1959.

Crenshaw, J. L. *Ecclesiastes: A Commentary*. OTL. London: SCM, 1988.

Davidson, R. *Ecclesiastes and the Song of Solomon*. DSBOT. Edinburgh: Saint Andrew, 1986.

Davis, B. C. "Ecclesiastes 12:1–8—Death, an Impetus for Life." *BSac* 148 (1991): 298–318.

De Moor, R. *God's Backyard: A Fresh Look at Ecclesiastes*. Grand Rapids: CRC Publications, 1993.

Delitzsch, F. J. *Commentary on the Song of Songs and Ecclesiastes*. Grand Rapids: Eerdmans, 1970.

Dell, K. J. "Ecclesiastes as Wisdom: Consulting Early Interpreters." *VT* 44 (1994): 301–29.

Dijk-Hemmes, F. van. "The Imagination of Power and the Power of Imagination. An Intertextual Analysis of Two Biblical Love Songs: The Song of Songs and Hosea 2." Pp. 173–86 in *The Poetical Books*. Ed. D. J. A. Clines. BSem 41. Sheffield: Sheffield Academic Press, 1997.

Eaton, M. A. *Ecclesiastes: An Introduction and Commentary*. TOTC 16. Downers Grove, Ill.: InterVarsity, 1983.

Ellul, J. *Reason for Being: A Meditation on Ecclesiastes*. Trans. J. M. Hanks. Grand Rapids: Eerdmans, 1990.

Farmer, K. A. *Who Knows What Is Good? A Commentary on the Books of Proverbs and Ecclesiastes*. ITC. Grand Rapids: Eerdmans, 1991.

Ferguson, E. "Some Aspects of Gregory of Nyssa's Interpretation of Scripture Exemplified in His *Homilies on Ecclesiastes*." Pp. 29–33 in *Studia patristica, 27: Cappadocian Fathers, Greek Authors After Nicaea, Augustine, Donatism, and Pelagianism*. Ed. E. A. Livingstone. Louvain: Peeters, 1993.

Forman, C. G. "Koheleth's Use of Genesis." *JSS* 5 (1960): 256–63.

Fox, M. V. *Qohelet and His Contradictions*. JSOTS 71. Sheffield: Almond, 1989.

———. *A Time to Tear Down and a Time to Build Up: A Rereading of Ecclesiastes*. Grand Rapids: Eerdmans, 1999.

Fredericks, D. C. *Coping with Transience: Ecclesiastes on Brevity in Life*. BSem 18. Sheffield: JSOT Press, 1993.

Freulich, R., and J. Abramson. *The Faces of Israel: A Photographic Commentary on the Words of Koheleth*. New York: Thomas Yoseloff, 1972.

Fuerst, W. J. *Ruth, Esther, Ecclesiastes, the Song of Songs, Lamentations.* CBC. Cambridge: Cambridge University Press, 1975.

Garrett, D. A. "Ecclesiastes 7:25–29 and the Feminist Hermeneutic." *CTR* 2 (1987–88): 309–21.

————. *Proverbs, Ecclesiastes, Song of Songs.* NAC 14. Nashville: Broadman, 1993.

Ginsburg, C. D. *The Song of Songs and Coheleth (Commonly Called the Book of Ecclesiastes).* The Library of Biblical Studies. New York: Ktav, 1970.

Ginsberg, H. L. *Studies in Koheleth.* TSJTSA. New York: Jewish Theological Seminary of America, 1950.

Gordis, R. *Koheleth, the Man and His World: A Study of Ecclesiastes.* 3d ed. Schocken Paperbacks. New York: Schocken, 1968.

Hall, J., E. A. Matter, and G. T. Sheppard. *Solomon's Divine Arts.* PCC. Cleveland: Pilgrim, 1991.

Halperin, D. J. "The Book of Remedies, the Canonization of the Solomonic Writings, and the Riddle of Pseudo-Eusebius." *JQR* 72 (1982): 269–92.

Harrison, C. R., Jr. "Qoheleth Among the Sociologists." *BibInt* 5 (1997): 160–80.

Hengstenberg, E. W. *Commentary on Ecclesiastes.* Philadelphia: Smith, 1860.

Holloway, G. *The Main Thing: A New Look at Ecclesiastes.* Abilene, Tex.: Abilene Christian Univ. Press, 1997.

Holm-Nielsen, S. "On the Interpretation of Qoheleth in Early Christianity." *VT* 24 (1974): 168–77.

Hubbard, D. A. *Beyond Futility: Messages of Hope from the Book of Ecclesiastes.* Grand Rapids: Eerdmans, 1976.

Johnston, R. K. "Confessions of a Workaholic: A Reappraisal of Qoheleth." *CBQ* 38 (1976): 14–28.

Jones, E. *Proverbs and Ecclesiastes: Introduction and Commentary.* TBC. London: SCM Press, 1961.

Jong, S. de. "Qohelet and the Ambitious Spirit of the Ptolemaic Period." *JSOT* 61 (1994): 85–96.

————. "God in the Book of Qohelet: A Reappraisal of Qohelet's Place in Old Testament Theology." *VT* 47 (1997): 154–67.

————. "A Book on Labour: The Structuring Principles and the Main Theme of the Book of Qohelet." Pp. 222–30 in *The Poetical Books.* Ed. D. J. A. Clines. BSem 41. Sheffield: Sheffield Academic Press, 1997.

Kaiser, W. C. *Ecclesiastes: Total Life.* Chicago: Moody, 1979.

Keddie, G. J. *Looking for the Good Life: The Search for Fulfillment in the Light of Ecclesiastes.* Phillipsburg, N.J.: Presbyterian and Reformed, 1991.

Kidner, D. *A Time to Mourn, and a Time to Dance: Ecclesiastes and the Way of the World.* BST. Downers Grove, Ill.: InterVarsity, 1976.

_____. *The Wisdom of Proverbs, Job, and Ecclesiastes: An Introduction to Wisdom Literature*. Downers Grove, Ill.: InterVarsity, 1985.

Kline, M. M. "Is Qoheleth Unorthodox? A Review Article." *Kerux* 13 (1998): 16–39.

Kreeft, P. *Three Philosophies of Life: Ecclesiastes—Life As Vanity, Job—Life As Suffering, Song of Songs—Life As Love*. San Francisco: Ignatius, 1989.

Kugel, J. L. "Qohelet and Money." *CBQ* 51 (1989): 32–49.

Levine, É. "The Humor in Qohelet." *ZAW* 109 (1997): 71–83.

Loader, J. A. *Ecclesiastes*. Text and Interpretation. Grand Rapids: Eerdmans, 1986.

Longman T., III. *The Book of Ecclesiastes*. NICOT. Grand Rapids: Eerdmans, 1998.

Machinist, P. "Fate, *miqreh* and Reason: Some Reflections on Qohelet and Biblical Thought." Pp. 159–75 in *Solving Riddles and Untying Knots*. FS J. C. Greenfield. Ed. Z. Zevit et al. Winona Lake, Ind.: Eisenbrauns, 1995.

Miller, D. B. "Qohelet's Symbolic Use of הבל." *JBL* 117 (1998): 437–54.

Murphy, R. E. *Ecclesiastes*. WBC 23a. Waco, Tex.: Word, 1992.

_____. "Recent Research on Proverbs and Qoheleth." *CR:BS* 1 (1993): 119–40.

Murphy, R. E., and E. Huwiler. *Proverbs, Ecclesiastes, Song of Songs*. NIBC 12. Peabody, Mass.: Hendrickson, 1999.

Ogden, G. *Qoheleth*. RNBC. Sheffield: JSOT Press, 1987.

Reitman, J. S. "The Structure and Unity of Ecclesiastes." *BSac* 154 (1997): 297–319.

Rudman, D. "A Contextual Reading of Ecclesiastes 4:13–16." *JBL* 116 (1997): 57–73.

_____. "Woman As Divine Agent in Ecclesiastes." *JBL* 116 (1997): 411–27.

Schoors, A., ed. *Qohelet in the Context of Wisdom*. BETL 136. Leuven: Leuven University Press, 1998.

Scott, R. B. Y. *Proverbs, Ecclesiastes*. AB 18. Garden City, N.Y.: Doubleday, 1965.

Seow, C. L. *Ecclesiastes*. AB. New York: Doubleday, 1997.

Shead, A. G. "Reading Ecclesiastes 'Epilogically.'" *TynBul* 48 (1997): 67–91.

Short, R. L. *A Time to be Born, A Time to Die*. New York: Harper & Row, 1973.

Spangenberg, I. J. J. "Irony in the Book of Qohelet." *JSOT* 72 (1996): 57–69.

Swindoll, C. R. *Living on the Ragged Edge: Coming to Terms With Reality*. Waco, Tex: Word, 1985.

Verheij, A. "Paradise Retried: On Qohelet 2:4–6." *JSOT* 50 (1991): 113–15.

Whybray, R. N. *Ecclesiastes*. OTG. Sheffield: JSOT Press, 1989.

_____. *Ecclesiastes*. NCB. Grand Rapids: Eerdmans, 1989.

Zimmermann, F. *The Inner World of Qohelet*. New York: Ktav, 1973.

Ecclesiastes 1:1–11

THE WORDS OF the Teacher, son of David, king in Jerusalem:

2 "Meaningless! Meaningless!"
    says the Teacher.
"Utterly meaningless!
    Everything is meaningless."

3 What does man gain from all his labor
    at which he toils under the sun?
4 Generations come and generations go,
    but the earth remains forever.
5 The sun rises and the sun sets,
    and hurries back to where it rises.
6 The wind blows to the south
    and turns to the north;
round and round it goes,
    ever returning on its course.
7 All streams flow into the sea,
    yet the sea is never full.
To the place the streams come from,
    there they return again.
8 All things are wearisome,
    more than one can say.
The eye never has enough of seeing,
    nor the ear its fill of hearing.
9 What has been will be again,
    what has been done will be done again;
    there is nothing new under the sun.
10 Is there anything of which one can say,
    "Look! This is something new"?
It was here already, long ago;
    it was here before our time.
11 There is no remembrance of men of old,
and even those who are yet to come
will not be remembered
    by those who follow.

 WE MOVE SWIFTLY, as the book opens, from the speaker to words that are spoken; yet the speaker intrigues us. He is, according to the NIV, "the Teacher" (vv. 1–2). Traditionally rendered as "Preacher" (KJV, NASB), the Heb. is *qohelet*, probably meaning "participant in an assembly" (Heb. *qahal*, Gk. *ekklesia*, "assembly"; see the Introduction), or perhaps "one who assembles (a group)." We will refer to him for the sake of simplicity as "Qohelet" in the commentary, without meaning the reader to take this as a proper name.

Qohelet addresses his gathered listeners, the Israelites. He is "son of David, king in Jerusalem" (v. 1). We immediately think of Solomon, yet it is not likely that the historical Solomon is truly the speaker. More likely Qohelet merely adopts the *persona* of a Davidic king for a while (probably to be identified with Solomon by his readers, although "son" itself need only imply a descendant) in order to facilitate those aspects of his exploration of "life under the sun" that require Solomon's type of experience. He "becomes" for a while a king within the world of the text (see the Introduction), later abandoning this disguise in favor of others.

In the same way that Qohelet thus presents himself to us in different guises so that we may explore different aspects of reality with him, so too Qohelet himself is "presented" to the reader by still another person—the one who transmits his words to us and who makes himself known to us explicitly in 12:9–14. For all we know, we only have access to Qohelet's words at all because this person thought them of sufficient value to pass on to his "son" (12:12).

Whether this "editorial voice" is also to be identified throughout 1:1–2 is unclear. It is true that Qohelet is referred to in 1:1–2, as in 12:9–14, in the third person, and it is possible therefore that our "second voice" is here adding to his later epilogue an introduction to Qohelet and his words. Yet it is also possible for authors to refer to themselves in the third person, especially when introducing previously delivered sayings or previous writings that were produced, as it were, by "another person" (the author as he was back then). It is therefore difficult to know for sure whether parts of 1:1–2 derive from Qohelet himself or not.

This issue in any case is only important if one believes there is some conflict of perspective between Qohelet and his admirer, so that the speaker and the transmitter of his words are not saying quite the same thing. It has indeed been suggested that 1:2, along with its parallel in 12:8, represents too much of an overstatement:

1:2:   "Meaningless! Meaningless!" says the Teacher. "Utterly meaningless! Everything is meaningless."

12:8: "Meaningless! Meaningless!" says the Teacher. "Everything is meaningless!"

Qohelet does not elsewhere, it is argued, speak of *everything* as *hebel* (the Heb. word behind NIV's problematic "meaningless"; see further below). It has even been suggested that 1:3 is overly anthropocentric, being focused on the usefulness of the world for human beings, whereas the remainder of the book is not (e.g., 12:1–7).[1]

The second of these points may quickly be addressed: It is not at all clear why one author (or an author with his editor) cannot look at the world now from one perspective and now from another. The whole book of Ecclesiastes, as we will see, contains such shifts in perspective, as human existence is considered from different points of view, with the aim of commending certain viewpoints over others. The first point, however, requires a more extended discussion, for everything depends on what we think *hebel* means. Here we come to a crucial matter of interpretation, given the frequency with which *hebel* occurs in Ecclesiastes (more than thirty times outside 1:2) and its importance in Qohelet's thought.

It is certainly true that to translate *hebel* as "meaningless," as the NIV does, causes serious difficulties for the interpretation of the book as a unified work, for even a cursory reading of Ecclesiastes demonstrates that Qohelet does not consider everything "meaningless." On the contrary, he is constantly to be found recommending certain ways of being to his listeners precisely because it is possible for human beings to know the goodness and joy of existence (cf., e.g., 2:24–26; 3:12–13, 22). "Everything" is *not* "meaningless."

Consideration of the use of *hebel* elsewhere in the Old Testament does not lead us in this direction for its meaning either. *Hebel* means "breath" or "breeze" (Isa. 57:13), and thus by extension things that are insubstantial or fleeting or actions that are in vain or to no purpose (BDB, 210–11). Ephemerality is thus one of the main associations of *hebel*, including actions that are "passing" in the sense that they make no permanent impact or impression on reality; they are futile or pointless, and their effects do not last. It is plainly true that everything to do with human (indeed, all mortal) existence, even if not meaningless, is nevertheless "ephemeral" or "fleeting." Consider the following texts (Ps. 39:5; 144:4; Prov. 31:30):

You have made my days a mere handbreadth;
the span of my years is as nothing before you.
Each man's life is but a breath [*hebel*]. (Ps. 39:5)

Man is like a breath [*hebel*];
his days are like a fleeting shadow. (Ps. 144:4)

Charm is deceptive, and beauty is fleeting [*hebel*];
but a woman who fears the LORD is to be praised. (Prov. 31:30)

---

1. Whybray, *Ecclesiastes*, 34–38.

Nothing lasts—neither beauty nor life itself. It is particularly clear that throughout Ecclesiastes 11:7—12:8, *hebel* most naturally refers to this transient nature of human existence. It makes little sense for Qohelet to advise a young person to be happy while living reverently before God only then to remind him that "youth and vigor are meaningless" (11:10)! It makes great sense for him, however, to offer this advice in the context of the *brevity* of youth, just as people generally are urged to enjoy all their years because "everything to come is fleeting" (11:8, pers. trans.). The summarizing conclusion that follows the graphic description of aging and death in 12:1—7 as well as all of Qohelet's words (12:8) most naturally refers likewise to the fleeting nature of all things, not to their meaninglessness. If 12:8 has this meaning for *hebel*, then 1:2 most likely does so as well. Other verses where *hebel* is best translated in a similar way include 6:12, 7:15, and 9:9.

There is no conflict between Qohelet and his editor. Both wish us to understand, as the foundational truth on which Qohelet premises all his words, that life is "like a breath." The seriousness with which they wish their readers to grasp the point is indicated in the structure of 1:2, which is better seen in the NASB than in the NIV: "'Vanity of vanities,' says the Preacher, 'Vanity of vanities! All is vanity.'" The fivefold repetition of the word *hebel* (translated here "vanity"), and in particular the repetition of the phrase *hᵃbel hᵃbalim*, "vanity of vanities"—a construction that conveys intensity and superlative, as in "heaven of heavens" (lit., Deut. 10:14; NIV "the highest heavens") or "Song of Songs" (Song 1:1, i.e., the best of songs)—drives home the message. We may translate Ecclesiastes 1:2 this way:

> "The merest of breaths,"
> says Qohelet,
> "The merest of breaths.
> Everything is a breath."

It is not, however, just the *ephemerality* of reality, from the mortal point of view, that Qohelet has in mind in using *hebel*. It is also the *elusive* nature of reality, that is, the way in which it resists our attempts to capture it and contain it, to grasp hold of it and control it. This is true at the level both of understanding and of action. The way in which the world works is in some measure comprehensible to us, yet in significant measure beyond our grasp. It resists our attempts to sum it up (thus passages like 1:12—18; 7:23—29). Connected with this is also a resistance to our attempts to manipulate the world through our actions so that it produces consistent and predictable outcomes. The world has its own rhythm and order, to be sure, but it is not controllable by mortal beings.

At times Qohelet underlines this truth by representing reality as a solid and relentless entity on which human activity does not have significant impact and in respect of which human achievement seems trivial and insignificant (e.g., 1:1−11). Here it is the ephemeral, phantomlike nature of the human being when contrasted to the larger ongoing reality that disallows mortal control, for mortal actions have a fleeting, insubstantial nature in respect of the universe. The case is similar to that in Psalm 39:6, 11 (following on from 39:5, cited above):

> Man is a mere phantom as he goes to and fro:
> He bustles about, but only in vain [*hebel*];
> he heaps up wealth, not knowing who will get it. . . .
> You rebuke and discipline men for their sin;
> you consume their wealth like a moth—
> each man is but a breath [*hebel*].

The very thought of Psalm 39:5 is found in Ecclesiastes 2:18−19 and elsewhere. However, the truth that human activity characteristically does not make the impact on reality that people hope for and may indeed have been led to expect—that it is from this perspective pointless or futile—is not only represented in terms of phantoms who are unable to exert force on solid reality. Qohelet frequently underlines the same truth by using a quite different metaphor—by combining a *hebel*-saying with a reference to "chasing after the wind" (Heb. *reʿut/raʿyon ruaḥ*, as in 1:14, 17; 2:11, 17, 26; 4:4, 6, 16; 6:9). Here the image is of something that is solid trying to grasp something that is not. To chase the wind is to seek to grasp hold of and control something beyond our grasp and uncontrollable. This is self-evidently futile; it makes no more sense for a person to expect to grasp wind than for a ghost to expect to get hold of a chair.

Again, the point is not that human activity intrinsically, whether in the realm of thought or action, is "meaningless"—Qohelet clearly does not believe this. He commends wisdom over folly (e.g., 2:13−14) and advocates all sorts of activity as good and worthwhile in itself (e.g., 9:7−10). The emphasis lies not on whether certain ways of being or doing possess *meaning in themselves*, but on whether these ways of being or doing succeed in *achieving the goals* that humans often set before themselves.

Qohelet thinks not. The human attempt to impose self on reality in this way is a foolish undertaking, which can only end in pain and frustration. Human goals should be set in accordance with the nature of reality, not in defiance of it; otherwise human existence becomes embroiled in pointless striving. The nature of reality is that human beings cannot grasp it and mold it to their own ends, any more than they can as solids grasp and mold the elusive and invisible wind, or as phantoms shape the universe in their own image. Their thought and actions in this regard cannot bring them the control they desire.

The term Qohelet often uses to signify that which mortals are aiming for and might achieve, if only they could gain control over reality, is found in the question that follows in verse 3: "What does man gain from all his labor at which he toils under the sun?" The Hebrew word *yitron* (NIV "gain") is unique to Ecclesiastes in the Old Testament; it derives from the verb *ytr*, meaning "to remain over, be left over." The idea is that of surplus, and the question is asked from the perspective of someone who thinks of life in a particular way, as if it were raw material to be invested in, manipulated and shaped, given added value by what is done with it, and marketed as a means of accruing capital. A closely associated word is *motar*, found in Ecclesiastes 3:19 and in Proverbs 14:23; 21:5 (where it is used of financial gain):[2]

> All hard work brings a profit [*motar*],
>   but mere talk leads only to poverty. (Prov. 14:23)

> The plans of the diligent lead to profit [*motar*]
>   as surely as haste leads to poverty. (Prov. 21:5)

The person who asks about *yitron* brings a capitalistic, consumer-oriented perspective from the world of business and commerce and applies it to life more generally. What kind of profit accrues, asks Qohelet from this perspective, from a person's labor "under the sun"—another unique Ecclesiastes phrase, which refers to life in this present world and is synonymous with the phrases "under heaven" (e.g., 1:13) and "on earth" (e.g., 8:14). What reward is there on the balance sheet of life for all the "labor at which he toils" (lit., "toil at which he toils," Heb. *camal*, often with the sense of sorrow and trouble, although in Eccl. one can also find joy in it, e.g., 2:10), that is, all the effort and hard work that human beings put into the business of living?

This question receives no explicit answer at this point in the book. The response is implicit, however, in the reflection that is offered in 1:4–11 on the nature of creation and history, particularly if we accept that NIV's "wearisome" in verse 8 is not the best translation. The rare Heb. word *yagea*c, if it has the idea of weariness in it at all, must refer here to the metaphorical weariness of "all things" as people endlessly and ceaselessly follow the circuit of life (and thus become, like any human worker toiling endlessly and ceaselessly, "tired"), rather than to the effect that watching their toils has on the human observer. The very rarity of the word (only found elsewhere in Deut. 25:18; 2 Sam. 17:2) should caution us in our understanding of it, however,

---

2. Other associated words are *yeter*, which can sometimes be used of abundance or affluence (e.g., Job 22:20), *yitra*, riches (Isa. 15:7; Jer. 48:36), and *yoter*, found almost exclusively in Ecclesiastes and used in different ways to express the idea of more (Eccl. 2:15; 6:8, 11; 7:11, 16; 12:9, 12).

for the verbal root *ygᶜ* is itself used to refer to the hard work that produces weariness as well as to weariness itself (cf. also the related noun *yᵉgiaᶜ*, which can refer to labor and its fruits).

Certainly a statement that "all things are hard at work" fits the context much better as a summary of verses 4–7 than the statement "all things are weary." The remainder of verse 8 (which commentators have struggled convincingly to connect with an opening statement about weariness) then makes good sense as a threefold response of human wonder to the threefold exposition of creation's workings in verses 5–7. Creation is a vast and intricate reality, which escapes the grasp of human beings in speech, sight, and hearing; we are unable to find the words for it, and all our looking at it and listening to it cannot comprehend it.

With such an understanding of verse 8 in mind, we may return to the remainder of verses 4–11, the argument of which proceeds as follows. The world is an essentially unchanging place, unaffected by the "generations" that come and go (v. 4)—those specific periods of time that elapse within the larger span signified by "forever," periods inhabited by human beings who enter a stage of history and exit again after only the brief performance of life. The sun rises and sets as it always has, only to "hurry" (lit., "gasp, pant," in its eagerness and speed to fulfill its mission) back to its starting point and rise once again in the new morning (v. 5).

In a similar manner, the wind blows south and north (directions chosen to balance the east-west movement of the sun), endlessly moving through the world yet remaining within its prescribed circuits (v. 6). The water cycle remains the water cycle, as moisture evaporates and returns as rain to feed the streams (v. 7); all the flowing of the waters does not change anything about the volume of the sea. All these various natural phenomena toil steadily away, around and around, going about their appointed tasks without variation (v. 8); there is "nothing new under the sun" (v. 9), no "thing" (v. 10) that breaks the rule of regularity and predictability seen in "all things" (v. 8).

The human participants in the drama of creation—those who pass across the stage that creation provides—are relatively insignificant when considered in this context. The sands of passing time sweep over and erase the marks they have made, so that they are obliterated: "There is no remembrance of men of old, and even those who are yet to come will not be remembered by those who follow" (v. 11). It is as certain as the erosion of footprints on the seashore, as they too concede to the overwhelmingly repeated reality of the tide. It is only because there is no remembrance, indeed, that the illusion of radical newness can captivate anyone: If there were remembrance, it would be acknowledged that the allegedly new things were already "here before our time" (v. 10).

The answer to the question of verse 3 is not explicit in this rumination on the nature of the world "under the sun" and the transience and fragility of human life when considered in this context. Yet a twofold implicit response may be detected. (1) There is indeed no "profit" worth speaking of, for history moves endlessly on, and the achievements of the individual person can only appear trivial when considered over the longer term. The massive reality of history overshadows all those tiny mortal beings who stand all too briefly within its reaches—ephemeral beings who soon pass away. Achievement does not last; the mark one makes on the world is soon erased.

(2) A second answer comes to the hearer as a question: Why do you imagine that a "surplus" for the puny individual is a realistic aim, when creation itself, in all its awesome mystery and complexity beyond mortal grasping, is not ordered to produce a surplus through its toil but is content, as it were, to go on with its tasks, endlessly and cyclically, in consistency with its nature? The massive reality of creation thus critiques the aspirations of all those tiny mortal beings who themselves stand within creation as transient creatures. There is no reason to assume that individuals should "gain" from their toil when creation as a whole does not, nor that some new profit should be individually attained by human toil "under the sun" when the general rule is that there is "nothing new under the sun."

We will find, as we proceed through the book, that Qohelet continually returns to these two themes, urging on his hearers the futility of human thought and activity in pursuit of common human aspirations, on the one hand, while urging a revision in their thinking and the embrace of reality as it actually exists, on the other. There is indeed much that is incomprehensible and futile (*hebel*), from one point of view, as mortal beings, whose life itself is fleeting, insubstantial, and unable to be grasped and retained (cf. "chase the wind"); but there is no need, Qohelet will tell us, for the chase. It is possible, acknowledging the way things really are, to live a contented life in harmony with reality.

The brutality of his unmasking of the world of human desire and action is thus balanced throughout the book by the gentler unveiling of a better way of being. There is no *yitron* to be found under the sun (2:11; 3:9; 5:16), but none need be found. To pursue *yitron* is pointless, but there is no need for the pursuit. There is sufficient reward in life itself, if it is received as a gift from God and lived well.

In sum, then, we will not be interpreting *hebel* in this commentary to mean something like "meaninglessness" or "absurdity," as the NIV and various other modern translations and interpretations have done. The view taken here is that this kind of interpretation is (perhaps unknowingly) too much indebted to an influential modern French existentialism and insufficiently grounded in biblical texts. Qohelet is not Camus.[3] With the word *hebel* he refers to the fragile, fleeting nature of existence, which should cause us to seize the moment and live well in it before God, while at the same time leading us to spurn the desire for any control of life and to disdain that insane grasping after *yitron*, which so often characterizes human activity. We will translate and interpret *hebel* in a manner that fits this general context, stressing the ephemerality of existence or its elusiveness and resistance to intellectual and physical control.

Qohelet's own alternative to the impossible attempt at "getting ahead of the game" in life is set out in numerous ways throughout the book, but perhaps nowhere is it stated more eloquently than in 4:6: "Better one handful with tranquillity than two handfuls with toil and chasing after the wind."

Bridging Contexts

IT IS ONE of the glorious curiosities of Christian faith that a book of ancient texts is held to represent in its totality the communication of God, not just to ancient but also to modern peoples: "All Scripture is God-breathed and is useful for teaching, rebuking, correcting and training in righteousness" (2 Tim. 3:16). When these words were written, the New Testament did not yet exist as a collected body of texts. Their primary reference is to that body of literature acknowledged as Scripture by Jews and Christians alike, known to the former as "Tanakh" and to the latter as "Old Testament." These are the foundational Scriptures of both church and synagogue, to which Christians have added their stories of Jesus and the early church, the apostolic letters, and apocalyptic visions.

The whole Christian Bible thus comes to be received as that which addresses the entire people of God. What God had to say to Israel through his various human agents is received as speech directed also at the church. From time to time throughout Christian history this attitude to the Old Testament has been questioned, whether by Marcion in the second century A.D. or by later Marcionites in the nineteenth and twentieth centuries. Yet the theological and historical grounds for adopting it are unassailable. It is impossible to see how we can be followers of Jesus and not regard his Scriptures as our own.

Thus, when Qohelet addresses the *qahal*, the assembled Israelites, we must also gather on the fringes of the crowd and listen to his words as the *ekklesia*—the word that is frequently translated in the New Testament as "church." We recognize, of course, that he speaks as a person of his own

---

3. In contrast to the moves in this direction by Fox, *Qohelet*, 13–15, 32–33, and elsewhere; see further now M. V. Fox, *A Time to Tear Down and a Time to Build Up: A Rereading of Ecclesiastes* (Grand Rapids: Eerdmans, 1999), 8–11, 30–33.

time, who stands at a particular juncture in history and therefore does not know everything we know about the world and about God's redemptive plans for it. He already speaks as one voice among many Old Testament voices that witness to the reality of God and to the truth inscribed in his creation and enacted in history; yet we must hear his utterance as one witness among a still larger cloud of witnesses stretching down through the Gospel writers and on to people such as Paul, James, and John.

We stand at a different juncture in history, and the concerted voices that offer testimony to us are many more than Qohelet could ever have known of. All this is only to say, however, that we must perhaps work harder than the first readers of Ecclesiastes to understand what God has to say to us through Qohelet. It is not to say that God does not speak to us through him and that we can afford to wander off and listen to an orator more to our liking. Whoever our anonymous and mysterious Qohelet is, he utters words that must be taken deeply seriously.

Qohelet's convictions about both the ephemerality of reality and its elusive nature are widely shared within the Old Testament, using imagery other than "breath." Psalm 90, for example, contrasts the eternity of God with the brevity and fragility of human life in this way (vv. 3—6):

> You turn men back to dust,
>   saying, "Return to dust, O sons of men."
> For a thousand years in your sight
>   are like a day that has just gone by,
>   or like a watch in the night.
> You sweep men away in the sleep of death;
>   they are like the new grass of the morning—
> though in the morning it springs up new,
>   by evening it is dry and withered.

Psalm 103:15—16 and Isaiah 40:6b—7 return to this same theme (cf. also Isa. 51:12):

> As for man, his days are like grass,
>   he flourishes like a flower of the field;
> the wind blows over it and it is gone,
>   and its place remembers it no more.

> All men are like grass,
>   and all their glory is like the flowers of the field.
> The grass withers and the flowers fall,
>   because the breath of the LORD blows on them.
>   Surely the people are grass.

The elusiveness of reality is also well captured in a passage like Job 28:12–28, as verses 20–28 show:

> Where then does wisdom come from?
>   Where does understanding dwell?
> It is hidden from the eyes of every living thing,
>   concealed even from the birds of the air.
> Destruction and Death say,
>   "Only a rumor of it has reached our ears."
> God understands the way to it
>   and he alone knows where it dwells,
> for he views the ends of the earth
>   and sees everything under the heavens.
> When he established the force of the wind
>   and measured out the waters,
> when he made a decree for the rain
>   and a path for the thunderstorm,
> then he looked at wisdom and appraised it;
>   he confirmed it and tested it.
> And he said to man,
>   "The fear of the Lord—that is wisdom,
>   and to shun evil is understanding."

The Old Testament is at pains throughout to remind us in this way of the nature of reality so that we are not deluded, and the New Testament communicates no different message. It too knows of a creation marked by *hebel*, albeit one that will one day give way to a new order of things. Romans 8:20, for example, speaks of a creation subjected to *mataiotes*, the Greek rendering of the Hebrew *hebel* in the LXX of Ecclesiastes. This noun and its related verbal and adjectival forms in fact appear in various New Testament contexts, characterizing many activities or objects of fascination that the New Testament authors consider to be futile, ephemeral, and lacking substance (a "chasing after wind"). Note the following verses (italics added):

> For although they knew God, they neither glorified him as God nor gave thanks to him, but their thinking became *futile* and their foolish hearts were darkened. Although they claimed to be wise, they became fools. (Rom. 1:21–22)

> You must no longer live as the Gentiles do, in the *futility* of their thinking. (Eph. 4:17)

> If anyone considers himself religious and yet does not keep a tight rein on his tongue, he deceives himself and his religion is *worthless*. (James 1:26)

For you know that it was not with perishable things such as silver or gold that you were redeemed from the *empty* way of life handed down to you from your forefathers. (1 Peter 1:18)

For they mouth *empty*, boastful words. (2 Peter 2:18)

The words in 1 Peter 1:18 are indeed followed, after a reminder about how Peter's readers *were* redeemed, by a characterization of their lives outside of Christ precisely in terms of the "grass that withers" in Isaiah 40. James echoes this thought in James 1:10–11 in urging the rich not to be arrogant, while also picking it up using different imagery in 4:14 in advising his readers that all life should be lived out in awareness of its fragility and ephemerality: "Why, you do not even know what will happen tomorrow. What is your life? You are a mist that appears for a little while and then vanishes."

We are reminded by this verse in particular of Jesus' teaching (e.g., Matt. 6:25–34) about getting on with life without worrying overly much about its extent or its practical aspects, which are ultimately beyond our control. The Old Testament use of "grass" as a metaphor for life is in the background of this teaching also, although here it is used as much to convince us of the preciousness of human life to God as to remind us of its brevity.

It is clear from all this that Qohelet is touching on an important biblical theme in emphasizing the ephemerality of reality and its elusive nature. Creation is indeed throughout the Bible a vast and intricate reality, which escapes the grasp of human beings in speech, sight, and hearing—incomprehensible and uncontrollable, to be reckoned with rather than owned or manipulated. It is, for those who refuse to accept this, a site of futility and emptiness; no "gain" can be made from it as a result of striving and struggling with it in pursuit of our own interests.

The New Testament in its own way underlines this theme again and again, assailing attempts to "profit" from God's world in this way. Just prior to his teaching on worrying in Matthew's Gospel, in fact, and connected with it, Jesus warns his listeners against storing up ephemeral treasure on earth and about worshiping money rather than God (Matt. 6:19–24). A central theme of his ministry, enacted in his own life, is that the proper way in which to respond to the nature of reality is to give away one's life rather than hold on to it, to open our hands and let things go rather than to close our fist around them, grasp hold of them, and try to use them for personal advantage (e.g., Matt. 5:5, 38–48; 16:24–25; 19:16–24; 20:24–28).

The apostle Paul, whose own life was characterized by a similar letting go of life, puts it forcibly when he writes to the Christians in Philippi: "For to me, to live is Christ and to die is gain" (Phil. 1:21). Life for the Christian is "Christ"—to hold him at the center of our attention, to trust him and follow him, and to imitate him. If there is "gain" at all, it lies only in death, whether the dying is daily and unto self or whether it is final and literal.

It is only in and through Christ that there is ultimately any "newness" that is worth speaking of in terms of creation—whether the newness of all things as they will appear in the future, when the kingdom of God fully breaks into our present age, or the newness of life that is lived in the present in anticipation of this amazing future (2 Cor. 5:17; Gal. 6:15; 2 Peter 3:13; Rev. 21:1). The Old Testament already knew of both aspects of newness (e.g., Isa. 65:17–25; Jer. 31:31–34), albeit without knowing the full story of how they would be realized.

As far as we can tell, Qohelet did not himself believe in such things; at least, he does not mention them. He restricts himself to the consideration of things as they can be observed within the limits of this present life. What he has to say is still fundamental, however, even to the Christian who knows more than he, for the Christian life is as much about living faithfully in the light of present God-given reality as it is about waiting expectantly for the dawning of the new reality that God will one day initiate.

From the day we arrive on the planet, and
    blinking, step into the sun,
There's more to be seen than can ever be seen,
    more to do than can ever be done. . . .
There's far too much to take in here, more to find than can
    ever be found;
But the sun rolling high through the sapphire sky
Keeps great and small on the endless round,
In the circle of life.

The Lion King, from which these words are taken, is one of those movies about which I have in recent years been warned by some of my Christian friends who have the best interests of my children at heart. "It's very 'New Age,' you know," they would say, in hushed and knowing tones. Undeterred, I took my family to see it anyway, and it is undoubtedly true, although unsurprising, that the movie betrays the influence of that strange mixture of ancient and modern idolatries known as *New Age spirituality*.

Yet many of its themes (and this too is not surprising in our "pick and mix" culture) are at least as indebted to biblical and Christian thinking as to anything else. My friends never mentioned this. I assume that they misunderstood the direction of the indebtedness. I assume this because I have so often before encountered similar things among Christians in the West, and particularly among those living in the United States or influenced by American religious culture.

To put the matter bluntly, many Christians do not possess a robust and biblical doctrine of creation (even if they spend much of their time arguing about "creationism" and why it is better than "evolutionism"). Lacking this, they often assume that ideas about creation they encounter are pagan, when in fact they are (or could be redeemed to be) biblical and Christian. They often fail to understand, indeed, that one reason why many idealistic people are uninterested in or hostile to Christianity is precisely because they consider Christians to have no place for creation in their thinking, with the result that they have contributed to the rapacious exploitation of our planet, which has brought us by degrees to the edge of global ecological disaster.

The theme song of *The Lion King*, at least in the edited version offered above, is almost a Christian song. It captures the wonder of creation—how it escapes our comprehension and control and yet mysteriously and effectively provides an environment in which the "circle of life" can continue. The "circle" is a deliberately chosen image, since it reminds us that human beings are themselves part of the matrix of life and do not stand in isolation from it. The emphasis of the song is on living in harmony with what is there, rather than objectifying it, manipulating it, and seeking to mold it to personal advantage. As the song tells us in another place, "all are agreed as they join the stampede, you should never take more than you give."

This too is (almost) a Christian thought. We find ourselves here almost in the world of Genesis 1–2 and of Psalms 8, 19, and 104—a world that comes to us as a wondrous gift to be cared for on behalf of its Creator and Owner, in which there is kinship between human beings and beasts and harmony between human beings and the earth; in which there is a glad and joyful use of the things God has given us, but always in an attitude of worship and praise that offers everything back to God, who gave it. The main difference between the Bible and *The Lion King* song lies, of course, not in the religious view of the world that both thus possess, but in the view that they take of the Giver and his relationship with his world.

We may contrast both these religious perspectives on the world with a common modern worldview that has both religious and secular forms, one that is not truly biblical at all. According to this view, the world may or may not have been created by God, but if it was, God does not continue to have much interest in it. It is passing away and set to be consumed by fire (1 Cor. 7:31; 2 Peter 3:10–13, quoted out of context). Thus, the created order should not figure in any central way in our understanding of human destiny. We should focus rather on our various human goals and ends, whether the redemption of our souls (the religious version of the heresy) or the pursuit of happiness and fulfillment (the secular version).

In practice both versions can coexist quite happily in the individual life, since the narrowing of the religious vision of life simply to the future state of the soul can leave plenty of scope (depending on which deprivations are thought absolutely necessary for the soul's good) for enthusiastic participation in the secular dream as far as the body is concerned. This is why many North American Christians can seemingly participate without a moment's religious self-doubt in a rapacious type of capitalism that pays no attention to the social and ecological costs it accumulates. This is why materialism generally (which is apparently not thought to jeopardize the arrival of the soul in heaven) is not spoken of in the church half as much as (the apparently much more dangerous) sex, whereas in the Gospels the emphasis falls in the opposite direction.

This brand of religious secularism is also why so many people in the modern world who take the name "Christian" are in many respects indistinguishable (aside from a few personal rules that make them eccentric) from their non-Christian counterparts, for they have largely bought into the secular dream. While talking a good Christian talk, they are in fact pursuing with all their might precisely the same goals as everyone else. They are looking for happiness and fulfillment in this life (albeit with an insurance policy for the next life in their pocket); they are looking to make their mark (or for their children to do so); they are looking to manipulate the world so as to achieve their own personal and family goals.

The fact that many Christians are doing this in a Christian subculture rather than in the world at large matters little. They are still approaching the world in a fundamentally irreligious manner, in the same way that a secular person will often do, and especially in these days of weariness with modernity, with even greater irreligiosity than a sensitive and idealistic person who is not a Christian.

To all those who try to "gain" from life, whatever it is they claim to be doing, Qohelet presents stark reality—reality that does not change simply because we wish it to, but remains fundamentally as it is in spite of all that comes under the heading "progress." The more things change, the more they stay the same. The universe is not designed to enable "gain" to happen, and those who attempt to fly in the face of reality can only ever know grief and frustration in the end. The universe is not designed to contain gods and heroes, but mortal beings who accept the limitations that have been set upon their lives and get on with them in quietness and humility.

This life on earth is intended to have as its center the God who created everything and who holds everything in his hand. He calls us to love him and our neighbor and to care for the "garden" he has entrusted to us. The culture at large has decided it would like reality to be different; thus, it dethrones God, worships gods and heroes who burst through life's limitations while patently failing to love their neighbor (think of most of the movies you have seen in the last decade), and exploits the earth for its own ends. The church cannot quite decide, it seems, which reality it will embrace, and it is so much caught between the two that it often even has a view of Christian leadership that has more of the god and the hero than the servant about it.

It is foolish for us to think, however, that we can walk on the world's path for the whole of our lives and then simply present our "insurance policy" to God at the end and to inherit the kingdom of God as well. Qohelet, by not even dwelling on the afterlife, helps us to get this much clear: There is a choice to be made *now* about which version of reality we will embrace and which path we will follow, and this choice has consequences for *now*. It also has consequences for later, for life everlasting comes, not as an arbitrary add-on to just any kind of life that is lived here and now, but as the natural extension of the life that is lived with God in the present and, because it is lived with God, is also lived in community with neighbor and earth.

The Christian writer C. S. Lewis grasped this thought clearly and expressed it beautifully in story form in *The Great Divorce*. The characters in this story, whose natural home and comfort zone is in hell, have never come to terms with, confronted, or lived out reality. Their lives have been lived in darkness and delusion. On a day-trip to heaven, a brief window of opportunity for redemption opens up before them, but they find reality unutterably painful to the touch. They are like wraiths and shadows suddenly facing the sunlight. Mostly they desire only to retreat from the light and from the pain. Having refused to come to terms with reality while alive, they cannot embrace it when dead. It is the embrace of reality that Qohelet urges upon us, for the good of our lives in the here and now. A Christian interpretation of Qohelet must make it clear, however, that it is also for our good in the hereafter.

What good will it be for a man if he gains the whole world, yet forfeits his soul? (Matt. 16:26)

Ecclesiastes 1:12–2:26

I, THE TEACHER, was king over Israel in Jerusalem. [13]I devoted myself to study and to explore by wisdom all that is done under heaven. What a heavy burden God has laid on men! [14]I have seen all the things that are done under the sun; all of them are meaningless, a chasing after the wind.

[15]What is twisted cannot be straightened;
    what is lacking cannot be counted.

[16]I thought to myself, "Look, I have grown and increased in wisdom more than anyone who has ruled over Jerusalem before me; I have experienced much of wisdom and knowledge." [17]Then I applied myself to the understanding of wisdom, and also of madness and folly, but I learned that this, too, is a chasing after the wind.

[18]For with much wisdom comes much sorrow;
    the more knowledge, the more grief.

[2:1]I thought in my heart, "Come now, I will test you with pleasure to find out what is good." But that also proved to be meaningless. [2]"Laughter," I said, "is foolish. And what does pleasure accomplish?" [3]I tried cheering myself with wine, and embracing folly—my mind still guiding me with wisdom. I wanted to see what was worthwhile for men to do under heaven during the few days of their lives.

[4]I undertook great projects: I built houses for myself and planted vineyards. [5]I made gardens and parks and planted all kinds of fruit trees in them. [6]I made reservoirs to water groves of flourishing trees. [7]I bought male and female slaves and had other slaves who were born in my house. I also owned more herds and flocks than anyone in Jerusalem before me. [8]I amassed silver and gold for myself, and the treasure of kings and provinces. I acquired men and women singers, and a harem as well—the delights of the heart of man. [9]I became greater by far than anyone in Jerusalem before me. In all this my wisdom stayed with me.

[10]I denied myself nothing my eyes desired;
    I refused my heart no pleasure.

My heart took delight in all my work,
　　and this was the reward for all my labor.
¹¹ Yet when I surveyed all that my hands had done
　　and what I had toiled to achieve,
　everything was meaningless, a chasing after the wind;
　　nothing was gained under the sun.

¹² Then I turned my thoughts to consider wisdom,
　　and also madness and folly.
　What more can the king's successor do
　　than what has already been done?
¹³ I saw that wisdom is better than folly,
　　just as light is better than darkness.
¹⁴ The wise man has eyes in his head,
　　while the fool walks in the darkness;
　but I came to realize
that the same fate overtakes them both.

¹⁵Then I thought in my heart,

　"The fate of the fool will overtake me also.
　　What then do I gain by being wise?"
　I said in my heart,
　　"This too is meaningless."
¹⁶ For the wise man, like the fool, will not be
　　　long remembered;
　　in days to come both will be forgotten.
　Like the fool, the wise man too must die!

¹⁷So I hated life, because the work that is done under the sun was grievous to me. All of it is meaningless, a chasing after the wind. ¹⁸I hated all the things I had toiled for under the sun, because I must leave them to the one who comes after me. ¹⁹And who knows whether he will be a wise man or a fool? Yet he will have control over all the work into which I have poured my effort and skill under the sun. This too is meaningless. ²⁰So my heart began to despair over all my toilsome labor under the sun. ²¹For a man may do his work with wisdom, knowledge and skill, and then he must leave all he owns to someone who has not worked for it. This too is meaningless and a great misfortune. ²²What does a man get for all the toil and anxious striving with which he labors under the sun? ²³All

his days his work is pain and grief; even at night his mind does not rest. This too is meaningless.

²⁴A man can do nothing better than to eat and drink and find satisfaction in his work. This too, I see, is from the hand of God, ²⁵for without him, who can eat or find enjoyment? ²⁶To the man who pleases him, God gives wisdom, knowledge and happiness, but to the sinner he gives the task of gathering and storing up wealth to hand it over to the one who pleases God. This too is meaningless, a chasing after the wind.

THE LEADING QUESTION of the book has been stated in the introduction: "What does man gain from all his labor at which he toils under the sun?" (1:3), and we have been reminded, in relation to this question, of the nature of the universe as an ongoing, solid reality on which it is impossible to make a lasting human impression. Human activity is fleeting and inconsequential in this regard.

The present long section now pursues in numerous ways this question of "gain from . . . labor" in the world as we find it, as Qohelet surveys that world from the perspective of the "king over Israel in Jerusalem" (v. 12). If any person might be expected to "gain from . . . labor" in Israel, it is the king—particularly a king like Solomon (whose reign is evoked in numerous ways in the passage), with the unlimited time and resources at his disposal and his famed wisdom to guide him (cf. 1 Kings 3–10). He is to all appearances in a wonderfully advantageous position, if "getting ahead of the game" is the goal.

Yet, as we will see, the report we receive from "the-speaker-as-Solomon" (this fiction is especially apparent in 1:16; 2:7, 9, which represent the perspective of Qohelet looking back over the whole history of Davidic kings in Jerusalem rather than the perspective of Solomon himself, who was preceded in Jerusalem only by his father David) is not particularly encouraging. Wisdom is useful as an instrument for understanding the world, yet what it mainly helps one to understand is just how impossible it is to control and to profit from the world as it has been created (1:12–18). Joy is possible as mortal beings go about their creative work and accumulate wealth and possessions, yet all the effort involved in all the work and accumulation does not leave a single cent of profit on the balance sheet of life (2:1–11). Death stands as the ultimate obstacle to human control of destiny, rendering the accumulation of both wisdom and wealth pointless—if the point is to make a profit of some kind.

This reality has the capacity to spoil the enjoyment of life itself, if one is not prepared to adjust one's aspirations to reality (2:12–23). It is this adjustment that Qohelet advocates as the whole section ends (2:24–26). For all their apparent advantages, it turns out that kings—even kings like Solomon—must content themselves with regarding life as an end in itself rather than as an object to be manipulated for profit. It is in the humble things, received as gifts from God—eating and drinking and finding satisfaction in one's work—that joy is to be found. The good life is the life centered on God and not on the striving self.

Wisdom As an Instrument for Understanding the World (1:12–18)

IT IS UNSURPRISING that we should begin with wisdom. Solomon's wisdom was famous—a gifting from God that brought him riches and honor, that produced justice and prosperity for his people, and that attracted admiration and visitation from people all over the ancient world (1 Kings 3:12–13, 16–28; 4:20–34; 9:10–10:29). Wisdom was the very foundation of the life of one of Israel's most successful and effective kings.

Yet the first-person testimony of "Solomon" tells us a different story from the one we might have expected on the basis of the narrative account of his life. It comes to us in two sections (vv. 12–15 and 16–18), each with its own statement of what Qohelet set out to do and what he discovered, and each with its own concluding proverb. The first section essentially tells us of the role that wisdom played in leading Qohelet to the point of view expressed in 1:1–11, while the second offers some comments on wisdom itself.

(1) "Solomon" first applies his wisdom to the business of "all that is done under heaven" (v. 13; cf. v. 3), and he discovers only that the burden that God has "laid" (the NIV's rendering of Heb. *ntn*, "to set, give") on human beings is a heavy one. It is a "sorry business" (NEB) or an "evil occupation"[1] that

---

1. The Heb. is *ʿinyan raʿ*, as in 5:14; cf. also 4:8. In the latter case the NIV offers what would also be a better translation in 1:13: "a miserable business." Words like "evil," which are frequently appropriate for Heb. *raʿ* in the Old Testament, are often best avoided (and are often thus avoided in the NIV) in translating *raʿ* / *raʿa* in Ecclesiastes, since they can give the modern reader the impression that Qohelet is referring to moral wickedness where this is not necessarily the case. The Heb. can refer (and often does in Ecclesiastes) simply or mainly to situations or outcomes faced by human beings that are experienced by them as, or thought by Qohelet to be, "bad," without moral blame being the explicit focus (e.g., 2:17, 21; 5:13, 16; 6:1–2; 7:14; 8:3, 5–6, 9). This is especially the case where God is concerned, who brings (and is entitled to bring) to human beings bad times as well as good (e.g., 7:14). As we will see shortly, a similar ambiguity is found in Ecclesiastes, as elsewhere in the Old Testament, with respect to Heb. *tob*, "good."

God has delegated to us, characterized by futile activity ("all of them are *hebel* [pointless], a chasing after the wind," v. 14; cf. comments on 1:1−11). The manner of the speech may at first suggest that there is some divine desire that human life should inevitably be of this character, yet passages like 2:24−26; 3:12−13 reveal that this is not Qohelet's opinion. We should understand God's "giving" of the "sorry business," therefore, in the wider context of biblical belief that whatever happens in the world has a general "God-ordainedness" about it, since nothing can happen outside of God's will.

To put this another way, God permits things to happen in his world that are his "will" only in the general sense that they will not happen if he chooses not to permit them. They are not his "will" in the narrower sense of representing his deepest desires and most heartfelt intentions with respect to his creatures. The judgment of God, for example, is not, biblically, something that proceeds from the deepest heart of God, which is to bless and to love his creatures (note, e.g., Lam. 3:31−33); God would, biblically, rather that his creatures repent of their sins and return to him (e.g., Hos. 11:8−9).

Nevertheless, God also allows people to suffer the consequences of their decisions, giving them over to these consequences and in a sense thereby "willing" them (e.g., Rom. 1:18−32). God ordains that their world should have a certain shape and content, but their own beliefs and decisions are themselves bound up with the kind of world they inhabit, and they have moral responsibility in respect of that world, which is not *inevitably* the one they must inhabit (cf. Eccl. 2:26). The Heb. verb *ntn* can itself often be translated "permit, ordain" rather than "give" (e.g., Gen. 20:6; 31:7; Ex. 3:19; Num. 20:21; 21:23).

That we should understand Ecclesiastes 1:13−14 in this looser way—that God has "ordained" that life should be a "heavy burden" for humanity in all its striving and struggling and chasing after the wind—is confirmed by the proverb that Qohelet cites in 1:15 in connection with this general human experience of life. The futility of life as it is characteristically lived out "under heaven" is captured here in terms of people trying to straighten what is twisted and to count that which is "lacking." The key to understanding the first line is found in 7:13: "Consider what God has done: Who can straighten what he has made crooked?" The emphasis there and in 7:14 is on accepting what comes from the hand of God rather than striving with it and struggling against it.

It seems likely, particularly in view of the suggestion in 1:1−11 that the fundamental human problem resides in a lack of harmony between common human aspirations and the very nature of reality itself, that the futility of 1:14 is to be understood precisely in terms of a human refusal to accept things as they are. There is a human insistence that the impossible can in fact be achieved—that what God has made "crooked" or "twisted" can indeed be made straight by human, mortal effort. It is all futile, for God is God, and the world is the way it is. Refusing to accept reality can only result in unhappiness and weariness (since wind cannot be caught, however hard the chase).

The second line of the proverb in 1:15 likewise presents us with an impossibility: counting what is "lacking." The Hebrew word here is *ḥesron*, from the verb *ḥsr*, "be lacking, deficient." The idea of "deficit" as the condition that people cannot accept and to which they foolishly respond by "counting," as if the deficit were in fact a surplus, ties this part of the proverb also to 1:1–11, with its question about where the human profit might occur in consequence of human effort. There is no "gain" of this kind from toil, Qohelet tells us; there is only and always a deficit. To pursue gain is therefore only and always futile. In due course this observation will lead him to suggest a different way of thinking about profit and toil, as he turns our attention away from toil as a means to the end of profit and presents profit, instead, as enjoyment of what God gives us (including toil itself).

(2) If the first part of 1:12–18 has viewed wisdom as an instrument through which to view reality and has found it useful in coming to a clear perception of the world in all its futility, the second part (vv. 16–18) now turns to consider wisdom in itself. Qohelet had previously devoted himself (*natan ʾet-leb*) to study the world (v. 13) and had found only pointless activity; now he applies himself (*natan leb*) to the understanding of wisdom (v. 17). Perhaps greater effort in sifting through what is known and separating out wisdom from "madness and folly" is the way ahead for human beings.

"Madness" (*holela*) carries connotations of a boastful arrogance that sets itself against God rather than praising God;[2] "folly" (usually spelled *siklut*, but here *śiklut*) is its occasional partner in Ecclesiastes (2:12; 7:25; 10:13) and the common antithesis to wisdom (2:3, 13; 10:1; cf. also 10:6 for a related noun and 2:19; 7:17; 10:3, 14 for the character called "the fool" [*sakal*]). Perhaps it is possible through concentrated intellectual effort to distinguish these things more accurately—to refine one's understanding of the world—and thus to escape from the trap set by life for the ordinary person.

Is there "profit" ("gain," cf. 1:3) here? Qohelet does not think so. It is not that wisdom is useless, for he has just used it in verses 12–15 to arrive at important conclusions about the world in which he lives, and he will go on employing "wisdom" throughout chapter 2 (e.g., 2:3), acknowledging that it is better than folly (2:13, and implicitly in 2:19, 26). Yet it is not itself something that can be grasped hold of and controlled (1:17), nor can it offer mortal

---

2. See BDB, 237–39, on the root *hll* (which can be used both of self-praise and the praise of God) and the nouns associated it with it.

beings release from the "evil business" of living. Although wisdom and knowledge are good and useful, they paradoxically bring with them "sorrow" (1:18; perhaps better, "frustration," Heb. *ka'as*) and "grief" (*mak'ob*, "mental pain")—not least, one suspects, because they enable people like Qohelet to gain particular clarity as to just how "evil" the "business" of living can be. We may note the recurrence of *mak'ob* and *ka'as* in that reverse order in 2:23 (NIV's "pain and grief"),[3] in the midst of a graphic account of the "sorry business" of life. The point is that wisdom and knowledge dispel illusions.

Joy, Work, and Profit (2:1–11)

THE KING HAS found wisdom limited in what it can achieve as he strives for profit from his labor. It has only succeeded in convincing him of the general pointlessness of human activity. Thus, he turns now to "pleasure," testing himself (addressed in the second person as "you") to discover whether a determined effort at enjoyment will somehow bring him a return on his investment. The Hebrew word is *simḥa* (2:1), which in other contexts means "joy, gladness, gaiety"; indeed in 2:26; 5:20; 8:15; and 9:7 it is described as a gift of God like wisdom and knowledge. The translation "pleasure" is thus an unhelpful one, if it carries for the reader the connotation of things forbidden or questionable.

Gladness of heart, joy, pleasure—it is not that these things are not good in themselves in Ecclesiastes. Yet Qohelet has discovered that the *pursuit* of them with the hope of gain is just as pointless as the pursuit of wisdom and knowledge for that purpose. The concept *simḥa* does not "accomplish" or achieve anything (v. 2). Indeed, it is as readily associated with fools as with the wise (cf. 7:4). The same is true of "laughter" (2:2), which is all too often uttered by those who have no profound grasp of reality (cf. 7:3–6).

The drinking of wine, likewise, is not of itself a necessarily foolish action (it is explicitly commended in 9:7), but it is not liable to "accomplish" anything. Qohelet's quest here is to use wine with a view to "embracing folly"—albeit consciously and intentionally, his wisdom-imbued mind still in control—until he is able to sift out what is "good" and to be embraced by mortals during their brief lives (v. 3; cf. also v. 1). The wine is a means to that general end, rather than a stimulus, more narrowly, to cheerfulness; the NIV's

---

3. The NIV's inconsistent translation brings with it unnecessary confusion; it would be better to translate "frustration and pain" in 1:18 and "pain and frustration" in 2:23. Heb. *k's* in noun and verbal forms appears also in 5:17; 7:3, 9; 11:10, where the NIV translates variously as "frustration," "sorrow," "anger," "provoked . . . anger," and "anxiety." There is no case in Ecclesiastes where it cannot refer to anger or suppressed anger (frustration), however (its normal use in the Old Testament), and several cases where it almost certainly does (5:17; 7:3, 9). It seems best to aim at a consistent translation throughout.

translation "cheering myself" is in fact an interpretative guess at the meaning of Hebrew *mšk*, which normally means "to draw, drag, lead."

The double path that Qohelet walks is better brought out by the following partial translation of 2:1, 3: "I said in my mind, 'Come, let me test you with joy and see what is good.' ... I searched with my mind to lead along [*mšk*] my body with wine—I myself shepherding my mind with wisdom—and to grasp folly until I saw what was good. ...'" He treads one path with his body while taking another with his mind, hoping in his intoxicated state to experience the full depths of "folly" and to arrive at discernment.

The overall intention of the experiment and the means by which it was conducted having been described, its detail is now laid bare. The "king" set out to transform his environment and thereby to facilitate his enjoyment of life. He "undertook great projects" (lit., "made great his works") in the line with his great wisdom of 1:16, but perhaps also with the connotation of godlike behavior (cf., e.g., the use of this verb *gdl* in the Hiphil positively of God in 1 Sam. 12:24; Ps. 126:2–3, and negatively of those who exalt themselves against God in Jer. 48:26, 42; Ezek. 35:13).

He put superhuman effort into what he did (Heb. *maᶜᵃśeh*, "works," is used in Ecclesiastes 1:14; 2:17, of all the "things" that are done under the sun). Houses, vineyards, gardens, and parks are all mentioned, the last of these words (Heb. *pardes*) deriving from the Persian word *pairi-daeza*, "an enclosure," from which we also ultimately derive our word "paradise." Paradise is indeed evoked by the reference to the "trees" that fill these gardens and parks, watered by their reservoirs (cf. Gen. 2:6–10)—a world that is then "populated" (cf. Gen. 2:15–25) by the king's own people: male and female slaves and the children born to them (Eccl. 2:7).

The enormous wealth of the king is portrayed (2:7–8) in terms of unparalleled numbers of herds and flocks, hoards of treasure that have been gathered in part from "kings and provinces" who have either been plundered or have brought tribute, and unspecified numbers of human beings devoted to the task of pleasing him, whether in song or in bed (if the last few words of v. 8, *taᶜᵃnugot bᵉne haʾadam šidda wᵉśiddot*, are indeed a reference to concubines). The first word, from the Hebrew root *ᶜng*, is often used simply of "delighting" in someone or something, whether it is God (e.g., Job 22:26; 27:10; Ps. 37:4; Isa. 58:14), material blessing (Ps. 37:11; Isa. 55:2), or maternal breasts (Isa. 66:11). Sometimes it refers to something or someone that is delightful or indeed tender, delicate, or soft, and particularly to a woman (Deut. 28:54, 56; Isa 47:1). The noun *taᶜᵃnug* (NIV "delights") also appears in Proverbs 19:10 of a fool living the lifestyle of the nobility, in Song of Songs 7:6 of the unspecified "delights" of a woman, and in Micah 1:16; 2:9 of children and homes that are the delight of adults.

From these references it can be seen that, although it is perfectly plausible to interpret *ta'anug* in 2:8 as referring to women, we cannot be entirely sure that this is what is meant. Yet the context favors it, since we expect a reference here to some counterpart to the singers—that is, to particular and specific "delights of the sons of men" (lit. trans.) rather than to delights in general. The play on words between *šarim w'šarot*, "men and women singers," and *šidda w'šiddot* itself implies this. It would greatly help us to know for certain the meaning of this last phrase, but we do not. Yet a derivation from Heb. *šad*, "breast," seems most likely, and we gain help as to meaning from Judges 5:30a, *raham rah'matayim l'ro'š geber* (lit., "a womb or two for each man"). A phrase like this is often explained in terms of synecdoche, whereby the part of something can stand for the whole—thus the NIV translation of Judges 5:30a, "a girl or two for each man." It is not always clear, however, that the intention is to refer to the whole female person rather than to the part in which the men whose perspective dominates the text are interested (whether "womb," because of childbearing potential, or "breast," where it is perhaps the potential for sexual fulfillment that is in mind). The best way in which to translate the second part of Ecclesiastes 2:8 may in fact be: "I acquired for myself male and female singers and the delights of the male— a breast or two."

Much of the description of what the "king" achieved and acquired echoes what we know of Solomon's reign from 1 Kings 3–11. He was a king who constructed many buildings, had many slaves and much treasure, and knew many women. Yet once again a distance from Solomon's time is suggested (Eccl. 2:7; cf. also 2:9), and it is clear that not all the details of our passage correspond to those that we find in the Kings account (note, e.g., the striking disclaimer in 1 Kings 10:21 about the relative worthlessness of silver in Solomon's day, when compared to Eccl. 2:8). Solomon is simply one of those many characters throughout history who have set out on the path described here, and his reign functions as a convenient backdrop for Qohelet's reflections. However, Qohelet himself (unlike Solomon toward the end of his reign),[4] kept wisdom by him throughout the entire experience (2:9; cf. 2:3), as he opened himself up to every "pleasure" (Heb. *simha*, better "joy," v. 10)— he remained in control of the experiment.

The closing verses of this section present in summary the mixed conclusions of Qohelet's experiment (vv. 10–11). First he tells us that he did in fact find joy in all his toil ("my heart took delight in all my work [*'amal*]," v. 10; the Heb. verb here is *šmh*, from which the noun *simha* in v. 10 also comes). Indeed, this joy itself was the "reward" (Heb. *heleq*) arising out of all his toil

---

4. See I. W. Provan, *1 and 2 Kings* (NIBC; Peabody, Mass.: Hendrickson, 1995), 84–102.

(Heb. *ʿamal*, NIV "labor"); it was what he "possessed" when all was said and done (cf. *ḥeleq* in 2:21, where the NIV translates it as "all he owns"; and in 11:2, where the phrase translated "give portions" might better be rendered "divide what you own").

Yet immediately the "king" proceeds to the final result of his experiment (v. 11). That is, he "surveyed" or turned to look at what he had done (Heb. *maʿăśeh*, cf. v. 4)—what he had toiled to achieve—and his assessment was that it was all pointless (Heb. *hebel*; see comments on 1:2). There was no "gain" (Heb. *yitron*). While engaged on the experiment on its inside, as it were (and even though mentally detached from it to some extent), he found joy as his reward; but considering it coolly from the outside after its completion and bringing to it the mentality of the balance sheet, he pronounced it all a "chasing after the wind." The reward was not an adequate one when measured by the aspirations that drove the experiment. His determined effort at enjoyment had not brought a sufficient return on the investment. Joy is as limited as wisdom in what it can achieve.

This insight will, in due course, lead on to Qohelet's important advice on how to live one's life contentedly, in some of which *ḥeleq* reappears:

3:22:   "There is nothing better for a man than to enjoy [*śmḥ*] his work, because that is his lot [Heb. *ḥeleq*, better trans. as reward]."

5:18–19: "Then I realized that it is good and proper for a man to eat and drink, and to find satisfaction in his toilsome labor under the sun during the few days of life God has given him—for this is his lot [*ḥeleq*, reward]. Moreover, when God gives any man wealth and possessions, and enables him to enjoy them, to accept his lot [*ḥeleq*] and be happy [*śmḥ*] in his work—this is a gift of God."

9:9:   "Enjoy life with your wife, whom you love, all the days of this meaningless [better trans. as brief] life that God has given you under the sun—all your meaningless [fleeting] days. For this is your lot [*ḥeleq*, reward] in life and in your toilsome labor under the sun."

The emphasis lies on enjoyment or joy as itself the reward that we may expect from life and all our effort expended in living it. There is no surplus, no profit beyond that. Indeed, the "reward" is itself a gift from God, an inheritance in which we share rather than a prize that we earn (cf. 9:6 for *ḥeleq* as our "share" [NIV "part"] of life under the sun; also Gen. 31:14; Num. 18:20; Deut. 10:9, etc., for the frequent use of *ḥeleq* in the sense of inherited land or property). It is in receiving life as a gift from God and in not striving to manipulate it and exploit it in order to arrive at some kind of "gain" that mortal beings can find contentment.

Further Reflections on Wisdom (2:12–16)

WE ARE NOT yet at this point of resolution, however. In fact, we are not yet done with Qohelet's reflections on wisdom, begun in 1:12–18. His return to this topic is clearly related to the completed experiment in respect of pleasure: He turned to look at (*pnh*) all that his hands had done (v. 11), and then he turned his thoughts (*pnh*) to consider once again wisdom and madness and folly (v. 12; cf. 1:17). His conviction is that his pursuit of joy has been comprehensive and that his use of wisdom in that pursuit has been thorough: "What more can the king's successor do than what has already been done?" (v. 12).[5] He is now in a good position, therefore, to reflect more fully on wisdom in itself. The movement of 2:1–16 is indeed somewhat similar to that in 1:12–18: Wisdom is seen to be a useful instrument through which to view reality and to come to a clearer perception of the world (1:12–15; 2:1–11), and yet wisdom in itself does not bring any real "profit" or "gain" (1:16–18; 2:12–16).

It is not that there is no profit in wisdom at all. When considered alongside folly, wisdom has everything to be said for it as something "better" (lit., "having a *yitron* over," v. 13), just as light is clearly better than darkness. The first part of verse 14 is in all likelihood another proverb, like those in 1:15 and 1:18, cited here to underline the point (cf. the similar thought in Prov. 4:18–19). Yet the fact remains that the same fate overtakes both the wise and foolish person: "Like the fool, the wise man too must die!" (Eccl. 2:16). Neither will be long remembered (cf. 1:11). Thus the question arises in Qohelet's mind: What does he "gain" (Heb. *yoter*, a noun related to *yitron*) by being wise (2:15)?

This question once again concerns ultimate, extrinsic gain, rather than the kind of intrinsic profit that is plainly acknowledged as a reality in verse 13. What is the point of excess in wisdom if it does not result in surplus of profit? In the end, in this sense, "death makes fools of us all," whether we were wise in life or not. There is nothing left over after life has ended; there is no surplus. Not only can wisdom not offer mortal beings release from the "evil business" of living, then (1:12–18); it also cannot solve the problem of death.

From Despair to Satisfaction (2:17–26)

THE REALITY OF death overshadows Qohelet's life, to the extent that he now confesses his hatred for life (v. 17). It is bad enough that there is no real

---

5. The Heb. of the line is difficult, lit., "for what the man who comes after the king? That which they have already done!" The NIV is surely correct to supply the verb in its first part and to understand the plural in its second part impersonally: "For what (is) the man (to do) who comes after the king? That which has already been done!" (GKC, §§117l, 144g, 167a). Yet the NIV's omission of "for" (*ki*) unfortunately obscures the connection between the two parts of v. 12.

personal "gain" in life from all the effort that is expended—an effort that is relentlessly emphasized throughout verses 17–23 through the repetition of the Hebrew noun ʿamal, "toil," in verses 18, 19, 20, 21, and 22, along with related verbal and adjectival forms of ʿml in each of those verses. But it is quite intolerable that to the extent that anything *has* been gained, it should be lost in the end to another person, who may himself be foolish rather than wise (vv. 18–19), yet will benefit from Qohelet's effort and wisdom (v. 19, where Heb. ḥkm, "be wise, act wisely," is rendered "poured . . . skill" by NIV; v. 21). Life is an "evil business" indeed when seen from this point of view, as 1:13 has already told us. It greatly helps comprehension at this point, in fact, to realize that the phrase ʿinyan raʿ in 1:13 (NIV's "heavy burden"; lit., "evil occupation/business") is echoed here in the NIV's "grievous" in 2:17 (raʿ), "work" in 2:23 (ʿinyan), and "task" in 2:26 (ʿinyan).

Life lived from such a perspective is full of pointlessness (vv. 17, 19, 21, 23), despair or hopelessness (v. 20), misfortune (raʿa "evil," v. 21), pain, grief, and restlessness (v. 23, noting that "pain" is the Heb. makʾob, translated by NIV as "grief" in 1:18, and that "grief" in 2:23 is Heb. kaʿas, translated by NIV as "sorrow" in 1:18). Those who seek control of life only and always "chase after the wind" (2:17), that is, grasp after what cannot be grasped. Death is the ultimate statement of mortal lack of control, which must always pass to another who will benefit from his predecessor's input (v. 19, where he will "have mastery/control over" the work, Heb. šlṭ). Only God has ultimate control, even though mortals may briefly possess some degree of it.[6]

The refusal to acknowledge this can only lead to misery—a lack of fulfillment in the daily work itself, perhaps heightened by a particularly clear perception of how pointless it all is (cf. 1:18) and an inability to sleep well at night. Such a person's body goes to bed, but his mind (lit.) "cannot lie down."

The confessions of a workaholic![7] There is an alternative way of being, however (vv. 24–26). This way of being represents the "good" life that Qohelet has been searching after (cf. Heb. ṭob, "good," in 2:1, 3). Thus the closing verses of chapter 2 contain four occurrences of ṭob (v. 24, NIV "better" and "satisfaction," and v. 26, "pleases") in parallel to the four occurrences of hebel, "pointlessness," that refer to the life of the person pursuing the wind in verses 17–23. The good life consists in eating and drinking and in the ability of the mortal being to "show himself what is good in his toil" (v. 24; NIV

---

6. We may note here Heb. šlṭ in 5:19 and 6:2 (NIV's "enable[s]") of God's control; the same verb occurs in 8:9 (NIV's "lords it over") of temporary human control.

7. So R. K. Johnston, "Confessions of a Workaholic: A Reappraisal of Qoheleth," CBQ 38 (1976): 14–28, citing the title of the book of the same name by W. Oates (New York: World, 1971).

"find satisfaction in his work"). It consists in viewing food, drink, and work as gifts from God and receiving them as such (vv. 24–25).[8]

This way of life, just as much as the "sorry business" described in the preceding verses, is "from the hand of God." There is more than one "God-ordained" path through life (cf. the earlier discussion of 1:13). The good life, indeed, has at its core an orientation of the mortal being toward God, such that God finds "good" in that mortal being: He or she "pleases" him (v. 26). With God the Giver at the center of things and the striving self displaced— we may note, by way of contrast, the centrality of the striving self and the absence of God in 1:16–2:23—there is now the possibility not only of wisdom and knowledge, but also of joy (Heb. *śimḥa*, v. 26).

The illusion that there is a "profit" to be made has been discarded, and creaturely limitations before the Creator have been embraced. It is now in fact made explicitly clear for the first time that the chasing of the wind is not only pointless but also a moral fault. It is the "sinner" to whom God delegates the task (*ʿinyan*, "business") of gathering and storing up wealth (cf. the use of the same Heb. *kns* in 2:8, where the NIV translates it "amassed"), only to lose it to another. It is the sinner whose life is "pointless" (v. 26), whose life is the "sorry business" of 1:13. The ultimate beneficiary of this loss is indeed "the one who pleases God," who has given up the striving after gain, but gains an inheritance in any case.

The fuller dimensions of wisdom, on the one hand, and madness and folly, on the other, are now clear. It is madness and folly, indeed sin, to seek for "profit" from life; and the consequence is misery for those sufficiently perceptive to see the pointlessness of it. Wisdom, by contrast, acknowledges God and not the self as the center of existence and gladly embraces the limitations of the creature set within the larger, massive reality of creation. Reality having been embraced, it is possible to know joy.

The quest for what is "good" for human beings in terms of their happiness and well-being (Heb. *rʾeh bᵉṭob*, "see the good," in 2:1, and *ʾerʾeh ʾe-zeh ṭob*,

---

8. The NIV follows most interpreters in assuming that MT is slightly corrupt in v. 25 ("without me who can eat . . . ?"), reading "him" for "me" (as in a few Heb. mss., LXX, and Syr.). This may well be correct, although it is also conceivable that we have here an interjection in the first person from God akin to those found in some psalms and in Lamentations. It is also the case that we should normally expect, in order to achieve the NIV translation at the beginning of v. 24 (which is clearly the correct sense in context), some further indication that Heb. *ṭob*, "good," is being used as the comparative "better" (cf. the closely similar expressions in 3:12, 22; 8:15). It is commonly assumed that a preposition *mem* has fallen out by haplography before *šeyyoʾkal* (as Syr., Vulg., and some LXX mss. perhaps imply). Finally, the NIV translation "find enjoyment" in v. 25 also requires comment, since it is a guess. The Heb. verb usually means "hasten." It is possible that the reference is to (speedy?) movement connected with work and that the sense is simply this: "Without God, who can eat or bustle about?"

"see what is good," in 2:3) has thus been successful. There is nothing better (*tob*) for a person than to eat, drink, and find ways of enjoying (lit., "cause his soul to see good in," v. 24, *weher²a ²et-napšo tob*) his work. It is indeed not only good *for* a human being to live in this way. It is also good (morally) *that* he or she should live in this way. That which is good in itself turns out, unsurprisingly, to be good for those who pursue it.

JOY AND WISDOM, the focal points of Qohelet's attention in this section of Ecclesiastes, are often mentioned elsewhere in the Old Testament. The first is found predominantly among family and friends (e.g., Song 3:11; or as it should have been in Gen. 31:27), in fellowship with God's people at festivals and at other times (e.g., Num. 10:10; 1 Sam. 18:6; 2 Sam. 6:12; 1 Kings 1:40), and (at least when the people of God are thinking straight) in company with God (e.g., Deut. 12:7, 12, 18; 28:47; Ps. 4:7; 16:11; 30:11; 100:2). It is an outcome of life that is lived within a set of good relationships, and it is abundantly present wherever one reads of life as God designed it to be. At the same time, it is also markedly absent when people sin, when disruption is caused to relationships, and when divine judgment falls on the land (e.g., Isa. 24:11; Jer. 7:34).

There is, indeed, a party atmosphere throughout much of the Old Testament when normal life lived out in God's presence is described. It is this general biblical context that makes Ecclesiastes 2:1–11 such extraordinary reading. The idea that joy should be *pursued* individualistically as a means to the end of "gain" is exceedingly curious within this context. The book of Proverbs, for example, views joy as the outcome of doing such things as righteousness and justice and promoting peace (Prov. 10:28; 12:20; 21:15), and in fact it warns against too great an attachment to joy in itself (21:17). The idea of "gain" from pursuing joy is entirely incomprehensible within this broader Old Testament context. Joy is a good in itself, which comes to us as a gift as we live unto God and in human community and experience the blessing of it all. The New Testament sees it in a similar way as a consequence of unexpectedly experiencing God's grace and mercy (Luke 1:58) or of finding the treasure that is the kingdom of heaven (Matt. 13:44), or as the unexpected result of a visit to Jesus' tomb (Matt. 28:8; cf. also Luke 24:41, 52). It is one of the gifts or fruits the Holy Spirit brings (e.g., Acts 13:52; Rom. 14:17; Gal. 5:22).

When Qohelet acknowledges in 2:10, then, that he found joy in his work, only then to pass on quickly to the question of "gain," he deliberately misses the point in the interests of describing what is truly, if insanely, a common view of the purpose of life. There is no surplus to joy beyond joy itself. There is indeed no pathway to joy except by refusing to pursue it and to grasp at it. Qohelet's own considered view of the matter as it is found in 2:24–26 fits the broader biblical context far better. At the same time, his description in 2:17–23 of the life of the person who will not accept the divinely ordained reality is as graphic as any other biblical description of the "way of the wicked." It is a sobering account of the relentless anxiety of the materialist who lives under the shadow of unavoidable death—an anxiety that disturbs both serenity in the daytime and sleep at night, in contrast to the joy that energizes daily life and leads on to peaceful slumber (Ps. 4:7–8; cf. 127:2).

If joy cannot be grasped and manipulated for "gain," biblically speaking, then neither can wisdom or knowledge. It is not that wisdom is at all an intrinsically bad thing; the remainder of the Bible agrees with Qohelet that it is certainly better than folly and that it is the necessary possession of mortal beings (e.g., Prov. 4:1–9; or Matt. 10:16, which advises that Christians be as wise as serpents). Jesus himself is presented as a wise teacher especially in Matthew's Gospel, constantly recommending that his hearers learn from observation of creation what is true about God and about themselves (e.g., Matt. 6:25–34).

Yet there are serious limitations to what empirical inquiry can do for us, as Qohelet shows and as the remainder of the Bible also teaches. Reality in the end evades our grasp as we pursue it by this method (as Eccl. 7:23–29 will underline; cf. Job 28:1–28). If in the end we cannot understand this, or if we perhaps refuse to accept it and decide to retain our own limited perspective on the universe at the center of our thinking rather than placing there the revelation of God who made it, then we are bound to go badly astray. For the great multitude of facts we may discover about the world require some greater Story about the nature of things, containing some central and undisputed larger Facts, in the context of which their meaning and significance may be comprehended.

In the absence of such a Story (often referred to as a *metanarrative*—a narrative that embraces and explains all others) with its important Facts, wisdom and knowledge can only ever bring to the perceptive and serious thinker "frustration and mental pain" at best (Eccl. 1:18), along with a sense of despair even about the purpose of "knowing" itself. At worst it leaves the person who is trying to understand the world caught up in a web of illusion, as "wisdom" is claimed where none exists, and falsehood is promoted as truth (1 Cor. 1:18–2:16). For the Christian, the necessary Story is told in the Bible, and among the many important facts that the Bible communicates to us, the central Fact is that "God was in Christ." It is this that provides the only safe and sound platform for the pursuit of wisdom.

Jesus himself is seen in some parts of the New Testament, indeed, as the personification of wisdom, referring and alluding back to those passages in Proverbs where wisdom is already personified as a charming female confidante and guide who addresses humankind, inviting people to accept her counsel (Prov. 1:20−33; 8:1−9:6; cf. Matt. 11:16−19, 25−30; John 1:1−3; 1 Cor. 1:24, 30; Col. 1:15−20). Thus, an important Old Testament theme is developed in a Christ-centered way: that wisdom derived independently of and even in opposition to God is no wisdom at all and brings no real enlightenment. This is already the message of Genesis 3, where Adam and Eve's grasping after godlikeness through wisdom resulted only in the knowledge that they were naked and in all the consequent alienation from God, from each other, and from the earth. Significantly, this is also the message of 1 Kings 1−11, which asks how a king so "wise" as Solomon could nevertheless be so foolish that in the end he departed completely from God's ways and lost his kingdom.

It is in fact generally kings, more than any other sort of human being in the Old Testament, who grasp after godlikeness in the manner we are discussing here, looking to burst through the confines of mortal life and to achieve "gain" of one kind or another. We have already noted the allusions to this kind of hubris in Ecclesiastes 2:1−11, as "Solomon" tries to reinvent his environment. One of the best examples in the Bible is presented by the Assyrian king Sennacherib, who in 2 Kings 18−19 presents himself to Israel as an alternative god who will lead the people out of bondage and into a new promised land (18:31−32); who has vanquished the true God, who is both powerless and deceitful (18:32−35; 19:10−13); and who has imposed himself in a godlike way upon creation (19:23−24). Nebuchadnezzar in Daniel 1−4 provides us with another good example.

These are the kinds of people, along with Solomon, who have the resources at their disposal to make a credible attempt at equivalence with the gods. Yet they only represent in a particularly blatant way what the Bible presents to us as the characteristic set of human choices. Faced with life set within the confines that God has ordained, even though this may involve living in a paradise where joy abounds and where wisdom can be sought in dependence on God, from the very beginning human beings have chosen to transgress the boundaries in search of something "more," turning the life that comes to us as a gift to be enjoyed into capital that might fund exploitation and expansion. Qohelet is only one biblical voice that seeks to persuade us that the "more" does not exist and that in pursuing it we lose ourselves.

A final comment needs to be made in this connection about the question of gender. It is obvious that the perspective of 1:12−2:26 is resolutely male. It is a king who undertakes these inquiries into wisdom and joy, and women appear only as his playthings. The question arises, therefore—as it always must arise when any biblical text is read in the wider biblical context that reminds us that we are created male and female and redeemed as such in Christ—as to whether there are any specific issues of gender that need to be addressed in moving toward a Christian reading of the passage.

It is difficult to see that there are such issues, however. It is certainly true that historically, and including biblical times, it is men who have mainly been in a position to indulge their lust for divinity in precisely the manner described here. Women, lacking independence and power, have most often been the victims, rather than the initiators, of such pretensions to deity. Yet beyond the particularities bound up with "Solomon," the passage concerns the essential human tendency (which is certainly not gender-specific) to try to shape and to fashion reality in our own image, rather than to receive it already shaped from God. As such, it speaks to all who are tempted in this direction, whether male or female.

We may note the offensiveness of the way in which women are referred to in 2:8, then, and how far short it falls of a biblical view of women overall (as indeed the attitude to human beings generally does in 2:7), without being distracted from the main point. For it is assuredly just as possible (although for reasons of unequal power distribution historically less common) for a woman who loves herself more than she loves God to abuse men as it is for a man of such character to abuse women. There are always, in the Bible, enormous social costs that arise from idolatry, whoever the idolater may be.

About 1883 something like a break occurred in my work. I had reached the end of "Impressionism," and I had come to realize that I did not know how to paint or draw. In short, I found myself in a deadlock.[9]

I'm the king of the world.[10]

There are not many kings (or queens) left in the world, and those who still exist often tend at least to try to behave like ordinary mortal beings. We have come a long way from the doctrine of the "divine right of kings" as it was commonly held and practiced in medieval and early modern Europe.

That is not to say, however, that we have fewer people in the world who aspire to *live* like kings (and queens). On the contrary, we have probably

---

9. Pierre Renoir, cited from M. Howard, ed., *The Impressionists by Themselves* (London: Conran Octopus, 1991), 194.

10. Movie director James Cameron, at the 1999 Academy Awards ceremony.

never lived in an age in which more people worldwide aspired to such a lifestyle, driven on in particular by a rapacious and immoral advertising industry that promises us the earth in return for our souls, and by a movie and TV industry that provides us with an ever-fresh succession of "role models" (if that is the correct term) for our imitation and an endless supply of fantasies that we can live out in preference to real life. Only kings and the elite few who surrounded them in the ancient world (and indeed for most of human history) could hope to fashion their environments to some extent after their own whim and liking. Most people faced a harsh reality every day, which allowed no self-deception about human nature and destiny. Modern life in the West, however, is full to the brim with illusion and delusion, as we are constantly told that there are "gains" to be made that will radically alter life itself. There is yet another way to increase our income, yet another way to improve our health and stave off illness and death, yet another way to increase our sexual pleasure. The Canadian radio station Z95.3 was found in mid-1999 to be offering "a new life for the millennium." Further inquiry revealed that this "new life" consisted in various material possessions (a new house, a new boat, and so on). To such an extent has real life become diminished in the midst of fantasy. It was with no apparent sense of inappropriateness that James Cameron prefaced his "king of the world" proclamation (above) during the 1999 Academy Awards ceremony, at which he received an Oscar for his fictional account of the sinking of the *Titanic*, with a brief (very brief!) moment of silence in memory of the real victims of the tragedy. No sense of outrage was apparent, either, in his audience.

If the aspiration to "kingship" is thus deeply rooted in our sickly materialistic and superficial culture, the pursuit of wisdom and knowledge is closely allied to it, at least in principle. The very foundation of the modern economic miracle in the West was indeed laid several centuries ago in the explosion of empirical inquiry that is often labeled "the scientific revolution" and in subsequent industrialization and technological advance. We understand better than any generation before us, we imagine, how to make the world work for us. We stand on the edge of yet a further revolution in genetics, which will give us substantial control, we believe, of human life itself. All this is the consequence of looking into the nature of things, and it has bred enormous self-confidence, culturally, in our ability to govern ourselves and in due course to usher in utopia. A politician can hardly ever get elected to office nowadays, in fact, unless he or she more or less promises that this goal is achievable—that things are always and only going to get better. Education has also formally been drawn into this lusting after paradise, as wisdom and knowledge are portrayed not simply as goods in themselves that enable us to live well in the world, but as ways of "getting ahead"—mechanisms that enable us to fulfill our own personal dreams. The point of education is to get good grades, and the point of getting good grades is to put oneself in a position to "gain."

The irony of all this is that it is often precisely those who have pursued wisdom and knowledge most relentlessly and have probed reality most deeply who understand most fully just how limited still is our understanding at the end of the quest. This is as true in the realm of art as in the realm of physics. In illustration of this we may add to the Renoir quote at the head of this Contemporary Significance section the following, written only a few months before his death in 1919:

> I feel I am still making some progress. I am beginning to get to know how to paint. It has taken me fifty years of work to get this far—and there's still more to do. . . .[11]

The culture marches confidently on, however, even in the face of such suggestions of inadequacy and limitation. There is even talk of conquering death itself:

> Death is an imposition on the human race, and no longer acceptable. Man has all but lost his ability to accommodate himself to personal extinction; he must now proceed to physically overcome it. In short, to kill death; to put an end to his own mortality as a consequence of being born.[12]

It is not difficult to understand the contemporary significance of Ecclesiastes 1:12–2:26, then, particularly when it is remembered what the reality of our modern culture is that underlies its confident, abrasive tone and its pretensions to divinity. The reality is the widespread sense of futility and weariness that Qohelet himself describes in this passage—the "first-person testimony" that contradicts (as the testimony of "Solomon" does in Ecclesiastes) the story that is usually told in public, and which provides a very different perspective on the culture. Empiricism has undeniably brought great gains to humanity, but it can only partially grasp what is true, and it cannot tell us the meaning of things.

One of my earliest memories as a university student is of standing at a party watching an extremely bright philosophy major, a bottle of vodka in one hand, sitting against a wall while banging his head rhythmically against it. He had thought deeply, and he would have known what Ecclesiastes 1:18

---

11. Cited from Howard, *The Impressionists*, 302.
12. Allan Harrington, cited in B. Cameron, "Wisdom Against the Power of Death," *Vocatio* 3:1 (December 1999): 13–15.

means, if he had ever read it. Empirical inquiry, which starts from myself and attempts to move outward to embrace what is true, can only do certain things for us; and they are not the most important things. The same is true of education more broadly.

It is likewise evidently the case just how unfulfilling is the accumulation of wealth in the pursuit of joy and how little "gain" there is at the end of the pursuit. Solomon's life is the life of many men in our culture: the carrying through of great projects, the building of personal monuments, the exertion of power over many other human beings, the amassing of wealth, and the possession of many women. What does it add up to? "A chasing after wind," with accompanying stress and anxiety (particularly about how to ensure that one's legacy is passed on) and sleepless nights, and at the end death—the ultimate auditor's report.

Why do people pursue "gain" in such obviously futile and unsuccessful ways? It is a mystery. It is the irrationality, in fact, of sin. It is an ancient phenomenon, of whom Alexander the Great is perhaps one of the best examples: a high-flying young man with the world literally at his feet, who pushed too far and died young. Modern forms of such world-beating include professional sports, with their endless quest for success and glory, even though no one can explain what winning really achieves. As a memorable episode of *The Simpsons* reminds us, "The road to the Superbowl is long . . . and pointless— I mean, when you really think about it."

Qohelet and the rest of the Bible advocate a different way of living. The biblical view of life is that it is designed to be lived in humility and obedience before God, accepting the limitations that are placed on us as mortal beings and finding joy and satisfaction in the ordinary things of life (including intellectual inquiry). As we walk this pathway, we will be "surprised by joy" (to borrow the title of C. S. Lewis's autobiography); but joy is only a signpost on the journey, not its end, and still less a means to some other human end beyond it. As we walk on this path, we should certainly engage our minds and our curiosity and use such gifts of intellect as we possess for all the good that they can achieve, but we should remember that our pursuit of truth is always carried out in the context of Truth's pursuit of and self-revealing to us and that it is certainly not to be used for selfish ends. Following this narrow pathway may not gain us entry into *Encyclopedia Britannica* or *Who's Who*, along with those many others who have pursued their own vision of life often at the expense of love for God and neighbor (although many famous people recorded on those pages have also loved as well). We will, however, be found in the book of life, which has different entry qualifications.

At the end of time, in fact, it is those who have done the ordinary things well who will "gain" something, not those who have sacrificed these things for some grander scheme. Those who have found joy in such things will know greater joy; those who have depended on God for wisdom will know yet more wisdom; and those who have lived their lives in the knowledge that death is the ultimate statement of human noncontrol will rise to new life beyond death. It is they, ultimately, who will receive the inheritance mentioned (incomprehensibly in the context of Ecclesiastes itself, who does not think of life beyond death) in 2:26. It is not those like Mr. Burns in *The Simpsons* who, in response to Homer's observation that "you're the richest man I know," replies, "Yes, but I'd trade it all for more."

It is C. S. Lewis who once again provides us with one of the best pictures of this reality, in *The Magician's Nephew*. A London cabdriver finds himself to his surprise in Narnia, where he meets the lion, Aslan, whom he vaguely recognizes. Aslan, however, tells him that he (Aslan) has known the cabby for a long time; and although the cabby and his wife are the most ordinary of people, they find themselves crowned king and queen of their new homeland, joyful and blessed in their new lives. The wicked witch-queen Jadis, by contrast, who has grasped after immortality and has become a goddess, flees to the far north and must endure endless unhappiness, for "length of days with an evil heart is only length of misery."[13]

> But the fruit of the Spirit is love, joy, peace, patience, kindness, goodness, faithfulness, gentleness and self-control. (Gal. 5:22–23)

---

13. C. S. Lewis, *The Magician's Nephew* (Harmondsworth: Puffin, 1963), 162.

Ecclesiastes 3:1-22

1 There is a time for everything,
   and a season for every activity under heaven:
2 a time to be born and a time to die,
   a time to plant and a time to uproot,
3 a time to kill and a time to heal,
   a time to tear down and a time to build,
4 a time to weep and a time to laugh,
   a time to mourn and a time to dance,
5 a time to scatter stones and a time to gather them,
   a time to embrace and a time to refrain,
6 a time to search and a time to give up,
   a time to keep and a time to throw away,
7 a time to tear and a time to mend,
   a time to be silent and a time to speak,
8 a time to love and a time to hate,
   a time for war and a time for peace.

9What does the worker gain from his toil? 10I have seen the burden God has laid on men. 11He has made everything beautiful in its time. He has also set eternity in the hearts of men; yet they cannot fathom what God has done from beginning to end. 12I know that there is nothing better for men than to be happy and do good while they live. 13That everyone may eat and drink, and find satisfaction in all his toil—this is the gift of God. 14I know that everything God does will endure forever; nothing can be added to it and nothing taken from it. God does it so that men will revere him.

15Whatever is has already been,
   and what will be has been before;
   and God will call the past to account.

16And I saw something else under the sun:

In the place of judgment—wickedness was there,
   in the place of justice—wickedness was there.

17I thought in my heart,

"God will bring to judgment
   both the righteous and the wicked,

for there will be a time for every activity,
a time for every deed."

18I also thought, "As for men, God tests them so that they may see that they are like the animals. 19Man's fate is like that of the animals; the same fate awaits them both: As one dies, so dies the other. All have the same breath; man has no advantage over the animal. Everything is meaningless. 20All go to the same place; all come from dust, and to dust all return. 21Who knows if the spirit of man rises upward and if the spirit of the animal goes down into the earth?"

22So I saw that there is nothing better for a man than to enjoy his work, because that is his lot. For who can bring him to see what will happen after him?

IF THE PRECEDING section of the book has advocated the embrace of reality, especially in the light of death (1:12–2:26), the present section underlines the nature of that reality, evoking as it does so the introduction to the book (1:1–11). The universe has a flow and a regularity to it that is beyond any human control and renders futile all attempts at "profit." The wise person lives life in the light of this massive truth.

Human Experiences As a Tapestry of Times (3:1–8)

THE OPENING VERSES picture human experience as a tapestry woven of "times." There is indeed a "time for everything, and a season for every activity under heaven" (v. 1). The totality of life is captured here, utilizing the literary figure of merismus,[1] in a series of opposites. The first pair of opposites is the most all-embracing as far as human life is concerned, and it connects chapter 3 especially with the closing part of chapter 2: There is "a time to be born and a time to die" (3:2). Aside from the placement of this first pair, however, there is no discernible purpose to the overall order in which the opposites are placed; they simply represent various aspects of human life between the two poles of birth and death, although they are often clustered together in groups in suggestive ways.

---

1. Merismus involves the statement of polar extremes as a way of embracing everything that lies between them (e.g., north and south; heaven and earth) and is a frequent feature of ancient Near Eastern literature. The totality of things is probably also implied by the fact that our list of opposites comprises twenty-eight items in fourteen pairs—multiples of seven, the number symbolizing completion or perfection in the Bible.

It is not always clear whether the pairs are to be understood literally or metaphorically. The second part of verse 2 gives us a case in point. The literal meaning of the words is plain enough: There is "a time to plant and a time to uproot." This is true in agriculture, in that both planting and plowing must be carried out in the appropriate season, and plants like vines eventually come to the end of their useful life (note, e.g., the dependence of the imagery in Isa. 5:1–6 on this reality). Literal planting also connects chapter 3 with chapter 2, in that "Solomon" planted both vineyards and trees (Eccl. 2:4–5). Yet it is also true metaphorically, that in life generally there are times of "planting" and putting down roots and times of "uprooting" and disruption. Jeremiah, one can remember, was called by God to be a prophet involved in such activities in Israel (Jer. 1:10). In a sense birth itself is a "planting" and death an "uprooting."

Life and death, creating and destroying, are still the themes in verse 3: There is "a time to kill and a time to heal, a time to tear down and a time to build." The second pair reminds one again of "Solomon" (2:4), yet also of Jeremiah (Jer. 1:10), underlining the difficulty of knowing whether the primary reference is to literal building or not. There are simply times in life for construction and times for dismantling. The first pair, likewise, speak of the termination and preservation of life in vague terms, not specifying what is in mind. Verse 4 is more straightforward: weeping, laughing (cf. 2:2), mourning, and dancing are all activities that form part of human existence, each in its proper time.

The purpose of scattering and gathering stones (v. 5) is somewhat unclear. It is possible, as some have argued, that the reference is to the ruining of another's field by scattering stones on it (2 Kings 3:19, 25), and conversely to the clearing of a piece of ground for agricultural use (Isa. 5:2). The emphasis of the line then falls on hostile actions against enemies on the one hand, and concern for one's own business on the other. Yet the verbs have different connotations in Ecclesiastes. "Scatter" (Heb. *šlk*) reappears in 3:6 (NIV "throw away") to describe the action opposite to "keeping," while "gather" has already occurred in 2:8, 26 of the amassing of wealth. It seems more likely, then, that this line in 3:5 concerns the accumulation and distribution of wealth and that the image of the gathering of stones is used to refer to the practice of accumulation. The Hebrew *'eben* (stone) can indeed be used of precious stones, even without any modifying noun that makes explicit their preciousness (e.g., Ex. 25:7; 35:9, where the NIV translates "gems"). It is interesting, in view of the echoes of Solomon in Ecclesiastes 1:12–2:26, that such precious stones are much in evidence in 1 Kings 10 (vv. 2, 10, 11). If this interpretation is correct, then the second line of Ecclesiastes 3:5 may well allude to the embracing (Heb. *ḥbq*) of wealth rather than to embrace more generally. We note that *ḥbq* appears again in 4:5, where the fool embraces (NIV "folds") his hands rather than his work and the wealth that follows from work.

The searching and giving up (Heb. ʾbd) of 3:6 may also refer specifically to the acquisitive search for wealth and its loss: ʾbd reappears in 5:14 of wealth "lost" in the course of life, and in 7:7, 15; 9:6, 18 of things or people perishing or being destroyed. The material on acquiring and relinquishing possessions is then brought to completion by the second line of verse 6: There is "a time to keep and a time to throw away."

Verse 7 contains a new thought. There is "a time to tear and a time to mend" or sew. This may well be connected to the following "time to be silent and a time to speak," on either of two understandings of the whole verse. The "tearing" and "mending" may refer to the breach and restoration of a relationship, which requires discernment in knowing when to speak and when not to speak. Alternatively, the imagery of "tearing" may itself refer to the opening of the mouth and the imagery of sewing to its sealing shut (the "sewing up of the lips"). Judgment in speaking and remaining silent is a frequent theme of the book of Proverbs (cf. especially Prov. 15:23, where a word in its proper "time" brings joy, Heb. śimḥa). Words are naturally integral to relationships (e.g., Prov. 15:1, "A gentle answer turns away wrath, but a harsh word stirs up anger"), so it is unsurprising that comments on words and their lack gives way in verse 8 to comments on love and hate, war and peace.

If there are some difficulties in 3:1–8 in understanding precisely what is being said in the detail, it is important to remember that it is not the individual elements of themselves that are important, but the elements taken together as an overall description of life. It is not even each *individual* life that is in view—not every person, for example, will find that killing or war feature as part of his or her experience. Still less are any of the aspects of human life that are mentioned here being *commended* by our speaker. There is no *prescriptive* aspect to this list of opposites. It is simply a generalized, *descriptive* account of the kinds of things that make up human existence as it can be observed (and has, indeed, been partially observed in the life of "Solomon," the representative human being in 1:12–2:26). Human beings in general spend their days in the ways described and in the activities that lie between the poles of activity represented by the opposites.

Life in the Context of the Creator (3:9–15)

HUMAN LIFE AS observed in this way has a shape and a regularity to it that matches the shape and the regularity of creation in general as described in 1:1–11. It is to be expected, then, that Qohelet should now return in 3:9 to the question first asked in slightly different words in 1:3 and already answered negatively in 2:11: "What does the worker [or better, simply 'the human actor/doer,' Heb. ʿośeb] gain from his toil?" We have returned to the perspective of the person interested in profit or gain from life, for whom the whole business of life is evil (cf. NIV's "burden" [*ʿinyan*] in 3:10 with the same Heb. word in 2:23, 26 and with "heavy burden" [*ʿinyan raʿ*] in 1:13). What is "evil" about life from this point of view, of course, is that it cannot be controlled and manipulated so as to render the rewards sought after.

The problem facing the human "actor" is that there is another "Actor" whose actions are decisive ones: "He has made [*ʿaśa*] everything beautiful . . . they cannot fathom what [lit., the work that, Heb. *maʿăśeh*, as in 1:14; 2:4, 11, 17] God has done [*ʿaśa*]" (v. 11). The verb *ʿśh* evokes the creation narrative (Gen. 1:7, 16, 25, 26, 31; 2:2–4) and reminds us that there is a Creator whose creatures we are. This Creator has made everything "beautiful" in its time— probably in the sense of "beautifully fitting," given the emphasis of Ecclesiastes 3:1–8, rather than in the sense of "intrinsically beautiful." There is an elegance about how life works, as "time" succeeds "time."

Yet Qohelet's point is this: Mortal beings "cannot fathom [*mṣʾ*; lit., find] what God has done from beginning to end." They cannot discover the key to unlock the mystery—the almanac that enables them to predict and to control the times and thus make the "gains" they so desire. They cannot find this key even though God has set "eternity" (*ʿolam*) in their hearts (v. 11). He has given them "a sense of time past and future" (NEB).[2] Their sense of time past and future is insufficient for the task of truly understanding the times. Only God, who made all things to fit their times, truly understands them; only God controls time and is able to "call the past to account" (v. 15).

The phrase here is literally "he will seek [*bqš*] what has been chased away" (cf. Isa. 17:13, of water chased before the wind like chaff). The imagery is perhaps drawn from shepherding, God seeking out the "lost" moments of past time in the manner of the human seeking lost animals (cf. *bqš* in 1 Sam. 9:3; 10:2, 14; Ezek. 34:6, 16). It is not explicit in Ecclesiastes 3:15 itself, but it is certainly implied by 3:1–15 as a whole passage and by what follows in 3:16– 22 (see below) that this divine "seeking" is effective and that it is quite unlike the human seeking after time that is referred to in 3:9–11, which results in not "finding" anything (*mṣʾ*; cf. the play on these same verbs in 7:23–29). Echoing in the background are other cases of *bqš* / *mṣʾ* used in combination, particularly those in verses that speak of seeking and not finding (e.g., Isa. 41:12; Hos. 5:6). That God "seeks the past" in order to settle accounts is also

---

2. Heb. *ʿolam* is normally used adverbially, as in 1:10 ("long ago"), 2:16 ("long"), and 1:4; 3:14 ("forever"), to denote virtually unlimited time past or future. Although commentators have often struggled with the syntax and the meaning in 3:11, it is difficult to imagine that the same notion of "foreverness" is not intended here, esp. in view of the close proximity of 3:14. The point is that mortals share with God a sense of the whole sweep of time, which has been given them by God himself, but that they cannot move on to comprehend it or control it; it is always slipping away from them (1:10–11; 2:16).

---

clear from what follows in Ecclesiastes 3:16–22, although this too is not explicit in 3:15 of itself.

If it is true that only God truly understands and controls the times and that the human sense of time is insufficient for the task of truly understanding or controlling them, then it is unsurprising that those who continue in the quest for gain (*yitron*) from toil will only know frustration—that they will perceive life as a "miserable business." As in chapter 2, however, there is an alternative course of action open to mortal beings. It is to give up on the quest for profit and to reorientate life toward the Creator.

Ecclesiastes 3:12–13 outlines for us the shape of such a life, in terms similar to those in 2:24–26. It involves the embrace of joy (*śmḥ*; NIV "be happy") as it comes to us; it involves eating, drinking, and "seeing the good" (NIV "find satisfaction") in our toil, rather than looking for the profit that may derive from it. All of this is to be received as a gift from God rather than sought for in our own efforts. The good life also involves *being* good—to "do good while they live" (v. 12, cf. 2:26). This is the kind of "doing" (Heb. *ʿśh*) that is consistent with the "doing" of the Creator (see comments above on 3:9–12; cf. the same phrase, *ʿaśa ṭob*, in 7:20).

This kind of "doing" is indeed the only kind that makes sense in a world where the actions of God are utterly decisive (note the use of *ʿśh*, NIV "does," twice more in 3:14–15)—a world where his work is the only work that lasts forever (*ʿolam*, v. 14), being incapable of alteration by human effort ("nothing can be added to it and nothing taken from it," v. 14; "whatever is has already been, and what will be has been before," v. 15; cf. 1:9–10). Only when what is done (*maʿaśeh*, 1:14, 2:4, 11, 17) under the sun takes account of and responds to what is done (*maʿaśeh*, 3:11) *by* God can it be other than "pointless." To struggle for anything other than harmony with this reality is to act insanely and with the utmost futility.

Instead, the only rational response to reality is to "revere him [God]" (v. 14), issuing in a life centered on God. This precise advice—to revere or fear God, acknowledging that he is Creator and that we are only creatures (5:2)—will be repeated forcefully in 5:7 and in the conclusion to the whole book in 12:13: "Now all has been heard; here is the conclusion of the matter: Fear God and keep his commandments, for this is the whole duty of man."

Divine Control and the Reality of Death (3:16–22)

IN THE CLOSING verses of chapter 3 we discover some new lines of thought that are nevertheless clearly related to what has gone before. Verses 16–17 pick up and develop the theme of divine control of "the times," using it to address the question of injustice in the world; verses 18–22 return to the theme of death as an ultimate reality, which renders the striving life futile, now developing this theme in relation not just to wise and foolish human beings (as in 2:12–26), but to human and animal life.

Verses 16–17 are clearly related to verses 1–15 both thematically and syntactically ("I saw something *else*," Heb. *ᶜod*). It is this world that is evoked in Qohelet's opening words, which pronounce that wickedness reigns where there should be impartial "judgment" and "justice" (or better, "right behavior"; Heb. *ṣedeq*, drawing attention to the connection with *ṣaddiq*, "righteous," in v. 17). Like every aspect of the world that is not in harmony with the reality of God, however, this present reality cannot last. God himself will "bring to judgment [i.e., provide impartial justice for] both the righteous and the wicked [i.e., everyone]."

A well-known prophetic theme is brought to the fore here. It may well be that the wealthy and the powerful often escape human justice, since they often control it; and it may well be that in such circumstances those who have fewer financial means and less power often fail to attain justice from their fellow human beings. Yet God himself is the ultimate guarantor of justice and brings it to everyone in the end (e.g., Isa. 10:1–4; Amos 5:7–13).

The second part of verse 17 is best translated in the present tense rather than in the future (as in NIV): "There is a time for every activity [*ᶜet lᵉkol-ḥepeṣ*, as in 3:1, where the NIV translates 'there is . . . a season for every activity'], for every deed there." As God sets the "times" for human existence, so also there are "times" for all of his activities, all of his deeds (*maᶜᵃśeh*, as in 3:11, "what God has done"). His deeds are, however, the decisive ones (as in 3:9–15), not those of the wicked. The curious "there" at the end of the verse (untranslated by NIV) is probably intended to underline this: ". . . wickedness was there [*šamma*] . . . wickedness was there [*šamma*] . . . God will bring to judgment . . . for there is a time for every activity, a time for every deed there [*šam*]." It should not be thought that God's inactivity in respect of wickedness signifies a concession of sovereignty to wickedness over the places in which it is found. In those very places God will, at the right time, bring justice.

Verses 18–22 are also, if more loosely, connected with verses 1–15, in that the "time to die" (v. 2) forms the basis of their reflection, and this reflection arrives at conclusions similar to those in verses 9–15. The verses are even more closely connected with 2:12–26, though with an emphasis on "death, which makes fools of us all." Here in 3:18–22, however, the emphasis falls on the apparent lack of distinction between humans and animals, rather than between the wise and the foolish, in death. God enables human beings to see that, in respect of their ultimate fate, "they are like the animals" (3:18).

The NIV implies that the means by which this knowledge comes is testing or trial, but this is far from clear in the Hebrew, which seems to be suggesting only that God purifies or cleanses (Heb. *brr*) human beings to enable them to gain this insight.[3] Purification can certainly come through trial, biblically speaking (cf. *brr* in Dan. 11:35; 12:10), but the two are not necessarily linked in general or specifically in Ecclesiastes 3:18, which may merely mean that God (by means unspecified) leads mortals to purity of heart and clarity of perception, to a place where they are able to see "straight," without illusions. In this condition they are, perhaps painfully, aware of the truth: For all that they like to think of themselves as gods, human beings are mortal, just like the beasts (cf. Ps. 49:12).

The similarity of human beings to the animals in this crucial respect is underlined in the fivefold use of Heb. *kol,* "all," in 3:19–20: "*All* have the same breath … *everything* is meaningless [better 'breath'; see comments on 1:1–11]. *All* go to the same place; *all* come from dust, and to dust *all* return." That all sentient life is comprised of the "dust" (ʿapar) of the ground and the "breath" (ruaḥ, often "spirit," as in the NIV translation of 3:21) of life, placed together by God and destined to be separated at death, is the common view expressed or implied in the Old Testament (e.g., Gen. 2:7, albeit that "breath" here is *nešamah*; 2:19; 7:15; Ps. 104:29; Eccl. 12:7).

The one "place" to which all the living go is Sheol, the world of the dead (e.g., Job 30:23, "the place appointed for all the living"), translated by NIV simply as "the grave" in Ecclesiastes 9:10. The Old Testament often speaks of death as if it were a final ending to human existence—a place of separation from God (e.g., Ps. 6:5; 88:10–12) that the righteous as well as the wicked will experience as darkness and chaos, and from which even they will not return (e.g., Job 10:20–22). Other texts, however, tell us that the *wicked* depart to Sheol (e.g., Ps. 9:17; 31:17), implying that the fate of righteous is ultimately (if not immediately) different—a point explicit in Psalm 49:13–15, where the righteous are ransomed from Sheol's power (cf. also 16:10–11). Proverbs 15:24 tells us that "the path of life leads upward for the wise to keep him from going down to the grave [Sheol]" (cf. 12:28; 14:32); Psalm 139:7–12 claims that God is not, after all, absent from Sheol, but present with the worshiper even in the midst of the darkness; and Job 14:13 pictures Sheol as a place in which God might hide Job until his wrath has passed, the passage envisaging a later time when God will remember him and the dead will be roused out of their sleep (14:12, 14–17; cf. the famous 19:25–26). In passages like Isaiah 26:19 and Daniel 12:2–3, moreover, there are clear references to resurrection from the dead.

---

3. The line is syntactically rather awkward, but its overall intention seems clear: "to purify them God (is intent), and to see that they are beasts," i.e., that they themselves should see that they are beasts, which is perhaps the reason for the curious final Heb. *hemma lahem,* "they to themselves." The complexity of the second part of the verse, in particular, may be due to syntax playing second fiddle to quality of sound: *šehem-behema hemma lahem.*

Qohelet does not commit himself to any particular view on what happens after death (3:21),[4] although he is clearly familiar with the idea that when the human body and "breath"/"spirit" are separated, the spirit does not go "down" with the body into the earth, as in the case of animals, but rather rises "upward" (presumably to God). His stance is agnostic: "Who knows?" He cannot be certain what will happen after death (cf. the same question in 2:19); it is unseen. He rests content with that which, in the grace of God, he *has* come to see (Heb. *rʾh*, 3:18), namely, that death renders pointless during life the quest for "gain" or "advantage" (*motar*, related to the *yitron* employed in 1:3; 2:11; 3:9) over the rest of creation.

It is in the light of this truth that Qohelet returns once again to the advice already offered in 2:24–26 and 3:12–13. Given the nature of reality, how should people live? What Qohelet sees (*rʾh*, 3:22) is that "there is nothing better for a man than to enjoy his work"—or better, "to find joy [*śmḥ*] in what he does" (cf. *maʿaśeh* in 1:14; 2:4, 11, 17; 3:11, 17). This itself is his "reward" (NIV "lot," but see comments on Heb. *ḥeleq* in 2:10, where NIV translates it "reward"); it is all that he holds as "profit" when all is said and done. We are to live life, not in the hope of gaining some advantage over the rest of creation with which we share dust and breath, but simply for its own sake, finding joy in it and receiving that joy as itself the reward that living brings us. When the dust settles and we arrive, out of breath, at the end of the journey, that will be all that remains (Heb. *ytr*). This was the insight that "Solomon" first gained in 2:10, even while journeying at that time on a different path.

THAT GOD, NOT mortal beings, controls the "times" is a fundamental biblical conviction. Thus the biblical account of Israel's past does not focus primarily on the social and political forces that drive history or on the great heroes who are said to shape its direction. It

---

4. It is sometimes claimed that the Heb. as it is found in the pointed text and translated accurately in the NIV footnote intends more certainty on the matter, and indeed that the pointing represents an "orthodox" revision of Qohelet's thought. Yet even as translated in the footnote, the verse is still best understood in context as expressing agnosticism in relation to claims about reality that cannot be demonstrated ("who knows the spirit of man, which rises upward . . . ?"); it is not clear how else it could plausibly be understood. Even as pointed, indeed, it is by no means clear that the translation in the NIV main text is not correct; see R. Gordis, *Koheleth, The Man and His World: A Study of Ecclesiastes*, 3d ed. (New York: Schocken, 1968), 238, on variety in pointing the interrogative particle. It is certainly how we are prompted to translate it in the light of 2:19.

portrays the past, rather, as an entity shaped by God, who acts in grace and judgment, in the midst of all the actions of its human and other participants, to move time along towards his own goal. The narrative of the later monarchy in 1–2 Kings, for example, although it tells us about kings and all their pretensions, policies, and battles—and indeed about more ordinary people and events than these—is a narrative basically about what God was doing in this period of Israel's history. The prophets of God who announce and interpret God's actions are in fact much more important figures in the book than the kings, who only *think* that they control their own and their people's destiny. God is the decisive Actor.

The same is true in the prophetic books of the Old Testament, where God reveals himself not only as the sovereign Lord who ruled the past but also as the governor of the present and the future. Human beings may scheme and plot as they will, but the plans of God are the ones that will be enacted (e.g. Isa. 10:5–19; cf. also Ps. 2). The book of Daniel, a unique combination of a narrative and a prophetic book, provides perhaps the best example of biblical thinking on this topic. King Nebuchadnezzar of Babylon thinks himself a god (Dan. 3) and requires worship. His delusions are shattered, however, by Daniel, who informs him that he has no control over either his kingdom or his person. There is only one sovereign God (Dan. 4). In order to learn that he has no control over the "times," Nebuchadnezzar is forced to endure seven periods of time (4:32) among the animals. His successor Belshazzar is forced even more abruptly to face reality when his life is taken away on the very night Daniel confronts him (Dan. 5, esp. v. 30). The succeeding chapters, which look to the future and promise the coming of the kingdom of God at the end of all the "times" (e.g., 7:25–27), underline the reality. It is God who is "sovereign over the kingdoms of men and gives them to anyone he wishes" (4:32).

The New Testament picks up the theme. At the appointed time Jesus came among humankind, announcing the kingdom of God and dying for our sins (e.g., Mark 1:15; Rom. 5:6; Gal. 4:4–5). He reminded all his hearers of the succession of times still to come—the appointed times in which the various aspects of God's plans will be carried through: the death of Jesus (e.g., Matt. 9:15; 26:18; John 13:1), the witness or the apostasy of his disciples (e.g., Matt. 10:19; 24:10, 23–25; John 16:32), the second appearing of the Son of Man (e.g., Matt. 24:30), and divine judgment and salvation (e.g., Matt. 8:29; 13:30). That he possesses knowledge of the times, which marks him out from all his fellow human beings, is unsurprising when it is realized that the triune God is Alpha and the Omega, the First and the Last (Rev. 1:8; 21:6; 22:13), and Jesus the very center of human time, as the apostles clearly understood (e.g., Acts 3:21; 1 Cor. 4:5; 2 Tim. 1:9; Titus 1:2).

Christians are to live their lives in consideration of this fact, looking ahead to the end times (1 Tim. 6:13–16; 1 Peter 1:3–5; Rev. 1:3; 22:10) without losing hope; for if God is seemingly inactive, it is to be remembered that "with the Lord a day is like a thousand years, and a thousand years are like a day" (2 Peter 3:8). That God is in control of time is thus a comfort to the faithful while at the same time being a warning to those who ignore reality and continue to try to manipulate the times to their own advantage as if they were gods.

In the rest of the Bible, including Ecclesiastes, whenever mortals think they are gods, suffering for other creatures is bound to follow. The Ten Commandments link love for God with love for neighbor (cf. also Matt. 22:37–40); equally as clearly is idolatry linked with social injustice and oppression (cf. the story of Ahab, king of Israel, esp. in 1 Kings 21:1–26; also the Daniel stories). Human beings get above themselves, and from this lofty position they pour down suffering on others. Qohelet seeks to deconstruct such human pretensions by reminding us of our fate in death, which we share with the animals—just as Nebuchadnezzar, who thought himself a god, had to become like an animal for a while in order to remember what it means to be a human being. For all that human beings like to think of themselves as gods, in control of their own destiny and able to construct their own reality, they are in truth just like the beasts. Implicit in the observation, in the context of Ecclesiastes 3 (esp. v. 22), is the suggestion that we are to live life not in the hope of gaining some advantage over the rest of creation with which we share dust and breath, but simply for its own sake, finding joy in it and receiving that joy as itself the reward that living brings us. We are in that sense, too, to be "like the animals," who rejoice only in the moment and do not make great plans for their lives.

This reminder about our commonality with the animal world (cf. also Gen. 2:7–20) is important not least because it is not just other human beings who typically are trampled in our rush for "gain," but also the rest of creation. Yet the human calling is to look after creation as agents of the Creator, not to exploit it for our own ends (Gen. 1:26–30). This, rather than self-worship, is what we are called to as those made in the image of God, who have eternity set in our hearts (Eccl. 3:11). Paradoxically, however, that sense of eternity can also lead us not only to fail to live in the present moment but also to mistreat creation around us, which is not perceived to be as important (or as "spiritual") as we are. The reminder that all living creatures are dust and die, therefore, is helpful to us in gaining a proper perspective on ourselves and on our calling. Having eternity in our hearts should not mean that we despise the earth and its other life, which indeed comprises just as much a part of God's redemptive plan as do human beings (e.g., Isa. 65:17–25; Rom. 8:19–22).

Nevertheless, what Qohelet has to say in 3:18–22 also leaves us with a question about his thinking. How does he imagine that God will in due course "bring to judgment both the righteous and the wicked" (3:17) if it is uncertain whether there is life beyond death? It is not a question that he himself answers in the course of his reflections. He is far more concerned to get his hearers thinking and living in a certain way in the present than he is to resolve all their questions about the future.

It is precisely here that there is a danger for the Christian reader of Ecclesiastes. Christians know about the resurrection and look forward to the future with a firmer hope than Qohelet ever gives expression to. It is all too easy to think that because we thus know more than he does, we need not pay much attention to what he has to say from his more limited perspective. Even those who live in hope of the resurrection, however, still need to live a life between birth and death, and to live it in the right spirit and in the right way. Death may not in fact necessarily be the end, as Qohelet allows that it might be, but it is still a significant reality that mocks our pretensions to human control of life.

As sure as we may be of the reality of *resurrection* beyond death, moreover, we are also clearer about the reality of divine *judgment* beyond death: "Man is destined to die once, and after that to face judgment" (Heb. 9:27). This should focus our attention, one might think, on the present. Yet significant sections of the modern church are far from focused on the present. They are obsessed with the future and seem to imagine that because they have a future, the present is not very important. Qohelet affirms that all will one day be well, apparently without understanding quite how this can happen, while focusing resolutely on what it means in the present to take God seriously. Modern Christians, by contrast, although understanding more about *how* all things will one day be well, ironically often seem to understand less about what this signifies for faith and life *now*.

We forget that the Bible has not been given to us primarily to satisfy our curiosity, but to engage our lives. We forget that the resurrection itself does not appear primarily in the New Testament as an idea about the future, but as a ground for present faith and holiness. Yet as George MacDonald puts it so well:

> ... to prove life endless is not a matter of the *first* importance. ... The man with life so in himself ... will not dream of asking whether he shall live forever. It is only in the twilight of a half life that the doubtful anxiety of immortality can arise.[5]

---

5. G. MacDonald, *The Curate's Awakening* (Minneapolis: Bethany, 1985), 203–4.

I've heard people talk about immortality,
but I ain't seen it.[6]

We live in a culture that is uncertain about life after death, although often interested in the concept—particularly if it can be grounded in some kind of "empirical evidence," such as is allegedly provided by those who have had near-death experiences. The empirical evidence for resurrection provided by the New Testament is for some reason not valued so highly. Presumably ancient testimony about such things is not to be trusted so implicitly as its modern counterpart. For many people in our suspicious, conspiracy-laden society, testimony itself of whatever age or nature is on principle to be doubted. Like Thomas in the Gospel of John, unless they see it for themselves, they will not believe (John 20:24–25).

It is an expression of the self-centeredness and paranoia of the age. The only person one can ultimately trust is oneself. This is not a world that will ever have much place for the immortal, invisible God of whom the Bible speaks or much patience with claims about life after death, unless by way of a completely irrational leap of faith from the scientific mind-set and into the spiritual fog. Weariness with modern life may indeed persuade many to make such a leap—thus the proliferation of "spiritualities" in North America as we enter the new millennium. These are on the whole highly individualized, personally tailored spiritualities, however, in which the untrusting self remains very much at the center of the universe as it pursues self-fulfillment.

Leaps of faith will never lead anywhere unless they are in the direction of the Truth that has already come to meet us, and then they will not be leaps at all. When the delusions and illusions of these spiritualities have been demolished, their possessors will still have to say, with the noble Private Witt: "I've heard people talk about immortality, but I ain't seen it." For it cannot be seen in the abstract; it can only be believed in, on the basis of what trustworthy persons who know the truth have to tell us, or glimpsed in the lives of people who already possess it—a subject to which we will return shortly.

A popular alternative to leaps of faith when confronted by the uncertainties surrounding life after death has been to seek to live life simply in the light of the reality that can indeed be seen—the reality of death. A well-known slogan associated with this way of looking at the world is *carpe diem,* a Latin phrase translated as "seize the day." Although it is an ancient saying, it has been given wider currency than it perhaps would otherwise have had in modern times by the movie *Dead Poets Society,* in which the comedian and

6. Private Witt, in the movie *The Thin Red Line.*

actor Robin Williams plays the role of a new teacher at a traditional private school. In an important scene early in the movie, he gathers his pupils around a cabinet in the school hallway that displays photographs of sporting heroes and trophies from the past, many of them now dead. Inviting his students to imagine what these ancient heroes, whose moment of glory has passed, would have to say to them, he moves among them whispering *carpe diem*. The scene is thus set for the remainder of the movie, in which the boys set out to squeeze all the life out of their schooldays that they can, with humorous and ultimately tragic consequences.

Qohelet's philosophy is also to some extent that all mortal beings should "seize the day." It is indeed the appropriate response to the reality of the "times" that are beyond our control, but lie in the hands of God, that we should cease to worry overly much about how things are going to work out and concentrate on living joyfully in the moment that is currently given to us: "I know that there is nothing better for men than to be happy and do good while they live. That everyone may eat and drink, and find satisfaction in all his toil—this is the gift of God" (3:12–13).

What is noticeable about what Qohelet says, of course, and what marks out his philosophy from modern secular views of the world with which it shares superficial similarity, is that it is centered on God. Qohelet's *carpe diem* is an expression of faith, not of self-fulfillment. It is not the greedy consumption of experiences and pleasures before oblivion consumes *us*. It is, rather, the patient and joyful embrace of daily life as it comes to us as a gift from God. That it involves ethics is also patently clear from 3:12; it is not a life centered on the self, but a life that is turned outward towards the neighbor, asking what is "good." We are indeed to seize the day, but we are to remember its divinely created nature as we do so. The biblical *carpe diem*, then, is not a self-centered response to the uncertainties surrounding life after death, but a worshipful response to the God of creation, who is also the God of new creation and resurrection.

It is important to stress the biblical *carpe diem*, however, in a religious culture in the Western world that has all too often given the impression to others that the point of the Christian faith is to repress life in the here and now in order to gain life in the future. It has given this impression because Christians have themselves often believed this to be the case. As Friedrich Nietzsche—who in many ways is the great prophet and moving spirit of the age in which we live—understood, what makes paganism attractive when set alongside this kind of Christianity is that the former can often seem to be life-affirming while the latter is perceived as centering on a holy God who imposes a life-denying ascetic spirituality on his worshipers. Thus the Christian life is defined for many in North America in terms of a certain number of activities in which we may *not* engage, rather than by the glorious freedom that is the inheritance of God's children. Christian communities everywhere are burdened with a legalism that has nothing at all to do with biblical revelation but is presented nonetheless as authentically Christian. This includes, tragically, many Christian colleges and seminaries, whose task is education and formation in the orthodox faith, yet whose students and faculty are often beset by a whole plethora of rules and regulations that they are required to keep even though they are merely cultural impositions and have nothing to do with obedience to God. A repressive, authoritarian spirit lies at the root of much of our religion.

Yet *biblical* religion is far from repressive and authoritarian. It knows of a God who made the world beautiful and fruitful, to be enjoyed by his creatures in fellowship with him—a God who says, "You are free to eat from any tree in the garden" (Gen. 2:16), with a single exception. It is the serpent who portrays God as repressive: "Did God really say, 'You must not eat from any tree in the garden?'" (Gen. 3:1); and the serpent is a deceiver. Those who believe him and adopt a defensive posture toward God and toward life are not honoring God, as they often claim, but are in fact dishonoring him and obscuring him from others. This is one of the reasons why Jesus often spoke so harshly to the scribes and Pharisees, for their legalistic approach to life missed the entire point and led others astray at the same time (e.g., Matt. 23:13, 15; Luke 11:46, 52). It was also a major issue in the early church, as the first Christians struggled to sort out what was really a gospel matter and what was merely a cultural matter (e.g., 1 Cor. 8:1–10:33).

The Christian faith is not about the repression of life in the here and now in order to gain life in the future. It is not about petty rules concerning the drinking of wine, for example—a particularly astonishing rule when it is found among Christians who hold a high view of Scripture, since Scripture routinely glories in wine as one of the finest of God's gifts (Deut. 7:13; 11:14; 14:26; 33:28; Ps. 104:14–15; Prov. 3:9–10; also in Eccl. 9:7, where the substance being drunk is explicitly wine). It is, of course, the case that we are called by Jesus to deny ourselves and take up our cross (Matt. 16:24), but that is a call for displacement of the self from the center of the universe, such as we already find in Ecclesiastes. It is not a call for a *life-denying* approach to existence, as Jesus' own life demonstrates (e.g., Matt. 9:14–15; Luke 7:33–34).

We may, of course, freely choose to give up certain good things for a shorter or longer time for the sake of the kingdom of God or out of concern for others (e.g., Rom. 14:19–21), and we should never abuse the good things God gives us (e.g., Eph. 5:18; 1 Tim. 3:8). Yet this too is already implied in Ecclesiastes, since the biblical "seizing of the day" is an activity of faith and is bound up with the doing of good. Whatever we do as Christians—even if it involves refraining from things—should be done out of joyful response to the God of extravagant blessing and grace, as we live *now* the abundant life that is also the life that stretches away into eternity (John 4:14; 5:24; 10:10).

Defensive living premised on a false and suspicious view of God is not something of which God approves (Luke 19:12–27). It makes him angry. It is indeed only as people live in joyful response to God that it is possible for any human being to "see" immortality in any sense. It cannot be seen in the abstract. It can, however, be glimpsed in the concrete, as a resurrection life lived out in the present that makes obvious sense of who we are as God's creatures, and thus confronts those living in rebellion against God with the irrationality and harmful consequences of their life-orientation. In this sense, "seizing the day" is what Christians are called to do not only in our own interests, but also in the interests of others (Matt. 5:14–16). We are summoned to demonstrate that Qohelet is right when he insists that the only rational response to reality is one of reverence for God, issuing in a life centered on God.

There is an old hymn by the famous hymn-writer Isaac Watts that captures well the essence of what we have been reflecting upon in this section:

Come, we that love the Lord, and let our joys be known;
Join in a song with sweet accord, and thus surround the throne.

The sorrows of the mind be banished from the place!
Religion never was designed to make our pleasures less.

Let those refuse to sing that never knew our God;
But children of the heavenly king may speak their joys abroad.

The men of grace have found glory begun below;
Celestial fruits on earthly ground from faith and hope may grow.

Then let our songs abound, and every tear be dry;
We're marching through Emmanuel's ground to fairer worlds on high.

We cannot truly understand or control "the times," and so we are cast back on God, who holds our times in his hands and alone knows the span of our individual days. Yet the God on whom we are cast is good, and he is *for us* (Rom. 8:31). Our response to his grace and blessing should be to seize the time that we have and live it well and joyfully to his glory and praise.

From one man he made every nation of men, that they should inhabit the whole earth; and he determined the times set for them and the exact places where they should live. God did this so that men would seek him and perhaps reach out for him and find him, though he is not far from each one of us. (Acts 17:26–27)

Ecclesiastes 4:1–16

AGAIN I LOOKED and saw all the oppression that was taking place under the sun:

I saw the tears of the oppressed—
  and they have no comforter;
power was on the side of their oppressors—
  and they have no comforter.
²And I declared that the dead,
  who had already died,
are happier than the living,
  who are still alive.
³But better than both
  is he who has not yet been,
who has not seen the evil
  that is done under the sun.

⁴And I saw that all labor and all achievement spring from man's envy of his neighbor. This too is meaningless, a chasing after the wind.

⁵The fool folds his hands
  and ruins himself.
⁶Better one handful with tranquillity
  than two handfuls with toil
  and chasing after the wind.

⁷Again I saw something meaningless under the sun:

⁸There was a man all alone;
  he had neither son nor brother.
There was no end to his toil,
  yet his eyes were not content with his wealth.
"For whom am I toiling," he asked,
  "and why am I depriving myself of enjoyment?"
This too is meaningless—
  a miserable business!

⁹Two are better than one,
  because they have a good return for their work:
¹⁰If one falls down,
  his friend can help him up.

But pity the man who falls
   and has no one to help him up!
¹¹ Also, if two lie down together, they will keep warm.
   But how can one keep warm alone?
¹²Though one may be overpowered,
   two can defend themselves.
A cord of three strands is not quickly broken.

¹³Better a poor but wise youth than an old but foolish king who no longer knows how to take warning. ¹⁴The youth may have come from prison to the kingship, or he may have been born in poverty within his kingdom. ¹⁵I saw that all who lived and walked under the sun followed the youth, the king's successor. ¹⁶There was no end to all the people who were before them. But those who came later were not pleased with the successor. This too is meaningless, a chasing after the wind.

IN THE SAME way that 3:16—17 and 3:18—22 pick up and develop themes from earlier in the book, so too 4:1—3 is related by theme to 3:16—17. The focus of attention is still the wickedness that exists "under the sun" (3:16; 4:1), now specified as "oppression" (from the Heb. root *ʿšq*, which appears three times in 4:1 to give emphasis to its reality; cf. the repetition of "wickedness" in 3:16). The world, as a place of striving after "gain," is a place of tears and of disproportionate power, in which many are ground down and "have no comforter" (also repeated for emphasis).

In the Bible, oppression involves cheating one's neighbor of something (Lev. 6:2—5 associates it with expropriation, stealing, retaining lost property that has been found, and swearing falsely), defrauding him, and robbing him. It involves making an unjust gain, including the profit made from interest on loans (e.g., Ezek. 22:1—29, esp. vv. 12, 29). It is the abuse of power, financial and otherwise, perpetrated on those who are not so powerful and are indeed vulnerable—the poor, widows, orphans, and strangers (e.g., Ezek. 22:7, 29; Amos 4:1; Mic. 2:1—2). Thus it is often associated with violence and bloodshed in the Old Testament and with the denial of rights and justice (e.g., Jer. 22:17; Ezek. 22:6—7, 12, 29; cf. also Prov. 1:10—19).

Oppression is accumulation—the seeking after profit—without regard to the nature, needs, and rights of other people. There is a fierce insistence in the Old Testament that people should not thus oppress each other. Note, for example:

Leviticus 19:13: Do not defraud your neighbor or rob him. Do not hold back the wages of a hired man overnight.

Deuteronomy 24:14–15: Do not take advantage of a hired man who is poor and needy, whether he is a brother Israelite or an alien living in one of your towns. Pay him his wages each day before sunset, because he is poor and is counting on it.

Zechariah 7:10: Do not oppress the widow or the fatherless, the alien or the poor.

Proverbs 14:31: He who oppresses the poor shows contempt for their Maker, but whoever is kind to the needy honors God.

Power, economic or otherwise, is not to be abused; people, whether less powerful than we or not, are not to be treated as objects out of which profit can be squeezed, but as human beings made by the same God who created us all. This includes our employees.

Human beings as we find them "under the sun" are, however, in rebellion against God and thus generally careless of the neighbor, as Qohelet sees all too clearly. They are out for "gain," and in their desperate attempts to climb the ladder of success they will happily kick and trample on the heads of those beneath them. This is simply the way the world is (cf. 5:8–9, with its injunction that we should not be surprised by it).

The world is, therefore, a miserable place for many people, who live without anyone to comfort them with the real prospect of change in their circumstances (cf. Ps. 23:4; 86:17, for the understanding of "comfort" not simply as empty words, but as carrying with it the promise of help and protection, and thus *real* comfort). They have been deprived even of the most modest means out of which to live their lives. In such a situation, Qohelet suggests, the dead are to be commended over the living (better than NIV's "happier than the living," which can be taken to imply a subjective state; cf. the more appropriate translation in Eccl. 8:15). They are to be congratulated in at least attaining rest.

More fortunate than both the living and the dead, however, are those who have never even seen what Qohelet has seen (cf. 4:1, 3) because they have not yet been born. It is a sorry sight (Heb. *raᶜ*, "evil," probably refers as much if not more to its misery as to the wickedness that produced it, cf. comments on 1:13 and the footnote there, as well as 4:8). They are blessed who have not yet looked on it.

The fuel that feeds the fires of this human striving after gain is now for the first time in Ecclesiastes identified (vv. 4–6): "All labor and all achievement [or better, 'all toil and success [*kišron*]'; cf. *kšr* in 11:6, 'you do not know which will succeed'] spring from man's envy of his neighbor." It is envy that drives us on in the mad rush after "gain." Notice 10:10, where there is a close connection between *yitron* and *kšr*, and 5:11, where *kišron* refers to a "gain" that is not truly a gain. It is the suspicion or realization that others are gaining more from life than we are that leads us on to compete with them in the insane rat race, striving to outdo them.

It is not by accident that the "neighbor" (*rea*) is mentioned in 4:4 as an object of envy, in the aftermath of the observations on oppression in 4:1−3 reminding us of various biblical injunctions about how we should correctly view and treat our neighbor (cf. *rea* in Lev. 19:13, 18). In pursuing out of envy the neighbor above us on the ladder, we inevitably step on the head of the neighbor below us. As disastrous as this is for the people who are trampled on, it is also futile for the person who is upwardly mobile at their expense. It is pointless, "a chasing after the wind" (Eccl. 4:4). It is true, on the one hand, that "the fool folds his hands and ruins himself" (lit., "embraces his hands and eats his own flesh," v. 5). The foolish person keeps his hands to himself rather than embrace work and the fruits of his labor that follow on from work (see comments on 3:5; also Prov. 6:10−11; 24:33). Consequently he has nothing to eat but himself! On the other hand, that is no reason to go to the opposite extreme, toiling and chasing after the wind (v. 6). "Two handfuls" are not better than none if they are gained at the expense of "tranquillity" (*naḥat*) or "peace of mind" (NEB), for the lack of tranquillity or contentment is *also* something that marks out the fool (cf. Prov. 29:9, where *naḥat* is contrasted with a striving marked by rage and mockery). The personal costs of giving up on contentment and capitulating to envy and oppression are well captured in a number of verses:

> Ecclesiastes 7:7: Extortion [*šq*] turns a wise man into a fool, and a bribe corrupts the heart.
> Proverbs 22:16: He who oppresses [*šq*] the poor to increase his wealth and he who gives gifts to the rich—both come to poverty.
> Proverbs 14:30: A heart at peace gives life to the body, but envy rots the bones.

Life for the body (Heb. *baśar* in Prov. 14:30) is no more achieved through grasping with both hands than through folding them (which actually results in self-destruction, 4:5—lit., the "eating of the flesh [*baśar*]"). The single handful symbolizes the way ahead.

The foregoing material has made it clear that the life of striving is fundamentally anti-neighbor. The point of life, when viewed from this perspective, is to get ahead of one's neighbors rather than to participate in community with them—just as, earlier in the book, it was to "get ahead" of creation as a whole rather than to live in harmony with it. It is not surprising, then, that in 4:7−12 we find material that first focuses on the loneliness of the striving individual and then moves on to offer a stirring and uplifting commendation of community.

Verses 7–8 paint the picture of a person "all alone" (lit., "having no second person"), without "son or brother" to inherit his wealth. This is a driven person, toiling endlessly with his eyes fixed resolutely on some unspecified, yet all-absorbing goal: "His eyes were not content with his wealth." It is a futile and miserable way in which to live (v. 8; cf. ʿinyan raʿ, "miserable [evil] business," also in 1:13; note also 2:23, 26; 3:10), because toil in pursuit of more wealth prohibits the person from "enjoyment" of life (lit., "the good," *ṭoba*, 4:8).

An alternative vision of the world involves at its heart the notion of community (vv. 9–12). In the world of the self-centered achiever there is only one person "all alone" (ʾeḥad weʾen šeni; lit., "one and not a second," v. 8), and that one person knows only toil (ʿamal) in place of "the good" (*ṭoba*). His individual life is futile, and it brings great pain and misery to others. In this alternative world, however, "Two are better than one" (tobim haššenayim min-haʾeḥad), and both have a "good return for their work" (sakar ṭob baʿamalam).

The language of verse 8 is consciously picked up in verse 9 in order to underline the difference between the two approaches to life and their consequences. Cooperation leads on to a rewarding life, both for the individual and for the neighbor (cf. sakar in this nonmonetary sense also in Ps. 127:3, where there is also an emphasis on the futility of human activity when out of harmony with God's ways). There may be pitfalls that confront the two of them as they journey (v. 10), but at least the troubles will be faced together and help will be available. There will be cold and dark nights as the travels progress (v. 11), but at least there will be the warmth that another's presence brings. There may be enemies lying in wait on the path (v. 12), but at least the battles will be fought alongside another and not alone.

The solitary traveler may get to the end of the journey faster, and indeed he may gain riches along the way as he leaves the weak and the slow behind him and is not required to share what he finds. However, he will also know pits out of which he must dig himself, unrelentingly cold nights, and lonely battles. He will in the end see no profit from it all, for the gain we make from our toil is found in the toil itself, completed in the context of our whole lives lived out before God and in the company of others to whom we are intrinsically and healthily connected as creatures of God. In community our lives are strong and enduring, like the rope "of three strands." The fool's individualistic life is, by contrast, weak and destined to be "broken."

The closing verses of chapter 4 (vv. 13–16), although their precise relationship with what precedes them has puzzled many commentators, seem clearly connected with what precedes by theme and by language (notice the common reference to what is "better" in vv. 6, 9, and 13; the reference to the "second person" [*šeni*] in vv. 8 and 15, unfortunately obscured by the NIV; and the occurrence of "there was no end to all" [*ʾen qeṣ lᵉkol*] in vv. 8 and 16). The king, as we have seen in 1:12–2:26, is the person who above all might be expected to "gain from toil" in Israel, and who might equally be expected to be a major source of oppression (cf. 1 Sam. 8:10–18). He represents the pinnacle of human success and the lifestyle to which many aspire. It is not surprising that in the course of reflections on the solitary yet unhappy and futile life we should return to consider once again the figure of the king.

The crucial matter of interpretation relates to the identity of the youth in verse 15, where the NIV translates "the youth, the king's successor," compressing and interpreting a Hebrew phrase that literally reads, "the youth, the second one who stood in his place." The view is thus taken that there is only one youth in verses 13–15 and that "second" refers only to his coming after and succeeding the king. It seems a more natural reading, however, to understand "he may have come from prison" in verse 14 (NIV's "the youth" is an interpretation not a translation) as referring to the king: The king himself had once been a poor but wise youth, and (a better translation) "came out from prison to rule even though in his future kingdom he was born poor."

A second youth from humble origins then supplanted the aged king, who in his (implicitly wealthy) dotage had become a self-absorbed fool living in a world of his own, unable to take advice or warning. Yet kingship for this youth himself did not turn out happily. "There was no end to all the people" deliberately recalls 4:8 with its complaint that "there was no end to [all] his toil," suggesting that the phrase does not refer so much to popular support for the king (as commentators have often assumed) as to the burden of royal office. That is, kingship is "toil," not least because of the sheer number of the royal subjects (cf. 1 Kings 3:8–9). The people before whom he stood (rather than the NIV's "the people who were before them") were too numerous.

What is more, there was no joy among later generations when this king came to mind (cf. Eccl. 1:11; also the similar fate of the poor wise man in 9:13–18). All in all, kingship is a thankless task—toil and trouble on the one hand, and a lack of appreciation on the other (cf. 2:12–26). The following translation results from this understanding of the Hebrew:

> Better a poor but wise youth than an old but foolish king who no longer knows how to take warning. For he [the old king] himself came out from prison to rule, even though in his [future] kingdom he was born poor. I saw that all who lived and walked under the sun were with the second youth who stood in place of him. There was no end to all the people, to all those whom he was before; and those who came later did not rejoice in him. This too is meaningless, a chasing after the wind.

In the real world of the ancient Near East the succession of one humbly born king by another would have been unlikely. It is not the real world of kings that is in view here, however, but the real world of human advancement and achievement in general. Qohelet's concern is to show that poverty with wisdom is better than advancement with folly, just as it is better to have one handful with tranquillity than two handfuls with toil (v. 6) and just as two are better than one (v. 9). Advancement all too often brings with it the loss of the self, as people lose touch with where they have come from (vv. 13–14). It brings with it even greater toil than before, but no greater thanks (vv. 15–16).

THE BIBLE HAS not been given to us to satisfy our curiosity but to shape our lives in a particular way in response to God. It is worth restating this rather obvious fact as we move from consideration of the "times" in chapter 3 to reflect on oppression and injustice in the world in chapter 4, for the religious culture we inhabit seems often to have forgotten it.

Comprehension of the times is beyond us, insists Qohelet, and Jesus agrees (e.g., Matt. 24:36–44). Yet significant numbers of modern Christians seem to regard the Bible mainly as a source of inside knowledge about the divine timetable for the universe, and they are much more interested in speculating about the future than about living faithfully in the present. They represent the mirror image of many secular academic students of the Bible (and not a few Christian ones, too), who understand the usefulness of the Bible, and especially the Old Testament, mainly in terms of a resource for their speculations about the past rather than as the Word of God that commands obedience in the present.

Attempts to control "the times" take many different forms. Abuse of the Bible itself in pursuit of this goal is common. When the Bible speaks about past or future, however, it does so not for our titillation or in the hope of advancing our academic careers but with a view to producing righteous living in the present:

Matthew 24:45: Who then is the faithful and wise servant . . . ?

1 Corinthians 10:6–7: Now these things occurred as examples to keep us from setting our hearts on evil things as they did. Do not be idolaters, as some of them were; as it is written: "The people sat down to eat and drink and got up to indulge in pagan revelry."

The Bible is resolutely focused on the *now*, even as it tells us enough about the past and the future to encourage us and challenge us about this *now*. An overwhelming aspect of the reality of the now, as Qohelet tells us, is that the world is a place of oppression and unjust gain. Other biblical texts agree. The foundational section of Scripture here is Genesis 1–11. God created human beings to live in harmonious community with himself and with each other; but the human desire to be gods disrupted that community, not just on the divine-human axis, but also on the human–human and human–rest of creation axes. Alienation is the new reality, seen especially in the relationship of Adam and Eve, then later in the relationship of Cain and Abel.

As Genesis 1–11 moves on, the alienation progresses even further outward from the center of the circle. As brother has been divided from brother, so neighbor is divided from neighbor (4:23–24). From that point on, community slides into complete chaos and anarchy, as violence fills the earth (6:11–13). Much of the point of Genesis 4 seems to be that even humankind's many achievements of culture (4:17–22) in its "knowledgeable adulthood" cannot disguise this slow but remorseless breakdown of community. Sophistication and technological expertise increase; but as they do so, community breaks down by stages until the alienation between God and humans, humans and humans, and eventually humans and the created order is complete. Sophistication and barbarism are perfectly compatible playmates.

One aspect of this alienation, as the rest of the Bible makes clear, is economic in nature. This is already hinted at in Genesis 5:28–31. Lamech's apparent interest, perhaps like Cain in chapter 4, is in avoiding the implications of the cursing of the ground in Genesis 3. He welcomes his new son Noah, therefore, not so much as *son*, but more as a *worker* who will release him from the toil imposed on all Adam's descendants (5:29). There is the suggestion in this of a grasping after divinity, since Lamech portrays Noah as having come "out of [NIV 'by'] the ground," alluding to the creation narrative in chapter 2 (2:7, 9 "the LORD God formed the man from the dust of the ground ... the LORD God made all kinds of trees grow out of the ground"). Lamech's apparent intention is to sit back and take life easy, enjoying the fruits of Noah's labor while contributing nothing of his own efforts to production.

We are reminded of that general alienation between human beings and the fruits of their labor that Karl Marx so eloquently expounded on, whose own vision of society itself had its roots in the Judeo-Christian tradition and was shaped by it. From a biblical point of view, as well as from a Marxist point of view, Lamech's hope of redemption from toil is not at all realistic or to be commended. Only a few verses further on, indeed, we find the story of the Flood, where the same Hebrew root *nḥm*, which means "give comfort" in 5:29, reappears of God's being "sorry" that he had made human beings at all (6:6).

It is a poorly based and futile hope that Lamech expresses. Noah is, however, a sign of hope, notwithstanding Lamech's misstatement of the hope.

Redemption for humankind comes through Lamech's son, even though it is not the kind of redemption he (or for that matter the Marxist) anticipates—that is, a redemption leading on to an earthly utopia. Redemption turns out to be the rescue of a remnant of human beings in the midst of a deluge of divine judgment.

The creation vision that places God at the center of the universe and human beings, when behaving rightly, in community together and living in harmony with the rest of creation continues to underpin the rest of the biblical story. This is why the Bible generally sets itself against any kind of political and economic hierarchy that rewards the powerful and the wealthy and sets them apart from the powerless and the poor. The biblical vision of society is resolutely one of community and common resources, not one of individual profit and upward mobility in which the elite enjoy the results of everyone else's work or even enjoy without a further thought the results of their own.

Israel is called out of Egypt to model for the world the way in which a righteous community should function. It is a community in which tribes and families hold property that cannot accumulate in the long term in the hands of others, and indeed which is to be viewed at all times as belonging to God and held only in trust (e.g., Lev. 25, esp. v. 23). The community must always allow access to its shared resources by those who need them, whether they are the poor and marginalized within the community or immigrants from outside it (e.g., Ex. 23:9–11; Lev. 19:9–10, 33–34; 23:22; Deut. 10:18–19; 15:1–11; 24:14–22; Ruth 2). The law places severe constraints on such things as lending money at interest, allowing the taking of interest only from non-Israelites (Ex. 22:25–27; Lev. 25:35–38; Deut. 23:19–20; Neh. 5:6–11); even in the case of loans to non-Israelites, the law forbids extortion and encourages generosity (Ex. 23:9; Lev. 19:33–34). When God's people cry out for a king, they are reminded of the *economic* consequences of the elevation of another human being to such a position of power (1 Sam. 8:11–17). The prophets regularly inveigh against Israel's economic sins as well as others, making clear that love of neighbor involves taking economic issues as seriously as any other kinds. No religion is acceptable to God that does not have at its heart questions of social justice in respect of the wider human community (e.g., Isa. 1:10–17; Amos 4:1–3; 5:11–12, 21–24).

It is no different (nor should we expect it to be) with God's people in the New Testament, who are also called to model the righteous community for the world. The socioeconomic organization of the early church, which recognizes that it stands in continuity with Israel, has its roots in the Old Testament. This is a body that shares everything in common (Acts 2:42, 44), ensuring that no one is in need (4:34), and that aims for economic and social equality (2 Cor. 8:13–15; James 2:1–7). The New Testament, like the Old Testament, recognizes economic repentance as intrinsic to the whole business of repentance (Luke 19:1–10), as it insists in general that the truly religious life is also the truly socially righteous life (e.g., Matt. 5:23–24). The only true test of our sincerity in respect of God is the level of our commitment to our neighbors (1 John 4:19–21). Christianity is, as much as its sibling Judaism, a way of life, not simply a set of doctrines.

All this represents the background against which the Christian reader must hear Ecclesiastes 4. Commentators have criticized Qohelet for resting content with his description of injustice and failing to propose action to put things right. This is a foolish criticism, which arises from the widespread modern conviction that it is somehow possible to "put things right" in this world in a general way. Historical experience tends to suggest, however, that although it may be possible to moderate the worst effects of societal evil and even replace evil with good in limited ways, the best-intentioned attempts to do so will be tainted by still further evils often unintended by the good and idealistic people involved in the projects. There are, at worst, spectacular examples from recent human history of groups of people who were utterly convinced of their ability to change the world for the better but whose ideas, when put into practice, resulted in widespread human misery.[1] Moreover, it is simply a fact that individuals usually have little power to change society at large, and their immediate need is to see the world clearly and to form some idea of how to negotiate it well. It is this latter, facilitating task that Qohelet sets for himself, lighting up the path ahead of the individual who wishes to dance to a different tune than the one often played by the world's pipers.

This is no less noble or important a task than the one carried through by the prophets, who for all their assaults on the human misery that they saw before them were never so naïve as to assume that utopia is humanly achievable. Jesus himself told his disciples that the poor would always be with them (Matt. 26:11) in the world, and he himself laid great emphasis on individual transformation as the heart of a societal transformation that would certainly not occur in the near future (e.g., 5:13–16). The prophets provide the larger canvas on which Qohelet paints his picture, but the picture is no less important for the fact that the canvas is its context. Both Jesus and the prophets agree: In the end it is God who must "put things right" (cf. Eccl. 3:16–17). In the meantime the person sickened by oppression and injustice should

---

1. One thinks, for example, of the period of the Khmer Rouge domination in Cambodia in the late 1970s, when a new "vision" of society resulted in the deaths of around one and a half million people.

follow the countercultural pathway sketched by Qohelet: hard work carried out for and in community rather than envy-driven, self-centered, and lonely toil, along with the striving for empty advancement.

SALLY: "Wake up, big brother."
CHARLIE BROWN: "Wake up?! Wake up?! Why are you waking me up?"
SALLY: "I thought you might like to get an early start."
CHARLIE BROWN: "For what? I'm not going anywhere . . ."
SALLY: "That's too bad . . . you could have been the first one there."[2]

I have been told that the noun used for a non-African white person in one of the African languages is "person who endlessly rushes around to no apparent purpose." This would be amusing if it were not for the fact that this insane desire to "be the first one there" is so personally and communally destructive, both nearer to home and globally. A contrast is provided by an increasingly popular soccer program in Europe that sets high standards of excellence but will not allow individuals to advance to the next stage of the program until the whole team is ready to advance. The community as a whole goes forward, or no one does.

Everything depends, of course, on what our goals are. Where are we going? Much of our Western culture answers this question individualistically rather than communally, whether in secular terms (I'm headed for the fulfillment of my dreams) or in religious terms (I'm headed for heaven). The two sets of goals are in practice often perceived to be perfectly compatible, allowing significant participation in "The American Dream" while still keeping alive the hope of an eternal welcome.

The Bible will have none of this. God's Word does, of course, teach us that individual human beings are precious to God, and it is from this wellspring that our modern individualism arises. Yet the Bible does not understand this preciousness as somehow residing within the human frame itself, which is simply "dust" or "grass," but only in the relatedness of the human being to God, who made him or her and bestowed his "image" (Gen. 1:27). The individual-in-relation-to-God is at the same time inseparable, biblically, from all those other individuals who as creatures are also in relation to God. This is why, biblically, it is impossible to drive a wedge between being in a right relationship to God and being in a right relationship to our neighbors (and indeed to creation generally); the one involves the other.

---

2. *Peanuts*, in *Vancouver Sun*, August 16, 1999.

The secular individualism that is often apparent in modern culture, which has everything to do with self-sufficiency and self-fulfillment and little to do with worship of God and social responsibility, has nothing in the end to do with the Bible. Even the religious individualism that lays great emphasis on a person's relationship with God but little emphasis on a person's social, economic, political, and religious relationships with other people, has little in the end to do with the Bible. The Bible is about *persons-in-community*, whether in the Godhead of Father, Son, and Spirit, or in the church, or in the world at large. The proper goal of the Christian is not an individualistic heaven but is to be found in right relationship with God, neighbor, and God's world *now* and in the future, which will include by God's grace a future stretching beyond death.

With this in mind—and remembering that Jesus himself taught us that our neighbor is whoever is in need of our help, even if it is our enemy (e.g., Matt. 5:43–48; Luke 10:25–37)—Christian readers need to respond to Qohelet's graphic description of the world as it is, and to his advocacy of a different way, with some serious commitments. The first is to root out from our hearts all the destructive and sinful thoughts that lead us to pursue a self-ish and individualistic path through life. Envy, which Qohelet mentions in 4:4, is certainly one of these; this vice is also highlighted in the New Testament (e.g., Mark 7:22; Rom. 1:29; 1 Cor. 13:4; Gal. 5:21; Titus 3:3). Excessive desire for our own advancement is another (Eccl. 4:13–16), and Christians are explicitly told not to set out on this road but to aim at servanthood (e.g., Mark 10:35–45).

Another sin to root out of our hearts is the refusal to accept that all other human beings do indeed have a stake in the world (in Heb., a *ḥeleq* or "portion"), which leads, for complex but often abominable reasons (e.g., greed, government policies framed "in the national interest"), to the turning of a blind eye to the reality that we have much more than others do. We also refuse to accept that many of these others have indeed been deprived even of the most basic means out of which to live their lives.

Along with our rooting out of these bad attitudes, and along with them the implicit belief that my family or my nation has some inherent right to more of the world's resources than others do, must come a commitment to do as much as we can to contribute to community and to alleviate the suffering of the world. It is impossible to be a follower of Jesus and simply observe "the tears of the oppressed" who "have no comforter" (Eccl. 4:1), nor is it acceptable simply to offer empty words. The contribution of our own lifestyle choices to their plight—in a world where the Market (or in traditional biblical terms, Mammon) dominates the agenda rather than human interests—is a factor here. There must also naturally be practical comfort in loving actions—such as caring for the widows and orphans, the immigrants and the poor—of which the whole Bible speaks. We do this for others—but at the same time we do it for ourselves, for what is good for others is also good for us. The life of selfish individualism leads neither to happiness nor to eternal life. The race run according to these rules leads only to the reality captured by a British movie of several decades ago: *The Loneliness of the Long-Distance Runner*.

One final comment is in order here. There is a truly depressing tendency, especially when matters like these are discussed among Christians in North America, to allow easy dichotomies to arise between allegedly *leftist* and allegedly *rightist* points of view on such issues as economic responsibility. This is only slightly less depressing than a more general tendency for Christians actually to identify themselves as *conservatives* or *liberals*, as if the label *Christian* were a secondary religious tag hung around the neck of what is essentially a political animal. Christians should have no other primary commitments than to love God and their neighbors and to look after God's world.

That task of love is far more complex than can ever be captured in a political ideology. The first question to be asked is not whether an idea is conservative or liberal (so what?) but whether it is orthodox and biblical. The Bible constantly strikes balances in order to catch the whole truth; political ideologies characteristically simplify and thus distort. Thus, for example, Qohelet both urges the virtue of hard work (in common with other parts of the Bible, e.g., Eph. 4:28; 1 Thess. 4:11) and yet draws our attention to the misery in the world and advocates community. Ideologues on the right have been known to use the first kind of text to justify inactivity in respect of the poor and oppressed, and ideologues on the left have been known to use the second kind of text to urge social reform that does not take individual sinfulness sufficiently seriously. The Bible presses a more complex world upon us and urges a more sensitive response. Truly loving one's neighbor (rather than simply being kind and polite) is always a challenge, yet it is the challenge that is set before us as we pursue a life of contentment-in-community, in which we do not "eat, drink, and enjoy" selfishly, but openheartedly.

> Then [Jesus] said to them, "Watch out! Be on your guard against all kinds of greed; a man's life does not consist in the abundance of his possessions."
>
> And he told them this parable: "The ground of a certain rich man produced a good crop. He thought to himself, 'What shall I do? I have no place to store my crops.'
>
> "Then he said, 'This is what I'll do. I will tear down my barns and build bigger ones, and there I will store all my grain and my goods. And I'll say to myself, "You have plenty of good things laid up for many years. Take life easy; eat, drink and be merry."'

"But God said to him, 'You fool! This very night your life will be demanded from you. Then who will get what you have prepared for yourself?'

"This is how it will be with anyone who stores up things for himself but is not rich toward God." (Luke 12:15–21)

Ecclesiastes 5:1–7

GUARD YOUR STEPS when you go to the house of God. Go near to listen rather than to offer the sacrifice of fools, who do not know that they do wrong.

²Do not be quick with your mouth,
  do not be hasty in your heart
  to utter anything before God.
God is in heaven
  and you are on earth,
  so let your words be few.
³As a dream comes when there are many cares,
  so the speech of a fool when there are many words.

⁴When you make a vow to God, do not delay in fulfilling it. He has no pleasure in fools; fulfill your vow. ⁵It is better not to vow than to make a vow and not fulfill it. ⁶Do not let your mouth lead you into sin. And do not protest to the temple messenger, "My vow was a mistake." Why should God be angry at what you say and destroy the work of your hands? ⁷Much dreaming and many words are meaningless. Therefore stand in awe of God.

THE WORSHIP OF Mammon has been a central feature of the preceding section of Ecclesiastes; now we turn to the worship of God. Worshipers should take care when they enter the temple to remember that God must be the focal point of worship, not the self, and that the Word of God should take priority, not the words of the worshiper.

In worship, the first task of the worshiper is to "go near to listen" (v. 1), with a view to obeying the divine voice (cf. the same language in Deut. 5:27). The activity contrasted with this listening is the offering of "the sacrifice of fools, who do not know that they do wrong." The second part of this phrase is (lit.) "who do not know to do wrong," which is perhaps better translated as "who sin without a thought" (NEB). Their sin is natural to them and does not require any conscious design. The whole line refers to those who perform the rituals of worship without any deliberate intention to bring the whole self before God in an attitude of reverence and awe. The "sacrifice of fools" is thus careless observance of religion, unattached to any genuinely

Godward movement of the soul and enacted out of custom, peer pressure, or habit. It is the kind of religion frequently attacked by the prophets, who associate it with oppression of one's neighbor (e.g., Isa. 1:10−20; cf. also 1 Sam. 15:22−23; Prov. 15:8−9; 21:3, 27).

The wise person comes before God carefully and with due attention, for such a person, unlike the fool, knows that God is really God. The wise person listens, therefore, rather than speaks (v. 2); for God is in heaven and is truly God, and mortal beings are mere creatures of dust found on earth. The fool, by contrast, is someone who is not in control of himself. As he sins without a thought, so too his speech pours out of his mouth just because the words are found in his heart (v. 3). It is as natural for the fool to be verbose as it is for dreams to come to those who toil pointlessly in search of gain. "Cares" is Hebrew *ᶜinyan* (as in 2:23), and the phrase is better translated "as a dream comes when there is overwork." Overproduction is the root problem in both cases. A heart attentive to God multiplies neither toil nor words.

The making of a vow is a particular form of speech and is the focal point of 5:4−6. Temple vows were a common feature of Old Testament worship and involved promises to consecrate such things as sacrifices or money to God in return for granting a request in prayer (Lev. 7:16−17; 22:18−23; 27:1−25; Num. 6). The temptation presented to the worshiper was to avoid fulfilling the vow once the prayer had been answered. Qohelet is insistent, however, on the need for integrity. There is no sin in refraining from speech (Eccl. 5:5), but one must do what one has in fact spoken (v. 4).

Other biblical passages also touch on this topic, emphasizing this same need for integrity (Prov. 20:25; esp. Deut. 23:21−23, with its closing admonition: "Whatever your lips utter you must be sure to do, because you made your vow freely to the LORD your God with your own mouth"). The mouth must be kept under control, or it can lead us into sin when our actions fail to be consistent with our words (cf. Prov. 10:14; 13:3; 14:3; 15:28, for general emphasis on control of speech as an aspect of wisdom). There must be no prevarication when confronted by the temple messenger (perhaps a priest) who comes to remind the worshiper of what has been said. God's anger is aroused by such dishonesty, and sooner or later this will result in the destruction of the works of the worshiper's hands.

The closing verse of the section represents a summary of the whole, picking up the vocabulary of verse 3 (the multiplying of dreams and words) and the central thought behind all seven verses (the worshiper must revere the living God), and contrasting the latter with the former. If the meaning is clear, the syntax is, however, admittedly unusual: (lit. trans.) "For [*ki*] in a multitude of dreams and futilities and many words therefore [*ki*] fear God." In the midst of all the foolish behavior that one sees round about, along with its consequences, the reader is exhorted to hold on to reality: "Stand in awe of God" (cf. Heb. *yrʾ* in 3:14; 7:18; 8:12–13; 12:13).

Bridging Contexts

THE BIBLE DOES not consider the worship of the one true God "in spirit and in truth" (John 4:24) to be an easy task. Our human passion is for idols made in our own image. Even when our doctrine concerning God is correct, we all too often deny its truth in practice by what we do and say. Qohelet's concern for integrity in the area of worship is thus a recurring concern in the Bible.

The book of Deuteronomy insists again and again that the one, undivided God who made the world and redeemed Israel must be approached and related to by one, undivided human person: "Hear, O Israel: The LORD our God, the LORD is one. Love the LORD your God with all your heart and with all your soul and with all your strength" (Deut. 6:4–5). It is a matter of heart as well as of sight (4:9) and speech (6:7). It begins with deep internalization of God's Word, which is to be the focus of life in all its aspects (6:7–8). There must be a constant, meditative "remembering" of reality, so that reality seeps into the interior of the being and becomes formative for all of life (4:10; 5:15; 7:18; 8:2, 18; etc.). The consequence should be that Israel, and the individual Israelite, is able "to fear the LORD your God, to walk in all his ways, to love him, to serve the LORD your God with all your heart and with all your soul, and to observe the LORD's commands and decrees" (10:12–13).

The prophetic books and other Scriptures constantly draw attention, however, to the way in which even biblical religion is in practice all too often merely a matter of externalism and pretense. It is lip-service (e.g., Ps. 50:16; Isa. 29:13; Jer. 12:2), offered by a people whose hearts are far from God. Jesus stands in the prophetic tradition when he criticizes many of his contemporaries for their practice of this kind of religion. In Matthew 23:27–28, for example, he describes the teachers of the law and the Pharisees as "whitewashed tombs, which look beautiful on the outside but on the inside are full of dead men's bones and everything unclean." Sincerity, by contrast, is to be the mark of the Christian (e.g., Acts 2:46; Rom. 12:9; 2 Cor. 6:6; 1 Tim. 1:5; 3:8). The New Testament, too, knows of a "form of godliness" that lacks the transformative power of true faith (2 Tim. 3:1–5).

The person who engages in this kind of "godliness" stands on dangerous ground, for he or she is toying with a God who is holy and good and who is therefore dangerous to those who cling to self-centeredness and sin. This too is a biblical theme found elsewhere than in Ecclesiastes. Holiness is, in fact, the characteristic most typical of God in the Old Testament. It refers to that mystery in the divine being that distinguishes God as God and marks him off from what is created, distinguishing him as wholly other (e.g., Hos. 11:9: "For I am God, and not man—the Holy One among you"). To say that God is holy is to say that God is God (cf. Amos 4:2 and 6:8)—that God is indeed in heaven while we mortals are on earth (Eccl. 5:2).

Isaiah 6:1–8 captures well the awe and fear that a vision of God in all his holiness induces when he is encountered by those who are aware of their own sinful condition. Holiness is in fact understood throughout the Bible in terms of a mysterious power that is dangerous, unapproachable, and fearsome. Nadab and Abihu died, for example, because they offered unholy fire before the Lord (Lev. 10:1–3). Many people in Beth Shemesh died when they looked directly into the ark of the covenant (1 Sam. 6:19–20), in response to which others said, "Who can to stand in the presence of the LORD, this holy God?" The people of Israel themselves trembled in Exodus 19 as they stood at the foot of Mount Sinai, as God revealed himself in a thunderstorm; they were right to do so, because they had been told that to come up onto the mountain or even to touch it meant death.

The people likewise had to be kept away from the tabernacle precisely because it was the place where God dwelt (Num. 1:47–53). Each step toward the Most Holy Place was controlled in terms of the people who were allowed to draw nearer to it and those who were not and in terms of the rituals that had to be performed in order to allow access to the divine presence. The rituals themselves were carefully spelled out in terms of what was allowed, who was allowed to perform them and who was not, what they were to wear, and so on. These rituals covered the whole of life. As the author of the letter to the Hebrews reminds us, "our 'God is a consuming fire'" (Heb. 12:29; cf. Deut. 4:24). That is why we must "worship God acceptably with reverence and awe" (Heb. 12:28). Our God is not One who will be mocked, as Ananias and Sapphira discovered to their cost (Acts 5:1–11).

This last instance of lack of integrity is a particularly powerful New Testament illustration of the expectation that our words and our actions should match up. If we speak at all, we should do what we say (Eccl. 5:4–6). The person who understands who God is will, however, be careful with words altogether. In fact, those who know God well understand that it is much more important that he addresses us than that we address him. The first requirement laid on his people in the Old Testament was not "speak, O Israel," but "hear, O Israel," and that exhortation is a common and insistent one—both in Deuteronomy and elsewhere (e.g., Deut. 4:1; 5:1; 6:3, 4; 9:1; Isa. 1:10; 7:13; 28:14). Without hearing there can be no understanding of the kingdom of God; thus Jesus repeats, "He who has ears, let him hear" (e.g., Matt. 11:15; 13:9, 43; John 8:47).

A time for speaking may, of course, follow (Eccl. 3:7), but even then human beings are not to manipulate and control God with words, as they may be accustomed to doing with their fellow human beings as they try to accumulate gain. As Jesus taught: "When you pray, do not keep on babbling like pagans, for they think they will be heard because of their many words. Do not be like them, for your Father knows what you need before you ask him" (Matt. 6:7—8). The speaking to God that follows on from our listening to God bears always in mind who God is—a Father who knows what we need before we ask. A holy God, certainly, but also a caring Father, whose holiness does not routinely bring destruction to human beings but has redemption as its utmost goal and who characteristically issues an invitation to embrace holiness (e.g., Ps. 51:11; Isa. 6:1—5; Hos. 11:8—9).

The insertion of this passage on the worship of God in the midst of reflections on the worship of wealth and advancement and its deleterious effects on humanness also reflects a broader biblical emphasis. "No one can serve two masters. Either he will hate the one and love the other, or he will be devoted to the one and despise the other. You cannot serve both God and Money" (Matt. 6:24). The first Master commands love of neighbor. The second applauds love of self and the trampling of one's neighbor. This is why false and hypocritical religion is so often linked with economic sin in the Bible (e.g., Mark 12:38—44). It is also why the presentation of the whole self as a living sacrifice in worship to God leads on to just and neighborly behavior with respect to our fellow human beings (Rom. 12:1—21).

It is better to remain silent and be thought a fool than to open your mouth and remove all doubt.[1]

Silence is undervalued in the noisy, intrusive world that most of us inhabit. Constant traffic and chatter surround us in our public spaces, and where these are mercifully quieted for a time, their place is taken by endless radio music and inanity. We retreat to our homes, but then we voluntarily recreate the noisy world there as well. The TV provides constant background noise, whether it presses on us the fantasies of soaps and movies or the horrors of the endless daily chat shows, with their multitudes who want their chance to speak but in truth have little to say.

The evidence suggests that we are afraid of silence—discomfited by it and

---

1. Lisa Simpson in *The Simpsons*.

unable to deal with it. There must be noise—any noise. I have personally witnessed in our home the panicked disorientation of a young child, visiting for the afternoon, who was unable to locate a TV in our main living space and, without this comforting presence, seemed unsure what to do with himself. We have all met his adult counterparts, and perhaps we ourselves are some of those. We have, in essence, made it extraordinarily difficult for ourselves in all our technological sophistication to "be still, and know that I am God" (Ps. 46:10).

This is a tragedy, but it is also a perceived necessity. Silence gives us too much time to think, and thinking raises too many awkward questions we do not wish to address about the nature of reality and our personal identity and destiny. We live in a culture that therefore feels a deep need to push reality as far away as possible and uses noise to this end. We have become, corporately, the man in the doctor's waiting room who feels compelled to break the silence with an asinine, jovial comment.

If it is bad enough that the culture should be of this inclination, it is entirely tragic that the people of God, who are called to witness to a different reality, should be found playing the same game. Christians, too, often inhabit all-too-noisy space. Their noise is more religious, perhaps, but it is still noise. "Worship services" provide little opportunity for silent awe in the presence of God but plenty of opportunity for performance on the part of a select few professional speakers and musicians, who fill all the space with their words and sounds. Other gatherings of the church are characterized by relentless activity. It is Christian activity, of course, but it still fills the space that might be taken by silent adoration. Thus, "church" comes to resemble simply another form of human group endeavor and indeed often comes to mimic in a serious way the culture around it that is supposedly governed by different values. "Church" is increasingly thought of in terms of organization rather than of people worshiping God together, and leaders bring business and management models to bear on its development—planning growth, programming success, and managing change.

Leadership itself is understood and evaluated from a secular point of view. What counts as "good leadership" in the church-as-organization has been borrowed from the secular world. The modern pastor is seen in this light as a kind of CEO of the company, trained as an expert in problem solving and management, and thus gains respectability in a world and in a church that no longer thinks in a truly Christian way, particularly about the church. He is "a CEO in his study and a shrink in his pulpit."[2] As Vinoth Ramachandra rightly notes, "Many seminary graduates are now skilled in management

---

2. O. Guinness, "America's Last Men and Their Magnificent Talking Cure," in *No God but God*, ed. O. Guinness and J. Seel (Chicago: Moody, 1992), 111–32 (quote on p. 123).

techniques, or counselling skills and even 'church-planting' methodologies, but lack any integrating theological vision."[3] The story is told of a Christian leader returning from a church-growth conference puzzled because he had heard no theology and no serious references to God—only the exaltation of technique and numbers.[4] Church advertising often reflects this ethos, as illustrated in these comments of an advertising executive regarding a contract from an Episcopal church in Minneapolis:

> Promoting one's church and marketing is a big part of evangelism. . . . George [the pastor] was used to getting on his knees a lot and asking for favors, and he wondered why he couldn't promote his own parish with messages as hard-hitting as a lot of the ads he'd admired.[5]

The narcissistic, self-absorbed church thus develops by degrees to respond to the narcissistic culture, mimicking that culture in its move from word to image, from passion for truth and righteousness to cultivating intimacy and "good feelings," from exposition to entertainment, from integrity to novelty, from action to spectacle.[6] A survey of sermons by evangelical ministers between 1985 and 1990 suggests, in fact, that over 80 percent of these made God and his world spin around the surrogate center of the self. This is related to the professionalization of the ministry, in which the fulcrum around which ministry turns is no longer God but the church, which itself thus turns out to be a kind of idol.[7] Of this kind of consumerist religion, Jacques Ellul commented rightly a number of years ago that it was not so much a "Jesus revolution" as a "gigantic religious expediency, in which Jesus and the revelation are served up to suit everybody's taste."[8]

Noise deafens us to reality. Silent reflection—deliberate inactivity—is necessary if we are to regain perspective and remember who God really is, what that really means, and what, therefore, the church is *for*. We need to hear again that injunction: "Do not come any closer . . . take off your sandals, for the place where you are standing is holy ground" (Ex. 3:5); and to hear it, we need to stop talking.

> It is necessary, if we are going to truly live a Christian life, and not just use the word Christian to disguise our narcissistic and promethean attempts at spirituality without worshipping God and without being

---

3. V. Ramachandra, *Gods That Fail: Modern Idolatry and Christian Mission* (Carlisle: Paternoster, 1996), 18.
4. O. Guinness, "Sounding Out the Idols of Church Growth," in *No God but God*, 174–88 (quote on p. 165).
5. T. Pruzan, "Angels in the Ad Field," *Print* (1998), 58–63 (quote on p. 61).
6. Ramachandra, *Gods That Fail*, 18.
7. D. Wells, "The D-Min-ization of the Ministry," in *No God but God*, 174–88.
8. J. Ellul, *The New Demons*, trans. C. Edward Hopkin (New York: Seabury, 1973), 154.

addressed by God, it is necessary to return to Square One and adore God and listen to God. Given our sin-damaged memories that render us vulnerable to every latest edition of journalistic spirituality, daily re-orientation in the truth revealed in Jesus and attested in Scripture is required. And given our ancient predisposition for reducing every scrap of divine revelation that we come across into a piece of moral/spiritual technology that we can use to get on in the world, and eventually to get on without God, a daily return to a condition of not-knowing and non-achievement is required.[9]

Therefore, since we are receiving a kingdom that cannot be shaken, let us be thankful, and so worship God acceptably with reverence and awe. (Heb. 12:28)

9. E. Peterson, *Subversive Spirituality* (Grand Rapids/Vancouver: Eerdmans/Regent College, 1997), 30.

Ecclesiastes 5:8–6:12

I F YOU SEE the poor oppressed in a district, and justice and rights denied, do not be surprised at such things; for one official is eyed by a higher one, and over them both are others higher still. ⁹The increase from the land is taken by all; the king himself profits from the fields.

¹⁰Whoever loves money never has money enough;
  whoever loves wealth is never satisfied with his income.
  This too is meaningless.

¹¹As goods increase,
  so do those who consume them.
And what benefit are they to the owner
  except to feast his eyes on them?

¹²The sleep of a laborer is sweet,
  whether he eats little or much,
but the abundance of a rich man
  permits him no sleep.

¹³I have seen a grievous evil under the sun:

wealth hoarded to the harm of its owner,
¹⁴ or wealth lost through some misfortune,
so that when he has a son
  there is nothing left for him.
¹⁵Naked a man comes from his mother's womb,
  and as he comes, so he departs.
He takes nothing from his labor
  that he can carry in his hand.

¹⁶This too is a grievous evil:

As a man comes, so he departs,
  and what does he gain,
  since he toils for the wind?
¹⁷All his days he eats in darkness,
  with great frustration, affliction and anger.

¹⁸Then I realized that it is good and proper for a man to eat and drink, and to find satisfaction in his toilsome labor under the sun during the few days of life God has given

him—for this is his lot. ¹⁹Moreover, when God gives any man wealth and possessions, and enables him to enjoy them, to accept his lot and be happy in his work—this is a gift of God. ²⁰He seldom reflects on the days of his life, because God keeps him occupied with gladness of heart.

⁶:¹I have seen another evil under the sun, and it weighs heavily on men: ²God gives a man wealth, possessions and honor, so that he lacks nothing his heart desires, but God does not enable him to enjoy them, and a stranger enjoys them instead. This is meaningless, a grievous evil.

³A man may have a hundred children and live many years; yet no matter how long he lives, if he cannot enjoy his prosperity and does not receive proper burial, I say that a stillborn child is better off than he. ⁴It comes without meaning, it departs in darkness, and in darkness its name is shrouded. ⁵Though it never saw the sun or knew anything, it has more rest than does that man—⁶even if he lives a thousand years twice over but fails to enjoy his prosperity. Do not all go to the same place?

> ⁷All man's efforts are for his mouth,
>> yet his appetite is never satisfied.
> ⁸What advantage has a wise man
>> over a fool?
> What does a poor man gain
>> by knowing how to conduct himself before others?
> ⁹Better what the eye sees
>> than the roving of the appetite.
> This too is meaningless,
>> a chasing after the wind.

> ¹⁰Whatever exists has already been named,
>> and what man is has been known;
> no man can contend
>> with one who is stronger than he.
> ¹¹The more the words,
>> the less the meaning,
>> and how does that profit anyone?

¹²For who knows what is good for a man in life, during the few and meaningless days he passes through like a shadow? Who can tell him what will happen under the sun after he is gone?

REFLECTION ON THE worship of Mammon and its consequences (4:1–16) has led to a brief digression on the topic of true worship (5:1–7). Now we return to the subject matter of oppression and the pursuit and hoarding of wealth. The key word in the whole section is "consumption" (Heb. *ʾkl;* lit. "eat," in 5:11, 12, 17, 18, 19, and 6:2, trans. variously by the NIV as "consume," "eats," "eat," and "enjoy"). If the good life involves what goes out of our mouths (5:1–7), it also involves what "enters" them and how it does so.

Ecclesiastes 5:8–9 picks up the thoughts of 4:1–3, making it clear to the reader that oppression is not merely a matter of individuals behaving badly in respect of their neighbors. Oppression has its structural, systemic aspects. The oppression of the poor and vulnerable and the denial of justice and rights are consequences of an entire hierarchical system of government that is corrupt. Each government official "is eyed" (Heb. *šmr*) by another, either in the sense that each looks out for the interests of the other, or in the sense that each is supervised by another and cannot behave in ways that are not to his superior's advantage.

In all this watching, however, no concern exists for the interests of the poor and for justice—for the powerless of 4:1–3. Government is in the interests only of the powerful. It has been forgotten that each person is supposed to be his brother's "keeper" (*šmr* in Gen. 4:9, i.e., to watch out for his interests), just as God himself watches out for the interests of his creatures (*šmr* in verses like Ps. 16:1; 41:2; 121:3–5, 7–8). It is the desire for "gain" that causes the lapse in memory (the NIV's "increase" in Eccl. 5:9 is the same Heb. *yitron* that we have encountered already in 1:3; 2:11, 13; 3:9 [see comments]).

The Hebrew of verse 9 is somewhat difficult; a literal translation would be: "Profit from land, in all, is this—a king in respect of a cultivated field." Syntactically awkward, it nevertheless seems likely that "profit" and "king" stand in parallel just like "land" and "cultivated field." Thus, the sense is that the only real "profit" made by workers from tending their crops is the king, who stands at the pinnacle of the corrupt regime and derives the ultimate benefit. We might paraphrase as follows: "In the end, the only 'gain' from hard work in the fields is the monarchy, which flourishes in the soil of the workers' labor." Note again 1 Samuel 8:10–18, with its picture of the king who takes and takes from his people, employing them to plow "his" ground and to reap "his" harvest, while ensuring that his officials and attendants are well cared for.

As in Ecclesiastes 4:1–16, we turn from oppression immediately to consider its root causes. Envy was the focus of 4:4–6; in 5:10 Qohelet fixes attention on the love of money itself. Like all false gods, money is incapable of satisfying the hunger and the thirst of the person who is devoted to it: "Whoever loves money never has money enough." Profit never fulfills those who pursue it but only feeds the insatiable desire for more. Indeed, the irony is that as goods increase, their owner finds not only that their consumption does not satisfy but that the number of those vying to consume them increases (5:11). His "benefits" from the whole business are only to "feast his eyes on them" before they disappear into other people's pockets and mouths.

The world of the rich is indeed a world of "abundance" (śbᶜ, v. 12), which does not in fact satisfy (śbᶜ, v. 10) and permits no sleep (cf. 2:23; 5:3). The world of the worker (ᶜbd, as in 5:9, "cultivated"), by contrast, is one in which there may be less consumption (he may not eat [ʾkl] much, v. 12; cf. "consume" in v. 11), but at least he has peace of mind that permits restful slumber. The one suffers the indigestion of materialism, being too full of good things. The other, tasting more selectively of life's bounty, knows sweeter dreams (Heb. *matoq/mᵉtuqa*, "sweet," often refers to what is eaten, esp. honey, cf. Judg. 14:14). Once again it is suggested that the pursuit of profit brings not only oppression to others but also damage to the self.

An explicit statement to this effect, looking back over 5:10–12, is found in verse 13. Qohelet has seen a "grievous evil" (lit., "sick evil," in the sense of "miserable outcome," cf. 5:16; see comments on 1:13) as he observes the world: wealth "hoarded" to the harm of its owner (cf. "owner" also in 5:11). The Hebrew verb behind "hoarded" is *šmr*, reminding us of 3:6 and, most recently, of 5:8. The rich man has kept his wealth when he ought to have been keeping his neighbor; but even though his goods have increased (v. 11), the end result for him has only been "harm" (lit., "evil," playing on the concept of whether "goods" are really good for the person).

This is not the only grievous evil that exists, however.[1] Qohelet has seen wealth both hoarded and also lost after being accumulated (5:14–17; cf. 3:6). The NIV ascribes this to "some misfortune" (5:14), but that is probably too specific; it is simply lost in the course of the wealthy person's involvement in the "evil/miserable business" of life (Heb. ᶜinyan raᶜ, 5:14, as in 1:13; 4:8[2]). The consequence is that this man, who unlike the driven man of 4:7–8 has a son, is

---

1. The NIV has laid the text out so as to imply that vv. 13–15 concern one grievous evil, apparently unconnected to what precedes, and vv. 16–17 a second grievous evil. Consideration of the content, however, reveals that both vv. 13 and 16–17 represent summary statements and elaborations of that which precedes them, not that which follows. A partial and paraphrastic translation of vv. 13–14, 16 that brings this out would be: "I have seen a grievous evil . . . wealth hoarded to the harm of its owner. Or (consider the case where) that wealth is lost . . . this too is a grievous evil. . . ."

2. The NIV translates this phrase in a variety of ways, such as "heavy burden" in 1:13 and "miserable business" in 4:8; here in 5:14 it is translated "some misfortune."

nevertheless unable to pass on any inheritance; there is literally "nothing in his hand" to give him (5:14). This is a bad state of affairs, for it means that no surplus survives his death. He arrives in the world naked, and thus he departs, with nothing from his "labor" (*ʿamal*) that he can "carry in his hand" (5:15). There is nothing to show for it all; he makes no "gain" (*yitron*, v. 16), for he "toils [*ʿml*] for the wind" that cannot be grasped and held captive.

The awareness of this fact leads this man, too, to "eat" in the midst of unhappy circumstances (in "darkness," v. 17, with all its connotations of chaos, imprisonment, and separation from God; e.g., Amos 5:18). Even the loss of his fortune does not lead to the abandonment of his futile approach to life but only to frustration, affliction, and anger, as his great plans are confounded.[3]

For those who pursue gain, then, and who oppress the poor in doing so—whether they possess wealth or have once possessed it and have now lost it—there is no contented consumption, but only dissatisfaction, restlessness, frustration, affliction, and anger. With this reality in mind, Qohelet returns to his earlier advice about how to gain or "find" contentment (v. 18; cf. 2:24−26; 3:12−13, 22). It is good for a person to eat and drink and to "see the good" (NIV "find satisfaction") in all toil. These things are, in themselves, our *ḥeleq*, our "share" in or "reward" from life (NIV "lot," 5:18). There is nothing beyond them during the few days of life that God gives to each of us as a gift.

Wisdom lies in accepting these things from the hand of the good God as they come to us as an aspect of the "times" he gives us. That is the force of the word "proper" (*yapeh*) in 5:18 (cf. also 3:11, where God has made everything "beautiful" or "fitting" for its time). As we adjust ourselves to the reality of the universe and to the reality of God who made it, it is possible to find peace of mind and joy in the midst of our lives (like the laborer of 5:12).

It is not that it is impossible to know God and to know joy even in the midst of wealth and possessions (5:19−20). Qohelet acknowledges the possibility that these things too can be received as divine gifts and that people might even be blessed with the ability to "enjoy them" (lit., "consume, eat them"; cf. 5:11, 12, 17, 18). Perhaps a wealthy person may, like the ordinary person, "eat" well while accepting what he has been given as his "share" in life (NIV "lot," v. 19) and finding joy (*śmḥ*) in his toil, rather than eating too much or eating in darkness (vv. 12, 17), striving always for more than his "share" (v. 10), and finding only frustration in his toil (v. 16). Perhaps a wealthy person may know so much joy (*śimḥa*; NIV "gladness," v. 20) in his heart that he will not be preoccupied with the brevity, cares, and frustrations of life (as in vv. 12, 17), but will, like the person in v. 18, gladly receive "the days of his

---

3. The Heb. text is again difficult here but is probably best rendered: "All his days he eats in darkness and is frustrated, and sickness and anger are his [lot]."

life" as gifts from God. The wealthy person, Qohelet acknowledges, can also be oriented toward God (notice the emphasis on divine giving throughout vv. 18–20, in contrast to vv. 8–17) and perhaps know contentment.

Yet what Qohelet himself seemingly gives with one hand he immediately takes away with the other, as he returns to reinforce what he has said in 5:8–17. The fact of the matter is that all too often God gives someone wealth, possessions, and indeed honor and yet does not grant him the ability to "enjoy them" (lit., "eat them," 6:2). A stranger "eats" them instead. This verse echoes the preceding passage (cf. 5:11, 14), even though we are not told here precisely why someone else, not the wealthy person himself, "consumes" what he has—as does the whole of 6:1–12. It is not clear, therefore, that the NIV's "another" in 6:1, which does not appear in the Hebrew text, is a correct interpretation. We are not dealing here with another "grievous evil" (v. 2) but are merely exploring further the reality already presented—an evil or bad situation that multiplies (Heb. *rabba*, NIV "weighs heavily," v. 1) just as quickly as riches multiply (cf. 5:11). It is possible to have all that the heart desires (v. 2) and yet to find no joy in it.

The paradigm case is the man who (presumably theoretically, and for emphasis) has a hundred children and lives many years. Long life and abundance of offspring are characteristic indicators of God's blessing in the Bible (e.g., Job 42:12–17; Ps. 127:3–5; Prov. 28:16). Yet of what use is the mere possession of multitudes of days and offspring if a person cannot be satisfied (Heb. *śbᶜ*, as in 5:10; NIV "enjoy") with these good things (Heb. *ṭoba*, as in 5:11, trans. by NIV as "goods"), if "he cannot enjoy his prosperity [*ṭoba*]" (6:3)? Without contentment—that is, "seeing the good" in things—the goods things of life are of little benefit. Verse 3 seems to envisage, indeed, only a frustrated life followed by a lonely death for this person; he "does not receive proper burial," or indeed any burial at all ("proper" does not appear in the Heb. text).

Certain passages of the Old Testament (e.g., 1 Sam. 31:11–13; 1 Kings 14:10–11; Isa. 14:19–20; Jer. 16:4–5) illustrate the importance of burial to the ancient Semitic peoples, as the community of the living sent the deceased person to be at rest with the community of the dead. A good life came to an end in a good death. Here in Ecclesiastes 6:3, a miserable life comes to an end in a bad death. Such a person is worse off than a stillborn child, the tragedy of whose birth is captured in verse 4: "It comes without meaning" (i.e., the birth is "pointless" [*hebel*] in that it does not lead on to life), and "it departs in darkness" (capturing the awful gloom that accompanies its departure from the land of the living; cf. the atmosphere of 5:17 and esp. Job 3:16 for the "infant who never saw the light of day"). In these respects the stillborn child is precisely like the wealthy person described in Ecclesiastes 6:3, for he too is born to a life that is not truly life and "departs in darkness."

It is not quite so clear whether the third element in verse 4, "in darkness its name is shrouded," also represents a similarity between child and man, in that the name of both is associated with darkness rather than with the light of life, or perhaps represents instead a contrast between them (the child has no descendants to whom to pass on his name). Even if the child is worse off than the man in this single respect, however, the overall picture is clear. Although the stillborn "never saw the sun or knew anything" and (perhaps this is the meaning) has no descendants, it is much better off than the man who knew long life and a large family but no "rest" (*naḥat*, 6:5). The Hebrew word *naḥat* has occurred in 4:6 ("Better one handful with *tranquillity* than two handfuls with toil and chasing after the wind"). The point in 6:5 is not to minimize the tragedy of the stillborn child but to emphasize, through the shocking comparison, the tragedy of the life that is lived without contentment or peace of mind (cf. Job 3:16—19; see comments on Eccl. 4:6). Such a life could last two thousand years and still be futile (6:6), if the person never learns to "see the good" (NIV "enjoy his prosperity [*toba*]"). Moreover, it will in any case end in death ("Do not all go to the same place?").

Verse 7 sums up the madness of it all: toil (NIV "efforts") undertaken in pursuit of things to consume, yet powerless to fill the gaping void that is human appetite. Verse 8, although the Hebrew of its second part might better be translated as "what advantage does a poor man have who knows how to meet life's challenges" (taking Heb. *ḥayyim* as "life," not "the living"), is best taken as the question to which verse 9 is the answer. What is the profit that wisdom has over folly, which the poor man is described as grasping in contrast to the rich (cf. 2:12—14 for the idea that there is some profit, at least, in wisdom)? It lies in understanding that we should rest content with what lies before us and resist the temptation to wander off in search of more (v. 9). "Better what the eye sees" (*tob marʾeh ʿenayim*) is related linguistically to the phrase "see the good" in verse 6 (*raʾa toba*; NIV "enjoys his prosperity"). The wealthy fool fails to "see the good" in what lies before him, but the wise pauper is content with it. The latter is happy simply to "walk" (v. 8; NIV "conduct himself"; Heb. *hlk*) well through life, while the former is determined to "rove" (*hlk*, v. 9) in search of gain.

Reality has once again been brutally exposed by Qohelet. As he brings this section of his reflections to a close (6:10—12), he underlines that it is something that must be accepted rather than debated. Verse 10 reminds us of our true nature as human beings. Everything that exists has already been "named" in accordance with its true character (e.g., Gen. 2:19—20). This includes "man" (*ʾadam*), who comes from the "dust" (*ʾadama*, Gen. 2:7) and will return to the dust (Eccl. 12:7). Human beings prefer to make a name for themselves (Gen. 11:4); but in fact they already possess one, and it is a name that signifies weakness ("dust") in the face of the almighty Creator God, with whom no one can "contend" or dispute, as Job discovered (Job 38—42).

There is simply no point in multiplying words, therefore, in a vain attempt to change the nature of reality (Eccl. 6:11; cf. 5:1—7): "the more the words, the less the meaning" (or better, "the greater the futility"). The wise person has the "advantage" (*yoter*, v. 8) over the fool, but there is no way for mortals to gain an advantage (*yoter* in v. 11; NIV "profit") over God.

Acceptance of reality is a necessity. "For who knows what is good for a man in life" (v. 12) other than God, who creates the good and blesses mortals with it (cf. 5:18)? No mortal being is in a position to challenge God on this point! "Who can tell him what will happen under the sun after he is gone?" No mortal being knows! We are ignorant and weak creatures, passing through life "like a shadow" that flits here and there and is gone after a few "meaningless" (better, "brief, insubstantial") days. It is certainly therefore not a rational course of action to seek anything other from life than harmony with creation as it really is and with God who made it thus. Life lived in any other manner can only end in tears.

THE IRRATIONALITY OF human rebellion against God is on open display in this section of Ecclesiastes, although its destructiveness to human beings is also painfully visible. What is it in human nature that leads us to "run after" material things (Matt. 6:32), behaving in adulthood as we behaved first as young children (accumulating and hoarding possessions that we were unwilling to share), rather than learning to trust and to worship the Creator God? Why are we so blind that we cannot see that this way of life is not even in our own best interests, much less in the interests of our neighbor or our planet?

It is the breathtaking stupidity of sin, rather than simply its wrongness, that often strikes our biblical authors. Even the ox knows its master, the donkey its owner's manger, but human beings are too stupid to recognize their Creator (Isa. 1:3). So they go on hoarding goods to their own harm (Eccl. 5:13), even though these possessions do the owner no real good while he or she possesses them but bring with them lack of satisfaction, worry, sleeplessness, frustration, and anger (5:11—12, 17; 6:1—6); and even though they are consumed in the end by other people, whether in life or in death (whither we go naked, 5:11, 15—16). This is a reality of human life reflected throughout the Bible, which identifies the human attachment to material things as one of the primary barriers that exists between God and his human creatures.

The book of Deuteronomy addresses the issue directly in its opening chapters. Note, for example, Deuteronomy 8:6—20, where the possibility is raised that Israel might forget God once they settled happily in the land and were enjoying God's blessings:

> ... then your heart will become proud and you will forget the LORD your God.... You may say to yourself, "My power and the strength of my hands have produced this wealth for me." But remember the LORD your God, for it is he who gives you the ability to produce wealth. (Deut. 8:14–18)

Likewise the book of Proverbs, while recognizing material abundance as a gift from God, also knows of the dangers:

> ... give me neither poverty nor riches,
>> but give me only my daily bread.
> Otherwise, I may have too much and disown you
>> and say, "Who is the LORD?"
> Or I may become poor and steal,
>> and so dishonor the name of my God. (Prov. 30:8–9)

This same theme figures prominently in the Gospels, which also place at the heart of prayer the request only for "daily bread" (Matt. 6:11). Material abundance is a blessing here too, but more importantly, an awesome danger:

> Do not store up for yourselves treasures on earth, where moth and rust destroy, and where thieves break in and steal. But store up for yourselves treasures in heaven, where moth and rust do not destroy, and where thieves do not break in and steal. For where your treasure is, there your heart will be also. (Matt. 6:19–21)

> There was a rich man who was dressed in purple and fine linen and lived in luxury every day. At his gate was laid a beggar named Lazarus, covered with sores....
> But Abraham replied, "Son, remember that in your lifetime you received your good things, while Lazarus received bad things, but now he is comforted here and you are in agony. And besides all this, between us and you a great chasm has been fixed.... (Luke 16:19–31)

First Timothy 6:5–10 captures particularly well the thrust of Ecclesiastes 5:8–6:12:

> ... men of corrupt mind, who have been robbed of the truth and who think that godliness is a means to financial gain.
> But godliness with contentment is great gain. For we brought nothing into the world, and we can take nothing out of it. But if we have food and clothing, we will be content with that. People who want to

get rich fall into temptation and a trap and into many foolish and harmful desires that plunge men into ruin and destruction. For the love of money is a root of all kinds of evil. Some people, eager for money, have wandered from the faith and pierced themselves with many griefs.

The present "grief" that often results from a materialistic lifestyle is thus as evident in the New Testament as in the Old Testament, although the New Testament also adds to this a grief that is eternal rather than simply temporal. Eternal consequences arise from the decisions we make about material goods and their place in our lives. What is equally clear from the New Testament, however—and this is also proclaimed in the Old Testament—is that such consequences affect not only us ourselves but other human beings as well. Oppression is as much associated with wealth in the Bible as blessing is, and this oppression is systemic as well as personal. It involves governmental and judicial power, which usually lies in the hands of the rich, and it all too often functions, whether with deliberate intent or simply through neglect, to establish the interests of the rich over against those of the poor (Eccl. 5:8–9).

This is one of the reasons why the words "rich" and "wicked" so often appear closely connected in the Bible and are sometimes used interchangeably (as in Isa. 53:9). The desire for possessions leads on to oppression of the neighbor, often pursued in judicial ways. Note the Old Testament example of Ahab, who desired Naboth's vineyard (1 Kings 21). A striking New Testament example of this phenomenon is provided by James 5:1–6: We lust as consumers after the good things of life; we end up consuming our neighbor, and eventually ourselves. We do this as groups of people and as individuals. Sin is structural— rooted in our institutions and customs—and not merely personal.

US Navy Radio Communiqué:

VOICE 1: Please divert your course 15 degrees to the north to avoid a collision.

VOICE 2: Recommend you divert *your* course 15 degrees to the *south* to avoid a collision.

VOICE 1: This is the captain of a U.S. Navy ship. I say again, divert your course.

VOICE 2: No, I say again, divert *your* course.

VOICE 1: This is the aircraft carrier *Enterprise*. We are a large warship of the U.S. Navy. Divert your course now.

VOICE 2: This is a lighthouse. Your call.

It is one of the great delusions of our time, and of some earlier, more ancient times as well, that the exertion of human power can change the shape of reality. The fact of the matter, however, is that reality is a solid rock with a lighthouse sitting upon it, and we can either alter our course to take account of it or keep on going until it imposes itself on us with force. We can insist all we like, with increasingly strident and authoritative words, that reality should be different, but all the words in the world will not make it so (Eccl. 6:10–12). The reality is this: God has created human beings in his image to love and honor him, to love and respect their neighbors, and to look after the planet on his behalf. That is how the universe is, and all who refuse to accept this in the short term will, sooner or later, have to come to terms with the truth.

The universe is not set up to allow human beings, in the end, to worship idols and, in their pursuit, to exploit other human beings and the rest of creation. It is not designed to allow the sacralization of created things, whereby they become central to human life and evoke religious-like awe and submission that is due only to God. This sacralization the Bible refers to is subsumed under the heading of the worship of Mammon—the idolatrous elevation of money and material things to the status of divinity, which leads on to sins such as covetousness (named as a form of idolatry in Eph. 5:5; Col. 3:5).

Karl Marx assailed this idolatry in these terms:

> Money is the Jealous God of Israel before whom no other god may exist.... Money is the general, self-sufficient value of everything. Hence it has robbed the whole world, the human world as well as nature, of its proper worth. Money is the alienated essence of man's labor and life, and this alien essence dominates him as he worships it.[4]

Yet it is not only the capitalist economic system attacked by Marx that has idolatry at its heart and so dehumanizes what is human. In truth, modern economic ideologies ranging across the entire political spectrum have at their core a utopianism that promises ever-increasing material prosperity. They all buy into the myth of progress via economic growth, facilitated by science and technology as means of control. Beneath the economic systems in themselves, as different as they may be in their strategies for reaching utopia, lies fundamental agreement that utopia exists and that its essence is *material* well-being. As Herbert Schlossberg puts it, "materialism, coupled with the productivity of machinery and electronics, has brought us the universal expectation of More."[5]

---

4. Cited in M. Habertal and A. Margalit, *Idolatry*, trans. N. Goldblum (Cambridge, Mass.: Harvard Univ. Press, 1992), 243.

5. See H. Schlossberg, *Idols for Destruction: Christian Faith and Its Confrontation with American Society* (Nashville: Nelson, 1983), 311, 139, for this and the next two quotes.

The Christian view of the world, however, does not make economics coterminous with life. The Sabbath is one great symbol of this truth, insisting that human beings are not defined in the first instance as workers but as people made in the image of the living God. The Christian view of the world does not confuse wealth with moral worth, nor does it promote greed as a virtue. It certainly does not consider the created order as humanity's own possession, to be endlessly manipulated and exploited in its own interest. As Schlossberg notes, this biblical view of wealth "seems odd only because we have adopted as normal a way of life that is hopelessly unable to produce what it promises and has demonstrated that inability to almost everyone."

In fact, it is the worship of the idol that is "odd," indeed insane, when one realizes that it cannot deliver well-being but only mars human life in its often oppressive demands on our time and energy as workers and in its production within us of unrest and discontent. Destruction is the end of such worship, for, to quote Schlossberg again, "insatiable greed placing infinite claims on finite resources can have no other end." From this point of view, there is for a Christian nothing to choose between capitalism and communism as economic systems. Both are idolatrous to their core.

The words that often drown out the Word of God on these kinds of issues are those of the advertisers—those great prophets and evangelists of Mammon, who present to us a world in which "mundane products take on magical powers and promise to shape new character, reinforcing the primal subtext of capitalism: one is what one owns/consumes."[6] Perhaps the first step toward defiance of the idols of Mammon among Christians is conscious resistance to their rhetoric and myth-making; yet we will not even realize that the advertisers are telling us lies about reality if we do not take steps first to deal with the hold that the idols they worship also have on our hearts. It is because we share their gods that we feel persuaded by their preaching. As Jacques Ellul rightly tells us:

> It is because man experiences consumption as a sacred delirium that he is plunged into the Orphism of yet more, and still more, and that advertising arouses such a sympathetic vibration in him. If he obeys advertising . . . it is, more than anything else, because he has been sensitized beforehand by the worship of consumer goods.[7]

This brings us to the heart of the matter: Does the church really want to give up the idols of Mammon? God's people have themselves always shown a propensity to idolatry, almost from the moment of their creation, whether

---

6. C. Myers, *Binding the Strong Man: A Political Reading of Mark's Story of Jesus* (Maryknoll, N.Y.: Orbis, 1988), 15.

7. Ellul, *The New Demons*, 146.

in their desire to construct images (Ex. 32:1–6) or to return to Egypt (14:10–14; 16:1–3; etc.). Their memory of idolatry's oppression is notoriously short. Paul warns the church in Corinth not to imitate these ancestors (1 Cor. 10:1–14), and John concludes his first letter with this admonition: "Dear children, keep yourself from idols" (1 John 5:21).

Yet only a moment's reflection should persuade us of the many ways in which the Christian church is caught up in the idolatries of the moment in North America, and among them materialism. Economic performance is widely seen, within the church as much as outside it, as an important measure of individual and societal worth, and the health, happiness, and security of the nuclear family is assumed as an ultimate good that justifies all human enterprise, including the acquisition and disposal of material resources. It is arguable, indeed, that it is love of the family more than anything that fuels the fires of materialism in the West, including among Western Christians. Capitalism is often routinely baptized as self-evidently Christian and other economic systems routinely excommunicated as not, and belief in endless progress, facilitated by scientific and technological control and sound management principles, abounds. It is because this kind of thinking is so deeply internalized among modern Christians that so many find it natural to think of the church in terms of business and management models. The fact of the matter is that the church often displays before the world, not true religion, but only a lightly Christianized version of the world's own most deeply held prejudices about the nature of reality. Idols are established within the temple itself.

Clearheadedness about reality is required. It is the necessary prerequisite of decisive action against idolatry in our midst. Listening more attentively to the words of Jesus would help: "I tell you the *truth*, it is *hard* for a rich man to enter the kingdom of heaven" (Matt. 19:23, italics added). It is *hard*, for wealth is routinely accumulated in our world through deliberate personal, or neglectful secondhand, oppression of others, and once we possess it, we are not keen to share it around. Christians sometimes behave as if, once we have made it clear that wealth is not necessarily and intrinsically evil in the Bible, we have said all there is to say; but this is not all the Bible has to say. "It is *hard* for a rich man to enter the kingdom of heaven." If we believed this, we could act. Even if we believed what is obviously and empirically true—that idolatry is bad for human beings—we could perhaps act. We might for these entirely humanistic reasons then be willing to engage in the unmasking of idols, as an expression of love of our neighbor as well as of the true God. For if idolatry is the investment of trust and hope in that which is unworthy of these things and incapable of rewarding them, or will in the short or long term destroy the worshiper and her community or society, then it can hardly be moral behavior to refuse to tell the truth of the matter.

Of course, we cannot necessarily expect that, because our motives are worthy, our message to others will be welcome. The unmasking of idols will always be received badly by society at large, for people do not appreciate it when things they hold to be sacred (gods they revere) are portrayed as, and persuasively argued to be, mere creatures of the worshiper, lacking in substance and benefit—or (worse) the conduits of demonic power. To threaten the position of the gods is to threaten the security of the worshiper, as the apostle Paul found out in Ephesus (Acts 19:23–41), and this will inevitably cause "no little disturbance . . . concerning the Way" (19:23 NRSV).

In a society that has come to think of the individual as a god, to dispute another person's interpretation of the universe and the ethics that follow from it has come to be regarded as tantamount to blasphemy. False gods cannot be named as such, for truth is only ever personal. If it is true for me, then who are you to say otherwise? To set out to unmask idols will only ever bring pain, then, especially in a culture that has learned to tolerate a wide range of things but remains highly intolerant of truth claims; for one person's idolatry is always another person's worship, one person's abomination always another's god.

We cannot expect a welcome for our message in society at large, then. What is tragic, however, is that we cannot be certain either of a welcome in the church, which has so widely conformed itself to the culture and has so broadly embraced a pseudogospel that uses Christian faith as an ideological support for "an American way of life," with all that this currently entails. I dare say I may have already outraged not a few readers of this commentary. This itself will be evidence of just how far whole sections of the modern church have moved away from what was recognized as orthodox Christian faith by our ancestors. Can we imagine many modern preachers in the affluent West addressing their congregations as Ambrose or John Chrysostom addressed earlier generations of Christians?

> Not from your own do you bestow upon the poor man, but you make return from what is his.

> This also is theft, not to share one's possessions . . . the rich man is a kind of steward of the money which is owed for distribution to the poor . . . not to share our own wealth with the poor is theft from the poor and deprivation of their means of life; we do not possess our own wealth but theirs.[8]

> Keep your lives free from the love of money, and be content with what you have. (Heb. 13:5)

---

8. Both cited from Ramachandra, *Gods That Fail*, 45.

Ecclesiastes 7:1–12

¹A good name is better than fine perfume,
  and the day of death better than the day of birth.
²It is better to go to a house of mourning
  than to go to a house of feasting,
 for death is the destiny of every man;
  the living should take this to heart.
³Sorrow is better than laughter,
  because a sad face is good for the heart.
⁴The heart of the wise is in the house of mourning,
  but the heart of fools is in the house of pleasure.
⁵It is better to heed a wise man's rebuke
  than to listen to the song of fools.
⁶Like the crackling of thorns under the pot,
  so is the laughter of fools.
  This too is meaningless.

⁷Extortion turns a wise man into a fool,
  and a bribe corrupts the heart.

⁸The end of a matter is better than its beginning,
  and patience is better than pride.
⁹Do not be quickly provoked in your spirit,
  for anger resides in the lap of fools.

¹⁰Do not say, "Why were the old days better than these?"
  For it is not wise to ask such questions.

¹¹Wisdom, like an inheritance, is a good thing
  and benefits those who see the sun.
¹²Wisdom is a shelter
  as money is a shelter,
 but the advantage of knowledge is this:
  that wisdom preserves the life of its possessor.

THE THE FIRST question of 6:12 ("Who knows what is good [*ṭob*] for a man in life?") is not meant to imply a complete lack of human knowledge about what is good, but is intended only to remind us of its contingent and limited nature, is already clear from everything that has preceded this verse in the book. Throughout his discourse on human folly and misery, and even as he has touched on the folly of expecting too much of wisdom (1:12–18; 2:12–16), Qohelet has never deviated from his conviction that some ways of being are better than others—indeed, wisdom is better than folly—and that the good life is bound up with knowing and accepting that this is so (e.g., 2:13, 24–26; 3:12–13, 22; 4:6, 9, 13; 6:9). The point is now underlined in the opening verses of chapter 7, as numerous "good" things (*ṭob*) are described and often compared to "better" (also *ṭob*) things.

The reality of death lies at the heart of the opening verses (7:1–6). If previously our author has used death to relativize wisdom, here it is introduced as an incentive to embrace wisdom rather than folly. There is a middle path to be walked between idolizing wisdom and despising it. As verse 2 puts it, "death is the destiny of every man; the living should take this to heart [*leb*]"; that is, death as human destiny should be deeply rooted in the inner person and be grasped by mind, emotions, and will.[1] It is part of the wisdom one needs to live the good life that we should embrace forthrightly the fact of death. Recognizing the brevity and preciousness of life, we should live life *seriously*.

In this spirit Qohelet commends to us in verse 2 mourning rather than feasting and "pleasure" (*śimḥa*, "joy," v. 4), and in verse 3 sorrow rather than laughter. The wise person mourns and listens to rebuke from those who are wise (vv. 4–5). It is the fool who pursues joy and listens only to the songs and the laughter of other fools (vv. 4–6). Qohelet has previously written of such things as joy and eating and drinking as aspects of the good life as it is received from God (e.g., 2:24–26). We are not to think, therefore, that these things in themselves are being criticized here. It is, rather, the *pursuit* of them as part of a frivolous and trivializing way of life that is under consideration.

There is a way of living that is *centered* on feasting, on the pursuit of joy, on empty laughter and singing. This is life lived in denial of the true nature of things, hoping to push reality to the margins by flooding the senses with

---

1. The Heb. word *leb* has a wide range of equivalents in English, and the common translation "heart" often does not do it sufficient justice. It refers to the inner person generally, as evidenced in thought, memory, inclinations, resolutions, emotions, and passions (see BDB, 524–25).

sensation and drowning out quiet contemplation with noise. For such a person, the heart's home is found in these activities (v. 4). The "day of birth" (v. 1) is life's defining moment—a day of celebration and unbounded optimism, looking ahead to the fulfillment of all manner of human potential. Given that reality is indeed reality, however, this mode of existence is ultimately futile (v. 6).

By contrast, there is a way of living that is centered on reality. It recognizes that there is a "day of death" (v. 1) as well as a day of birth and that, at least from the point of view of focusing the mind on the business of living, the day of death is the "better" of the two (just as the possession of a good "name" or reputation is of more lasting value than the possession of "fine perfume," even if people are in due course forgotten after their deaths [2:16; 9:5]). Here death, as well as birth, defines life, and there is an underlying personal seriousness alongside other things (the heart's home is the "house of mourning," v. 4). Depth is, in fact, a characteristic of the person who lives in the light of reality, just as superficiality is the mark of the life in denial. The wise person knows the value of things. This is clear from verses 5−6, where words having moral content and directed at the important question of how we should live (the "rebuke") are preferred to the inane, pointless (*hebel*, NIV "meaningless") sounds produced by fools, whether in song or in laughter.

The same theme is probably to be found in verse 3, translated thus: "Anger [*ka'as*; NIV "sorrow"] is better than laughter, for a glowering countenance is good for the heart." The Hebrew word *ka'as* is used more often of anger than of sorrow in the Old Testament, particularly of God's response to sin (e.g., 1 Kings 14:9; 16:2; see also comment on Eccl. 1:18 and below on 7:9). It is only the deeply lost fool who, in response to his folly, prefers sycophantic laughter to redemptive disapproval. Laughter in the midst of folly brings nothing to the situation other than noise (7:6, unless the thought is also that it positively contributes to the fool's downfall; cf. Ezek. 11:1−11 for the imagery of the pot in the context of divine judgment). Rebuke brings the possibility of change (cf. Prov. 15:31; 17:10).

Verse 7 appears at first sight to have little to do with the theme of verses 1−6, until it is noticed that it, too, concerns the state of the inner personal life (the "heart," *leb*), the health and orientation of which has been the subject of verses 1−6. Perhaps it is the thought of associating with and being influenced by fools that leads on in particular to the scenario in which the wise person submits to the temptation to gain wealth through economic oppression and bribery.

The pursuit of wealth has already been characterized as folly on numerous occasions in Ecclesiastes (cf. especially 4:1−12, with its treatment of oppression, Heb. ʿošeq, translated in 7:7 as "extortion"). The wise person who joins the insane race after possessions, compromising integrity in the process, becomes just as much a fool as the wise person who joins with fools in empty laughter (note that Heb. hll, "turns . . . into a fool" [7:7], is used of laughter in 2:2 [it "is foolish"]). It is the pursuit of God, rather than the pursuit of either laughter or wealth, that in turn reintegrates laughter and wealth into the good life and makes them wholesome.

Verses 8–9 pick up the general idea from verse 1 that it is the end of things that should dictate wise behavior rather than their beginning, but they apply this idea now to specific matters rather than to the whole of life. Qohelet advocates a patient attitude toward life. A wise person will not react immediately to circumstances but will take a longer term view, waiting to see the full measure of a matter before deciding how to respond. It is the fool who arrogantly or angrily makes an immediate response (cf. Prov. 12:16; 14:29), giving speedy expression to the anger that has been nursed in his "lap" as if it were a young child in need of being kept warm. Note that "anger" in verse 9 is again kaʿas, as in verse 3. Anger directed at foolish behavior for the purposes of bringing the fool to his senses is a good thing. Anger as an indication of impatience and arrogance is itself a mark of the fool.

The precise connection between verse 10 and what precedes it is unclear. Perhaps the question represents one particular example of the impatience and anger described in verses 8–9, in that it expresses dissatisfaction with the present and suggests a questioner unwilling to take a patient, long-term view of life. An early assessment has rather been made, in which present experience is contrasted unfavorably with past experience and a conclusion reached that disputes the statement of verse 8 ("the end of a matter is better . . .").

Alternatively, it may simply be that the connection between verse 10 and what precedes it lies in the idea of what is "better" more generally. All sorts of things may be assessed as "better" than others in the context of inquiry into how human beings should presently live their lives, and this inquiry is worthwhile, since it leads immediately to practical consequences. To ask why the past was better than the present, however—even if it is true that it was—is to ask a question that by comparison is of little value. "It is not wise to ask such questions," whereas it is wise to ask whether, for example, patience is better than pride.

Verses 11–12 sum up the value of wisdom for "those who see the sun," that is, for all human beings. It is like an "inheritance" passed down through the generations so that those who now receive it may live well. It brings "benefit" (yoter) to those who are its recipients. It is similar to a monetary inheritance in that it provides "shelter" or protection from much of the harshness of life. Yet wisdom has this advantage (yitron) over money: It brings continuing life to the one who possesses it, as opposed to the living death so often enjoyed by the wealthy that has been graphically described in the preceding chapters. As Proverbs 3:13–18 puts it:

> Blessed is the man who finds wisdom,
> the man who gains understanding,
> for she is more profitable than silver
> and yields better returns than gold.
> She is more precious than rubies;
> nothing you desire can compare with her.
> Long life is in her right hand;
> in her left hand are riches and honor.
> Her ways are pleasant ways,
> and all her paths are peace.
> She is a tree of life to those who embrace her;
> those who lay hold of her will be blessed.

The contrasting case is given in Proverbs 11:28:

> Whoever trusts in his riches will fall,
> but the righteous will thrive like a green leaf.

To embrace wisdom is to embrace life itself, along with all the gifts that may be bestowed with life—length of days and riches and honor. But to embrace and pursue riches and honor of themselves is to head for disaster; as we have seen, even length of days is of itself not necessarily a blessing (Eccl. 6:1–6). Money is something of a shelter against the winds of misfortune that so often blow through life, yet it cannot match the sort of comprehensive protection provided by wisdom. It is for this reason that the father in Proverbs 4:5–7 urges his son:

> Get wisdom, get understanding;
> do not forget my words or swerve from them.
> Do not forsake wisdom, and she will protect you;
> love her, and she will watch over you.
> Wisdom is supreme; therefore get wisdom.
> Though it cost all you have, get understanding.

Bridging Contexts

THE PATH THROUGH life that is an expression of, and leads on to, everlasting life is defined in the Scriptures as a narrow path (Matt. 7:13–14). The point about most narrow paths is that it is possible to stray from them on either side. Christian theology rooted in the Scriptures likewise tries to walk a narrow and difficult path, holding complex truths together in the center rather than giving in to the temptation to resolve things simplistically at the extremes and margins.

On the topic of wisdom and the proper attitude that mortal beings should strike in relation to it, the narrow path lies between the extremes of the idolization of wisdom on the one hand, and the despising of it on the other. It is this middle road on wisdom that is mapped out for us in Ecclesiastes 7, as Qohelet first of all extols wisdom and provides us with some specifics for our journey (7:1–12), before going on to mix further similar material with reflections on wisdom's limitations (7:13–29).

The heart of Qohelet's concern is that his listeners should live life seriously, with the whole course of the journey in mind. Christian readers are immediately reminded of the second beatitude in Matthew 5:4 ("Blessed are those who mourn, for they will be comforted"), reflected also in the third beatitude of Luke 6:21 ("Blessed are you who weep now, for you will laugh"). Qohelet's ultimate "journey's end" is different from the one described in the Gospels, of course, in that he does not betray any definite conviction about an afterlife, but the idea that the "end" should determine our view of the journey is the same. There is no room for frivolity in life, given that it ends in death and beyond that (as the Gospels make clear) divine judgment and redemption. Life is a deeply serious matter.

The "blessed" form of saying in the beatitudes is itself a form found in the wisdom literature of the Old Testament and in other texts influenced by the wisdom tradition (e.g., Prov. 3:13, 18; 8:32, 34). Perhaps the most famous example is Psalm 1, which speaks of two paths through life and their eventual destinations. That person is blessed (knows a life that is deeply rewarding) who does not follow the advice of the wicked rather than God's guidance, nor shares the way of life of those who deviate from God's standards, nor gathers together and spends time with those who mock God and his law (Ps. 1:1). This person rather delights in the law of the Lord and meditates on it throughout his or her waking hours (1:2), seeking to have it imprinted on both mind and emotions. The consequence is that there is a solidity and a fertility about this person's life, and he or she is able to withstand even the fiercest storms of life's experience (Ps. 1:3). The wicked, on the other hand—the self-ruled, self-grounded, self-centered, and self-seeking—are like the husks of corn thrown up in the air during the winnowing process at harvest. Their lives are insubstantial, and they will not stand in the judgment (1:4–5). Here is wisdom, then, and wisdom leads on to blessing, whether in Psalm 1 or in Matthew 5:3–12.

Jesus' beatitudes in Matthew 5 set a larger context in which the whole of Qohelet's message can in fact be more clearly heard. It is only in this larger context that it becomes clear that those who mourn (Eccl. 7:2—4) will indeed be comforted; that those who refrain from grasping after "gain" (3:12—13) but instead adopt the attitude of the poor and the meek, will in due course inherit the earth that they have not sought to control; that those who hunger and thirst after righteousness and are merciful to others, rather than hungering and thirsting after success and power and trampling on their neighbors to possess it (4:1—3), will be filled with good things and will know mercy; that those who have integrity and pursue peace instead of domination will see God and be owned by God; and that those who know the world's anger because of the pursuit of righteousness will receive their due reward from God.

The serious way of life that Jesus also recommends is not in the New Testament any more than in Ecclesiastes, of course, a way of life that is joyless and repressive, for it is a seriousness lived out before the God of grace and goodness. The blessed who mourn are the same blessed people who are already invited to the wedding supper of the Lamb (Rev. 19:9) and in the meantime know that God has "blessed us in the heavenly realms with every spiritual blessing in Christ" (Eph. 1:3). They know blessing already in the keeping of "the perfect law that gives freedom" (James 1:25; cf. Luke 11:28). A serious life is not a gloomy life.

Jesus himself models for us what it looks like. It is a life firmly based on reality, one that does not allow itself to be distracted from the right path by illusion or delusion; yet it is a way of being that, in being focused on God who is ultimate reality, knows liberation and joy—and is capable of knowing this even in the midst of adversity and grief. The language of blessedness thus attaches itself even to persecution and suffering in the New Testament (e.g., James 1:2, 12; 1 Peter 3:14; 4:14), as does the language of joy (e.g., 2 Cor. 7:4; 8:2; 1 Thess. 1:6). The "man of sorrows" himself knew joy (Isa. 53:3; John 15:11; 17:13) and did not refrain from enjoying the good creation that the triune God has provided for the blessing of all mortal life.

The serious life does involve anger, however (Eccl. 7:3, 5). Anger, like wisdom, can be both a good thing and a bad thing as far as the Bible is concerned. God, who is good, is frequently described as being angry with his creatures because of their wickedness. Jesus, who is God incarnate, is likewise often portrayed in the Gospels, whether explicitly or implicitly, as expressing anger (Mark 3:5; John 2:14—16). There is such a thing as righteous anger, which is provoked by sin; ordinary human beings are in principle capable of this anger too, as the apostle Paul implies in Ephesians 4:26, when he urges Christians not to allow anger to become the occasion of sin (and thus suggests that it need not; cf. Ps. 4:4).

There is no essential virtue in not being angry when confronted by wickedness, and there is certainly none in failing to rebuke another person for engaging in wickedness. Such a failure is a failure to love one's neighbor. Yet righteous anger is not easy for human beings to achieve; after all, this sort of anger is bound up with other aspects of God's character, like grace and compassion, and its expression in speech and action is therefore slow and measured (e.g., Ex. 34:6; Num. 14:18; Ps. 86:15). There is a need for human beings also not to be quickly provoked (Eccl. 7:9; cf. Prov. 29:11). Beyond that, however, it is clearly the case that anger in human beings is almost inevitably bound up with far from righteous thoughts and motivations. Righteous anger is difficult to achieve because we are not righteous in general. Thus many biblical references to human anger presuppose it to be a wicked or at least a dangerous thing (e.g., Matt. 5:22; 2 Cor. 12:20; Eph. 4:31; Col. 3:8; James 1:20). Anger must be kept under control, so that when we relate to others, we are able to remember that we should be acting for their good and not for our satisfaction. The wise person's rebuke must always be uttered in such a spirit (e.g., Gal. 6:1; 2 Tim. 2:23–26; Heb. 5:2), even if the actions that provoke the rebuke are reprehensible and have made the wise person rightly angry.

This is not unconnected to Qohelet's insistence that we should not look back wistfully to the past (Eccl. 7:10). The Bible does not commonly assess the present in terms of the past, but much more typically does so in terms of the future, with all its potential for change. Those who insist on harking back to the past often impose burdens on those who live in the present, from which they cannot escape. But to set the present in the context of the future is to set a path before someone else that allows the past to be left behind and a new way of being to be embraced.

It is such continuing "life" that is said to derive from wisdom as this section of Ecclesiastes comes to a close (7:11–12). It is not at all clear within the confines of Qohelet's thought what exactly such an assertion may mean, for Qohelet knows very well that wisdom does not always preserve the physical life of its possessor (e.g., 7:15). We find similar sayings about "life" in the book of Proverbs, where they are equally puzzling (e.g., Prov. 3:18; 12:28; 15:24). In the end their meaning only becomes clear as books like Proverbs and Ecclesiastes are read in the context of the whole of Christian Scripture and we realize that the "life" being spoken of refers not only to present, temporal existence but also to ongoing, eternal existence. It is in the whole eternal scheme of things that the truth of such sayings is recognized, as what is lacking in "life" here is made up as life continues with God.

I see the Raves as a religious ritual. The God is technology. The music is Techno. . . .

The Rave experience is a spiritual cleansing from the stressed out politically correct technological society.[2]

We live in an escapist culture. The materialist mansion that we as modern people have constructed for ourselves has become for many an unbearably oppressive prison whose spiritual emptiness is all too apparent. The sensible course of action is to visit the archives, find the building plans, and begin a discussion of what has gone wrong. This would be to admit, however, that a mistake has been made, and there is widespread unwillingness to consider that option—not least because, even in our heartfelt misery, we still rather like our living quarters and do not want to move out.

The alternative choice is escapism, that is, the modern attempt to have our materialist cake and to eat it, but to drown its taste with strong wine. We embrace modern reality to the extent that it is convenient for us to do so for the purposes of income and security, but we make it palatable by fleeing from it as soon as we are able and entering the world of fantasy, where the mind need no longer be engaged and the senses and the appetites can take over.

The object is to shut out the pain of the everyday world. Movies and TV soaps achieve this for some; parties and "raves" for others. Drugs can be combined with almost any such activity to increase one's personal distance from what is ordinary and mundane. This is *homo sapiens* in party mode, who borrows his or her motto for partying, perversely, from Qohelet (albeit it in corrupt form): "Let us eat, drink, and be merry" (cf. Luke 12:19). It is a motto well understood by those who work in the advertising industry, who exploit it relentlessly in their pursuit of sales. The human desire for wild, uninhibited "fun" can always be relied on, apparently, to increase the consumption of goods. Advertisers have grasped this truth: that we seem perfectly willing, as a culture, to party our way into oblivion.

That the escapism often has religious overtones is made clear by the quote at the head of this section. It is "spiritual cleansing" from modern culture that is sought—a way out from under the crushing weight of a world that defines our humanness in terms of our economic usefulness and productivity, constricts our imagination and creativity, and can tell us nothing about what it all means. The answer lies, it is thought (whether consciously or not), in using modern technology itself to liberate us from the everyday

---

2. Jack Bowman, "Rave on and on and on and on" website (February 1993).

society that oppresses us. We feel better about it all once we have spent an evening watching our favorite TV shows or have danced the night away while drugged with Ecstasy or alcohol to heighten the experience, that is, once we have entered a "sacred" space away from the normal secular and enslaving space we regularly occupy. As Bowman again puts it with respect to his version of escapist religion:

> Techno music is the only place that technology is used for the benefit of primal man. The beat of Techno is made to match the beat of his primal heart. The rhythm is made to match the rhythm of his primordial soul.

Modern religion is enlisted in the pursuit of primal man—our "real selves." Ancient religion is also not far away, however:

> Dayton Ohio's first Raves coincided with the full moon. Those that felt the vibrations cleansed their soul as primal man had done a million years earlier. But it was different! This time there were two Gods. One was represented by the moon, the other by technology.

Against all such escapism, whether outside or inside the Christian church (some of whose modern worship bears a striking resemblance to non-Christian escapism in both its motivations and form), Qohelet should help us set our face, even as we empathize with and grieve over the sense of personal alienation that produces it. Biblical faith is not escapist. It does not advocate the evacuation of the mind in the face of unpleasant facts, the embrace of fantasy in the face of a harsh reality, or the increase of both noise and activity lest the silence frighten us and our inactivity give us time to think. It certainly does not advise us to seek redemption by dancing the night (or the morning) away to songs with meaningless or banal lyrics that awaken our "primal" instincts (as if that were a good thing). Biblical faith does not advocate a "party culture," as Qohelet makes clear.

The healing of our pain of which the Bible speaks requires us to confront reality rather than to seek to escape from it. One of these realities is death. It invites us to embrace that reality rather than to push it away; all the partying in the world will not push it away forever. It invites us to allow the fact of death, looked squarely in the eye, to do its work in us. It invites us to pursue the question of death to the end rather than to pursue joy, and to help us to accept this implausible invitation, it claims that to make joy our focus is only in any case to know death now and also forever.

The work that death and its friend illness must do in our lives is to break in on us and confront us with this important reality, namely, that we are mortal beings who only live for a short time, whereas God is God. Death is an evangelist. It helps us to see that there is a great gulf fixed between Creator and creature and places us in a position therefore truly to worship and to repent of our sins. In God's grace death and illness offer us the gift of knowing the preciousness of mortal life, which must soon pass away, and therefore of knowing the importance of not wasting time. In God's grace death and illness also offer us the beginnings of wisdom and insight about how to live life well during our time here, for death, if looked courageously in the eye, allows the embrace of wisdom and thus of life, even in the midst of death. Death allows the embrace of serious living before God, which has at its heart "the fear of the LORD."

True, death is our great enemy (1 Cor. 15:26); yet paradoxically in God's grace, it becomes our friend, because it convinces us to die to self and abdicate the throne of our lives to God, who is the sovereign King. It is, in the end, only this dying to self that removes death's sting; for there is then nothing left, in the end, to lose (15:55–56). Death is not to be escaped—and indeed, *will* not be escaped. It is best met face to face on the road and studied.

Only those who have truly met and understood death and have thus understood themselves can truly understand who God is and what Christian faith means. Only such people fully understand what it means that immortality does not reside in us as a property of our being and that resurrection must come to us as an utter and surprising gift and not (even for Christians) as a right. The path to resurrection passes through death's citadel, both in the reality and in the comprehension of it. Death must teach us things that no one else can.

This wisdom and more "benefit those who see the sun" (Eccl. 7:11). They walk in darkness who deliberately put themselves in places where they cannot find such wisdom, preferring the worship of their modern, escapist gods.

> They did not love their lives so much as to shrink from death. (Rev. 12:11)

Ecclesiastes 7:13-29

CONSIDER WHAT GOD has done:

Who can straighten
what he has made crooked?
¹⁴When times are good, be happy;
but when times are bad, consider:
God has made the one
as well as the other.
Therefore, a man cannot discover
anything about his future.

¹⁵In this meaningless life of mine I have seen both of these:

a righteous man perishing in his righteousness,
and a wicked man living long in his wickedness.
¹⁶Do not be overrighteous,
neither be overwise—
why destroy yourself?
¹⁷Do not be overwicked,
and do not be a fool—
why die before your time?
¹⁸It is good to grasp the one
and not let go of the other.
The man who fears God will avoid all ˻extremes˼.

¹⁹Wisdom makes one wise man more powerful
than ten rulers in a city.

²⁰There is not a righteous man on earth
who does what is right and never sins.

²¹Do not pay attention to every word people say,
or you may hear your servant cursing you—
²²for you know in your heart
that many times you yourself have cursed others.

²³All this I tested by wisdom and I said,

"I am determined to be wise"—
but this was beyond me.

> [24] Whatever wisdom may be,
>   it is far off and most profound—
>   who can discover it?
> [25] So I turned my mind to understand,
>   to investigate and to search out wisdom and the
>   scheme of things
>   and to understand the stupidity of wickedness
>   and the madness of folly.
>
> [26] I find more bitter than death
>   the woman who is a snare,
>   whose heart is a trap
>   and whose hands are chains.
>   The man who pleases God will escape her,
>   but the sinner she will ensnare.
>
> [27] "Look," says the Teacher, "this is what I have discovered:
>
> "Adding one thing to another to discover the scheme
>   of things—
> [28]   while I was still searching
>   but not finding—
>   I found one ⌞upright⌟ man among a thousand,
>   but not one ⌞upright⌟ woman among them all.
> [29] This only have I found:
>   God made mankind upright,
>   but men have gone in search of many schemes."

WISDOM IS A good thing and is certainly better than folly. However, Qohelet has been insistent throughout the book that human knowledge is contingent and limited. Moreover, possessing wisdom does not enable anything approaching total comprehension of or control of the universe or autonomy in respect of God who created it and rules over it. There is a certain amount of "profit" in wisdom (cf. *yitron* in 2:13; see comments). It is a good and useful thing that allows us to arrive at important conclusions about the world and dispels our illusions about it. It points us in the direction of contentment (although it can paradoxically bring sorrow and grief in that it enables clear insight about the nature of things, 1:18). Nevertheless, possessing wisdom is far from enabling complete mastery over existence, and it certainly does not solve the problem of death (e.g., 2:14—16). Wisdom operates within fixed parameters.

In the current section we return to consider this broader reality within which wisdom operates. Wisdom, leading on to righteous living, is an excellent thing (7:19, 21, 26). Yet it is only partially grasped by mortal beings (7:23–25), and righteousness is always mixed in with wickedness (7:20–22, 27–29). The pursuit of wisdom and righteousness brings no guarantees, moreover, about how the individual life will work out (7:15). The wise person accepts as reality the mixed nature of experience and does not struggle against it (7:13–14, 16–18). He or she accepts the limitations that God has set on mortal life. Thus does Qohelet continue to balance appreciation for wisdom with critique of its potential and, no doubt, of the way that it was sometimes used within his own culture and time.

The crucial thing to be remembered about the universe is that God has created it (vv. 13–15). Wisdom is not a key that can be used in independence of the Creator to unlock the secrets of the universe, to shape existence after mortal desires, and to control life. Although certain ways of being and behaving are wiser than others and in general tend toward life rather than death, yet in the end we must remember that the universe is not a predictable machine but a personally governed and complex space. Wisdom is not magic. God is not an object to be manipulated, nor does God's world belong to human beings. If God makes something crooked, it is beyond human power to make it straight (v. 13; cf. 1:15).

Thus, the wise person accepts the world as he or she finds it, receiving both good and bad from God and acknowledging that either might lie in the future (v. 14). The wise person knows that righteousness does not infallibly produce life in the short term (in spite of the advantage that wisdom has over money), just as wickedness does not inevitably lead on, in the short term, to death (v. 15). The embrace of wisdom does not give one leverage in respect of God, so that the future becomes predictable. As chapter 3 has reminded us, it is God who controls the "times," and the times are extremely varied.

To those who accept these limitations (i.e., conform themselves to reality), there is clearly "benefit" (*yoter*, 7:11) in wisdom. To those who do not and think of life not so much as something to be lived as something to be capitalized upon—who are committed to striving with and struggling against reality rather than living in harmony with it—life will ultimately seem to have no benefit worth speaking of (cf. *yoter* in 2:15, NIV "gain").

The surprising advice of 7:16–18, based on what Qohelet has seen (v. 15) during his "brief," perhaps even "puzzling," (but not "meaningless") life should be understood in this context. Wisdom is clearly attractive to many people, as the book has shown, precisely because it appears to offer the possibility of control over life. The wise, and consequently righteous, person (it is thought) can guarantee for herself divine blessings, including long life and wealth, while the foolish, and consequently wicked, person guarantees for herself only doom.

Yet this represents, for Qohelet, a profound misunderstanding of the nature of things. While he agrees that people should avoid excessive foolishness and wickedness, since (in spite of acknowledged exceptions, v. 15) this does represent a path to destruction (v. 17), he is equally concerned that they should avoid excessive righteousness and wisdom (v. 16). The dogged pursuit of the latter, just as much as the committed quest after the former, brings bad consequences, for both are incompatible with the fear of God (v. 18). Both represent, in their own way, a refusal to accept the limitations God sets on mortal beings.

Those who pursue wisdom or righteousness for "profit" in this sense (note that "neither be overwise" in v. 16 is in Heb. *weʾal titḥakam yoter;* cf. the comments on *yoter* at 2:15; 6:8, 11; 7:11), hoping to gain an edge over God and force his hand, are in no different a position to those who pursue foolishness and wickedness. Both are guilty of *hubris*—the arrogant self-deification in which mortal beings so regularly indulge as they seek to fashion reality after their own liking. Both are guilty of sin. It is, indeed, self-delusional to think it possible to escape sin and become the kind of blameless person that verse 16 implies, as Qohelet will go on to argue (7:20, 27−29).

The truly wise person (v. 18) will grasp hold of both the pieces of advice contained in verses 16−17, therefore, embracing not only the obvious truth of verse 17 but also the perhaps less obvious truth of verse 16.[1] That the fear of God thus sets the boundaries within which mortal life should be lived out (see comments on 3:9−15, noting also 12:13) makes it clear that Qohelet is not, in suggesting that the two extremes are equally problematic, implying at the same time that any actions between the extremes are equally acceptable. Reverence for God requires not only the avoidance of foolishness and wickedness but also the pursuit of wisdom and righteousness. If indeed it is reverence for God that motivates the pursuit, then it is a good thing.

Verses 19−22 further explain the message of verses 15−18. Although wisdom may be pursued from bad motives and its pursuit may result in bad consequences, yet in itself it is a good thing. It is vastly superior, in fact, to political or military power (v. 19; cf. 9:13−18; Prov. 21:22; 24:5−6), which

---

1. The second part of v. 18 is best translated, not as the NIV has it (which implies that a general statement about avoiding extremes is being made, even though the word "extremes" itself does not appear in the Heb. text), but as follows: "For the person who fears God will avoid/proceed [Heb. *yṣʾ*] from both" (understanding Heb. *kol,* "all," in the sense of "both," as in v. 15 and in 2:14). Heb. *yṣʾ* means "to go out," and the meaning is therefore either that the God-fearer, having grasped both pieces of advice in vv. 16−17, should proceed to live life on that basis, or that he or she should avoid doing both the things mentioned.

is dependent on wisdom for its success. One wise person is "more powerful than ten rulers [perhaps better, officials] in a city." Yet the wise person will still be a flawed person, because he or she is a human being. No one is sinless (Eccl. 7:20; cf. 1 Kings 8:46), no matter how intent a person is in pursuing God. To err is human.

Verse 22 identifies by way of example one such flaw (cursing others in one's heart), drawing from the reality of universal human sinfulness in this regard the advice that people should not be too attentive to the words of their servants and (presumably) take punitive action against them. One's attitude to other human beings should be conditioned by the awareness of one's own flawed humanity. The truly wise person who fears God and remembers who he is (vv. 15–18, 20) will also remember who one's neighbor is and will behave accordingly.

With verses 23–25 we move toward the conclusion of the whole chapter. Qohelet's reflections on wisdom in this section ("all this," v. 23), motivated by a determination to be wise, have convinced him of the complexity of it all. No one can "discover" (mṣʾ; lit., "find") wisdom itself in all its mystery (v. 24); it is "beyond" (lit., "far off from") the inquirer (v. 23). No one can come to a comprehensive understanding of the universe, for the data[2] are "far off and most profound" (lit., "deep, deep"); that is, the ocean of knowledge is too wide and deep. It is impossible to grasp the whole "scheme of things" (ḥešbon, v. 25; cf. also v. 27), to articulate the whole sum of the matter.[3] Understanding, investigating, and searching out have not led Qohelet to the achievement of this larger goal (v. 25). This is not surprising, for as Job 28:20–23 tells us:

> Where then does wisdom come from?
> Where does understanding dwell?
> It is hidden from the eyes of every living thing,
> concealed even from the birds of the air.

---

2. The NIV's "whatever wisdom may be" in v. 24 is in the Heb. *mah-šehaya*, which in 1:9; 3:15; and 6:10 refers simply to "that which has happened/has come into existence." A more literal translation is preferable here also, for it is crucial to understand that Qohelet refers in these verses to the attempt to grasp the whole "scheme of things" rather than to individual discriminations between wisdom and folly.

3. The NIV's "so" at the beginning of v. 25 is unfortunate if it suggests to the reader an action consequent upon the discovery in vv. 23b–24 that wisdom is beyond Qohelet. In fact, it is fairly clear that the "turning of the mind" in v. 25 is consequent upon the "determining to be wise" in v. 23a and that vv. 23b–24 represent a perspective attained by Qohelet only after the experiment was over. It is after the great effort (indicated by the accumulation of verbs in v. 25) to grasp the "scheme" or "sum" of things has been expended that Qohelet understands that the "data provided for analysis" (NIV "wisdom" in v. 24) are too complex to allow great comprehension of them.

> Destruction and Death say,
>   "Only a rumor of it has reached our ears."
> God understands the way to it
>   and he alone knows where it dwells.

Yet although wisdom in itself may not be found and a comprehensive grasp of reality cannot be attained, some individual findings are possible, as chapter 7 and other sections of the book have illustrated. Verses 26–29 recount some such findings. As the futile attempt to build a systematic account of wisdom was progressing, one "fact" being added to another and yet no "finding" of the more general kind taking place (Heb. *mṣ²*, vv. 27–28; NIV "discovered" and "finding"), Qohelet did manage to come to some conclusions about men and women.

For example, the kind of woman who sets out to entrap and enslave a man is "more bitter than death." The good man, walking on the right path and embracing wisdom rather than folly, will "escape" (*mlṭ*) her "snare" (lit., "nets"; Heb. *mᵉṣodim*), just as the wise man of 9:13–18 saves (causes to escape, Heb. *mlṭ*) the city from the "nets" (Heb. *mᵉṣodim*) of the invading king. The book of Proverbs devotes considerable space to the arming of a young man for such a sexual battle (e.g., Prov. 2:12–19). The sinner, on the other hand, has no motivation to avoid the trap and thus falls straight into it.

A more fundamental conclusion (*mṣ²*, "discovered," v. 27) to which Qohelet has come is that human beings generally (and not just women), although created "upright" by God, have gone astray. The precise manner of their straying, as described in verse 29, is significant: They have "gone in search of many schemes" (Heb. *biqšu ḥiššᵉbonot rabbim*). The verb *bqš* is used in verses 25 and 28 ("search out," "searching") of Qohelet's own quest for comprehensive knowledge—that is, his own inquiry into the "scheme of things" (*ḥešbon*, vv. 25, 27). The language is deliberately chosen to suggest that Qohelet's quest is itself an indication of departure from God's ways. One of his individual findings, in fact, is that the larger attempt at finding wisdom is not only futile but sinful—an act of irreverence toward God (cf. vv. 15–18).

The precise way in which we are to understand the second part of verse 28 in this context is a matter of debate. Most commentators have understood "man" and "woman" (which is all that actually appears in the Heb. text) to mean "upright man" and "upright woman" (cf. NIV). If this is correct, then the verse anticipates verse 29, stressing just how little righteousness humankind exhibits (cf. also v. 20). It is unlikely that Qohelet intends any particular comment on women by the admittedly awkward way in which the finding is expressed. The point of the line in context, if "uprightness" is the focus, is not that there are more righteous men than righteous women in the world but that there are hardly any righteous people at all, whether men or women. Yet it is curious, if this is what Qohelet means, that he does not qualify "man" and "woman" explicitly with Heb. *yaṣar*, "upright," or some similar term. It seems more natural, in fact, to link verse 28 to verse 27 in the first instance, as a more literal translation of verses 27–29 makes clear:

> See, this I have found, says Qohelet:
> one to one to find a sum,
>> which I still seek but have not found.
> One man among a thousand I found,
>> but a woman among all these I did not find.
> See this only I have found:
> that God made humans upright,
>> but they sought many sums.

In order to come to a cumulative understanding of the world, one must be able to make connections between things, between the experiences of this person and that ("one to one to find a sum"). What Qohelet seems to be saying in his rather compressed way is that summation has proved impossible, because it has proved all but impossible to make connections. He has only occasionally (one time in a thousand) been able to connect a particular primary datum (presumably derived from his own experience and observation) with that provided by another to make any kind of "sum," and even then, it has only ever been another man. Women have remained clothed in mystery.

The overriding perspective of the whole book of Qohelet is, of course, resolutely male, as has been most recently demonstrated by verse 26 (it does not speak of the man who is a snare to women). Qohelet's "findings" thus represent a drop in the ocean of experience (one part in a thousand), and they are a male drop at that. The futility of the common human enterprise of "adding" in order to arrive at conclusions about life is thus made especially clear.

WISDOM, QOHELET TELLS us, brings in its train power (7:19); to know and to understand the ways of the world places one in a position of great advantage in respect of others who may have some power but no understanding. This is why the history of the ancient and indeed modern world is full of stories of people who were the real "power behind the throne." It is because wisdom brings power that it is so attractive to so many (note Matt. 13:54). It offers godlike control over destiny—one's own destiny and that of other people. This is also the reason why it is so dangerous in a world where sin has touched every life and every heart. It offers the illusion that one is indeed a god, and with this comes inevitable damage to the rest of creation and ultimately to oneself.

It is necessary when considering wisdom, therefore, constantly to remind ourselves—and to be reminded by the Bible—of the true nature of things. What can wisdom really achieve? What is it really for? The biblical answer is that wisdom can never achieve for human beings the kind of control over life and destiny that they aspire to. At all times it is God who controls the times; at all times it is God who rules the universe, and his ways are inscrutable:

> Oh, the depth of the riches of the wisdom and knowledge of God!
> How unsearchable his judgments,
> and his paths beyond tracing out! (Rom. 11:33)

One of the first steps in true wisdom, in fact, is the acceptance of this reality and thus the truth that while wisdom is indeed *light for* life, it cannot be a means of gaining autonomous *control of* life. The New Testament achieves the necessary balance here by linking true wisdom firmly with the person of Jesus and by attacking any wisdom that ultimately stands apart from him. There is a human wisdom that opposes God and that God opposes. It is a wisdom he intends to frustrate (1 Cor. 1:17–21). Christ, by contrast, is himself "the power of God and the wisdom of God" (1 Cor. 1:24, cf. v. 30), the firstborn over all creation (Col. 1:15, alluding to the personified figure of wisdom in Prov. 8:22–31; cf. Col. 2:3 and John 1:1–5). All truth and wisdom are ultimately focused on him and derive from him (e.g., 1 Cor. 12:8; Eph. 1:8; Col. 1:9).

Already in the Old Testament we have the similar insistence that "the fear of the LORD is the beginning of wisdom" (e.g., Ps. 110:10; cf. Prov. 1:7). Various passages make clear just how far beyond human grasp wisdom is. To Job 28, mentioned above, we may add by way of example the closing chapters of the book of Job (chs. 38–42), where the speeches of God persuade Job (and us) of exactly the same point. Job was not present at the creation of the universe and knows little of what happens within it. He has neither adequate knowledge nor power to contend with God. Thus he acknowledges in the end, "I spoke of things I did not understand, things too wonderful for me to know" (42:3).

It is, of course, because Christ *was* present at the creation of the universe that he understands what the universe is about and teaches therefore with authority, unlike the teachers of the law (e.g., Matt. 7:29). He brings as divine wisdom both light and liberation. The purveyors of religion bring only darkness and slavery.

This brings us neatly to the religious expressions of this innate human desire for power and control, for it is not only those who *say* that they pursue control over reality in neglect of or in opposition to God who in fact do so. Religion can itself represent, in many of its expressions, an attempt by human beings to control their own destiny—an attempt that does not reckon seriously with the true nature of things. It is clear, for example, that much of the non-Israelite religion in the Bible is presented as being of this kind (cf. 1 Kings 18, where the prophets of Baal dance around the altar and mutilate themselves in an apparent attempt to manipulate their god into action).

However, even those who assert belief in the true God can be found engaging in this kind of false religion. Jeremiah assails his contemporaries, for example, for repeating the mantra "the temple of the LORD" (Jer. 7:4), as if their religion, focused on the Jerusalem temple, provides security against divine judgment. More to the point in reference to Ecclesiastes 7:13–29 are the New Testament's various attacks on those who seek to manipulate God by means of the accumulation of righteousness (cf. the letter of the apostle Paul to the Galatians). Even the pursuit of virtue, when it is the pursuit of control over God and his actions present and future rather than the pursuit of God himself, is false religion. True religion has at its heart *love for God* and *love for neighbor*, in which the self looks outward and gives itself away to others. It knows nothing of the selfish manipulation of God and the self-interested helping of my neighbor that is part of such manipulation. It is reverence for God (which is connected to love for neighbor) that must motivate the pursuit of righteousness, as indeed the pursuit of wisdom. The true wisdom is in fact biblically always connected with love for neighbor as well as for God (cf. Matt. 11:19; James 3:13–17).

Our neighbors are women as well as men. This means that we must consider carefully how to handle a passage like Ecclesiastes 7:26–28 in the context of the whole Christian Bible, which knows that all human beings are made in the image of God and redeemed equally in Christ. It is, of course, true that some women set out to entrap and enslave a man (v. 26), but there is no reason, biblically or experientially, to think that they are greater in number than those men who set out to entrap and enslave a woman. There is some reason to think, on the contrary, that they are fewer. It would be a hermeneutical error of the gravest kind not to recognize this, and in failing to recognize it to perpetuate a tendency throughout the history of (mainly male) biblical interpretation to suggest that women are much more the cause of sexual sin than men. Qohelet's "findings" here are the findings of one man, as in the case of the psalmist who tells us in Psalm 37:25 that he has "never seen the righteous forsaken or their children begging bread." Although Qohelet's words are words of Scripture, they are only some of those words that together speak to us as the Word of God. They must be correctly located within the entirety of the Bible if we are to understand how they are to be heard. Were Qohelet indeed a misogynist, as some have claimed, then we should have to deal with that fact within the whole context of Scripture. Even though he is not, on the view taken in this commentary, a misogynist, he still speaks from a male perspective. The "drop in the ocean of experience" that his findings represent must not be confused with the ocean itself—at least, not if we want to sail with Jesus.[4]

 The fundamental reason why the best that a government can give a great society of free men is negative, is the unalterable ignorance of any given mind, or any organization that can direct human action, of the immeasurable multitude of particular facts which must determine the order of its activities. Only fools believe that they know all, but there are many.[5]

It may seem that Friedrich Hayek is only stating the obvious when he tells us that the universe is beyond our grasp; yet as he himself reminds us, those who believe otherwise are "many." The majority in Western culture have long ago ceased to believe that empirical inquiry is only a limited inquiry into the universe God made ("thinking God's thoughts after him")—as many of the founders of modern science believed—and have come to think of it as an all-embracing method that enables us, stone by stone, to demolish the wall that separates us from true and complete knowledge, to arrive some day on the other side.

We retain, culturally, the Christian view of the world, which understands it as rational and law-governed and therefore in principle comprehensible to some extent by human beings. But we have long ago abandoned, theologically, the larger idea that it is rational and law-governed because it was created so by God. Our group aim, indeed, is to displace God from his throne and to put ourselves there instead, as we come to understand and thus (so we imagine) to control the universe, shaping it to our own ends. We are the modern inheritors of the legacy of Babel (Gen. 11:1–9), seeking to build through our wisdom and our technology a new city "with a tower that reaches to the heavens, so that we may make a name for ourselves" (11:4). At the same time technology coexists with barbarism, as in Genesis 4–6, and the earth is "full of violence" (6:11).

---

4. See further D. A. Garrett, "Ecclesiastes 7:25–29 and the Feminist Hermeneutic," *CTR* 2 (1987–88): 309–21.

5. F. Hayek, *Law, Legislation and Liberty*, vol. 3, *The Political Order of a Free People* (New York: Routledge and Kegan Paul, 1979), 130.

The conceit that lies at the heart of our empiricism is found across all the fields of human inquiry. It reveals itself, for example, among those who gaze on the wonders of our universe and, faced with the opportunity for worship, see only the promise of bringing all the vastness under intellectual control:

> After a century of discoveries that opened the cosmos to our gaze, astronomers are now poised to uncover the universe's most fundamental properties—its size, age, origin and destiny.[6]

Such conceit is found among historians who imagine they can reconstruct the past more truly and objectively than any of their predecessors and who miss the opportunity of learning from it because they are so busy recreating it in their own image. It is the conceit of the social scientist who observes groups of people or asks them questions in the belief that he or she can discover deep truths about human nature generally and does not have any concept of just how trivial these findings are when thrown into the vast ocean of human findings. As Hayek suggests, it is the conceit also of the economist and of the government that depends on this modern-day "wise man at court" (Dan. 2:1–24), who imagines that the economic world is a material system that can be understood, predicted, and manipulated. It is, finally, the frightening conceit of the geneticist who proclaims that we are on the verge of understanding the nature of human beings and of being able to manipulate (and to buy and sell) humanness, in pursuit of a much better world. This one stands arm in arm with the biologist when he or she speaks, for many biologists "know" that humanness is simply a matter of evolutionary selection and see no reason why human beings should not themselves contribute proactively to their own future development.

It is all about control of the times—past, present, and future. It is about power—the power to define, create, and act in freedom from all constraints. It is not that this mode of empirical inquiry has not brought with it many societal benefits. With these benefits has come a forgetting of God, however (Deut. 8:10–20), and a dark and mistaken belief that we are the masters of our own destiny. "Only fools believe that they know all, but there are many," and ordinary people seem more than willing to trust them. There is a tremendous public appetite for new discoveries, new steps forward on the path of progress, new cures, and new means of self-advancement. The latest "wisdom" is eagerly devoured and turned to profit by all who hear of it.

On September 1, 1999, the *Vancouver Sun* reported that Frances Rauscher (a psychologist at the University of Wisconsin) had demonstrated empirically

---

6. I. Semeniuk, "The New Cosmology: A State of the Universe Report," *Sky News* (Sept./Oct. 1999), 8–11, 14–15, 22 (quote on p. 8).

in 1993 that ten minutes of listening to Mozart's *Sonata for Two Pianos in D Major* could boost a person's score on a portion of the standard IQ test. Soon teachers and parents took advantage of the discovery, hoping that their children might attain a few extra points in their SAT scores. An entrepreneur turned Rauscher's preliminary finding into a seemingly authoritative self-help book, while others released compact discs of Mozart music that bore extraordinary health claims. The governor of Georgia decreed that every newborn should leave the hospital with a state-purchased cassette or CD of classical music, and catalogues began offering stethoscope-like devices so that pregnant women could introduce babies in the womb to Mozart. It is the way of the modern world. The universe is seen only as raw material for me to shape, through technological control, in pursuit of my educational, financial, and other goals. Wisdom is sought because it brings power.

In the world of the Bible this kind of phenomenon is referred to as idolatry, that is, the worship of some created thing in place of the living God. Any Christian person caught up in it needs to repent. It is not that intellectual curiosity is forbidden by God, nor is scientific inquiry into the world God has made sinful. Yet we should remember fundamentally that God is God and we are not. When we forget this, we make the basic human mistake. The consequences of this mistake, when human power is wielded in defiance of divine power, is disaster for other people, for creation more generally, and eventually for ourselves.

The only safe kind of human wisdom is wisdom rooted in God and centered in Jesus Christ, which thus knows its limitations and boundaries. The nature and character of God as revealed in Jesus Christ and in the Scriptures that testify to him is also the reference point that Christians need to use when confronted by claims about reality others may make and when faced with plans that others may have that arise out of these claims.

It is only a matter of consistency, of course, that we should not object to other people's attempts to control the universe if we ourselves are practicing a religion that seeks such control rather than exercising true biblical faith. In this regard it is important to remember that the Bible itself was never intended to give us complete inside knowledge and understanding of the universe, so that we ourselves might exercise a godlike power over our own lives and over others. It is an amazing indication of just how deep our human rebellion against God goes, however, that the very Bible that tells us the truth about God, the world, and ourselves should have been so frequently used by Christians to fight power with power. We object to other people's claims to possess the truth by asserting that we possess it instead, and all humility before God, who cannot be possessed and whose universe can never be fully comprehended by mortal beings, disappears. The Bible, we should remember, has not been given to the church so that we as Christians, rather than some other human beings, should behave like gods, knowing all things and being capable of all things. It has not been given to the church so that we can control "the times." It is given only so that we may have sufficient light to live by, as we worship the God of mystery and wonder and move humbly through his amazing creation as the brief, mortal beings that we are.

We do not truly understand anything, even if we know the contents of the Bible, if we do not understand this. The Bible itself can become an obstacle to our redemption, in fact, if it receives more of our devotion and trust than God does. It can become itself an idol we worship. Even the Bible cannot function properly in God's universe unless it is read in dependence on the living God and as a witness to the One who is alone the fount of all wisdom. The Bible should never be used as a means of placing ourselves, rather than God, at the center of the universe.

Who is wise and understanding among you? Let him show it by his good life, by deeds done in the humility that comes from wisdom. (James 3:13)

Ecclesiastes 8:1-17

¹Who is like the wise man?
    Who knows the explanation of things?
    Wisdom brightens a man's face
        and changes its hard appearance.

²Obey the king's command, I say, because you took an oath before God. ³Do not be in a hurry to leave the king's presence. Do not stand up for a bad cause, for he will do whatever he pleases. ⁴Since a king's word is supreme, who can say to him, "What are you doing?"

⁵Whoever obeys his command will come to no harm,
    and the wise heart will know the proper time
        and procedure.
⁶For there is a proper time and procedure for every matter,
    though a man's misery weighs heavily upon him.

⁷Since no man knows the future,
    who can tell him what is to come?
⁸No man has power over the wind to contain it;
    so no one has power over the day of his death.
As no one is discharged in time of war,
    so wickedness will not release those who practice it.

⁹All this I saw, as I applied my mind to everything done under the sun. There is a time when a man lords it over others to his own hurt. ¹⁰Then too, I saw the wicked buried—those who used to come and go from the holy place and receive praise in the city where they did this. This too is meaningless. ¹¹When the sentence for a crime is not quickly carried out, the hearts of the people are filled with schemes to do wrong. ¹²Although a wicked man commits a hundred crimes and still lives a long time, I know that it will go better with God-fearing men, who are reverent before God. ¹³Yet because the wicked do not fear God, it will not go well with them, and their days will not lengthen like a shadow.

¹⁴There is something else meaningless that occurs on earth: righteous men who get what the wicked deserve, and wicked men who get what the righteous deserve. This too, I say, is

meaningless. ¹⁵So I commend the enjoyment of life, because nothing is better for a man under the sun than to eat and drink and be glad. Then joy will accompany him in his work all the days of the life God has given him under the sun.

¹⁶When I applied my mind to know wisdom and to observe man's labor on earth—his eyes not seeing sleep day or night—¹⁷then I saw all that God has done. No one can comprehend what goes on under the sun. Despite all his efforts to search it out, man cannot discover its meaning. Even if a wise man claims he knows, he cannot really comprehend it.

SCHOLARS HAVE DEBATED whether 8:1 is better read with what precedes it or what follows it. It seems difficult, however, to make sense of the verse, and particularly its second part, as merely the continuation of 7:29. But it is possible to understand verse 1b as the quotation of a proverbial saying, the significance of which is then expounded in the verses that follow. The first part of verse 1 is then to be understood as an introduction to the saying and translated thus: "Who is like the wise man? Who knows the interpretation of the saying [*pešer dabar*] . . . ?"

The word *pešer* is frequently found in the Qumran literature regarding the interpretation of hidden meanings in biblical texts. Equivalent or cognate forms appear in Genesis 40–41 and in Daniel of the interpretation of dreams. The "saying" in this case is the proverb of Ecclesiastes 8:1b, which at one level might be taken to refer to the beneficial effects of wisdom in cheering a person up and relieving gloom or harshness. Qohelet, however, has not only found that wisdom often brings sorrow and grief as much as joy (e.g., 1:18); he has also advocated a glowering countenance over a happy one (7:3).

So what can the proverb of 8:1b mean? To what does it truly refer? The material that follows suggests that Qohelet interprets it[1] to refer to behavior at the royal court, where a glowering countenance will do no good and may bring great personal danger. It is wise not to show one's disapproval of, or disagreement with, a despotic monarch. The proverb now speaks of things as they should be made to appear rather than as they actually are.

As the focus of the passage now shifts more explicitly to the wise man at court, the emphasis falls in the first instance on obedience (8:2). The command of the king is paramount and must be obeyed. The implication of this

---

1. That it is his own particular interpretation of an already existing proverb is suggested by the enigmatic "I" (Heb. ⁾ᵃ*ni*) at the beginning of v. 2, which is itself interpreted (rightly) by the NIV as "I say."

instruction, however, and the assumption of the verses that follow are that there will be occasions when the wise man will not approve of the king's command and be tempted to ask: "What are you doing?" (v. 4).

This much is clear, even though the best way precisely to understand verses 2b–3 is not. The Hebrew syntax of verse 2 (lit., "obey the command of the king and because of the oath of God") makes it a little awkward to read the line as in the NIV, which has led to the suggestion that verse 2b should be read with verse 3a: "as for the oath before God, do not be hasty." The remainder of verse 3 would then read: "from his presence go out; do not remain in a bad situation [a better translation than the NIV's 'do not stand up for a bad cause'; cf. comments on 1:13], for he will do whatever he pleases."

Taken together the verses should then be read as advocating withdrawal from the royal court rather than opposing the king, which may involve the uttering of an oath by way of indicating the seriousness of the opposition (cf., e.g., 1 Kings 17:1, 12; 19:2, for oaths that underline words). The wise man will think more than twice before opposing the king in this way. He will not rush to speech and action. We may note similar general advice, also employing Hebrew *bhl*, "be hasty," in Ecclesiastes 5:2 and 7:9:

> Do not be quick with your mouth, do not be hasty in your heart to utter anything before God.

> Do not be quickly provoked in your spirit, for anger resides in the lap of fools.

The Masoretic text as it stands, however, takes a different view of the oath, clearly understanding it as providing the reason, or perhaps even an additional reason over and above the pragmatics of the matter (a desire for self-preservation), why the king should be obeyed: "Obey the king's command, (especially) because of the oath of God."[2] An oath of loyalty sworn to the king before God by the wise man himself could be in mind, or perhaps an oath sworn to the king by God, guaranteeing the king's rule. Mortal rule, and especially Davidic rule over Israel, is commonly regarded in the Bible as legitimated by God, and rebellion against the king is closely associated with rebellion against God, as in Proverbs 24:21–22:

> Fear the LORD and the king, my son,
>   and do not join with the rebellious,
> for those two will send sudden destruction upon them,
>   and who knows what calamities they can bring?

---

2. Although the precise syntax found here is indeed awkward, the manner of usage of Heb. *wᵉ* found here is by no means unparalleled; see GKC, §154a, note 1.

If verse 2 is thus read as a unit, then verse 3 should be understood either as providing balanced advice to the wise man on how to react to a foolish command (he should not storm out of the king's presence in a rage, but neither should he tarry in a bad situation), or, syntactically better (given the absence of any adversative particle that might be translated as "but"), as suggesting how a wise person should react and then what he should do ("Do not be dismayed3; leave the king's presence. Do not tarry in a bad situation . . .").

The difference between the two interpretations lies in the role of the oath. In both cases, however, it is clear that the wise person is advised to disguise his true feelings while in the king's presence, for "a king's word is supreme" (v. 4). The theme of power, especially expressed in Hebrew *šlṭ* ("supreme" [v. 4]; "power" [2x in v. 8]; "lords it over" [v. 9]), is indeed prominent throughout the passage. It may be true that wisdom makes one wise man more powerful than ten rulers (Heb. *šalliṭim*, 7:19), but the truly wise person knows not to flaunt his wisdom when confronted by a foolish ruler, for there is a serious risk of "harm"4 if he does so (v. 5).

The way to avoid "coming to" (v. 5a; lit., "knowing," Heb. *ydᶜ*) harm is to "know" (v. 5b; Heb. *ydᶜ*) the "proper time and procedure" (lit., "both time and judgment") for everything. This phrase is probably not best understood as in the NIV, however, since the Hebrew reminds us of chapter 3 in general, where we are told that there is a time for everything (3:1; see esp. 3:16–17, which speaks of a time for judgment). The linguistic connections here are striking:

3:1:	"There is a time for everything, and a season [*ᶜet*, time] for every activity [*ḥepeṣ*, pleasure, business, matter]."
3:16–17:	"In the place of judgment [*mišpaṭ*], wickedness was there. . . . God will bring to judgment [*špṭ*] . . . for there will be a time [*ᶜet*, time] for every activity [*ḥepeṣ*]."
8:6:	"For there is a proper time [*ᶜet*, time] and procedure [*mišpaṭ*] for every matter [*ḥepeṣ*]."

In 5:8, moreover, we have been told that we should not be surprised by "such things" (*ḥepeṣ*) as the denial of justice (*mišpaṭ*) and rights. Taking these

---

3. Heb. *bhl* in the Niphal more often means "be disturbed, dismayed, terrified" than "be hasty"; see BDB, 96.

4. It is difficult in English translation to catch all the nuances of the passage, and esp. the way in which the words *raᶜ* / *raᶜa*, "evil," and *dabar*, "word, thing, situation," are used in vv. 3–6. It is because the king's "word" is supreme (v. 4) that "harm" (lit., "an evil thing," v. 5) may be experienced by the wise person who disapproves of or opposes it. That is why the wise person should leave the king's presence rather than remain in a "bad cause [situation]" (lit., "an evil thing," v. 3). He recognizes that in a time characterized by great "misery" (lit., "evil," v. 6), the wise thing to cultivate is patience.

other passages as our guide, it seems best to interpret 8:5—6 as exhorting the wise man at court, faced with a foolish ruler, to exercise patience rather than to give free rein to his true feelings—to remember that there is a time for everything, including divine judgment on foolishness and wickedness.

This interpretation is supported by the observation of a play on words in verses 3 and 6. In verse 3 the wise man should not futilely oppose the king, for the latter will do "whatever he pleases [*ḥpṣ*]." He should recognize, rather, that such a royal "matter" (*ḥepeṣ*, v. 6) is a temporary feature of reality, which will meet its appropriate recompense in due course. This he should know in his "heart" (v. 5), even while behaving outwardly as if he knows no such thing. The recognition that what is good and just will prevail in the end will help him to endure in the meantime what is admittedly "misery" (*raʿa*, v. 6; lit., "evil"; cf. the "evil" of 6:1, which also "weighs heavily" on humankind).

With the exegetical platform thus laid in 8:1—6, it is now more obvious than it otherwise would be precisely how verses 7—9 should be construed. Verse 7 reaffirms the lack of control that human beings have over "the times" (cf. ch. 3). The wise heart "knows" about "time and judgment" (v. 5), and this influences both his thinking and his actions when confronted with his king, but no one "knows" exactly how and when things will work out (v. 7).

Various images of mortal lack of control are then given in verse 8 to underline the point. No one has power over the wind (cf. 1:6) or over the number of the days of one's life. Once a war is under way, no one has the ability freely to walk away from the army. Wickedness, finally, will not allow "those who practice it" (i.e., its possessors; Heb. *baʿal*; lit., "master, owner," as in 5:11) to escape—a clever line, which is better translated more literally than in the NIV, since it raises the question of whether anyone ever really "possesses" wickedness rather than being enslaved by it. One would expect an *owner* to try to prevent the *slave's* escape rather than vice versa.

These truths are general ones that might apply to anyone, and in particular to the wise person, who may be tempted to think that he can change things by his words and actions that cannot in fact be changed for the moment (at this "time"). The deliberate twofold use of Heb. *šlṭ* (NIV "power") in verse 8, however, which reminds us of the "supreme" word of the king in verse 4, already makes us think of the king in particular—the one who appears to be completely in control when in reality he is not. It is the king's word that has the potential for harm or evil (*raʿ*) in verses 3 and 5 and that creates misery (*raʿa*) in verse 6. Yet verse 8 suggests that wickedness (*rešaʿ*) ends up possessing its possessor.

Verses 9—10 then bring the whole section to an intermediate conclusion. The present "time" that is under consideration is characterized (v. 9) as that in which a man exercises power (Heb. *šlṭ*) that results in "hurt" (*raʿ*, "evil"). The statement is ambiguous (lit., "there is a time when a man exercises power over a man for hurt to him"), and perhaps deliberately so in the light of the preceding verses. Does the "hurt" fall only on the king's victims, or ultimately on the king himself? The passage as a whole suggests that Qohelet intends us to think of both outcomes. Evil intended for others ultimately damages the perpetrator (cf. 5:13). In the end, in fact, the reign of the wicked person comes to an end—even the wicked are buried (v. 10).[5] As prominent and as visible, perhaps as self-important and self-righteous, as kings once were (symbolized by their coming and going from the temple), yet they die, are buried, and are soon forgotten[6] even in the city where they were most visible and well known. Their reign is not so imposing as they think and as their subjects fear. Even the memory of it soon fades.

The final sentence of verse 10, referring to futility (Heb. *hebel*; NIV "meaningless"), is better taken with what follows it than what precedes it, just as the *hebel*-statement in verse 14 also refers forward rather than backward. It is one of the unfortunate results of divine patience with human beings in their sinfulness, which may mean that "the sentence for a crime is not quickly carried out" (v. 11), that foolish hearts are "filled with schemes to do wrong." Wrongdoing meets no opposition, and the wrongdoer is thus encouraged to continue on his or her chosen path. It is this way of thinking and doing that is "pointless."

Qohelet himself as a wise person "knows" (v. 12; cf. v. 5) that reality will not ultimately conform itself to the fantasies of fools. The wicked may sin massively—a hundred times over (cf. 6:3 for a similar use of the number)— and yet live a long life. This is admittedly puzzling if God is good and just and truly governs the universe. Yet Qohelet resists the conclusion that wickedness pays. He continues to affirm that it will go better with the person who fears God than with the person who does not (vv. 12–13), and he explicitly states that the days of the wicked "will not lengthen like a shadow," by which is probably meant that the life of the wicked is a fleeting and insubstantial thing that does not last long (cf. 6:12).

The puzzle presented by the affirmation of ultimate justice is to understand how Qohelet imagines things will in practice work out. As he has noted already in the book, it is not just the foolish who die and are forgotten (2:16). Nor is it only the life of the wicked that is a fleeting shadow (6:12).

---

5. The connection between vv. 9 and 10 is perhaps not adequately represented by the NIV, whose "then too" in v. 10 might suggest a new observation unrelated to what has gone before. Heb. *ub'ken* certainly connects the two verses closely, however (cf. the use of the term in Est. 4:16 as indicating consequential action: "when this is done . . ."). There is a time when the wicked oppress others, but death and burial follow.

6. I prefer the majority Heb. reading here over the minority reading accepted in the main text of the NIV.

He maintains that the days of the wicked will not lengthen (Heb. *ʾrk*, v. 13), yet he has just observed that the wicked may live for a long time (Heb. *ʾrk*, v. 12), and he goes on immediately in verses 14–15 to suggest more generally not only that wicked people sometimes get what the righteous deserve but that righteous people sometimes get what the wicked deserve (cf. 7:15).

The clear implication of his thinking must be that there is some "time" beyond the "times" of life in which wrongs can be righted and imbalances corrected; yet as we have seen, Qohelet is agnostic about life after death (3:18–21). His agnosticism is proclaimed, indeed, precisely at that point in chapter 3 when the reality of God's judgment on the righteous and the wicked is first articulated. So how is justice to be done? Qohelet never explains himself. He simply expresses his confidence in the moral nature of the universe while noting various data that bring this into apparent question. Unable finally to resolve the puzzle himself, he then characteristically advocates that the reader get on with life and not worry too much about the details, which lie with God.

That is precisely the direction in which he moves in verses 15–17. If it is ultimately unclear how justice is to be achieved and precisely how, in the longer term, it is "better" (*tob*, cf. its use in vv. 12–13) to fear God than not to, then at least this much is clear: There is nothing "better" (*tob*, v. 15) for someone living in the present time "under the sun" than to eat, drink, and be glad—to know joy in the presence of God in his world. The business of living well before God in this way must not be sacrificed in the pursuit of truth that is ultimately beyond our grasp.

With the closing remarks of chapter 8 we return to the theme of much of the second part of chapter 7. Qohelet has set out to understand the business of life (Heb. *ʿinyan*, NIV's "labor"; but cf. 1:13; 2:23, 26; 3:10; 4:8; 5:3, 14) at which mortal beings are constantly busy ("not seeing sleep day or night"). He has examined the work (*maʿaśeh*) or action of God, and, as in 3:11, 17 (where the work of judgment is in view), he has found it unfathomable. All efforts at knowing wisdom (*ydʿ ḥokma*, v. 16, as in 7:25), in the sense of "finding" a comprehensive account of reality (Heb. *mṣʾ*, three times in 8:17, as in 7:24, 27–28), have failed. A more literal translation of part of verse 17 communicates the emphasis with which the failure is announced:

> No human being can find out [*mṣʾ*] the work [*maʿaśeh*] that is done under the sun. Despite all human effort to search it out, one cannot find [*mṣʾ*] it. Even if the wise man claims to know, he cannot find [*mṣʾ*] it.

It is this reality that leads to the advice of verse 15. It is not the ultimate justice of God that Qohelet doubts. It his own ability to understand how that justice works out in practice. He does not consider it wise to pursue that question at the expense of living well the life God has given him.

*Bridging
Contexts*

THE BROADER BIBLICAL context in which Ecclesiastes 8 must be understood is provided by all that
voluminous material that speaks of the foolish
and wicked rulers of this present age, under
whose power God's people must live for a time, and that offers models of and
advice about what righteous living should look like. That much human government is wicked, even though government as such is instituted by God for
human good and should not lightly be opposed, is simply taken for granted
by the Bible, which characteristically sees idolatry as lying at the root of the
problem. Kings, made in God's image to govern creation as his representa-
tives, come to "worship the image" or the self and set themselves up as gods
in opposition to the living God. The consequence is "harm"—to other human
beings, to the rest of creation, and, ultimately, to the king himself.

The most fundamental picture of this reality in the Bible is provided by
the Exodus narrative. God's people find themselves in Egypt, enduring harsh
oppression at the hands of a human being who is considered within his cultural and religious context to be a god—the pharaoh of Egypt, son of the sun-
god Re, and becoming, after death, the god Osiris. This god-king requires
servanthood from Israel—a harsh, oppressive slavery, ruthlessly imposed
(Ex. 1–2; cf. 20:2).

Opposed to this "god" is the living God, who contests the sovereignty of
Pharaoh over his world. An almighty, cosmic battle between the god of
Egypt and the God of the burning bush ensues, which proves beyond doubt
that we are dealing here with the only true God, who has ultimate power over
both creation and history, and that other gods are not truly gods at all, albeit
that they are often regarded as such. Ten plagues—environmental disaster
in the main—suffice to make the point that the God who has addressed
Moses, not Pharaoh or any other Egyptian god, is the God of fertility and
blessing; in the end he is God of life and death (Ex. 12:12).

The events at the Reed Sea confirm his identity, as creation is replayed
in the divine control of the watery chaos and the divine judgment on the
forces of darkness. All God's enemies are dismissed as the Spirit-wind sweeps
across the earth (cf. Gen. 1:1–10; Ex. 14:21–29). The Lord God, who
promised to deliver his people from the Egyptians—to shape history in
terms of his own will rather than permit it to be shaped by Egyptian gods (Ex.
3:7–12)—has proved able to deliver on his promises, for he is the true and
living God who creates, redeems, and blesses.

The kingdom that Israel's God governs is unlike Pharaoh's kingdom, for
it has at its heart a seventh day of rest, in which there is space for all creatures to remember that life is more than work and the universe more than an

object to be manipulated in pursuit of gain. The kingdom of Pharaoh is one in which there is no rest but only feverish productivity for God's people (Ex. 1–2). The kingdom of God offers a clear alternative. There is no comparison between the good society ordained by God and the oppressive society ordained by the gods.

Thus is a fundamental contrast set up early in the biblical story between two kingdoms, and the battle between them is replayed in different forms throughout the remainder of the Bible. Isaiah 14 exults over the downfall of the king of Babylon, one who said in his heart, "I will ascend to heaven; I will raise my throne above the stars of God. . . . I will make myself like the Most High" (Isa. 14:13–14).

Second Kings 18–19 presents us with the Assyrian emperor Sennacherib, who suggests that the Lord God cannot deliver Jerusalem because he is merely one of many powerless gods (18:33–35)—and a deceitful one at that (19:10). Sennacherib portrays himself as the true provider of material blessings and life itself, and indeed as the provider of a new exodus for Israel to a "promised land" (18:31–32; cf. Deut. 8:7–9). Invited by the Assyrian king to turn his back on this deceitful and powerless god and so save himself from the fate of all those other kings who went to their doom clinging to their idols, Hezekiah of Judah offers a memorable prayer (2 Kings 19:14–19), in which he reaffirms that the God enthroned between the cherubim, who has taken Israel for his special people, is not merely one god among many, but God alone. All earthly kingdoms should know the difference between God and the gods. Thus, Hezekiah asks that Jerusalem be delivered from the Assyrian's hand. Isaiah's reply (19:21–34) makes clear just how much exception the living God takes to Sennacherib's pretensions to divinity.

Ezekiel 28:1–10 addresses the prince of Tyre, who has said, "I am a god; I sit on the throne of a god in the heart of the seas" (v. 2), but in reality is mortal and destined to die at the hands of foreigners because of his pride (cf. Ps. 82).

Finally, Daniel 3–4 tells us of Nebuchadnezzar of Babylon, a king who imagines he has, in defeating Judah, defeated Judah's God and symbolically places vessels from the Jerusalem temple in the treasury of his gods (Dan. 1:1–2). His sense of godlike control is revealed in his construction of a massive golden image on the plain of Dura and in the subsequent demand for political and religious allegiance (Dan. 3). Three Jewish exiles refuse to bow down, intent on avoiding confusion between an idol and the living God. After their escape from royal power, Nebuchadnezzar himself receives an object lesson in reality (Dan. 4), as he is cut down while flourishing, driven out among the animals, and made to eat grass for seven "times," until he realizes the truth of his existence as king, namely, "that Heaven rules" (v. 26).

An inscription of the Assyrian king Assurnasirpal gives deep insight into the idolatrous nature of power as it is wielded by such rulers:

> And now at the commands of the great gods, my sovereignty, my dominion, and my power, are manifesting themselves: I am regal, I am lordly, I am exalted, I am mighty, I am honored, I am glorified, I am preeminent, I am powerful, I am valiant, I am lion-brave, and I am heroic. (I), Assur-Nasir-Pal, the mighty king, the king of Assyria, chosen of Sin, favorite of Anu, beloved of Adad, mighty one among the gods.[7]

It is undoubtedly because of this tendency among foreign kings and states to self-divinization that Deuteronomy 17:14—20 instructs Israel, in respect of her own kingship, that the king should not be a foreigner, should not imitate foreigners, and should have constant recourse to the law of Moses, lest he forget that he rules under God. The oft-succumbed-to temptation to be like the other nations was, after all, a strong one (1 Sam. 8)—the temptation to make "strength . . . their god" (Hab. 1:11).

Whether in these Old Testament books, or later in a New Testament book like Revelation, the Bible is not naïve about the nature of human government. Nor is it pessimistic, however. It knows that individual kings die (as in Eccl. 8:1—17), and beyond that it knows that one day all earthly powers will pass away, when "one like a son of man" (Dan. 7:13) comes to bring in the kingdom of God in a final way and deals decisively with all those "beasts" or nations who have governed up to this point (7:14). Kings do not control their own destiny, much less anyone else's. They have no grasp of the times, which lie in the hand of the Alpha and Omega, the First and the Last, the Beginning and the End (Rev. 1:8; 21:6; 22:13).

The question for believers, of course, is how to live "between the times"— in the present, where government is flawed and often wicked, before the end times come and the kingdom of God is fully among us. Qohelet, although he seems to have little explicit interest in the end times, offers some helpful advice. He counsels caution when confronting power, for although that power in relation to God is no power at all, it is still capable of doing great harm. A wise person may well be more powerful than ten rulers in a city (7:19); but he is unwise if he thinks that wisdom gives him precisely the same kind of power as the king, and he is likely to regret it if he fails to make the appropriate distinction between them. What Qohelet is saying here comes under the New Testament heading of being "as shrewd as snakes and as innocent as doves," precisely because as sheep it is not wise to attract

---

7. *Annals of Assur-Nasir-Pal*, 1.33, as cited in Schlossberg, *Idols for Destruction*, 40.

attention from any wolves (Matt. 10:16). There is no virtue in running deliberately into the jaws of death for no good reason.

To caution, Qohelet adds patience. The wise person who understands the nature of things will not struggle foolishly against reality as it is presently found, as if an individual could singlehandedly change the world for the better. There must be a steady and a patient waiting for God's judgment and redemption, knowing that (as 2 Peter 3:8–9 puts it) "with the Lord a day is like a thousand years, and a thousand years are like a day. The Lord is not slow in keeping his promise, as some understand slowness. He is patient with you, not wanting anyone to perish, but everyone to come to repentance."

This patience is naturally allied to faith. It is necessary to keep our heads clear when confronted by the idols of power, lest we come to think that the pretensions of the powerful have some basis in reality, and lest we are tempted therefore to view the world from their point of view. The present nature of the world should not determine our thinking, however. We should not be persuaded by those who scoff and follow their own evil desires, saying "Ever since our fathers died, everything goes on as it has since the beginning of creation" (2 Peter 3:4). Mortal power *will* pass away, sooner or later. The wicked powers *will* face judgment, and "their days will not lengthen like a shadow" (Eccl. 8:13).

To caution and patience Qohelet adds, finally, integrity. Above all we must not be drawn into living falsely just because we live in a world where falsehood is normal. We are to go on living our lives before God, eating and drinking and being glad, and in doing this undermining all those ideologies that exalt power as a means to human happiness. We are to stay on the narrow path, refusing the temptations and ignoring the threats of power. In this way we witness to the futility of power and shine light on the broad path that leads to destruction. We do this, not because we understand all of God's ways, but because we know that God is God (Eccl. 8:16–17). It is a false religion, indeed, that teaches or implies that we can somehow comprehend or control God—a religion hinted at in the case of Nicodemus (John 3), who seeks rational control of the truth and needs to be reminded as to the ungraspable nature of God, who is like the wind.

Shrewd caution, patient faith, and integrity are all on display when we read those many biblical stories that are most directly about God's people living under foreign rule. In the Old Testament we think most notably of the story of Joseph in Genesis 37–50 and of the books of Esther and Daniel. The Joseph and Esther stories remind us that living under such rule is frequently complex and certainly not morally unambiguous—there is always a fine line between accommodation and compromise. The Daniel stories tell us something that Qohelet does not: that even when the people of God make a sincere attempt to live under the "beastly empires," displaying due loyalty to governmental power and exercising caution, faith, and integrity, they will still face persecution and danger and will sometimes be called upon to stand up and be counted for God.

Even though wise people have no interest in running deliberately into the jaws of death for no good reason, there will sometimes *be* good reasons to do so. For God is God, and loyalty to God comes first and above all other loyalties. The early church preaches the same message to us: "We must obey God rather than men" (Acts 5:29). Christians have always struggled with what exactly this means, particularly when it comes to the question of how far human powers are to be opposed in the name of God (e.g., as far as violent revolution?). What is clear, however, is that those who hold to biblical faith can never accede to any mortal demand that they blur the sharp boundary between God and the created order, whether that demand comes from an individual "god" or from a nation-state or other community that has divine pretensions.

God, who entered Israel's story so mysteriously as a voice speaking from a burning bush, possessing a name whose meaning cannot be pinned down—"I am who I am; I will be what I will be" (Ex. 3:14)—thus announced that he possesses unhindered power beyond all human power to contain, to objectify, and to control. There can be no compromise on that fundamental truth.

The greatest joy is to conquer one's enemies, to pursue them, to seize their property, to see their family in tears, to ride their horses and to possess their daughters and wives.[8]

Power corrupts, and absolute power corrupts absolutely. This maxim is amply demonstrated throughout history, and not only by Ghengis Khan, whose words are cited above. Power is gasoline thrown on the fire of our ordinary self-worship, turning it into a blazing inferno. Out of the fire all too often steps a god, risen from the ashes of humanity, and these megalomaniac gods do great harm. They take names for themselves like "Ghengis Khan," which means "universal ruler," or "divine Caesar." They define all time and space as their possession; constructing chronology in terms of the godlike self has been one of the basic moves of the egomaniac since ancient times (e.g., the Roman emperors) and down to the present (year 0 in Cambodia). Oppression and bloodshed are their stock in trade.

---

8. Ghengis Khan (1162–1227).

The modern deification of the state—the philosopher Hegel once called the state "the march of God through the world"—has much to do with the collapse of Christendom, as the nineteenth-century German thinker Friedrich Nietzsche foresaw. Looking ahead in a world shaped by Enlightenment and scientific thought in which God was dead and in which there was therefore no universal truth or morality, Nietzsche foresaw a point in the future when this reality would dawn widely on Western culture, leading to widespread nihilism—that is, a pervasive sense of purposelessness and meaninglessness.

Nietzsche also correctly foresaw, however, that most people would be unable to accept the intrinsic meaninglessness of existence and would seek alternative absolutes to God as a way of investing life with meaning. He thought that the emerging nationalism of his own day represented one such surrogate god, in which the nation-state would be invested with a transcendent value and purpose. The slaughter of rivals and the conquest of the earth would follow, even while people were proclaiming universal brotherhood, democracy, and socialism. It was Nietzsche's world in which we lived in the twentieth century—a century of unparalleled butchery and brutality. The god of the nation-state has exacted a heavy price on its worshipers.

What this god offers us, however, is so attractive that we are prepared, culturally, to turn a blind eye to its darker side, for the idols of power are always to be found intermarried with the idols of Mammon, and the combination is potent. It is potent enough to draw us to listen carefully to those who advocate politics as the only means of redemption available to us and to justify, in terms of necessary sacrifice, all the bloodshed and oppression that such idolatry has produced. For the state has this godlike capacity, apparently, to supply us with all blessings and to fulfill all our material needs. That is why we are devoted to it.

We like the utopianism that promises ever-increasing material prosperity—the utopianism that modern economic ideologies ranging across the entire political spectrum have at their core. We are comforted by the myth of endless progress via economic growth, facilitated by science and technology as means of control. The idols of power and Mammon are seductive. That is why Satan paraded them before Jesus on the high mountain, when he showed him all the kingdoms of the world and their splendor and said, "All this I will give you . . . if you will bow down and worship me." Jesus was thinking clearly and biblically at the time, however: "Away from me, Satan! For it is written: 'Worship the Lord your God, and serve him only'" (Matt. 4:9–10).

It is this biblical clarity that modern Christians must strive for when confronted by power in the present, remembering that it does not always reveal itself to us in its terrifying aspect, but often in its more seductive aspect. The first and foremost conviction we must possess is that we are called to "worship the Lord our God, and serve him only." We are always servants of God first and the servants of others second. There is no place in Christian thinking for any "God and . . . ," for "God and . . ." is idolatry.

One of the most serious of these idolatries is "God and country." It has milder and stronger forms. In its milder form, there is only a subtle, but certainly dangerous, elevation of the nation-state to a position in one's life in which it is spoken of in the same breath as God. It is only a short step to the stronger and more deadly form, however, in which God is enlisted in support of one's country, one's culture, and one's way of life; and it is assumed that to be Christian is to be, for example, American or English. Faith, flag, and country are an unholy trinity. The real Trinity has no interest in it and opposes it, for the whole earth is the Lord's (Ps. 24:1), and the Lord has no interest in artificial human barriers and boundaries constructed out of self-interest, nor does he have any intention of being used to legitimate them.

God will not tolerate being located as one among a pantheon of gods. God is the only God there is. The modern nation-state, so deeply rooted in the affections of many—as we see not only in the wars of twentieth century but also in such areas of life as international sporting events (warfare by another name)—arose only in the aftermath of the dissolution of Christendom as a God-substitute. Thus it remains for many today.

Qohelet and those other biblical writers who touch on the matter of power and our response to it point us in a different direction. They remind us that God is Other, who cannot be recruited to any of our crusades or enlisted in support of the "American way of life"—or indeed any way of life. They remind us that God's interests do not in any way coincide with our national interests. They allow that we must live within a particular culture and society and that we must come to terms, in various ways, with our context. They assume, however, that we will always be dancing to a different tune and responding to a different voice, even if we are doing it quietly. The biblical writers assume a distance between Christians and their culture or society— an alienation and a discomfort, at least, with the situation. They counsel due respect for authority, up to a point, and advocate caution and patience, but they do so in the assumption that sooner or later conflict will arise, at which time the worshipers of the living God will have to name as idols what others think of as gods.

To put the matter bluntly, the Bible, when read as a whole, does not advocate social conservatism, if by that is meant a passive, quietist acceptance of the way things are and a submergence of Christian identity beneath some other identity. It does not present the law-abiding citizen as a paragon of all virtue or offer support for the idea that it is always better to keep things more or less the way they were in the old days. It tells us, rather, that we must resist the pretensions of the powerful and keep their claims in divine perspective, that we must resist the suggestion that the state is our real provider and the real guarantor of our future happiness and security, that we must resist the notion that any person or institution has such mortal control over our destiny, whether temporal or eternal. We are always citizens of the kingdom of God first and citizens of our state second; and we are always to live in a way different from those who worship the idols of power and Mammon.

This represents something of a challenge, to put it mildly. To focus on the United States, where this commentary is most likely being read, I remember a conversation a few years ago with an American Christian, just after the U.S. government had arranged for the bombing of Libya. The discussion revolved around whether a Christian could support his government in carrying out such an action. After an extended debate involving much mutual incomprehension, he looked at me incredulously and said: "What you're saying is that a Christian ought to be an internationalist!" The incredulity that accompanied what ought to be a statement of the obvious is the truly worrying thing.

Yet we are speaking here of a country in which many Christians place their hands over their hearts and talk to the flag (what *is* the religious significance of this action, exactly?), in which the national flag is commonly found positioned prominently in churches (often near the pulpit), in which "God and country" language is frequently and loudly heard, and in which Christians are as likely to become as angry as anyone else if American national interests are harmed in some way, especially if something is said or done to hurt the American economy. We can always tell what our real devotion and trust are given over to by noting when we feel most threatened, frightened, and angry. Noting this is the first step towards repentance.

To those who already understand this, a different word is necessary, for those who are already walking on the costly Christian way often feel estranged and homeless in the communities where they live (even in church communities). It is a difficult path to walk when even their Christian neighbors are not truly walking it with them. They admit they are "aliens and strangers on earth . . . looking for a country of their own . . . longing for a better country" (Heb. 11:13–16), but few are up for the journey. It is painful to be a Jeremiah, forced to choose between loyalty to God and loyalty to one's country. It is still worse to suffer the persecution that Christians have always suffered as a result of making such choices, from the days of the Roman Empire until now. For these readers, it is important to remember texts like these:

> Blessed are those who are persecuted because of righteousness, for theirs is the kingdom of heaven. (Matt. 5:10)

For I am convinced that neither death nor life, neither angels nor demons, neither the present nor the future, nor any powers, neither height nor depth, nor anything else in all creation, will be able to separate us from the love of God that is in Christ Jesus our Lord. (Rom. 8:38–39)

And having disarmed the powers and authorities, he made a public spectacle of them, triumphing over them by the cross. (Col. 2:15)

And I saw the souls of those who had been beheaded because of their testimony for Jesus and because of the word of God. They had not worshiped the beast or his image and had not received his mark on their foreheads or their hands. They came to life and reigned with Christ a thousand years. (Rev. 20:4)

Ecclesiastes 9:1–12

S O I REFLECTED on all this and concluded that the righteous and the wise and what they do are in God's hands, but no man knows whether love or hate awaits him. ²All share a common destiny—the righteous and the wicked, the good and the bad, the clean and the unclean, those who offer sacrifices and those who do not.

> As it is with the good man,
> so with the sinner;
> as it is with those who take oaths,
> so with those who are afraid to take them.

³This is the evil in everything that happens under the sun: The same destiny overtakes all. The hearts of men, moreover, are full of evil and there is madness in their hearts while they live, and afterward they join the dead. ⁴Anyone who is among the living has hope—even a live dog is better off than a dead lion!

> ⁵For the living know that they will die,
> but the dead know nothing;
> they have no further reward,
> and even the memory of them is forgotten.
> ⁶Their love, their hate
> and their jealousy have long since vanished;
> never again will they have a part
> in anything that happens under the sun.

⁷Go, eat your food with gladness, and drink your wine with a joyful heart, for it is now that God favors what you do. ⁸Always be clothed in white, and always anoint your head with oil. ⁹Enjoy life with your wife, whom you love, all the days of this meaningless life that God has given you under the sun—all your meaningless days. For this is your lot in life and in your toilsome labor under the sun. ¹⁰Whatever your hand finds to do, do it with all your might, for in the grave, where you are going, there is neither working nor planning nor knowledge nor wisdom.

¹¹I have seen something else under the sun:

The race is not to the swift
  or the battle to the strong,
nor does food come to the wise
  or wealth to the brilliant
  or favor to the learned;
but time and chance happen to them all.

¹²Moreover, no man knows when his hour will come:

As fish are caught in a cruel net,
  or birds are taken in a snare,
so men are trapped by evil times
  that fall unexpectedly upon them.

 THROUGHOUT THE PRECEDING material and reaching back into chapter 7, Qohelet has been anxious to affirm the superiority of wisdom over folly and of righteousness over wickedness. At the same time he has sought to make his readers think about what wisdom and righteousness really are and how far they are truly attainable, about the expectations that the wise person should have about how life will work out, and about the best way of thinking and living in the light of all the facts. He has particularly emphasized the way in which wisdom and righteousness often do not seem to bring sufficient reward, highlighting the challenge that this reality (and the reality that wicked fools prosper) presents to the notion of a morally coherent universe. The present section continues in this vein, as Qohelet continues his reflection on all he has observed and thought about ("all this," 9:1).

The NIV rendering of the opening verse is somewhat unsatisfactory. It implies that the first part of the verse is intended as a comforting statement along the lines of 8:12, affirming that the righteous are in a "better" place overall than the wicked. Its second part presumably provides alternatives (love and hate) that lie in the future, although human beings do not know which one lies ahead. It is then difficult to see how verses 1 and 2 cohere together, since verse 1 speaks of two possible fates, whereas verse 2 speaks of a common destiny for all. A more literal rendering of the admittedly terse Hebrew in 9:1–2 should help us toward a more satisfactory understanding:

... the righteous and the wise and their deeds are in the hand of God. Both love and hate—humankind does not know—both are before them. Both—just as for everyone (there is) one fate.

The point of verse 1 is to emphasize that the righteous and the wise, perhaps against their expectation, will experience in life both "love and hate," which may simply be another way of saying "good and evil." Their experience is in this respect no different from that of the wicked and the foolish—*everyone* has a mixed experience of life. The lack of knowledge mentioned then refers either to general ignorance that this is indeed the case (perhaps especially among the wise and righteous themselves) or to specific ignorance as to the precise mix of "love and hate" that each individual will have to endure. Human beings cannot know in advance how much of each they will encounter.

The point is then developed in the remainder of verse 2, as those who share both the common life and the common fate are enumerated—the "destiny" in question (Heb. *miqreh*, as in 2:14) being death, as will become clear. The righteous and the wicked have already been mentioned in connection with death in 7:15; 8:14. The Hebrew text next refers to those who are "good and clean" on the one hand, and "unclean" on the other. Since the phrase "good and clean" disturbs what would otherwise be a neat list of opposites (righteous/wicked, clean/unclean, etc.), the LXX has often been appealed to for the reading "good and bad, clean and unclean" (cf. NIV).

Whether neatness was ever Qohelet's concern is, of course, an important (and unanswerable) question. It may be that the combination "good and clean" is intended to clarify that it is not simply ritual cleanness to which Qohelet refers, but moral cleanness (cf. Heb. *ṭhr*, e.g., in Job 4:17; Ps. 51:10; Prov. 20:9), as in another contrasting pair, "good man/sinner." It would have been as natural for an early translator (i.e., in the LXX) as it has proved for modern ones, who did not read the text in this way, to supply a reference to "evil" after "good."

The ritual and sacrificial realm is not in any case excluded from the area of Qohelet's concern, for he mentions next "those who offer sacrifices and those who do not." If we are to imagine, as the progression of the list of pairs itself suggests overall, that the first-mentioned attribute is that of a righteous person, then it is assumed here, as it was in chapter 5, that the righteous and good person will engage in temple worship. The point of 5:1–7 was simply to draw attention to the dangers of engaging in the rituals of worship without possessing any intention to bring the whole self before God in an attitude of reverence and awe.

The final word pair in verse 2 refers to "those who take oaths" and "those who are afraid to take them." The latter are presumably reluctant to swear an oath because they lack integrity. They do not intend to follow through on their words and therefore shy away from making a clear commitment of a binding nature (cf. the force of the oath in 8:2, whether uttered by the wise man or by God).

Both the virtuous in moral conduct, religious observance, and social relationships, then, and those who lack virtue share a common—indeed, an "evil"—destiny (v. 3). The emphasis is on the unfortunate nature of the fate, as is often the case when Hebrew *ra‘* / *ra‘a* is used in Ecclesiastes (cf. comments on 1:13). This being the case, and given the clear distinction in 9:1–2 as to character (if not fate) of the righteous and the wicked, it is more likely that Qohelet has in mind, in referring to the "evil" found in human hearts in verse 3, the misery that is commonly endured rather than the moral corruption that produces at least some of that misery.

Human "hearts . . . are full of evil" in the same sense that in 8:6 "the evil of a person is great upon him" (NIV, "a man's misery weighs heavily [Heb. *rab*] upon him"). The heart experiences its full measure of misery (cf. also the Hiphil of *rbb*, "multiply," of having great experience of something in 1:16; 5:17). It is likewise probable, given that Qohelet has just distinguished wise from foolish, that he is maintaining that the "madness" that is linked to folly throughout the book (cf. Heb. *holela* in 1:17; 2:12; 7:25; also the forms of *hll* in 2:2; 7:7; 10:13) is commonly *experienced* by all people rather than *characterizing* them all.

We should thus understand 9:3 as somewhat reiterating, in reverse order and with emphasis on the negative, the contentions of 9:1–2. There is a common human destiny (death), and during life both the righteous and the wise are by no means untouched by misery and folly. In the terms used in verse 1, they know hate as well as love. The following translation of 9:3 results:

> This is the miserable thing in all that is done under the sun: One fate comes upon all. Moreover, the human heart knows its full measure of misery and folly during life—and after it, they join the dead.

The unsatisfactory life, at least in degree, comes to an unfortunate and absolute end. Verse 4 probably does not hold out "hope" in this context (NIV) but speaks rather only of "certainty" (Heb. *bittahon*, which connotes trust and security): Anyone who is currently among the living may be certain that he or she will know some misery and then death. It is the fact that the living thus know *something*, however, whereas the dead know nothing (v. 5), that brings to Qohelet's mind what looks like another traditional proverb: "A live dog is better off than a dead lion" (v. 4).

We may well imagine that this proverb was not widely used in Israel in quite the way that Qohelet uses it here. Of itself, it looks like a piece of wisdom designed to encourage dishonorable self-preservation (the dog not being highly regarded among ancient Near Eastern peoples) over glorious and heroic death (such as a "lion-hearted" warrior might welcome). Qohelet's scope is not so large. His interest here, so far as we can tell, is only in the contrast between life and death in the single regard that the living are conscious while the dead are not. The dead have no further "reward" (*sakar;* cf. 4:9) or return on their investment in life and are not even held in *other people's* consciousness (they are forgotten, 9:5, as in 2:16). They no longer possess a "part" (Heb. *ḥeleq,* cf. 2:10, 21; 3:22; 5:18–19) of or share in life (9:6).

In the context, in view of the apparent meaning of "love" and "hate" in 9:1, we should probably interpret the first part of verse 6 as once again concerning their *experience* of love, hate, and jealousy. The dead are beyond all such experience of life, whether good or bad. They cannot know these intense emotions. Experience of and reflection on life may bring its own trials, and it may sometimes seem that it would be better to be without them (1:18; 4:2–3); yet in the end, life is better than death.

With this stark description of reality articulated, Qohelet now turns once again to advice for the living (vv. 7–10), picking up the thread from 8:15. Life is indeed a mixed bag; death awaits us all. What is the wise response? It is to seek joy where it may be found. We should eat and drink in "gladness" (*simḥa*), knowing that God himself delights in what we do (v. 7).[1] We are "always [lit., in every time] [to] be clothed in white" and to have our heads anointed with oil (v. 8)—outward signs of joy, indicating a festive and celebratory atmosphere (cf., e.g., Ps. 23:5; Est. 8:15). If married, we are to "enjoy" (lit., "see") life with our spouse throughout our days, albeit that those days are brief (NIV "meaningless"; Heb. *hebel,* v. 9). For this is indeed our "share" (*ḥeleq* again; NIV "lot") in life—the reward for all the toil and effort that we invest (cf. 2:10; 5:18–19). This is the only "profit" that there is, and we had better enjoy this lot because after death it disappears (9:6). That reality is what should spur us on to live our lives wholeheartedly and with commitment (v. 10). Whatever our hand "finds" to do, we should do.

The play on the impossibility of "finding" any large-scale explanation of the universe throughout the preceding chapters is obvious. If the reality of death is to set the context for the living of life (7:1–12), then "finding" should best be directed at the business of living in itself. For there is not only no doing or "working" in the place of the dead, but no "planning" (Heb. *ḥešbon;* better, "attempt to comprehend the scheme of things," cf. 7:25, 27), knowledge, or

---

1. The NIV's wording implies that a distinction is intended between "now" and some other time when God's "favor" might be withdrawn. If the "now" of life is being distinguished from the "then" of death, then this is true. The line might better be translated, however, so as to remove any idea that particular moments within life are being distinguished from others. The combination of general context, the meaning of Heb. *kᵉbar* (NIV's "now") elsewhere in the book (e.g., 1:10; 2:12), and the full range of meanings of Heb. *rṣh* and the cognate noun *raṣon* (BDB, 953) certainly do not suggest this. What Qohelet is saying is that those who eat and drink joyfully may be sure (always) that this is the will of God, for already "God favors what you do."

wisdom. It would be best in life, as it is inevitable in death, to abandon the futility of pursuing a comprehensive grasp of the universe.

Verses 11–12 provide a tailpiece that underlines the message of verses 1– 10. Life's outcomes (other than death) are not predictable in their specifics; good and bad come to all. We might expect that the swift would always win the race and the strong the battle, and that the wise, the brilliant, and the learned would receive all of life's rewards. This is not so, however. The things that human beings so often covet and seek to develop and that are by no means bad things in themselves—bodies fit and strong, and minds well educated and sharp—do not bring control of the "times" (ʿet, "time," v. 11 [cf. 3:1– 11]). Things often happen to people[2] that are unforeseen and beyond their control, and no one knows when a particular "time" will occur (ʿet again in v. 12a, which does not refer to the "hour" of death, but to any particular "time" that lies in the future).

The human situation is somewhat akin to that of fish or birds. A fish does not anticipate the moment of capture in a "cruel" (lit., "evil") net, nor does a bird have any idea that in a moment it will find itself entrapped in a snare. Thus do evil or bad times come on us "unexpectedly" or suddenly.

OVER AGAINST WHAT is claimed in much modern pseudo-Christian theology, the Bible never promises that any human being will know in this life only good health, financial prosperity, and happiness. Moreover, it certainly never ties faith and righteousness to the attainment of these things in any simplistic way. It is true that the way of faith and obedience to God is in the end the blessed way, and God's blessings can include good health, financial prosperity, and happiness. It is untrue, however, that the faithful and obedient person will only and ever possess such things and can somehow be sure of avoiding illness, disaster, and death if he or she can simply muster enough religious devotion. To believe this is to believe something profoundly unbiblical; to teach it is to insult every Christian throughout the past two thousand years who has known illness, poverty, and misery; and to press it on the sick, the poor, and the unhappy of the present day is to place a millstone around the neck of those who are drowning,

---

2. The NIV's "chance" (pegaʿ) is an unhappy choice of translation, since this word connotes an impersonal and random force, whereas Qohelet is clear throughout the book that human fate lies ultimately in God's hands, no matter how random and impersonal what befalls us may appear. The verbal form pgʿ means "to meet, encounter." A pegaʿ is simply something we encounter on the path of life—a circumstance or situation over which we have no control.

rather than offering them the comfort and hope of the gospel. God is much more concerned to make us holy and to shape us in the image of Christ than he is to make us happy, rich, and healthy.

Qohelet emphasizes that each of us is destined to experience both good and evil, both love and hate, both misery along with the effects of folly, and joy along with the effects of wisdom, and in the end to know death. In doing so, he is speaking the truth—a truth widely proclaimed elsewhere in the Scriptures. Job knew God's blessing in life, for example, especially wealth and good health (Job 1–2). But God's sovereign plan for his life involved the removal of both wealth and health and the loss of almost everything else. God has given, and God may take away (1:21), and the point is that Job never got to understand why God had done this. We, the readers of the book of Job, understand something of why bad things happened to Job, for we have access in the opening chapters to the heavenly court. Job was kept in the dark, however, and had to remain content as his trials came to an end simply with encountering the God Who Is (Job 38–42). God's plans remained undisclosed, even when Job's material blessings were restored (42:12–17). God remains God.

At the center of the biblical story stands our Lord and Savior himself. He walked a pilgrim path, lacking a place to lay his head (Matt. 8:20). Although he did heal the sick, he certainly did not teach that faith in and obedience to God bring inevitably in their wake prosperity, health, and happiness; rather, he warned his disciples to beware of wealth (e.g., Matt. 19:16–26; Luke 16:19–31) and to know that they would face constant threats to life and limb (e.g., Matt. 5:11, 44; Luke 21:12–19). Jesus' own life was a life marked by alienation, pain, and eventually death. His followers could not avoid a similar fate. The apostle Paul is a good example, knowing constant danger, frequent need, and ever-present illness (2 Cor. 11:23–30; 12:7–10), which prayer to God did not affect. His conclusion from this last experience was not that his faith was weak or that God did not exist but that God's power was being revealed in his weakness. He goes on to say something that those who are devotees of modern pseudogospels can never say:

> Therefore I will boast all the more gladly about my weaknesses, so that Christ's power may rest on me. That is why, for Christ's sake, I delight in weaknesses, in insults, in hardships, in persecutions, in difficulties. For when I am weak, then I am strong. (2 Cor. 12:9–10)

Biblical faith is not about control. Nor is it about manipulation of God so that God will do as we wish. It is idolatry, not true faith, that has at its heart control and manipulation, as one recent author has clearly seen and has powerfully expressed in respect of modern religious forms, particularly in North America:

The Good News is packaged and marketed ... as a religious prod-uct: offering "peace of mind," "how to get to heaven," "health and pros-perity," "inner healing," "the answer to all your problems," etc. What is promoted as "faith in God" often turns out, on closer inspection, to be a means for obtaining emotional security or material blessing in this life and an insurance policy for the next. This kind of preaching leaves the status quo untouched. It does not raise fundamental and disturbing questions about the assumptions on which people build their lives. It does not threaten the false gods in whose name the creation of God has been taken over; indeed, it actually reinforces their hold on their wor-shippers. This kind of "gospel" is essentially escapist, the direct descen-dent of the pseudo-gospels of the false prophets of the Old Testament. It is simply a religious image of the secular consumerist culture in which modern men and women live. It lays itself wide open to the full blast of the savage criticism of Marx and Freud.

... At the heart of idolatry is the attempt to manipulate "God" or the unseen "spiritual world" in order to obtain security and well-being for oneself and one's "group" (whether family, business corporation, ethnic community or nation-state). Biblical faith, in contrast, is the rad-ical abandonment of our whole being in grateful trust and love to the God disclosed in the life, death and resurrection of Jesus Christ: so that we become his willing agents in a costly confrontation with every form of evil and unjust suffering in the world.[3]

Qohelet does not yet express a *fully* Christian faith, of course. This is most clearly seen in our section, perhaps, in his insistence that life is better than death and in his reasons for thinking so. Those who know of the res-urrection of the dead cannot be so stark in their differentiation of the two (note Paul's statement that he desires "to depart and be with Christ, which is better by far," Phil. 1:23). Yet Qohelet's faith is *truly* Christian faith in its insistence that God is God and we are not, that God's ways in the world are beyond us and beyond our control, that believers live the same human life as anyone else, and that they encounter the same range of human experiences even while God is present in their midst. He reminds us that "biblical faith ... is the radical abandonment of our whole being in grateful trust and love to ... God," not something we practice out of self-interest. He also reminds us at the same time, however, that this expression of trust and love to God is not consistent with the wrong kind of self-denial.

There has always been within the Christian tradition an ascetic tendency that understands true spirituality as involving the shunning of created things

---

3. Ramachandra, *Gods That Fail*, 40–42.

(e.g., food, wine, sex) rather than the enjoyment of these things in thankfulness to God who has blessed us with them. Qohelet helps us see that the latter is the truer spirituality. We are certainly not to worship created things, but neither are we to behave as if God did not make the world *good* (Gen. 1). Recognizing that our experiences in life will be mixed, we should not spend time worrying about the future while failing to live well in the present. We should concentrate instead on living out the present before God (Eccl. 9:7–10; cf. Matt. 6:25–34)—acting out our existence heartily and joyfully as we eat, drink, and enjoy our most intimate relationships.

Jesus himself, although he knew alienation, pain, and eventually death, was also to be found feasting and partying with his friends (e.g., Luke 7:34; John 2:1–10). He set his face against gloomy religion and insisted that serious religion should be wedded instead to joy (e.g., Matt. 6:6–18, noting the possible allusion to Eccl. 9:8). His generous, joyful faith was opposed, of course, by the teachers of the law and the Pharisees (e.g., Luke 7:31–50), who, like the poor, are always with us. Those who follow Jesus need to know, as he did, the difference between the laughter of fools (Eccl. 7:1–6) and the joy of the wise.

The war in Vietnam is going well and will succeed[4]

We are people much given to prediction, and prediction implies control. We imagine we understand the world; we can see how it is going. Yet we are constantly surprised. The *Quarterly Review* of 1825 asked, "What can be more palpably absurd than the prospect held out of locomotives travelling twice as fast as stagecoaches?"—to which one might respond, "human beings who ask questions like this."[5] Seven years before the introduction of anesthesia in 1846, French surgeon Dr. Alfred Velpeau said that "the abolishment of pain in surgery is a chimera." Eight years before the first successful operation for stomach cancer in 1881, British surgeon Sir John Eichsen gave the opinion that "the abdomen, the chest and the brain will be forever shut from the intrusion of the wise and humane surgeon." In the computer field, IBM chairman Thomas Watson predicted in 1943 a world market for about five computers. Finally, Richard van der Riet Wooley, the British Astronomer Royal, said in 1956, "space travel is utter bilge."

---

4. Robert McNamara, U.S. Secretary of Defense in 1963.
5. The source for this and some of the other examples cited here is the *Vancouver Sun* (Aug. 28, 1999).

All were mistaken. It has been calculated, further, that two-thirds or more of the forecasts made by American social scientists between 1945 and 1980 have likewise proved to be mistaken, giving them a batting average substantially lower than the three witches in Shakespeare's *Macbeth*. The fastest runner in the Olympic Games and a "sure bet" for the title is tripped in the course of the race and falls. One of the least favored horses in the British Grand National wins because of an unprecedented and chaotic mess at one of the fences, which put many other horses out of the race. One of the best-trained and mightiest armies in the world fails to win a guerrilla war, despite confident predictions. Highly qualified and educated people end up in poverty, hunger, and dishonor.

"The race is not to the swift or the battle to the strong, nor does food come to the wise or wealth to the brilliant or favor to the learned; but time and chance happen to them all." This seems obvious. Yet we are highly resistant to believing it. We live in a world in which cause and effect are often visibly in connection with each other. I press a light switch, and the light comes on. The swift usually win races. It is this visible connection between cause and effect that makes plausible the idea that somehow the universe can eventually be mastered by human beings, given enough time and sufficiently well-developed technique. It is, after all, only a large and complex machine (isn't it?), and we are in so much control of it already.

This promise of control is a seductive one and lies at the heart of much of the advertising with which we are every day deluged. To control our lives—so it is suggested—we need only buy this product, eat this kind of food, and avoid that sort of drink. No longer need we be the victims of our frailty and mortality. We can define and shape ourselves and become the persons we really want to be. Self-expression, self-fulfillment, and self-actualization lie at the heart of our cultural agenda as we tread the path towards superhuman status through self-empowerment. Their advocates are found in every corner of society—from the advice columns of newspapers and magazines through to schools, where sometimes the point no longer seems to be to learn things but to "find oneself" and be the best person one can be. We are constantly urged, in fact, to believe in ourselves and to better ourselves—in our individual choices and actions. In accordance with our personal ambition, we are encouraged to make and remake ourselves in our own image or in some other human image of perfection.

We are invited to pursue the body beautiful, to take control of our personal health and fitness, to invent our own value and belief systems, all with a view to gaining personal fulfillment. We are given ever-increasing permission to ignore—and if necessary to dispense with—whatever and whoever stands in our way in this quest, be it life in the womb, children, spouses, the poor, foreigners, or the aged. Churches often play the same kind of game, although what they advertise as the means of human control is religion rather than irreligion. The fundamental belief is the same, however: Correct belief and correct technique can give me the edge (in respect of life temporal and, in this latter case, eternal).

The idea that we have any such control, Qohelet and other biblical writers remind us, is a myth. It is true that the universe is an ordered place and that cause and effect are features of its reality. Yet the universe is not a machine. It is a personally created and governed space, whose Originator and Sustainer is the living God. Our human vocation is to love God, to love our neighbor, and to look after the earth—not to take advantage of the order of the universe to engage in self-centered and manipulative living. Indeed, cause and effect will only get us so far in life. The pursuit of health and education, for example (perfectly good things in themselves), will only disappoint us in the end, if they are invested by us with ultimate value. For beyond cause and effect there is God, who will not allow the idolatry of the self ultimately to exist.

The God of order, therefore, brings chaos to life, so as to remind us that we are not in fact gods who control the present or the future. Instead, we are mortals in need of repentance in dust and ashes. Every time a prediction fails, every time the swift do not win a race and the strong a battle, every time our health breaks down, or we find ourselves poorer rather than richer, or we discover we are miserable rather than happy—every such occasion is a moment of grace and an opportunity to look reality straight in the eye. It is a moment in which we are helped to remember who controls the times.

All the occasions are important, for as the preacher used to thunder in the movie version of *Pollyanna*: "Death comes unexpectedly." Qohelet puts it this way: "No man knows when his hour will come . . . men are trapped by evil times that fall unexpectedly upon them" (9:12). Death is the ultimate proof, if we need one, that our pretensions to be gods are utterly foolish, but death is also the phenomenon that makes it too late to address our error.

The reminders of reality that we graciously receive from God are necessary in a world so utterly conceited about itself and its achievements and so determined to convince us all how wonderful it is. A Merrill Lynch advertisement appearing on Canadian TV around May/June 1999 captures the conceit well. Against the background of various events from the end of the 1980s (among them the fall of the Berlin Wall and the crumbling of apartheid in South Africa), the words "Human Achievement" appear on the screen and a voice says, "The world is ten years old. Go get 'em, kid." As I pointed out earlier, constructing chronology in terms of the godlike self has been one of the basic moves of the egomaniac since ancient times. We proclaim mastery of the universe by taking control of time itself. The world is not ten years old, of course, and it is God who carries out his plans in it, not mere mortals. As we did not create it, so there is a limit (unacknowledged in the advertisement, naturally) to what we can achieve in it.

The Christian path through the madness and folly of our culture is this: to fear God and live to God's glory, to keep ourselves from idols (1 John 5:21), and to do what we do in life, in this context, with all our might (Eccl. 9:10). This includes the ordinary things of life (eating, drinking, loving). Neither our evident mortality and vulnerability nor our sense of the complexity of everything must be allowed to distract us from following this path. We are not (or should not be) Christians in the first instance, after all, because we want to escape mortality and vulnerability or because we want to understand everything about the universe. We are Christians first of all because God is God.

It is this reality, in turn, that gives us our true hope that despite all the trials and puzzles of life, things will work out well in the end. The 1999 movie *Shakespeare in Love* captures the truth well, and at the same time captures the truly Christian optimism about the world we find in Shakespeare's writing—an optimism so noticeably lacking in many modern plays and novels (in which there is no notion of a governing Providence that oversees all). At various times in the movie, characters are moved to proclaim their belief that everything is going to work out. When asked how this will happen, they reply, "I don't know—it's a mystery." Christians know something of this mystery (e.g., Rom. 16:25–27; Eph. 1:9–10), but not all.

Who has known the mind of the Lord? Or who has been his counselor? (Rom. 11:34)

Ecclesiastes 9:13–10:20

I ALSO SAW under the sun this example of wisdom that greatly impressed me: ¹⁴There was once a small city with only a few people in it. And a powerful king came against it, surrounded it and built huge siegeworks against it. ¹⁵Now there lived in that city a man poor but wise, and he saved the city by his wisdom. But nobody remembered that poor man. ¹⁶So I said, "Wisdom is better than strength." But the poor man's wisdom is despised, and his words are no longer heeded.

¹⁷The quiet words of the wise are more to be heeded
than the shouts of a ruler of fools.
¹⁸Wisdom is better than weapons of war,
but one sinner destroys much good.

¹⁰:¹As dead flies give perfume a bad smell,
so a little folly outweighs wisdom and honor.
²The heart of the wise inclines to the right,
but the heart of the fool to the left.
³Even as he walks along the road,
the fool lacks sense
and shows everyone how stupid he is.
⁴If a ruler's anger rises against you,
do not leave your post;
calmness can lay great errors to rest.

⁵There is an evil I have seen under the sun,
the sort of error that arises from a ruler:
⁶Fools are put in many high positions,
while the rich occupy the low ones.
⁷I have seen slaves on horseback,
while princes go on foot like slaves.

⁸Whoever digs a pit may fall into it;
whoever breaks through a wall may be bitten by a snake.
⁹Whoever quarries stones may be injured by them;
whoever splits logs may be endangered by them.

¹⁰If the ax is dull
and its edge unsharpened,
more strength is needed
but skill will bring success.

¹¹ If a snake bites before it is charmed,
    there is no profit for the charmer.

¹² Words from a wise man's mouth are gracious,
    but a fool is consumed by his own lips.
¹³ At the beginning his words are folly;
    at the end they are wicked madness—
¹⁴   and the fool multiplies words.

No one knows what is coming—
    who can tell him what will happen after him?

¹⁵ A fool's work wearies him;
    he does not know the way to town.

¹⁶ Woe to you, O land whose king was a servant
    and whose princes feast in the morning.
¹⁷ Blessed are you, O land whose king is of noble birth
    and whose princes eat at a proper time—
    for strength and not for drunkenness.

¹⁸ If a man is lazy, the rafters sag;
    if his hands are idle, the house leaks.

¹⁹ A feast is made for laughter,
    and wine makes life merry,
    but money is the answer for everything.

²⁰ Do not revile the king even in your thoughts,
    or curse the rich in your bedroom,
    because a bird of the air may carry your words,
    and a bird on the wing may report what you say.

THE LIMITATIONS OF wisdom as well as its benefits have been explored throughout the preceding section of the book (7:1–9:12). We now return to the kind of generally affirming material with which chapter 7 opened. Wisdom may be limited, but it is a good thing. It is particularly necessary when dealing with foolish and wicked rulers, who function in this section of the book as the central illustration of what fools looks like.

The keyword of 7:1–12 was *ṭob*, "good, better" (also found in 7:14, 18, 20, 26; 8:12, 13, 15; 9:2, 4, 7). This word lies at the heart of 9:13–18 as well, where Qohelet opines that "wisdom is better than strength ... wisdom is better than weapons of war" (9:16, 18). The event associated with this opinion that impressed Qohelet "greatly" (*gadol*) is first described. "A powerful [*gadol*] king" once besieged a city, throwing up "huge [*gadol*] siegeworks" around it. Bad times had arrived for this city; indeed, the Hebrew word behind the NIV's interpretative "siegeworks" is *mᵉṣodim*, "nets," the singular of which appears in 9:12 (cf. also 7:26). Here is a city caught, like a bird, in nets. The language is reminiscent of what the Assyrian king Sennacherib has to say about his siege of Jerusalem in 701 B.C.:

> As to Hezekiah, the Jew, he did not submit to my yoke, I laid siege to 46 of his strong cities, walled forts and to the countless small villages in their vicinity, and conquered them.... Himself I made a prisoner in Jerusalem, his royal residence, like a bird in a cage. I surrounded him with earthwork in order to molest those who were leaving his city's gate.[1]

Qohelet then reflects on the way that wisdom can come to human aid in the midst of snares and nets. Set over against the powerful king is the poor man who is "found" (*mṣ'*) there, meaning either that the king found him there or that he happened to live there (as in the NIV). He is a good counterpoint to the king, for no one would have expected much from him by way of either intellectual or physical power (cf., e.g., Prov. 14:20; 18:23; 19:7, for some evidence of societal attitudes in Israel toward the poor). Yet it turns out that this particular poor man possessed wisdom, and by means never disclosed to us (a subterfuge perhaps, or wise and eloquent speech), he was able to save the city where others could not have done so. Truly "wisdom makes one wise man more powerful than ten rulers in a city" (Eccl. 7:19). That is why "the quiet words of the wise are more to be heeded than the shouts of a ruler of [or better, 'among'] fools" (9:17). Noise is no substitute for astute judgment.

Yet having read his words to this point, we do not expect Qohelet to fail to offer qualifications of his praise of wisdom, or at least its efficacy in human life. The qualifications are found in latter parts of verses 15–16 and 18. Verse 15b tells us that even after the extraordinary deliverance of the city, the poor man was forgotten. Even though he had proved himself wise, he found himself disregarded once the danger passed—as unvalued as he had been beforehand. Verse 16b reads like a generalization from the particular case rather than a further reference to the particular (as in the NIV): "The poor man's wisdom is despised, and his words are no longer heeded."

This incident had proved beyond doubt the value of wisdom, and it might have been assumed that this would have made a difference in people's attitudes

---

1. See *ANET*, 287–88.

towards poor people who happened also to be wise. But no! The implication of verses 15–17 is that wealth and social class are far more impressive to people, generally speaking, than wisdom and that people will listen more readily to people of great wealth and high social class than to a poor but wise man (they should "heed" the wise man's words, v. 17, but they do not thus "heed" them, v. 16). It only takes one shouting fool (here "sinner," v. 18, again underlining the connection between folly and wickedness) to persuade the masses of the rightness of his cause and so to nullify the truth of the statements that "wisdom is better than [*toba*] strength . . . wisdom is better than [*toba*] weapons of war," for one such sinner destroys much "good" (*toba*).

We are reminded here of the dangerous woman of 7:26, from whose "nets" (*mᵉsodim*, as in 9:14) a good man escapes (*mlt*, as in 9:15), while the sinner (*hoteʾ*, as here in 9:18 and earlier in 2:26; 8:12; 9:2) is captured (*lkd*, often used of the capture of a city in war). In 9:18, the foolish sinner destroys, in his folly, the advantage that wisdom gives over "weapons of war"—the advantage that in the case described had prevented the capture of a city. The sum of the matter is this: Wisdom is not only better than folly (2:13) but is also found to be better than military strength (9:16). It offers a way ahead when bad times befall (cf. 9:11–12). Yet in practice wisdom and its purveyors are undervalued, so that remedies are not found when needed.

This reaffirmation of wisdom's value, albeit accepting its limited efficacy in the face of human (and particularly a leader's) folly, leads to a number of sayings concerning wisdom's value, many of them dealing with leaders and with foolish or wise speech. We begin with a proverb that underlines the truth of 9:15–18. As a fact of experience, contrary to the real worth of things, folly is often valued above wisdom and honor (10:1). That is the sense in which folly "outweighs" wisdom and honor—it is given more weight than it should by those who are doing the evaluating, so that only a small amount of it tips the weighing scales, as it were, in its favor.

A better translation than in the NIV of 10:1b is thus the more literal one: "More precious than wisdom and honor is a little folly." Two weighty things[2] are commonly undervalued in contrast to the one lightweight item against which they are weighed; the worldview described is very different from the one found in passages like Proverbs 3:13–15.

The first part of Ecclesiastes 10:1 is obviously designed to drive home the point through the use of striking imagery, although the precise meaning has proved difficult to determine. The common assumption that the flies are

---

2. The genuine "weight" of the second of these things, in particular, is suggested to the reader of the Heb. text by the similarity between the noun *kabod*, "honor," and the verbal root *kbd*, "be heavy."

doing something to the perfume (cf. the NIV and many commentators) is, however, to be questioned, which in turn extricates the reader, among other things, from the task of explaining convincingly how "dead flies give perfume a bad smell." It seems more likely that the two verbs in this line (of which the NIV apparently only renders one) refer to two different actions.

The first verb (*b'š*) in the Hiphil refers to the bad smell associated with things dead and/or decaying, as in Exodus 16:24 (the manna "did not stink or get maggots in it"); thus "flies of death [i.e., the flies that infest corpses] emit a stinking odor." The second verb (*nb'*) in the Hiphil is only ever used elsewhere in the Old Testament of words "pouring forth" from the mouth (Ps. 19:2; 59:7; 78:2; 94:4; 119:171; 145:7; Prov. 1:23; 15:2, 28; cf. the Qal form in Prov. 18:4); thus, "they pour forth scented oil." Spices and perfumes have been used throughout history to disguise the smell of decaying bodies (e.g., 2 Chron. 16:14, where Heb. *rqḥ*, which lies behind "scented" in Eccl. 10:1, reappears in reference to "spices" placed in King Asa's tomb).

The associations of 10:1a, then, are with a dead body in terms of both its true and its apparent "smell." "Flies of death" may simply be a colorful way of referring to such a body, through the literary figure of synecdoche, where one aspect of something (here the flies that cover it) stands for the whole thing (see comments on 2:8).[3] At the same time, it seems obvious that behind the imagery here Qohelet has a real plural subject in mind, namely, those "fools" whose words so often prevail in public discourse. The general context and the particular use of the verb *nb'* of the flow of "scented oil" suggest this. But this is not all. We may also note Proverbs 13:5, the only other place in which the imperfect Hiphil of *b'š* appears and which should be translated thus (rather than as in NIV, which accepts an unsupported emendation):

> The righteous person hates a lie, but a wicked person emits a stinking odor and is put to shame.

The parallelism clearly suggests that "emits a stinking odor" is a reference to deceitful speech. We may add to this that the Hebrew word *šemen*, "oil," is itself used of wicked and deceitful speech in Psalm 55:21 and Proverbs 5:3. The words of fools are foul-smelling words of death (Prov. 5:5; 14:12), then, yet they are scented sufficiently to lead the majority of people to value them above the words of life, since oil is a precious commodity. People prefer the gushing, oily utterances of the wicked to the bubbling brook that is the fountain of wisdom (Prov. 18:4).

---

3. It is striking that the verbs are singular, yet the subject is formally plural. One possible explanation for this, although it is not a *necessary* explanation, is that Qohelet's thought is flitting between the images he is using and the reality to which he is really referring.

Verses 2–3 develop the general point about the bizarre and different choices that people make in life. The inner lives ("hearts") of the wise and foolish persons are set in completely different directions. The fool has no idea, in fact, of his destination and how to get there: "His heart is lacking/deficient" (Heb. *libbo ḥaser*; NIV, "the fool lacks sense"). This is connected with listening to the words of fools rather than to the wise, for "the lips of the righteous nourish many, but fools die for lack of judgment" (*baḥᵃsar-leb*, Prov. 10:21).

The final part of verse 3 is ambiguous in the Hebrew (lit.): "He says to all he is a fool." Has listening to foolish words in turn produced further foolish speech (the one who is in fact a fool calls everyone else a fool)? Or is it simply that he proclaims to everyone by his attitude and actions that he himself is a fool? Or are these the words of the heart, pictured as having abandoned him on the journey and now denouncing him to anyone who will listen?

The launching pad for this whole section was the contrast between the wise poor man and the rich and foolish "ruler" (*mošel*) in 9:13–18. Thus, we now focus in 10:4–7 on the figure of the "ruler" (*mošel*, 10:4, also called šalliṭ in 10:5). The advice of verse 4 is directed to the wise person at court and is similar to that in the Masoretic text of 8:3, although we are clearly dealing with the noisy, angry ruler of 9:17 rather than merely with the strong-willed king of 8:2–9. Faced with such a person, abandoning one's post is not a wise option (since this will presumably lead to further anger and perhaps even more severe punishment). Quiet and soothing words are still the best approach (9:17; cf. Prov. 16:14). This advice is sharpened by the double use of Hebrew *nwḥ*: "Do not *leave* your post; calmness can *lay . . . to rest*." Whether the "errors" belong to the courtier or the king is not clear.

Verses 5–7 further elucidate the kind of foolish behavior that such rulers indulge in, preferring as they do to promote and to take advice from people who share their foolish outlook: "Fools are put in many high positions." The antithesis to fools here, "the rich," is perhaps at first sight surprising after 9:13–18. The point of that passage, however, was to argue that wisdom ought to be heeded regardless of the social class of the wise person; it was not to argue that all poor people are wise and capable of roles in government. Qohelet's concern in 10:6–7 is not with the individual case—he does not elsewhere equate riches with wisdom any more than he equates folly with poverty (nor, for that matter, "princes" with good leadership, v. 16, and those of humble origins with bad leadership, 4:13–16).

It was a societal reality in the ancient Near East, however (as in many societies since), that those found at the royal court, and therefore the sort of "wise men" who are here under consideration, generally also possessed wealth and influence. It is interference with this general order of things to which Qohelet objects (cf. Prov. 19:10; 30:21–23): social upheaval in which those ill-equipped for government are elevated to high positions above those with wisdom and experience.[4]

Verses 8—9 have in common that they concern unforeseen happenings in which a person suffers hurt. The completion of everyday tasks—the digging of pits, the demolition of walls, the quarrying of stone, and the splitting of logs—result not in satisfaction and well-being but in injury. The context suggests that the figure of the angry and foolish king with his unpredictable policies is still at the forefront of Qohelet's mind, although the truth that "no one knows what is coming" (v. 14) is also a general one that has been articulated more than once in the book. It is a risky occupation being a courtier in such a royal court, for even mundane and straightforward tasks may turn out to have hidden dangers. The royal "snake" may bite (vv. 8, 11) before it is charmed by the snake charmer (lit., "master of the tongue"), that is, the wise man with his soothing words (v. 4).

Verses 12—14 speak further about the wise man's speech (which is "gracious" in the sense of winning him favor; cf. Prov. 28:23) in contrast to the self-destructive words of the fool, which begin in folly and end in wicked and verbose madness (cf. "folly" and "madness" in 10:13; also 2:12; see also the injunctions against verbosity in 5:2–3, 7; 6:11). The fool's words devour him.

The agenda of the syntactically awkward verse 10 in the midst of all this is apparently to urge the wise person to greater effort in his work, so that he will know some "profit" (*yitron*, v. 11; also in v. 10; NIV, "success") from it. Even a blunt ax (a metaphor here for the wise man who is not having great success) may succeed in its set task if more strength and wisdom (*ḥokma*; NIV, "skill") is brought to that task. It is worth persevering in the business of speaking wise words even when dealing with a fool.

The conjunction of the foolish "multiplying of words" and the reminder that no one knows the future in verse 14 is most reminiscent of 6:11–12. This suggests that the connection between the two parts of 10:14 (which is not explicitly made within the verse itself) has to do with the fool's illusion that he possesses control over life. The number of his words is in inverse proportion to the extent of his understanding, in that he does not understand the nature of the universe as a succession of "times" over which he has no power (cf. also 7:14; 8:7). He does not know enough, as it were, to find his way into town (cf. 10:3)! The wise person, although he also does not control the times, at least

---

4. Since this is clearly the thrust of the verse in context, it should also be considered whether the terms "rich," "princes" (lit., "leaders"), and "slaves" are meant metaphorically rather than literally, the first two referring to those who are "wealthy" in wisdom and possess obvious leadership skills, and the third referring to those who possess neither wealth nor skills of leadership. The whole passage is marked by this kind of use of language (cf., e.g., the use of "snake" in vv. 8, 11, and "town" in v. 15).

knows that he does not, and his "toil" (*ʿamal*, v. 15; NIV, "work") is therefore not the wearisome business endured by the fool. We are reminded here of passages like Ecclesiastes 2:10–24, with its extended reflections on "toil" (*ʿamal*, also in 3:13; 4:4, 6, 8, 9; 5:15, 18, 19; 6:7, 8:15; 9:9) as something experienced by many as profitless, yet capable of being engaged in with joy and fulfillment when a correct (wise) view is taken of the world. The wise person may not be able to map the universe, but he at least grasps sufficient geography for the task of living everyday life. He "knows the way to town" (cf. v. 15).

The closing verses of chapter 10 again return explicitly to reflect on the ruling classes and their oft-displayed vices and to offer advice on wise behavior when dealing with them. Qohelet envisages two contrasting scenarios (vv. 16–17): A land whose king was previously a "servant" (and/or possibly a youth or child; Heb. *naʿar* has both connotations) and, being ill-equipped for government (unlike the poor wise youth of 4:13–16), presides over a ruling class that is dissolute and neglectful of responsibility (cf. Isa. 5:11–12, 22–23 for the associations of the kind of feasting referred to here); and a land whose king himself originates from the ruling classes and who keeps a firm hand on the reins of government.

It is the first scenario that is developed in verses 18–19 in terms of the consequences that follow from weak and dissolute government. If a man is lazy with respect to maintaining his house, eventually the roof falls in (better than NIV's "the rafters sag") and everyone gets wet! The unique Hebrew *mᵉqareh*, referring to the roof beams, is likely a clever play on *miqreh*, which appears in 2:14–15; 3:19; 9:2–3, of the death that is the "fate" of everyone. It is the inevitable consequence of idleness in government that disaster follows for the land.

Verse 19 speaks further of the great illustration of, and perhaps the partial cause of, the idleness, which is the inappropriate banqueting mentioned already in verses 16–17. The NIV does not translate it in the best way, however. A more literal translation is: "For laughter they prepare food, and wine that brings joy to the living; and money meets the demands of [lit., 'answers'] both." Qohelet often uses Hebrew *kol* to express "both" of two options rather than a global "all, everything" (cf. 2:14; 7:15, 18). The implication is that money that may have been well used for "house repairs" has been squandered on partying.

It is not surprising that verse 20 goes on to speak of reviling the king and cursing the rich, for in a country governed in such a way, the temptation to indulge in such bad-mouthing would be great. Yet it is unwise in an autocratic and corrupt state even to think such thoughts, for thoughts can easily spill out into words, and even words spoken in private may find their way back to the rich and powerful, who can do the subject damage.

Bridging Contexts

WE DO NOT know whether Qohelet has in mind a real, historical example of a siege as he writes 9:13–18, nor do we know which siege it might be—although this has not prevented commentators from speculating wildly on the matter, sifting through the historical records especially of the third century B.C. to find a siege they can claim as their own. The most famous biblical siege that illustrates the general point that "the battle [is not] to the strong" (9:11), while not truly corresponding in detail to the story told here, is the one described in 2 Kings 18:17–19:37. Sennacherib, king of Assyria, besieges King Hezekiah of Judah in Jerusalem and taunts him about his own and his God's powerlessness. Hezekiah's "wisdom" is to pray and indeed to seek advice from the prophet Isaiah.

Another biblical story that comes to mind concerns the siege of Abel Beth Maacah in 2 Samuel 20, where a wise woman saves the city by advocating the sacrifice of the refugee Sheba. Wisdom takes many forms in the Old Testament, but it is always at least as necessary as strength, even though it is constantly undervalued.

It is the undervaluing of wisdom and the consequences of this in which Qohelet is mainly interested in the current section. At the heart of human existence there is a "madness" (10:13) that leads us to value what we should not and to despise what is truly valuable. The human tragedy is that we are incapable even of enlightened self-interest, much less the disinterested love of God or neighbor. "Even the stork in the heavens knows its times; and the turtledove, swallow, and crane observe the time of their coming" (NRSV); but human beings are, apparently, too stupid to know when the time has come to repent of idolatry, with all the damage it brings to self and society (Jer. 8:7). "The ox knows its owner, and the donkey its master's crib" (NRSV), but Israel in her perversity does not know the living God (Isa. 1:3).

God's appeal to his people is to reason it all out (Isa. 1:18)—to come to their senses. It is not by accident that when Nebuchadnezzar's *reason* returns to him he praises God, recognizing that "all his works are truth, and his ways are justice" (Dan. 4:37 NRSV). The first lie of the serpent goes deep, however (Gen. 3:1–5), and reason is not easy to come by. We prefer to believe that we are gods-in-waiting and capable of living in our own way and on the basis of our own insights. Thus, folly is valued above wisdom, whether by ordinary people or by those who govern them.

The ordinary fool is characterized in our passage fundamentally as someone who is lost, yet verbose. He talks a good game, but he does not know where the goal line is. The number of his words are in inverse proportion to the quantity of his knowledge. Of the two paths through life described for us in Psalm 1, he has chosen the second. He walks in the counsel of the wicked, he stands in the way of sinners, and his life is as insubstantial as chaff blown away in the wind. He is like those described in Psalm 107:4–5:

> Some wandered in desert wastelands,
>> finding no way to a city where they could settle.
> They were hungry and thirsty,
>> and their lives ebbed away.

The fool walks in the way of evil people (Prov. 4:14)—the way of the wicked who will perish (Ps. 1:6). As he does so, he talks incessantly. He "sits in the seat of mockers," ridiculing those who take a different path (1:1) and uttering wicked and deceitful words designed to wound and hurt the righteous (36:3; 55:21; 64:3; 94:4) and to draw them away from the truth (Eph. 5:6; 2 Peter 2:18). He even babbles before God, thinking to be heard because of his many words (Matt. 6:7). Proverbs 2:12–15 speaks instructively of just such people

> whose words are perverse,
> who leave the straight paths
>> to walk in dark ways,
> who delight in doing wrong
>> and rejoice in the perverseness of evil,
> whose paths are crooked
>> and who are devious in their ways.

The righteous person, on the other hand, knows the way on which he or she is walking and the destination that lies at the end of the road. That individual does not know everything about the universe or even about God and his ways, but he or she "knows the way to town," depending on God for direction and light for the path:

Make straight your way before me. (Ps. 5:8)

He guides the humble in what is right and teaches them his way. (Ps. 25:9)

Teach me your way, O LORD, and I will walk in your truth. (Ps. 86:11)

Walk in the way of understanding. (Prov. 9:6)

Jesus answered, "I am the way and the truth and the life." (John 14:6)

He went to the high priest and asked him for letters to the synagogues in Damascus, so that if he found any there who belonged to the Way, whether men or women, he might take them as prisoners to Jerusalem. (Acts 9:1–2).

The righteous person also knows that "when words are many, sin is not absent, but he who holds his tongue is wise" (Prov. 10:19). Moreover, "a man of knowledge uses words with restraint, and a man of understanding is even-tempered" (17:27). The righteous person therefore does not babble on, seeking to disguise lostness with verbosity. He or she chooses words carefully.

Folly is also frequently valued above wisdom by those who govern, who prefer to promote and take advice from people who share their own foolish outlook. The best narrative example from the Old Testament is found in 1 Kings 12:1—11, where Rehoboam is confronted with the question of how his kingship is going to be exercised so that it is consonant with the nature of God's covenant people. The Israelites complain, in fact, that they are no longer the people set free to live in freedom in the Promised Land but have become once more a people under harsh labor, as they were in Egypt. Rehoboam receives wise advice from the elders, who may have had the benefit of Solomon's own wisdom (cf. 1 Kings 10:8) and had little hope of or desire for further advancement from his son—the advice that effective leadership comes from below and not from above (12:7). But the new king does not like what they have to say. Thus, he chooses instead to accept the foolish advice of his younger contemporaries, who are currently in his own service (12:8). They owe their position in life to him, and they give him the advice he evidently wishes to hear. Rehoboam in consequence behaves like Pharaoh, increasing the oppression on the people (cf. Ex. 5:1–21). Such foolish government, in Kings as in Ecclesiastes, leads inevitably to disaster. All authority exercised under God, in fact, is to be exercised with humility and with love for one's neighbor, whoever that neighbor may be (note, e.g., Matt. 23:8–12; Eph. 6:4, 9).

WOMAN: "Teach me things!"
MAN: "What do you want—information or wisdom?"[5]

WOMAN: "Do you believe everything the authorities tell you?"
MAN: "Why not?"
WOMAN: "They're *authorities*—that's reason enough!"[6]

We live in a world where information is widely privileged over wisdom. We are bombarded with "facts" and expected somehow to accommodate all of them and to integrate them into our lives. But we are like the readers of a

---

5. From the movie *Atlantic City*.
6. From the movie *Kafka*.

complicated novel who read all the sentences yet cannot grasp the plot. The information highway runs directly through our homes in the form of TV and the Internet, and we are exhilarated at the chance of catching a ride and ending up in exotic places. But there is too much traffic and it moves too fast, so we are more likely to find ourselves playing the role of dead squirrel, caught beneath its wheels, than the role of daring hitchhiker.

It is a world in which no one ever thinks to ask whether twenty-four-hour news channels are a good thing (it is thought to be obvious that they are), a world in which it is self-evident that information technology is a more important school or college subject than philosophy, a world in which "Have you heard the latest?" is a more pressing question than "Do you know the truth?" It is a world in which it is estimated that by the time a child born today reaches the age of fifty, 97 percent of everything known in the world at that time will have been learned since her birth. The truth is that we have never known so much and understood so little.

We live in a world, in fact, in which wisdom—at least insofar as it derives from authority and tradition—is routinely suspected, mocked, and despised. Long gone are the days when the venerable age of an idea was thought to be an indicator of its value. Long gone, too, are the days when trust was placed in authorities, whether ancient or modern. These are more suspicious, fractured times. We are all the distant heirs of the Enlightenment idea that truth must be rediscovered from the ground up, all previous truth claims notwithstanding.

What we have discovered, however, as we have pressed our suspicion of "authorities" further and further, is just how difficult it is to know any truth at all. Truth has thus become a personal matter, which changes with the life circumstances of the person who proclaims it. The only wisdom that counts is the wisdom that has been collected experientially along the way. Swimming in the midst of the ocean of "facts," each individual must somehow work out how at least some of them cohere with each other and make sense. The best he or she can hope for in terms of help from the outside is that some other individual may be able to offer a few words of knowledge, and even then, it is a fairly forlorn hope.

The depths of the dilemma are clearly seen in many of our more recent movies, which offer for our inspection a variety of incompetent adults who clearly have not the first idea of what life is about. Contrasted with these are various wise and competent youths (or even children or babies) who, understanding all things, certainly have no need of listening to any adult and have a thing or two to teach most of the adults they know. As in the consumer culture generally, it is the new that counts, not the ancient; the young, not the old. The movies reflect the culture, in which parents have themselves lost confidence or interest in teaching and disciplining their children (after all, what do *we* know?), and even school and college teachers are uncomfortable with the idea that they have a body of wisdom to pass on to their pupils, taking refuge instead in the (frightening) idea that education is about drawing out what is already "in" the child. This atmosphere was nicely captured by a "back-to-school" section in a local newspaper,[7] which carried headlines "Words from the Wise" over comments and advice to incoming students from children as young as six and seven.

It is not that children have no wisdom of their own. Of course they do—and it is indeed sometimes superior to that of adults. It is not that adults cannot accumulate wisdom as they walk the path of life, although many appear to manage to avoid doing so. Nor should we always believe what authorities tell us and do what they say. Authorities can lie and be mistaken, and they can certainly be corrupt. Yet in the end, it is impossible for the solitary, transient individual to make sense of the universe, or even for a band of transient individuals to do so.

We all need some larger story to inhabit, with an Author who knows the beginning and the end and who controls the plot. We all need wisdom from above and from outside us—and from before us—if we are to know who we are, what it is all about, and where we are going. We all need to know Truth, if we are to make even the beginnings of an attempt to sort out truth from fiction in all the claims and counterclaims of human experience—in all that passes for "wisdom" in society, whether it comes from children or adults, from authorities or those who are suspicious of authority.

We will not find this Truth by watching TV chat shows (the great symbol of the modern desire to share experiences without ever having to be committed to truth that relativizes or criticizes experience). We will not find it by listening to powerful politicians, to famous actors or performers, or to people who are both (and thus illustrate just how far what is novel has overtaken in importance what has substance). We will find it only in God's revelation in Jesus Christ, who is the touchstone of all reality and the focus of all wisdom. It is in Jesus and in the great story of human history woven around him as its center that we will find the solid rock on which to stand and against which to measure the truth of all the truth claims that people make about the world—the authority that can be trusted. It is the house built on this ancient Truth that will still be found standing at the end of time, when the waters have washed all other more modern and attractive houses away:

> Therefore everyone who hears these words of mine and puts them into practice is like a wise man who built his house on the rock. The rain came down, the streams rose, and the winds blew and beat against

---

7. *Vancouver Sun* (Aug. 18, 1999).

that house; yet it did not fall, because it had its foundation on the rock. But everyone who hears these words of mine and does not put them into practice is like a foolish man who built his house on sand. The rain came down, the streams rose, and the winds blew and beat against that house, and it fell with a great crash. (Matt. 7:24–27)

It is as we stand on the Rock that we will learn to recognize and embrace wisdom, wherever it is found (e.g., whether in a poor man or in another, Eccl. 9:16), filtering out all the noise of the culture that distracts us and distorts our values (9:17). It is as we stand on the Rock that we will learn to value wise words over oily words (10:1, 12), whether they come from politicians, advertisers, or indeed preachers. It is as we stand on the Rock that we will learn those necessary skills required even to survive the autocratic and corrupt state (10:4–11).

On this last point we should remind ourselves that it is always possible for one loud fool to persuade the masses to go along with him or her, even on the most implausible and mad of crusades. One thinks of the shocking absurdity of Adolf Hitler, an unimposing man with dark hair, ranting to large crowds about the supremacy of the blond, Aryan warrior race, and of all the misery and wickedness that followed the suspension of disbelief among those who heard him. It will always be the case, however, that a fool (precisely because he or she is a fool) will eventually come to grief. A German friend remembers well the day that Hitler's troops invaded Russia, for he saw his father stalking around his home muttering, "The fool! The fool!" So it always ends for those who think themselves wise but are not. So it always ends for those who are fools or listen to fools.

He said to them, "How foolish you are, and how slow of heart to believe all that the prophets have spoken!" (Luke 24:25)

Be very careful, then, how you live—not as unwise but as wise, making the most of every opportunity, because the days are evil. Therefore do not be foolish, but understand what the Lord's will is. (Eph. 5:15–17)

Ecclesiastes 11:1–8

¹ Cast your bread upon the waters,
    for after many days you will find it again.
² Give portions to seven, yes to eight,
    for you do not know what disaster may come
        upon the land.

³ If clouds are full of water,
    they pour rain upon the earth.
Whether a tree falls to the south or to the north,
    in the place where it falls, there will it lie.
⁴ Whoever watches the wind will not plant;
    whoever looks at the clouds will not reap.

⁵ As you do not know the path of the wind,
    or how the body is formed in a mother's womb,
so you cannot understand the work of God,
    the Maker of all things.

⁶ Sow your seed in the morning,
    and at evening let not your hands be idle,
for you do not know which will succeed,
    whether this or that,
    or whether both will do equally well.

⁷ Light is sweet,
    and it pleases the eyes to see the sun.
⁸ However many years a man may live,
    let him enjoy them all.
But let him remember the days of darkness,
    for they will be many.
    Everything to come is meaningless.

QOHELET'S ADVICE ON living wisely continues, although it is now more generalized and not focused so specifically on the business of bad government and how to survive it. It is, rather, life in its broader scope that appears as the challenge to be met in chapter 11, although there are backward glances to 10:16–20 in the advice given about what to do with "bread" (11:1; cf. 10:19) and about diligence in work (11:6; cf. 10:18).

The opening verses (vv. 1–6) remind the reader of our human inability to control "the times," emphasizing the lack of knowledge (Heb. ydᶜ, vv. 2, 5, 6) that mortals possess. (1) None of us knows "what disaster may come upon the land" (v. 2; lit., "what evil may be upon the earth/land"). Bad times as well as good lie ahead for each of us (cf. 7:14).

(2) As both the movements of the wind and the formation of the body in the womb are deeply mysterious (v. 5),[1] so too is the work of God, who made "all things" (*hakkol*, which can also be translated "both of them"; cf. 2:14; 7:15, 18; 10:19). None of us "understands" (*ydᶜ*, v. 5b) what God does in his world, and none of us has any control over it. When "clouds are full of water" (v. 3), rain inevitably falls; there is nothing that the farmer can do about it. Nor does anyone have control over whether trees, wherever they may be,[2] fall over when the wind blows. Whether such events are predictable or unpredictable, in other words, the point is that mortal beings cannot control them.

(3) Nor is anyone of us able to predict ("know," v. 6) which of all *our* various projects and activities (*our* work) will be successful. We dwell in significant ignorance about what is and will be happening in the world.

In the light of all that we do not know, Qohelet offers his advice. In the midst of uncertainty, but in the expectation sooner or later of trouble, various kinds of actions are to be considered wise. Verse 1 counsels long-term investments: "bread" sent out (rather than NIV's "cast") like a ship on an ocean voyage, apparently wastefully in the short term, but surprisingly floating back to the thrower when the storm is over.

Verse 2 advises distribution of risk, so that when disaster strikes we are not found with all our eggs in one basket (to mention a modern, rather than a biblical, proverb). There has been much discussion among commentators about the precise meaning of this advice. Is it directed at business people, perhaps

---

1. Many Heb. mss. (reading *bᶜsmym* for *kᶜsmym*) suggest that it is not a comparison between "wind" (*ruaḥ*) and "bones" (NIV "body") that is in mind in v. 5, but the entry of the life-breath (another meaning of *ruaḥ*) into the embryonic human being. Whether this reading is correct or not, there is certainly a wordplay apparent in the use of *ruaḥ* in vv. 4–5, as there is in the use of *mlᵓ*, "full," in v. 3 and *mᵉleᵓa*, "full (i.e., pregnant) woman," in v. 5. The world is a mysterious place, whether at the macro- or micro-level, whether one considers full clouds and wind, or full women and the life within them. The play perhaps continues in the use of "seed" in v. 6, since Heb. *zeraᶜ* often refers to semen or offspring.

2. The NIV "to the south or to the north" (v. 3) is better translated "in the south and in the north," i.e., anywhere. The Heb. provides an example of merismus, whereby the extremes are cited as a way of including everything between. "Morning" and "evening" in v. 6 are likewise intended to communicate constant activity throughout the day.

suggesting that they engage in sea-trade, but using several boats? Is it exhorting everyone to generosity and almsgiving, assuring them of help in the future when they find themselves in difficulty? Most likely the advice given here does not have one precise meaning. Instead, Qohelet is inviting his readers to embrace a certain way of looking at the world. They are to take a long-term view of life, which accepts the good with the bad; they are to sit loose to their lives and their possessions, not becoming too attached to them. Certainly such a view of life should affect both business practice and everyday relationships, but it is far from clear that the latter are the primary focus of Qohelet's concern at this point.

What these same readers should *not* do is described in verse 4. They should not try to "beat the system," attempting to find some patterns in the complex combination of predictable and unpredictable events that will enable them to manipulate reality to their own ends and profit. Again, the imagery is drawn from farming, though farming is not likely primarily in view. The danger faced is that in the end people will neither "sow" nor "reap" in life because they are waiting for a more propitious time in which to begin, thinking that they can control the outcome. Qohelet's view throughout the book, by contrast, is that life should be embraced for what it is, good and bad, and that people should give up the pursuit of "profit" from their toil, understanding that living life fully is its own reward.

Thus, in verse 6 Qohelet advocates a course of action opposite to that described in verse 4. Given that reality is the way it is, the wise course of action is not to refrain from sowing and reaping but to engage vigorously and continuously in these activities, knowing that some projects will succeed and some will fail. It is a recapitulation of 9:10: "Whatever your hand finds to do, do it with all your might." He is exhorting his readers not to give in either to the fear of failure or to the false promise of godlike success. At the same time, it is in its own way a call for distribution of risk (as in 11:2). The person who knows he or she does not control destiny, yet launches into life with enthusiastic abandon, will know at least some reward. But the person who thinks it may be possible to control one's destiny and seeks somehow to avoid the risk inherent in living cannot know any reward.

It is the theme of living life to the full while not being unaware of the darker side of things that is taken up in verses 7—8. There is no reason to think that one cannot "enjoy" (śmḥ, v. 8) life under the sun. Yet all will not always be sweetness and light. It should never be forgotten that there will be dark days as well. Although the darkness referred to here may include those dark days of life that represent the invasion of death into the realm of life (cf. 5:17; 12:2), the primary reference is to death itself (since the light with which darkness is contrasted refers to life "under the sun"), which stretches away eternally in the future.

This advice is broadly similar to that in 9:7–10: Live life in the context of the reality of death. If the Hebrew word *hebel* refers to futility, as the NIV suggests, then it is likely a reference here to the futility that awaits us in death. Yet in 9:7–10 the focus is much more likely the *brevity* of the life to be enjoyed, as is also the case with *hebel* in 11:10 (see below). The contrast here in 11:7–8, then, between the days of life that are brief and the days of death that are many likewise suggests that we should understand verse 8 in the following way: "Let him bear in mind the days of darkness, for they will be many; [by contrast] all the days to come [in life] will be brief."

IT IS AS TRUE for the Christian as for the pre-Christian reader of Ecclesiastes that none of us understands what God does in his world and none of us has any control over it. We still dwell in significant ignorance about what is and will be happening in the world. If there is a difference between Qohelet's frame of reference and ours, it lies in what counts as the "long-term view of life" of which he speaks and in the context of which we are counseled to sit loose to our lives and possessions and to live life exuberantly and to the full. Christians have a clearer idea than is ever expressed by Qohelet of what happens beyond death and of what difference this makes to how one views life.

The specific advice about sitting loose to life and possessions and living life to the full is paralleled on many occasions in the New Testament. Jesus counsels his followers not to store up treasures on earth, where they will eventually be lost, but to think in the long term and invest in heaven (Matt. 6:19–21). He illustrates the folly of hoarding possessions out of self-interest in the parable of the rich fool in Luke 12:16–21, going on to advocate a carefree attitude to life in the context of real faith in God and a generosity toward the poor (12:21–34). He teaches us not to try to hold on to life but rather to give it away:

> If anyone would come after me, he must deny himself and take up his cross daily and follow me. For whoever wants to save his life will lose it, but whoever loses his life for me will save it. (Luke 9:23–24)

> I tell you the truth, unless a kernel of wheat falls to the ground and dies, it remains only a single seed. But if it dies, it produces many seeds. The man who loves his life will lose it, while the man who hates his life in this world will keep it for eternal life. (John 12:24–25)

Jesus is particularly opposed to defensive living, as the parable of the talents reveals (Matt. 25:14–30). The two servants who are entrusted with money and use it to make yet more are commended, but the servant who buries it in the ground is not (vv. 24–26):

> "I knew that you are a hard man, harvesting where you have not sown and gathering where you have not scattered seed. So I was afraid and went out and hid your talent in the ground. See, here is what belongs to you."
> His master replied, "You wicked, lazy servant!"

The parable is not really about money, of course, but about the life that we are gifted by God in Christ. The wicked servant, suspicious and distrusting of his master, refuses to live out this life and have it bear fruit. He essentially refuses to "sow and reap" (Eccl. 11:6) because he has capitulated to the lie of the serpent in the garden (Gen. 3:1–5) that God is a "hard man" who harvests where he has not sown and gathers where he has not scattered seed—and even then the servant does not live consistently with that mistaken belief.

The faithful response to divine generosity is generous and exuberant living, in the awareness that Jesus came to give us life "to the full" (John 10:10)—an eternal life that begins in the present (John 5:24). Enjoying this life before and with God, we see everything else from this perspective, behaving as the wise rather than the foolish. The immediately preceding parable in Matthew 25, in fact, develops this very theme of wisdom and foolishness in the context of having a long-term view of life that is taken seriously. The wise virgins are so committed to the project of welcoming the bridegroom (25:1–13) that they ensure a ready supply of oil for their lamps. The foolish virgins have not seriously planned for the event, and they are caught unprepared.

There is never a more propitious time—such as some time in the future—to begin living. Life is to be lived now, and it is to be lived unto God, the generous Giver. "Remember this: Whoever sows sparingly will also reap sparingly, and whoever sows generously will also reap generously" (2 Cor. 9:6).

Man as we know him is a poor creature, but he is half-way between an ape and a god, and he is travelling in the right direction.[3]

Modern people tend to view the movement of history, as far as human beings are concerned, as being from primeval swamp to divinity. The beginning was unpromising, but quite against expectation the forces of evolution

---

3. W. R. Inge, *Outspoken Essays* (1922), cited from *CDRSQ*, 159.

have propelled us along, to a point where we stand on the verge of greatness. We have already overcome so many of the limitations of human life as it was experienced by most of our predecessors. Control of life itself, it seems, is now within our grasp, as we come into possession of the mysteries of DNA and pronounce ourselves capable of manipulating genetic codes so as to bring in utopia—the land of ultimate consumer choices (which hair or skin color do you prefer in your baby? which gender?), freedom from illness and deformity, and happiness for everyone. We look forward to a fresh millennium of endless opportunity.

The Bible presents us with a rather different view of history as it moves from a garden (Gen. 1–3) to a city (Rev. 21). It tells us of a promising rather than an unpromising beginning, as human beings knew and revered their Creator. It replaces the myth of endless rising up toward divinity with the harsh fact of fallenness, as the mortal seeking of immortality brings with it alienation and wickedness. It knows of technological progress but also knows that it can coexist with barbarism. Whereas those who tell the first story look ahead to boundless possibilities stretching into the future, the Bible knows of a sudden ending to everything, as God's sovereignty over his universe is displayed in an ultimate way. Here is the reality that must be juxtaposed with our modern myths.

It is the reality captured many times throughout history in art, literature, and music, but it has perhaps not been better grasped, at least in the description of our present existence, than by Johann Wolfgang Goethe (1749–1832) in his poetic tragedy *Faust*. The character of Faust represents the human dilemma as we stand at a distance from God. We are created with an inherent capacity for creation and for control over nature, yet as we restlessly pursue these things apart from the worship and love of God, we inevitably destroy each other and damage both the natural world and ourselves.

At a more trivial level we may recall the episode in *The Simpsons* where Bart meets a self-help guru who is of the opinion that the obnoxious and out-of-control child has "fully developed ego-integrity," because he does what he feels. As Bart tells his sister: "Lisa, today I am a god." Societal mayhem follows. It is a telling snapshot of the therapeutic culture that treats all social evils as if they were simply problems in the individual psyche and does not even recognize evil as evil. We are, after all, far too adult at this point in our evolutionary development to believe in *evil*.

If we are indeed halfway between an ape and a god ("a little lower than the heavenly beings," Ps. 8:5), the fact of the matter is that, out of relationship with the living God, we are capable of behaving vastly more badly than any ape, and we are traveling precisely nowhere. We cannot control "the times" any more than we can, as a species, control ourselves.

Faced with this awful truth, what are we to do? The wise thing to do is to adjust ourselves to reality. We are to turn to God in repentance for all our foolish vanity about ourselves and for all our mad schemes for gaining control of his universe and using it for our own selfish ends. We must learn to be content with the life God has actually given us to live, rather than pursuing the life that we imagine we might have preferred, and in our contentment learn to live each moment well and to be generous to others. The long-term view must dominate our thinking and our living and inform all our decision making—whether about personal matters, such as what to do with our possessions and investments, or about larger social issues, such as what to do about genetics. All must be judged in the light of the Truth and not in the light of self-serving myths, in the sure and certain knowledge that it is living in the context of the long term that is also best for human beings in the short term.

It is at this point that a particularly Christian repentance may well be necessary, for Christians have all too often managed to give the impression that our faith is about refusing to live a full life in the present so that we may inherit a better life in the future. We have thus seriously distorted the gospel, which is about love, joy, peace, and freedom, as much as it is about patience, kindness, goodness, faithfulness, gentleness, and self-control (Gal. 5:22–23). We are not called to suspend earthly life in the hope of eternal life but rather to live out eternal life *as* earthly life, embracing the reality of the latter as firmly and as affirmingly as God did in becoming incarnate in Jesus.

> Let us not become weary in doing good, for at the proper time we will reap a harvest if we do not give up. Therefore, as we have opportunity, let us do good to all people, especially to those who belong to the family of believers. (Gal. 6:9–10)

Ecclesiastes 11:9–12:8

9 Be happy, young man, while you are young,
and let your heart give you joy in the days
of your youth.
Follow the ways of your heart
and whatever your eyes see,
but know that for all these things
God will bring you to judgment.
10 So then, banish anxiety from your heart
and cast off the troubles of your body,
for youth and vigor are meaningless.

12:1 Remember your Creator
in the days of your youth,
before the days of trouble come
and the years approach when you will say,
"I find no pleasure in them"—
2 before the sun and the light
and the moon and the stars grow dark,
and the clouds return after the rain;
3 when the keepers of the house tremble,
and the strong men stoop,
when the grinders cease because they are few,
and those looking through the windows grow dim;
4 when the doors to the street are closed
and the sound of grinding fades;
when men rise up at the sound of birds,
but all their songs grow faint;
5 when men are afraid of heights
and of dangers in the streets;
when the almond tree blossoms
and the grasshopper drags himself along
and desire no longer is stirred.
Then man goes to his eternal home
and mourners go about the streets.

6 Remember him—before the silver cord is severed,
or the golden bowl is broken;
before the pitcher is shattered at the spring,
or the wheel broken at the well,

> ⁷and the dust returns to the ground it came from,
>   and the spirit returns to God who gave it.
> ⁸"Meaningless! Meaningless!" says the Teacher.
>   "Everything is meaningless!"

QOHELET HAS ADVOCATED the embrace of joy while our brief life lasts, before the darkness of death overshadows us. His thoughts now turn in particular to the young man who, because the time of youth is also brief (11:10), has a still shorter period in which to make the most of his opportunities. In view not only of death (12:6–7) but also of the slow and steady intrusion of death into life as people age (12:1–5), the young man is urged to live life to the full (11:9–10).

Qohelet's view of what a full young life looks like is articulated in 11:9–10. The young man is urged to pursue joy (Heb. *śmḥ*, as in 11:8; NIV "be happy"), to allow his heart to do him good (Heb. *ṭwb*; NIV "give you joy"). This is to be achieved by following the leading of the heart and the eyes—by experiencing the good things in life that are first imagined, desired, or seen. Once again Qohelet affirms the goodness of creation and the rightness of enjoying all that is gifted to us by God in it. The young person is to make the most of it all.

That this is not an invitation to hedonism, especially not to atheistic hedonism, is already clear from our reading of Ecclesiastes to this point. The language used in 11:9a also indicates this, for *yeṭib leb* ("let your heart give you joy") reminds us of *yiṭab leb* ("is good for the heart") in 7:3 (in the midst of a passage exhorting the adoption of a serious attitude to life), while *marʾe ʿenayim* ("whatever your eyes see") reminds us of *marʾeh ʿenayim* in 6:9 ("what the eye sees"), in the midst of a passage advocating that we should rest content with what lies before us rather than wandering off in search of more. It is not foolish behavior that Qohelet advocates here, but life lived out joyfully in the world God has made and governs.

This is what he explicitly reminds us of in the last part of 11:9. The following of the heart and the eyes is to be carried out in the sure knowledge that there is moral accountability in the universe: "God will bring you to judgment [*mišpat*]" (as in 3:16, leading on to the mention of divine judgment in 3:17; 5:8; 8:5–6; cf. also in the final verse of the book, 12:14). Joy is to be pursued within the boundaries set by goodness and virtue—the boundaries set by God.

Yet joy *is* indeed to be pursued. The young man is to make the most of his brief moment of youth (11:10). He is to banish from his heart "frustration" (*kaʿas;* not "anxiety," as in NIV; see comment on 1:18). He is also to cast off "troubles" (*raʿa;* lit., "evil") from his body. In other words, he is to embrace with his whole being (his inner and outer life) the pathway through life that Qohelet has advocated throughout the book (e.g., 2:24–26; 3:12–13, 22; 5:18–20; 9:7–10), rather than conforming himself to and defining himself by the world of frustration and evil that has also been described therein (cf. *kaʿas* in 1:18; 2:23; *raʿa* in, e.g., 5:13, 16).

The world may well be marked by frustration and evil, and indeed "futility" (*hebel;* NIV "meaningless" in 11:10; see comments on 1:3), but a life marked by "brevity" (another trans. of *hebel*) need not also be a life of futility, if life is embraced for what it is and joy is pursued therein. Qohelet's advice is to start early on this pathway of joyful existence before God (Heb. *šaḥᵃrut,* "vigor," in 11:10 is most likely derived from *šaḥar,* "dawn," referring to the dawn of life), in the sure knowledge that life will only ever become more challenging as time passes and as we move inexorably toward the darkness of death: "Remember your Creator in the days of your youth, before the days of trouble [*raʿa*] come" (12:1).

The days of trouble Qohelet particularly has in mind are those of advancing years, which are now graphically described in 12:1b–5, culminating in the description of death and burial in 12:6–7. These are days in which people eventually "find no pleasure" (12:1) because of the challenging circumstances in which they find themselves. They are times of darkness (12:2), similar to the darkness at the close of day (cf. 11:8; contrast the sunlight that is enjoyed in the early morning of life, 11:7, 10) but of a more ultimate nature. For at nightfall the sun, the moon, and the stars themselves do not normally "grow dark," as they do in 12:2. This is the language of the unmaking of creation (note the "light" in Gen. 1:3–5, and the sun, moon, and stars in 1:14–18)—the apocalyptic language of the end times (cf., e.g., Isa. 13:9–10; Joel 2:31; Amos 5:18; Zeph. 1:14–15), in which "clouds" also often feature.

A particularly striking example of the application of this language to the life of an individual is found in Ezekiel 32:7–8:

> When I snuff you out, I will cover the heavens
>   and darken their stars;
> I will cover the sun with a cloud,
>   and the moon will not give its light.
> All the shining lights in the heavens
>   I will darken over you;
> I will bring darkness over your land,
>   declares the Sovereign LORD.

As Ezekiel brings this kind of language to bear on the pharaoh of Egypt, so Qohelet uses it to describe the end of every person, for every person is in the end "unmade" (cf. Eccl. 12:7). It is forceful language with which to address the young man, who is thus confronted with the unmaking of creation as his inevitable future, so that he may take seriously the exhortation to remember his Creator in the present (12:1).

The description of the "unmaking" that follows in 12:3—8 has often been interpreted entirely allegorically by commentators, who have found in the powerful imagery veiled references to multiple aspects of the aging process in the individual.[1] In this kind of reading the trembling "keepers of the house" in verse 3, for example, become the legs or the arms, and the few "grinders" are understood as the teeth. It is, however, difficult convincingly to read bodily parts out of much of the material, which in turn calls into question whether such reference is truly intended in the few examples where there is some plausibility to the idea. This interpretation is not adopted here.

Others have noted funerary aspects to some of the description in verses 3—5 especially and have wondered whether a funeral is in fact being described. The question is, however, whether such language, insofar as one can find it in the passage (again, it is difficult to account convincingly for many of the details in terms of a funeral), is employed so much to depict a funeral as to depict the funereal-type emotions of those who face the apocalyptic darkness just described in verse 2.

The interpretation offered here takes seriously as its cue precisely this apocalyptic introduction to the section and moves on to interpret verses 3—5 as for the most part a generalized description of advancing old age, using the analogy of a community facing the end times. It is not until verse 5b that death and burial come into the picture. Since every translation is also an interpretation, and the NIV translation seems to be influenced by the allegorical approach, the translation offered here of verses 3—5a is different in places from that in the NIV, and it is probably best for the sake of clarity to provide it at this point:

> . . . in the day that the men looking after the house tremble
>   and the powerful cringe,
> and the women grinding corn cease from toil because they are few,
>   and those peering from their windows draw back into the gloom;
> and the doors to the street are closed
>   and the sound of the mill is quieted—

---

1. See Fox, *Qohelet*, 281—98, for a good discussion and analysis of the history of interpretation of 12:1—8.

one used to rise in the morning to the sound of birds,
    but now all the singers are silent.
Yes, they are all afraid of what is above,
    and great terrors lie along the path,
where the almond tree spurns,
    and the locust carries a heavy load,
    and the caper plant fails . . .

As metaphorical darkness falls across the land, various reactions are to be found among its inhabitants, who are characterized in verse 3 as "keepers of the house," "strong men," "grinders," and "those looking through the windows." The "strong men" (ʾanše ḥeḥayil) are probably those of high social status (cf. the use of ḥayil in verses like Ruth 2:1; Isa. 30:6), while the "keepers of the house" are male servants (cf. 2 Sam. 20:3 for the function, albeit that these are females). Likewise, the "grinders" are female servants, whose responsibilities include crushing grain with millstones to make flour for bread (cf. Isa. 47:2, where a princess becomes a servant), and "those looking through the windows" are likely women of higher social status, who have the leisure to sit and watch the world go by.

These four types of people represent the totality of the community— everyone, whether servant or noble, male or female. The male servants "tremble" in response to the apocalyptic darkness, while the male nobility "stoop" (lit., "make themselves crooked"—the same verbal root as in Ecclesiastes 1:15; 7:13, suggesting a fearful cringing in response to the divinely ordained darkening). The female servants cease their work because their numbers have dwindled—presumably because they have fearfully left their workplaces and retired indoors (cf. v. 4). Similarly, the women of leisure "grow dim" (ḥšk, v. 3) in response to the darkening (ḥšk, v. 2), which in context must refer either to emotional darkness and dread or (more likely, in view of the parallel case of the servants) to abandonment of their viewing point at the windows, so that they are (from the perspective of the observer) lost in the gloom.[2]

Verse 4a certainly presents us with a picture of general withdrawal inside the home in the face of the terrors outside. One would expect a similar reference to the cessation of normal activity in verse 4b (which the NIV translates in a way that leaves me puzzled), particularly given the similar meanings of Hebrew špl, "become low" (NIV "fades") and Hebrew šḥḥ, "be bowed down/prostrated" (cf. Isa. 2:11, 17, for the two verbs in parallel). It is better

---

2. It is interesting that Heb. ḥšk, "grow dark," is indistinguishable in an unpointed text from Heb. ḥśk, "refrain from doing something" (as, e.g., in Isa. 54:2; 58:1), which in turn provides a better parallel to Heb. bṭl, "cease," in Eccl. 12:3b. One wonders if it is ḥśk that Qohelet intended, or whether, indeed, a deliberate play on words is present here.

to understand the line in this way: "One[3] used to rise [in the morning] to the sound of birds, but [now] all the singers [lit., daughters of song] are laid low." Either this refers literally to the effect of the darkness on the birds, who depart from their normal activity because of the unexpected darkness (cf. the behavior of birds during a solar eclipse), or it refers metaphorically to the female servants, shut indoors and now no longer audible early in the morning as they go about their everyday tasks. All "sound" (*qol* in both cases) has vanished as its makers have abandoned their everyday activities.

Verse 5 is best taken as a summarizing and climactic review, as well as an expansion in terms of detail, of the apocalyptic events introduced in verses 2−4. It is introduced by Heb. *gam* (not trans. by NIV): "Yes, they are afraid of what is above, and great terrors lie along the path." "They" are all the people mentioned in verses 3−4, both male and female, and the "high thing" (*gaboah;* NIV "heights") of which they are afraid is what is happening above them in the heavens.

The details that are then provided in the admittedly difficult Hebrew text of the middle part of verse 5 are best understood as earthly events that accompany the heavenly darkening—the "great terrors" (*hathattim,* in intensive, duplicated form) that would be encountered if one were brave enough to venture outdoors and walk through the countryside.

The key to understanding the triplet of images in verse 5 (almond tree, locust, caper plant) is found in the mention of the locust (NIV "grasshopper") that "drags itself along" (*sbl* in the Hithpael, only here in the Bible) because it has eaten too much. The Hebrew verb *sbl* means "to bear a heavy load" in the Qal, and (once) in the Pual seemingly refers either to being fat or to pregnancy (Ps. 144:14—the precise sense is uncertain). The sated locust dragging itself away from the fields containing crops would not be a heartening sight to the observer (cf. 2 Chron. 7:13, where the locust [*hagab,* as here] devouring the land is a sign of divine judgment).

The third image, when the line is understood more literally than in the NIV, confirms that the symbolism here is of agricultural disaster: "the caper plant fails [Heb. *prr,* lit., 'breaks (covenant), does not keep its promise to be fruitful']." The NIV's rendering arises from the fact that the fruits of the plant *capparis spinosa* (Heb. *ᵃbiyyona;* i.e., capers) were used in the ancient world not only to stimulate the appetite for food but also as an aphrodisiac (to stimulate sexual appetite). This being so, it must be the case that if the NIV's under-

---

3. The verb is masculine singular, but it is difficult to know why the NIV renders it "men," since nothing in the context suggests that males to the exclusion of females are in view. This is even more the case in v. 5 ("men" again), where it seems clear that *both* men and women are indicated by the plural verb. Among all the many texts in the NIV crying out for revision into inclusive language, these two are prominent.

standing of the first line of our triplet is correct ("the almond tree blossoms," taking Heb. *yane'ṣ* as an incorrectly written form from Heb. *nṣṣ*),[4] the blossoming can only be the brief and unfortunate precursor to the feeding of the locusts. A better option, however, is to take *yane'ṣ* as an unusual form from *n'ṣ*, "to despise, spurn": "The almond tree spurns" those who look to it for fruit.

Ecological disaster is very much a part of apocalyptic descriptions of the end times elsewhere in the Old Testament (e.g., Isa. 24:1–23). The choice of almond tree, locust, and caper plant (among many possible candidates) to represent the disaster here is no doubt significant. The almond tree blossoms in early spring, a time of youth, and its fruitlessness therefore speaks of youth that is past. The locust has devoured the years (as in Joel 2:25; note the ecological destruction throughout the book), so that there are none left. The absence of capers speaks powerfully of the absence of pleasure, whether in food or in sex (cf. Eccl. 12:1). Thus is apocalyptic language brought to bear on the realities, for many, of the individual aging process. These are dark days indeed.

The end times for the individual human being are here pictured, then, in terms of the end of the world: darkness, terror, cessation from normal activity, and an ecological nightmare. It is in this manner that a "man goes to his eternal home" in the grave, mourned by those who knew him. Verses 6–7, with their imagery associated with death and burial, drive the point home. The young man is to remember his Creator "before the silver cord is severed, or the golden bowl is broken [better, 'crushed']; before the pitcher is shattered at the spring, or the wheel broken [better, 'crushed'] at the well." The middle two images communicate the complete destruction of a vessel containing liquid and the consequent escape of the liquid, correlating with the dissolution of the human body and the return of the human spirit to God, who gave it (v. 7b; cf. Gen. 2:7).

The Creator encompasses this whole section (vv. 1, 7), just as he encompasses the whole of life. That the bowl is golden and the cord from which it hangs is silver speaks of the preciousness of the life that is thus given by God and then in due course taken away.[5] The word *bor*, "well," is also used more generally of a pit, including the pit that is a person's grave (e.g., Prov.

---

4. This is the suggestion in GKC, §73g.

5. The first verb in v. 6 is lit. "distanced" according to the Ketib, or "bound" according to the Qere—slightly curious verbs to use in either case. It should be remembered with respect to the Ketib, however, that from the perspective of the "bowl" (i.e., person) heading toward the earth, the silver cord of life is indeed moving upward and away into the distance. The text represented by the Qere, by contrast, seems to have been influenced by the use of Heb. *ḥebel*, "cord, rope," in texts like Ps. 18:5; 116:3, which picture death as a captor entrapping the victim: "before he is bound (with) a silver cord."

28:17; Isa. 14:19). Thus the mention of the well also carries with it connotations of burial—the grave is the site of the breaking of the "wheel."

This reference to the "wheel" (*galgal*) is the only really puzzling element
of the description, since "wheel" does not correlate with "bowl" and "pitcher"
in terms of imagery (especially since well wheels are not well attested in
ancient Palestine). In attempting to explain the appearance of *galgal* here, it
is important to realize that both this word and Hebrew *gulla* ("bowl") earlier
in the verse are both derived from Heb. *gll*, "roll, roll away," along with Heb.
gulgolet ("skull," "head"). In the older Semitic language of Akkadian, indeed,
the word *gulgullu* can refer to "skull," "water pitcher," or "cooking pot."

We may further note that the Hebrew *rṣṣ*, "to crush" (NIV "broken"), which
appears twice in our verse in reference to both *gulla* and *galgal*, is the verb used
in two other places in the Old Testament of the crushing of heads or skulls
(Judg. 9:53, comparing *wattariṣ ʾet-gulgalto* with *wᵉtaruṣ gullat* and *wᵉnaroṣ haggalgal*
in Eccl. 12:6; cf. Ps. 74:14). It is likely, then, that whatever precisely *galgal*
means in Ecclesiastes 12:6, its presence along with *gulla* has as much to do
with wordplay as with anything else.

Thus, Qohelet seems here to be playing on the idea of skulls, as well as
bodies, being broken in death. Whether we are justified in suspecting that
galgal itself does not mean "wheel" in 12:6, but uniquely here in the Old Testament refers to a container such as a cooking pot, is less certain. The shift
in imagery to the broken wheel, which presumably refers to the breaking in
the individual case of the ongoing patterns of life—the successive "times" of
human experience (3:1–8)—may be deliberate, especially if Qohelet is seeking a word similar to *gulla* and connoting "skull." Poets are not by any means
required to conform themselves to audience expectations.

It is worth noting in this connection that 12:8, which brings our section
to a conclusion, is virtually identical to 1:2 (see comments), thus bringing all
the words of Qohelet to a conclusion as well. In fact, both 1:3–8 and 12:1–
7, associated with these summary statements of Qohelet's message, concern
the circularity of things (which a "wheel" well symbolizes). The ongoing circularity of nature is the theme of 1:3–8; the circle of the individual life, however, is eventually broken (12:1–7), although in another sense there is the
completion of a circle as the body is reabsorbed into the ground from which
it came (12:7). It is, of course, the ephemeral nature of human life in contrast
to the ongoing reality of the universe that makes the attempt to wrest extrinsic "profit" out of life a futile one (cf. 1:3 and throughout the book).

All of Qohelet's words are to be understood in the context of this beginning in 1:2 and this end in 12:8. The context of the closing remarks makes
it particularly clear, however, that "meaningless" is not a good translation for
the Hebrew word *hebel*, for the whole thrust of 11:9–12:8 (and 11:7–8 before-

hand) has been that life is a precious gift to be enjoyed, albeit that the days of life are brief (cf. *hebel* in 11:8). A better translation is this:

"Fleeting, fleeting," says Qohelet, "everything is fleeting."

THE RESOLUTELY MALE focus of Ecclesiastes is particularly clear in this passage, addressed as it is to the "young man" (v. 9). Yet there is nothing in the passage that cannot also be taken seriously—and without any real need for "translation" with reference to the whole biblical context—by the young woman. Qohelet's advice is good advice regardless of one's gender.

The advice is premised once again on the idea of the goodness of creation as portrayed in Genesis 1–2. The good Creator God has made all things well and offers creation to human beings not only so that it may sustain them physically as they look after it but also so that they may enjoy it. It is a world of abundance, to which there is free access (Gen. 2:15–16)—a beautiful world as well as a functional one (2:9). Why should anyone *not* follow the lead of heart and eyes in experiencing this abundance and beauty and know joy in God's presence as he or she does so (Eccl. 11:9)? Why is it that so many religious people's lives are instead characterized by fear and defensiveness, by a joy-suppressing legalism that is more concerned "to do the right thing" than to revel in God's blessings?

Qohelet is himself concerned that people "do the right thing," but the first and foremost "right thing" is to revere God as God, and we do not do this by suggesting through the way we live our lives that God is a mean-spirited and harsh tyrant. We do not honor God by proclaiming (falsely) in our attitudes and actions that he is the kind of person to create a wonderful world and then systematically to forbid his creatures to enjoy it. All other "right things" have to proceed, rather, from the primary "right thing" of rightly relating to God as God truly is. It is when this is a reality that virtue flows out of love (for God and for neighbor), rather than out of fear, defensiveness, and legalism, for "perfect love drives out fear, because fear has to do with punishment" (1 John 4:18), and "love is the fulfillment of the law" (Rom. 13:10).

The broader biblical context in which Qohelet's advice must be heard, therefore, includes all those passages in the Gospels where Jesus assails the Pharisees and others for legalism and defensive living, which have entirely missed the point of the Old Testament, and those other New Testament passages that remind us that we are not to be bound by rules of behavior unrelated to the business of loving God and neighbor. This includes many types of Old Testament law (e.g., concerning clean and unclean food), which, it turns out, were temporary measures unreflective of God's broader plans for his world. Colossians 2:13—16 and 1 Timothy 4:1—5 are particularly relevant:

> God . . . forgave us all our sins, having canceled the written code, with its regulations, that was against us and that stood opposed to us; he took it away, nailing it to the cross. And having disarmed the powers and authorities, he made a public spectacle of them, triumphing over them by the cross.
>
> Therefore do not let anyone judge you by what you eat or drink, or with regard to a religious festival, a New Moon celebration or a Sabbath day.

> The Spirit clearly says that in later times some will abandon the faith and follow deceiving spirits and things taught by demons. Such teachings come through hypocritical liars, whose consciences have been seared as with a hot iron. They forbid people to marry and order them to abstain from certain foods, which God created to be received with thanksgiving by those who believe and who know the truth. For everything God created is good, and nothing is to be rejected if it is received with thanksgiving, because it is consecrated by the word of God and prayer.

Everything God created is good! Yet from the beginning human beings have misperceived who God is and failed to appreciate the true freedom that worship of God brings with it, even as we revere and obey him. It is for this reason that Qohelet has also been misread, from ancient times and down to the present, as advocating hedonism in Ecclesiastes 11:9—10. Religious readers of the text have often not been able, in their religiosity, to understand how reverence for God and reveling in life are compatible.[6] They have failed to realize that God is as interested in what we do with our lives as he is with what we refrain from doing. It is worth noting, in fact, that the latter part of 11:9 ("but know that for all these things . . ."), which may be thought in the NIV translation to imply that we should not be too extravagant in our "following," can just as easily be understood as suggesting that God will hold us to account if we do not make it our business to enjoy what he has given us to enjoy.[7]

---

6. Fox, *Qohelet*, 279, notes the ways in which this incomprehension, or at least a fear that Qohelet might be misunderstood as advocating hedonism, already affected translation, interpretation, and discussions about canonical status in early times.

7. Gordis, *Koheleth*, 335—36.

Throughout Ecclesiastes, of course, joyful living is also serious living: We live in remembrance of who God is and of who we are. The great reminder is death—the reality graphically expounded upon in this section as a spur to the young person to live life well. Death constantly breaks in on life in the Old Testament, in the form of illness and other threats to existence, and eventually and noticeably in the aging process. It is for this reason that many psalms speak of the person who is sick or under assault from other chaotic forces as already having one foot in Sheol, the world of the dead. Note, for example, Psalm 18:5–6:

> The cords of the grave coiled around me;
>   the snares of death confronted me.
> In my distress I called to the LORD;
>   I cried to my God for help.
> From his temple he heard my voice;
>   my cry came before him, into his ears.

It is because death breaks in on life all too soon that Qohelet advises young people to make the most of their youth, when they have the strength and the vigor to do so. The apocalyptic language also reminds all readers, however, that there is not only an ending to each individual life but also an ending to all things. This more comprehensive ending is also a reason, biblically, to make the most of our lives while we still possess them:

> Immediately after the distress of those days
>
> > "the sun will be darkened,
> >   and the moon will not give its light;
> > the stars will fall from the sky,
> >   and the heavenly bodies will be shaken."

At that time the sign of the Son of Man will appear in the sky, and all the nations of the earth will mourn. . . .

So you also must be ready, because the Son of Man will come at an hour when you do not expect him. (Matt. 24:29–30, 44)

From the New Testament perspective there are eternal implications bound up with our present decisions. Qohelet does not know of these, even if 12:7 perhaps gives a hint that 3:20–21 is not his last word on the matter—for the human spirit is at least said here to return to God. His concern is, as ever, with the present implications of our decisions. These are not less important, however, than the eternal implications with which they are entirely bound up, for the life that is lived with God now is, for the New Testament, continuous with the life that is lived in eternity.

I had no idea there was a demand for such a thing, but since we suddenly seem to be in a world of don't-trust-anyone-over—20, I guess I shouldn't be too surprised. I don't mind teenagers, really. But the idea of books for teens, written by teens—that gives me the horrors. I have this funny idea that teenagers might benefit from reading work by somebody with a world view a little less limited than their own.[8]

Do not seek death. Death will find you. But seek the road which makes death a fulfilment.[9]

We all need the wisdom that derives from those who possess a worldview a little less limited than our own; but young people, who do not have the advantage of wide experience of life in the present, perhaps require this wisdom more than most. The question is: What should we tell them? We live in a time when there is a palpable crisis of confidence among many adults as to what to say to their children. Having lost hold on God, the culture has by degrees lost hold of any larger story that make sense of our individual and group stories and that provides us with shared codes of ethics and with role models who enact them.

This loss of narrative and direction makes life difficult enough for the adults who have experienced it and who no longer know where they are heading or why, but it makes the task of instructing those younger people who accompany us on the journey particularly difficult. There is a justifiable antipathy to the older, authoritarian "Do as I say, not as I do" approach to parenting, for which young people have little respect in any case; but this leads in practice simply to saying less and less—and having less and less conviction about it. Parenting becomes by degrees a matter of the blind leading the blind and is often simply delegated to those professionals who are thought to know something that we do not—schoolteachers, doctors, psychologists—or to those willing amateurs, like sports coaches, who seem to get on well with children. The delegation of parenting to the TV is not unknown, for the TV speaks with authority and has role models in abundance. "Who are we to tell our children how to live," we cry, "when we have made such a mess of our world and our lives?" And in our lostness, we become more interested in their approval of us and their friendship with us than in being an adult-in-relation-to-a-child at all. We may even look to them for the wisdom that we lack, for they seem to know so much and to be so confident about it.

---

8. Sara O'Leary, *Vancouver Sun* (Aug. 21, 1999).
9. Dag Hammarskjöld, *Markings* (1964), cited from *CDRSQ*, 167.

The biblical narrative—and all the texts that are bound up with it, reflect on it, and comment on it—provides us with the map we need both for our own journey through life and for helping others find the best path. The Bible tells us of the God who creates a good world and, despite all our tendencies to spoil it and to damage both ourselves and others, is *for us* in Christ (Rom. 8:31). It tells us both who we really are and what we are destined to be in this same Christ. It gives us our bearings, fixing our location and lighting the road ahead; it provides us with rules for the journey that will keep us from danger and with stories of others who have made it, so that we can be both warned and encouraged.

This divinely inspired map represents one of the most precious gifts that any adult can be given and that any adult can give a child. It provides us with wisdom beyond our own experience, as worthwhile and yet as flawed as that can be. It gives us a worldview a little less limited than our own.

Qohelet paints a corner of the map. He suggests to us that the young person needs to be told two things. (1) He or she needs to be told about the reality of decay and death and what this signifies about God and ourselves. This is important, because young people often think themselves indestructible and all-but-eternal, and youth culture often seems designed to establish this self-understanding. It is a culture of reality-avoidance—of image rather than substance. As we do not love people if we fail to warn them of the cliff toward which they are running, so we do not love people if we fail to speak to them of death and what it means.

Reality must be proclaimed, especially since many of our young people today, unlike most of their predecessors throughout history, gain little direct experience of death even through their family experience. They have little contact with the dead, even when it is a relative, and little experience of nursing the dying. It is all too easy, therefore, for mortality never to have stared them in the face and to have challenged them about their identity and value.

(2) The young person also needs to be told, however, about the goodness of God and to be encouraged to live responsively to that goodness. This involves virtue, of course, but it also involves joy. It is important to speak about both. We cannot as adults absolve ourselves of the responsibility to speak of right and wrong and of guiding younger people through example and loving discipline to a place where they know the difference and hopefully choose the better option. The first task of a parent is not to win a child's approval or even friendship, but to be a parent.

It must be said at the same time, however, that Christian adults have sometimes been better at telling their children *what* they should do rather than explaining *why* they should do it, forgetting the important distinction drawn in this comment from the seventeenth-century English philosopher John Locke: "It is easier for a tutor to command than to teach."[10] The problem has been created in part because parents *themselves* have not known why various Christian rules should be kept. The point about God's law, however (which is not necessarily the same thing as traditional Christian rules), is that it is good, not only in itself but in respect of its benefits for human life. It is not intended to be repressive but to bring joy. This is the reason why it is so often extolled in the Old Testament, as in Psalm 19:8:

> The precepts of the LORD are right,
>   giving joy to the heart.
> The commands of the LORD are radiant,
>   giving light to the eyes.

God's law is good, and it is attractive. It is the beauty of what is good that adults must above all communicate to children, so that they not only learn to *do* it but also to *love* it. The adults themselves must first be captivated by this beauty, however, for if they themselves are only burdened by the duty of it all, they will not be able to speak convincingly of the joy. Perhaps one reason why religious readers of Ecclesiastes 11:9—10 have not liked the passage very much, indeed, is because it makes them wonder whether they ever really needed, in their younger days, to trade joy for duty as much as they did. They rather resent the idea that young people now should be allowed the privilege of combining the two. Resentment and envy must be replaced by generosity if parenting is to be experienced as liberation as well as discipline. There must be an acceptance that true religion involves true humanness in all its dimensions.

The young person must be presented, in other words, with adults who, even though they presumably (though never certainly) stand nearer to death than the young and are prepared to speak frankly about its reality, do not insist that death should intrude into life too early. They do not refrain from proclaiming God's life-affirming goodness to them nor refuse to enjoy the world in which they live. Young people need those who are prepared to say: "Do not seek death. Death will find you. But seek the road which makes death a fulfilment." Seek a life that, because it is lived seriously (as well as joyfully) before God and in reverence and awe of him, draws the sting of death as "the spirit returns to God who gave it" (Eccl. 12:7).

The counterexample, of the adult as he or she is sometimes encountered by the young, is provided by Victor Meldrew in the British TV series *One Foot in the Grave*—an uncharitable, irascible man possessing little joy and even

---

10. Cited from *CDRSQ*, 70.

less tolerance. If we do indeed stand with one foot in the grave (and we will be perceived by most youngsters as doing so if we are older than about twenty-five), we should at least do so graciously, lovingly, and encouragingly in relating to those who do not. There are too many Victor Meldrews in church and society and not nearly enough St. Augustines, who are prepared to say with that church father: "Love God and do what you like."

Children, obey your parents in the Lord, for this is right. . . .
Fathers, do not exasperate your children; instead, bring them up in the training and instruction of the Lord. (Eph. 6:1, 4)

Children, obey your parents in everything, for this pleases the Lord.
Fathers, do not embitter your children, or they will become discouraged. (Col. 3:20–21)

Ecclesiastes 12:9–14

NOT ONLY WAS the Teacher wise, but also he imparted knowledge to the people. He pondered and searched out and set in order many proverbs. ¹⁰The Teacher searched to find just the right words, and what he wrote was upright and true. ¹¹The words of the wise are like goads, their collected sayings like firmly embedded nails—given by one Shepherd. ¹²Be warned, my son, of anything in addition to them. Of making many books there is no end, and much study wearies the body.

¹³Now all has been heard;
  here is the conclusion of the matter:
Fear God and keep his commandments,
  for this is the whole duty of man.
¹⁴For God will bring every deed into judgment,
  including every hidden thing,
  whether it is good or evil.

WITH THE CLOSING verses of Ecclesiastes 12 we once again hear the voice of the person who has been reporting the words of Qohelet to his "son" (v. 12) and to us but who has only occasionally and ambiguously indicated his presence throughout the book to this point (1:1–2; 7:27). Now he "adds" to the words of Qohelet his own more extended comments. The Hebrew word *yoter* at the beginning of verse 9 (cf. the same word in 2:15; 6:8, 11; 7:11, 16) seems to mean something like "conclusion, epilogue, footnote." We may paraphrase verse 9a in the following way: "I want to add my own perspective on all this: I consider Qohelet a wise man and someone who taught knowledge to the people." This is presumably the very reason why he has passed on Qohelet's words at all. It is not likely that he would otherwise have done so.

Verse 9b further describes the author's view of what Qohelet has been about. Qohelet has listened (Heb. *ʾzn*, although uniquely in the Piel, probably refers to "listening" rather than "pondering," as in the NIV) to many proverbs. He has "searched them out" or examined them thoroughly (cf. Heb. *ḥqr* in verses like Job 29:16; Prov. 18:17, of the thorough examination of legal cases). He has "set them in order" (lit., "straightened them"; *tqn*, as in

Eccl. 1:15; 7:13); that is, he has arrived at just the right interpretation ("got the meaning straight"), understanding what individual proverbs can and cannot mean in the context of traditional and empirically derived wisdom more generally.

The fact that human beings should accept what comes from the hand of God rather than striving with it and struggling against it (i.e., seeking to straighten what is crooked, 1:15; 7:13) does not mean that getting proverbs "straight" in terms of what they mean and do not mean is impossible. This Qohelet has achieved.

Qohelet's task, then, has been to gather and reflect on proverbial wisdom, arriving at its proper interpretation. What he has to say, moreover, is not only "upright" (honest) and "true" (v. 10) but is also expressed in "just the right words," which he has taken pains to find. The Hebrew here is *dibre-ḥepeṣ* (lit., "words of pleasure"), and the reference is probably at least partly to the high aesthetic quality of Qohelet's writing, which we have noted throughout the book (e.g., in the frequent wordplays that are present). The aesthetics are not to be considered simply as dispensable ornamentation, however, but as intrinsic to the communication of what is true—form and content belong together. Qohelet's words are at the same time "words of pleasure" (*dibre-ḥepeṣ*) and "words of truth" (*dibre-ʾᵉmet*, also v. 10).

As his "words," moreover, set the individual proverbs in context and communicate wisdom and knowledge to the people, so too these words themselves have a broader context. They are only some of the many "words of the wise" (*dibre-ḥᵃkamim*, v. 11), which serve a similar function to the "goads" (staffs with sharp nails embedded in them) that were used by drovers in the ancient world to keep animals on a straight path (akin in function, though not in form, to the spurs sometimes used by horse riders today). Wise words not only bring pleasure and truth, therefore, but they also bring pain, as they dispel illusions and confront folly, thereby preventing the receptive listener (however reluctant a listener may be) from straying from the straight and narrow path through life.

The wise themselves are represented in verse 11, indeed, as "masters of collections" (*baʿᵃle ʾᵃsuppot*; NIV "collected sayings"),[1] which has a double meaning. It is not only that they collect and interpret proverbs, as Qohelet did; they are also experts in shepherding the people, prodding them along like the "nails" embedded in goads (cf., e.g., Heb. *ʾsp*, "gather in," of shepherding

---

1. It is not easy to extract the NIV's meaning from Heb. *baʿᵃle ʾᵃsuppot*. It is much better simply to assume that the first part of the verse refers to the words of the wise and the second to the wise themselves with whom the words are closely identified: "The words of the wise are like goads, and the masters of collections like embedded nails given by one Shepherd."

in Gen. 29:3; Mic. 2:12). They are undershepherds, in fact, to the one Shepherd, from whom ultimately comes everything that is beautiful and truthful, if painful—the Creator God, who gives sages to his people for their instruction and benefit.

If the transmitter of Qohelet's sayings has allowed himself a brief commentary and summation (*yoter*, v. 9), this is not because he truly has anything himself to add (*yoter*, v. 12). He has simply been commending Qohelet's words, not adding to them. Indeed, his exhortation is that his "son" should himself beware of making any addition in respect of the words of the wise.

The reason for this is given in verse 12b. The point is probably not, however, that the writing of books goes on endlessly (since it is redundant to say that the making of *many* books is endless), but that the creation of many books is pointless (it has no purpose or "end"). The "father" who thus advises his "son" wishes him to use the books that already exist, not as a foundation for his own literary activity, but as the foundation for living. Qohelet and his company have already thoroughly investigated the "many proverbs" (*mᵉšalim harbeh*, v. 9). There is no profit in adding to their exhaustive work "many books" (*sᵉparim harbeh*, v. 12), nor indeed in engaging in "much study" (*lahag harbeh*) to that end, for such study only "wearies the body" to no good purpose.

The commendation of Qohelet and the warning to the son are thus two sides of the same coin: Wisdom is to be embraced and employed wisely rather than used for one's own foolish ends. The "father" is at this point underlining some of Qohelet's own teaching, in fact, for it is Qohelet who, while commending wisdom, warns the reader to use it well and not unwisely (cf. 1:12–18 and, esp. significant, 10:15, where "a fool's work wearies him" employs Heb. *ygᶜ* in verbal form, as here in 12:12 in noun form).

The commendation of Qohelet and the wise and the warning about a possible *foolish* response to their wisdom are now followed finally by the father's perspective on the *wise* response (vv. 13–14). It is once again based, unsurprisingly, on Qohelet's own teaching: "Fear God and keep his commandments, for this is the whole duty of man [better, 'this is everyone's duty'; lit., 'this is all people']. For God will bring every deed into judgment, including every hidden thing, whether it is good or evil."

Qohelet's consistent advice throughout the book has been to live joyfully and reverently before God in the midst of what is often a complex world, believing that God himself will judge every human work (Heb. *maᶜᵃśeh* in v. 14; NIV "deed"). We remind ourselves here of passages like 2:24–26; 3:12–17, 22; 5:1–7, 18–20; 7:15–18; 8:11–13; 9:7–10; and 11:9–10. This is what the words of Qohelet and the wise are truly for, says the father to his son. They are not primarily designed for use in pursuing our own literary and intellectual ends. They are designed so that we may live well before God, reverencing him and bearing always in mind that the universe is a moral place in which there is accountability for the way in which we spend our days.

I cannot offer a better summary of the end of the book of Ecclesiastes, as it draws together the threads of what has gone before, than the one offered by Craig Bartholomew:

> ... central to the structure of Ecclesiastes is the juxtaposition of the *carpe diem* passages with the enigmatic passages and ... this juxtaposition creates gaps which the reader has to fill. Chapter twelve of Ecclesiastes is fundamental to the book in the answer it gives as to how the gaps should be filled, namely by remembering one's creator....
>
> Ecclesiastes is an ironical exposure of an empiricistic epistemology which seeks wisdom through personal experience and analysis without the "glasses" of the fear of God. This empiricistic epistemology keeps running up against the enigma of life when pursued from this direction, and it appears impossible to find a bridge between this enigma and the good that is visible and which the biblical tradition alerts one to. The resolution of this paradox is found in the fear of God (rejoicing and remembrance) which enables one to rejoice and apply oneself positively to life in the midst of all that one does not understand, including and especially death.[2]

Bridging Contexts

WE ONLY HAVE the Scriptures at all because people have passed them on to us—people like Qohelet's epilogist, Jeremiah's scribe Baruch (Jer. 36:4), or Isaiah's disciples (Isa. 8:16)—and beyond these, the communities of faith who treasured them and lived by them. The mere possession of the Scriptures, however, will do us no good if we do not know how to read them or if we misappropriate them for purposes other than their intended purposes. It will do us no good if they are disabled in any way in respect of their role as goads that should keep the flock of God from straying off the path, or, in New Testament terms, as words "useful for teaching, rebuking, correcting and training in righteousness" (2 Tim. 3:16). It is to the danger of "mere possession" that the author now turns as he brings his book to a close, addressing his "son" (but through him all of us, male and female, who read the book).

Knowledge of how to read the Bible is not something that humans beings innately possess. Acts 8:26—40 tells us of an Ethiopian official on a journey from Jerusalem to Gaza, who is reading from the book of Isaiah. "Do you

---

2. C. G. Bartholomew, *Reading Ecclesiastes: Old Testament Exegesis and Hermeneutical Theory* (AnBib 139; Rome: Pontificio Istituto Biblico, 1998), 268.

understand what you are reading?" Philip asks him. "How can I," he replies, "unless someone explains it to me?" He is reading the words, but he does not know what it all means, in relation to the other Scriptures and to his own existence. Earlier, Jesus had met with his disciples, whose Bible knowledge was presumably fairly good (Luke 24:13–49). Yet it was necessary for him to explain the Scriptures to them so that they could understand what the texts meant (24:25–27, 44–45).

The Bible is a vast ocean of literature that requires steady and patient exploration, under the guidance of both the Holy Spirit and other students, if we are to begin to comprehend how it all fits together and speaks to us with God's voice—if we are to become those who "correctly handle the word of truth" (2 Tim. 2:15). An important part of the process is to know how to "set things in order," as Qohelet did with his proverbs, for we only truly understand what one part of Scripture means when we set it in relation to another, which may be emphasizing rather different things. What can truly be made of a single proverb can only be seen if we set it rightly in the context of another, and God's Word can only be heard as we engage in that process of ordering. Scripture must interpret Scripture, each part playing a role in forming our view of the whole. That is essentially what we have been doing in these Bridging Contexts sections—setting Ecclesiastes in the broad biblical context in order to hear what God might be saying to us.

Misreading the Scriptures is not, however, as serious an error as misappropriating them for purposes other than their intended purposes. The devil himself can misappropriate God's words for his own ends, as we see all too clearly in the narrative of Jesus' temptation in Matthew 4:1–11. There Satan quotes from Deuteronomy and Psalms in his attempt to lead Jesus astray, before openly revealing his real agenda ("All this I will give you . . . if you will bow down and worship me," v. 9). Scripture is sometimes used in the cause of the idolatry of the self.

The teachers of the law and the Pharisees are often criticized by Jesus, likewise, for using the Scriptures in pursuit of their own agendas while completely missing the point of what they are saying (Matt. 21:33–44; John 5:36–47). Similar criticisms are found elsewhere in the New Testament, as in Peter's comments on the apostle Paul in 2 Peter 3:16:

> His letters contain some things that are hard to understand, which ignorant and unstable people distort, as they do the other Scriptures, to their own destruction.

The author of Ecclesiastes is concerned about a particular form of the idolatry of the self that is often found among scholars. It occurs when the main purpose of the Holy Scriptures is perceived to be not to contextualize, relativize, and challenge the scholar as a frail creature of dust who exists and prospers by the grace of Almighty God but rather to provide the scholar with a platform on which to construct a writing career. The text becomes the raw material out of which he or she constructs beautiful idols.

It is all too easy, says the author, to use even wisdom completely foolishly in this way and to utterly, utterly miss the point. Wisdom must be allowed to do its painful work on our lives, as the goads bite; we must resist the temptation to reach for the painkiller, which is scholarly success, especially in publishing. The "ordering" of things is all well and good, so long as chaotic disruption to our lives is not thereby excluded—that is, so long as we do not arrange things in order to keep God's Word at arm's length, rather than with the intention of hearing it yet more clearly and obeying it.

The "professor" is really the analogy to Don Quixote. Perhaps he will become an even more profound comic figure. Someone who has no idea or humanness in the direction of personally wanting to act and live in imitation of prototypes but who believes that it is a scholarly question. "The truth" is crucified as a thief, is scorned, spit upon before it cries out, dying: Follow me. But the "professor" does not understand a word of it; he conceives of it as a scholarly question.[3]

Much learning does not teach understanding.[4]

To know the Bible is not necessarily to know God, and to cite it is not necessarily to communicate God's Word. The history of the misuse of the Bible in legitimizing human agendas and institutions that Christians should never have been found supporting is, in fact, a long one; American slavery in the nineteenth century and South African apartheid in the twentieth are only two of the more recent examples.

Much of the problem has its roots in a failure to "order" properly the whole redemptive history of which the Bible speaks, such that the church has sometimes come to think of its role as being the socially conservative one of legitimating and perpetuating the fallen state of things as described in Genesis 3, rather than the socially progressive one of being the light by means of which God at least partially transforms society and restores his kingdom as envisioned

---

3. Soren Kierkegaard's *Journals and Papers*, vol. 3 (L-R), trans. H. V. and E. H. Hong (Bloomington: Indiana Univ. Press, 1975), entry 3568. Entries 3585, 3578, and 3872 are also worthy of consideration.

4. Heraclitus, *Fragments* (6th century B.C..), cited from *CDRSQ*, 120.

in Genesis 1–2. Thus, at different times Christians have opposed the introduction of anesthetics in childbirth (on the grounds that women are supposed to suffer during childbirth, 3:16) and equal-rights legislation for women
(on the grounds that a husband should rule over a wife, 3:16).

Such interpreters have had no grasp of the larger movement of that Scripture that should guide us in the interpretation of its parts, and in particular
they have failed to understand what it means that history, for the Christian, not
only has a beginning and an end, but also a center in Christ, which casts light
both backward and forward. Much learning does not necessarily teach understanding, nor does it necessarily prevent us from shutting the kingdom of
heaven in people's faces and traveling over land and sea to win a convert, only
to make that one twice as much a child of hell as we are (see Matt. 23:14–15).

Of all the many misappropriations of the Bible that are possible, however,
there can scarcely be one that is more grievous than that which the scholar
commits when he or she takes the words of Holy Scripture and uses them
for self-promotion and self-worship, multiplying these words endlessly in
parody of the story of the loaves and the fishes (Matt. 14:15–21). If it is the
mark of the fool, indeed, to overproduce everything—including words (Eccl.
5:1–7)—then we are living in exceedingly foolish times. Never have so
many books and articles touching on biblical texts been written and published
as in the past fifty years. Yet this explosion of literature has had little to do
with genuinely new and worthwhile insights as to how God is addressing us
through his Word. It has had much more to do with the fact that the Bible
has proved itself useful to those whose business is "gain."

Research and publication are necessary footholds on the ladder of academic success, and few can progress without them. They are also important
for the institutions that employ the scholars, in their quest to climb higher
up the ladder of success and to receive funding from the various bodies who
are impressed by such things. So it is that we have had our literary explosion,
yet little of what has been written is at all comparable in worth to the ancient
classics, which were written in different times and by scholars with different
motivations. The usefulness of much of our modern scholarship can easily be
assessed, in fact, simply by asking of any particular piece of work: "So what?"

This has not deterred publishers from publishing it, even though it be of
such an intellectual and moral quality that it would have been instantly
returned to the author half a century ago. For publishers, too, make vast
sums of money out of the Bible industry, and they are not anxious to ask too
many questions of it. They are not likely to refuse to publish a book simply
on the basis that we have too many books already and that another book is
not necessary. Much more relevant as a consideration is whether a projected
book will sell. Publishers constantly and actively canvas authors to write

books, in fact, so that the overproduction will continue and the money will keep rolling in. It is a pity that one cannot say that Christian publishers generally dance to a different tune, but it is not visibly evident that they all do.

It is important to consider what Jesus would do—he who cleared the temple of those who had defiled it in pursuit of their own gains (Matt. 21:12–13)—if he were to come into the midst of this Bible industry and execute judgment on it. It is terrifying to imagine (and I speak now as a scholar myself) what he *will* do when each of us stands before him—when it is no longer enough to defend our own readings against all-comers, because it is only his reading that matters; when it is no longer enough only to have been interested in the artistry of the text and not in its truth; when our own books are judged not on their popularity among others who also cannot see that the emperor has no clothes, but only on their intrinsic worth when assessed in the light of God's kingdom. As a friend of mine once said, "There is only one book review that really matters," and that final book review is one that allows no objection or response. Much learning does not necessarily teach understanding, and it cannot absolve us from accountability before the truth.

All this brings us in the end to the question of what this commentary on Ecclesiastes is *for*. There is the distinct possibility that it was never necessary in the first place—that it is simply one more example of the unnecessary multiplication of words to which Qohelet's "epilogist" refers. I think I have learned something about Ecclesiastes in writing it, however, and something more about God and the Christian life. I hope that the reader will also have learned something and will not simply be better informed as a result, but be a truer worshiper of the triune God.

It is certainly the case that my work can only be justified if it has indeed enabled the reader to hear Qohelet more clearly and through him to hear God more clearly. There is no other defense of the exercise. Nor is there any defense of the act of reading the commentary if it does not result in obedience to the Word of God as it is heard in the Scriptures. We will not be saved simply because we have read commentaries and taken notes. We will not even be saved because we have read the Bible or have preached brilliantly from its texts.

> See to it, brothers, that none of you has a sinful, unbelieving heart that turns away from the living God. But encourage one another daily, as long as it is called Today, so that none of you may be hardened by sin's deceitfulness. We have come to share in Christ if we hold firmly till the end the confidence we had at first. As has just been said:
>
> > "Today, if you hear his voice,
> > do not harden your hearts
> > as you did in the rebellion." (Heb. 3:12–15)

Introduction to Song of Songs

UNLIKE THE BOOK of Ecclesiastes, which is explicitly associated with King Solomon only in the tradition and not in the text, the Song of Songs is clearly connected with this particular king of Israel, not only by way of references to him in the body of the text (1:5; 3:7, 9, 11; 8:11–12), but also by way of the heading to the whole song itself. Song of Songs 1:1 translates literally: "The Song of Songs which is to Solomon."

It has been the common Jewish and Christian view up until modern times (although it has not been universally held)[1] that Solomon indeed wrote this song—something reflected in the NIV's translation of 1:1 as "Solomon's Song of Songs." Yet Solomon only appears in this book in third-person references, and none of the first-person speeches are explicitly connected with him. Even at this level, then, it does not read most naturally as a composition *authored* by Solomon. Moreover, when the essentially negative character of most of the material mentioning Solomon or "the king" is recognized (see further below), the case for Solomonic authorship is further weakened.

The heading itself certainly does not demand it, for Heb. *lᵉ*, "to," can also signify that the song was written *for* Solomon (although it is unlikely that a song critical of Solomon would have been composed *for* him by a contemporary scribe) or that it *concerns* Solomon. It is this last possibility that is accepted in this commentary. The Song of Songs is *about* Solomon to some extent, just as Ecclesiastes also concerns Solomon to some extent. In Ecclesiastes, this king appears as a famous character who represents power and wealth, enabling Qohelet to explore these aspects of human reality and to offer his readers an alternative vision of life to the one Solomon represents. In Song of Songs, the king also appears as a character who represents power and wealth, but the real focus of attention is on his famed possession of women (alluded to in Eccl. 2:8 and described above all in 1 Kings 11:1–8). This feature allows the biblical author to explore important aspects of human reality—on this occasion love and sexual intimacy—and to present to us a particular vision of the world for our consideration. Solomon is the foil for this author's broader purposes, for Solomon's relationships with women represent the antithesis of the relationship between a man and a woman that the author wishes us to admire and (implicitly) to imitate.

---

1. Jewish tradition has also suggested Hezekiah or Isaiah as the author.

Our author's agenda is already announced in the first part of the heading, for the expression "Song of Songs" communicates, like "vanity of vanities" in Ecclesiastes 1:2 and elsewhere, a superlative.[2] We are reading, we are told, the very best, the most sublime of songs, as we read of the love between a man and a woman that is expressed here. That is quite a claim when one considers how many songs (Heb. *šir*) there are in the Old Testament (see the titles, e.g., of Ps. 30, 45, 46, 48, 65).

The identity of this author is unknown, as it is in the case of Ecclesiastes. The date of the composition is likewise uncertain. Although the Song of Songs clearly evokes the Solomonic era, whether in general terms (alluding to the wealth and luxury of Solomon's court as we hear of it in 1 Kings 2–11; see esp. comments on Song 3:6–11) or in its specific details (e.g., the mention of the city of Tirzah in 6:4, an important city of the time, 1 Kings 14:17), it is not clear whether it does so from near or far, chronologically speaking. The broad connections between the Song of Songs and other ancient Near Eastern literature of a comparable sort do not help us to be precise even about the century or two within which this song might be placed. The language of the book probably indicates a postexilic rather than a preexilic date overall (e.g., the Persian loanword *pardes*, "orchard," in 4:13; cf. Neh. 2:8), but that is as far as we may go.[3]

The usual manner and extent of speculation exists in the commentaries as to whether some parts of the Song of Songs are earlier than others and whether

---

2. M. H. Pope, *Song of Songs* (AB; Garden City, N.Y.: Doubleday, 1977), 294, provides other examples of the same kind of construction. I will repeatedly cite Pope's work in this commentary, since it is by far the most detailed reference commentary on the Song and frequently gives excellent treatments of matters that are important in themselves but cannot be pursued at length in our own reflections on the text.

3. Thus R. Gordis, *The Song of Songs and Lamentations*, rev. ed. (New York: Ktav, 1974), 23, is almost right when he says of the Song of Songs (which he regards as a *collection* of songs): "Being lyrical in character, with no historical allusions, most of the songs are undatable." His choice of the word "most" is dictated by his inexplicable insistence that Tirzah could only have been mentioned in a text predating 876 B.C. and that 3:6–11 could only have been composed on the occasion of one of Solomon's marriages. Pope makes a similar kind of error when he claims that "the antiquity of at least parts of the Songs cannot be doubted in light of the Ugaritic parallels" (*Song*, 27). That which cannot actually be doubted is the antiquity of some of the language and imagery that the Song employs, whether reflected in Ugaritic cultic texts or in ancient Egyptian love lyrics (see M. V. Fox, *The Song of Songs and the Ancient Egyptian Love Songs* [Madison, Wis.: Univ. of Wisconsin Press, 1985]). It is also true, however, of *modern* Palestinian songs that offer parallels to the Song (Pope, *Song*, 56–66) that they employ language and imagery used in ancient times, and no one suggests that this makes these songs themselves ancient. See further A. Brenner, *The Song of Songs* (OTG; Sheffield: JSOT Press, 1989), 41–47, 57–61; R. E. Murphy, *The Song of Songs* (Hermeneia; Minneapolis: Fortress, 1990), 41–57.

it is really only the final form of the book that is as late as the postexilic period. But since it is only the final form of the book that we have and on which we are commenting, it is a waste of precious time and energy to engage with such discussion. We pass immediately to a much more important matter: How has the Song of Songs been read, and how should we read it now?

The "Original Meaning" of the Song of Songs

HISTORICALLY THERE HAVE been two primary ways in which the Song of Songs has been read by Jews and Christians: (1) as a text that concerns the love and sexual intimacy of human beings, and (2) as a text that uses the language of human love and intimacy to speak of something else—the relationship between God and Israel, perhaps, or between Christ and the church or individual members of the church (including the Virgin Mary). These two ways of reading have commonly been referred to as the *literal* and the *allegorical* respectively.

(1) The former way of reading the text is perhaps reflected already in the words attributed to Rabbi Akiba ben Joseph (c. A.D. 40–135) by *t. Sanh.* 12:10, where he attacks those who chant the Song of Songs "in the banquet house," which has commonly been interpreted as an ancient tavern.[4] It is certainly found later in the writing of the church father Origen (c. A.D. 185–254), who allowed that the Song of Songs might be a marriage song related to Solomon's marriage to Pharaoh's daughter (1 Kings 3:1), even though he was more interested in its "higher sense" as it applied to Christ and the church or the individual believer.

It is also alluded to in various other writings of the fathers (e.g., Gregory of Nyssa and Jerome in the later fourth century), albeit usually only in their cautionary or prohibitive statements about how other people should *not* read the Song of Songs. It is already clear from such allusions that a literal reading was certainly practiced by substantial numbers of Christians in the postapostolic period. We will probably never know how widespread it was, however, since great efforts were expended in suppressing the views of even well-known exponents of such a reading.

It is only from the attacks that others made on it, for example, that we know about Theodore of Mopsuestia's fourth-century commentary, which interprets the Song as erotic literature sung by Solomon in defense of his love

---

4. See Pope, *Song*, 210–29, however, for a different view. Gordis, *Song*, 9, also points out that rabbinic discussion of the order of the Solomonic composition of Song of Songs, Proverbs, and Ecclesiastes implies a literal interpretation of the Song, when it is claimed that it is young men who sing songs like the Song and older men who write proverbs and then, later, voice disenchantment with life.

for and his marriage to an Egyptian princess. Jovinian, a Roman monk who made it his business around the same time to attack asceticism in the church and in contrast to Theodore (who opposed the Song's place in the canon) cited the Song of Songs as a defense of the virtue of marital sexual love, was roundly condemned by both Augustine and Jerome. The Council of Constantinople in 550 famously outlawed the literal reading of the Song of Songs altogether, enshrining the allegorical interpretation henceforth as the only right interpretation. The immediately succeeding centuries provide little evidence of literal reading in our surviving sources (although absence of evidence is not, of course, evidence of absence).

It was in the post-Reformation period that a more literal approach once again surfaced among Christians, although there were many Protestant writers who initially continued to read the text allegorically in the manner of the Targum (see below), understanding it as an account of church history rather than of God's history with Israel. The literal reading often became in the succeeding period a weapon in the hands of rationalist writers, who wished to exclude the Song of Songs from the canon of Scripture altogether on the grounds that its graphic sexual content was obscene. At the same time, continuing resistance to the literal reading seems often to have been grounded, not so much in any deep initial conviction that the book was originally intended to be read allegorically, but in the belief that the content, if read literally, would indeed *be* obscene, and therefore problematic for the Christian.[5] This latter belief, being culturally rather than biblically rooted, has increasingly come to be questioned as time has passed and as readers have asked why a description of human love and sexual intimacy should trouble a Christian reader. The consequence is that the literal approach has become much more popular among Christian readers in modern times than it ever was (so far as we can tell) in ancient times. The popularity of such a reading is shared among modern Jewish and nonreligious readers of the text.

(2) The allegorical reading of the Song of Songs is probably at least as old as the literal reading. There is no solid evidence that it is older. The LXX translation of our text (dating from around 100 B.C.), for example, reveals no explicit evidence of allegorization. Akiba himself, one of the principal founders of rabbinic Judaism, stands at the origin of the establishment of normative Jewish interpretation of the song as an allegorical account of the history of the relationship between the Shekinah (the divine presence) and Israel from the Exodus to the Exile and beyond, but our sources present

---

5. Thus, John Wesley was of the opinion, e.g., that the description of the woman and her lover could not *with decency* be taken to refer to human characters (see Pope, *Song*, 130).

Akiba as contributing to an ongoing debate about the interpretation of this song, which is already to be found at his time among the Scriptures.

We have no idea (despite the misleading impression that has sometimes been given on this point) how the Song of Songs came to be regarded as Scripture in Judaism in the first place and which kinds of reading were adopted by those who embraced it as such.[6] All we know is that at a certain point toward the end of the first century A.D., a dispute arose in the Jewish community about whether the Song of Songs should indeed be regarded (as it already was) as Scripture and that the issue of how to interpret it was tied up with that dispute. Akiba championed both its scriptural status and its allegorical reading, but we cannot deduce from this that every other first-century Jew who viewed it as Scripture also read it allegorically.

It is certainly the case that after Akiba the allegorical reading predominated among Jews for many centuries (although literal reading was by no means unknown). The Targum, for example, understands the Song of Songs as a history of salvation in five movements (Exodus and Sinai, 1:2–3:6; Solomon's temple, 3:7–5:1; the monarchy, 5:2–6:1; the return from Exile, 6:2–7:11; the end times, 7:12–8:14). The medieval exegete Rashi (eleventh century) characterized it as speaking of this history in the language of a woman saddened by living as a widow and longing for her love. Some medieval and early modern Jewish readers read it as referring to the union of individual body and soul, or of the active and passive intellects, or of Solomon and his "bride" Wisdom.

Christian interpreters have tended on the whole to follow the Jewish lead, beginning with Hippolytus (c. 200) and then Origen. The real focus of the dispute between Jews and Christians in the postapostolic period was not, indeed, on whether the Song of Songs should be read as an allegory (this was widely agreed) but on the true reference of the allegory. Whereas Jews

---

6. A recurring claim throughout the history of interpretation has been that the Song would never have been accepted into the canon of Scripture had it not been understood allegorically. This claim tells us much more about what has been conceivable to those who have made it, however, than it does about any factual historical reality that can be described. It arises not from evidence but from a refusal to believe that anything "profane" or "earthly" could be found in Holy Scripture—as if all the Scriptures were not profoundly human as well as divinely inspired, and as if creation and redemption had nothing to do with each other. An alternative view (albeit just as unproveable) is attributed by Gordis, *Song*, 43, to M. Jastrow: "It entered the canon not by vote, but because of its inevitable human appeal. Love is sacred even in passionate manifestations"; we may also note M. Goulder, *The Song of Fourteen Songs* (JSOTS 36; Sheffield: JSOT Press, 1986), 86: "The Song won its way to favor and into the Canon by virtue of its message [it takes a broad view of whom Jews may rightly marry, i.e., Gentile women], its beauty, its eroticism and its false ascription." See further the excellent discussion of all the historical uncertainties in Murphy, *Song*, 12–16.

predominantly read the book as concerning God and Israel, Christians naturally read it as concerning God or Christ, on the one hand, and the church or the individual Christian, on the other. Bernard of Clairvaux (twelfth century), for example, wrote voluminously on this book as a text concerning the Word of God and the human soul in a love relationship.

The medieval period saw the progressive development of Christian allegorical reading, with more and more of its details interpreted as referring to some aspect of the God-human relationship. The period since the Reformation has seen progressive disillusionment with the approach in its traditional Jewish and Christian forms as readers first began to ask whether much of the allegorization of the detail was not fanciful and then began to doubt whether ancient nervousness about the literal reading was justified. The notion that the text truly speaks of something other than what is apparent on the surface level survives, however, in approaches that understand this song as about, among other things, sacred marriage and ancient fertility rites.[7] While it is not to be questioned that various connections (unsurprisingly) exist between the Song of Songs and its broader ancient Near Eastern environment, some of the work done in this area is no more plausible than the most extreme of the medieval efforts at reading behind the text to find out what is "really" there.[8]

---

7. Thus, rightly, Gordis, *Song*, 4: "The most modern form of the allegorical theory regards our book as the translation of a pagan litany." The critique throughout pp. 4–10 is, though dated, still worth reading.

8. It is one of the rich ironies of modern biblical scholarship in general that it is precisely those who most resolutely desire to be "modern" and so roundly condemn the medieval search for Christian meanings beneath the literal sense of the text, who are so often to be found insisting that the "real" meaning of a biblical text is to be found, likewise, somewhere other than in the literal sense of the text as it stands. The thoroughgoing attempt to interpret the Bible as if it were "really" much more like the surviving literature from surrounding ancient Near Eastern cultures than is actually the case is only one spectacular example of the phenomenon, and it is scarcely any more helpful than the attempt to do the opposite (i.e., to interpret the Bible as if it had no significant points of contact with surrounding cultures). The fact is that there are indeed many echoes of other ancient Near Eastern literature to be found in biblical texts like the Song (described at length by Pope, *Song*, passim), esp. where the language and imagery concern fertility and sexual activity, but this does not of itself prove that, e.g., the Song is "really" about a sacred marriage rather than about an ordinary human relationship. It only means that the Hebrew poetry has been influenced in various ways, unconsciously and consciously, by its wider literary environment, which it may be echoing as much to distance itself from it (cf. the case of Gen. 1–11) as to embrace its governing ideology. We might as well suggest, with J. G. Snaith, *Song of Songs* (NCB; London: Marshall Pickering, 1993), 5, that "perhaps the Song was included in the canon because it was a non-mythological, non-cultic, outright, open celebration of God-given sexual love." Texts must first and foremost be interpreted in their immediate literary, cultural, and historical environments and must not simply be passed through a reductionist sieve in order to suit some prior theory about unified cultural and religious development.

If literal and allegorical readings of the Song of Songs have thus been in evidence throughout the history of interpretation, the question that arises and must be addressed here in the first instance is this: Which manner of interpretation is most likely to correspond to the manner of interpretation intended by the original author[9] of the book? This is an extraordinarily difficult question to answer. It is somewhat difficult to believe that an ancient Hebrew author primarily intent on speaking of a relationship between God and God's people would have composed the Song of Songs in precisely the way that he or she did, with such heavy emphasis on the erotic aspects of love and particular passages such as 8:5b–7, where the woman (i.e., on this reading, the people of God) takes the initiative in "rousing" the man's (i.e., God's) love. We cannot *rule out*, of course, the possibility that allegory is primarily intended, especially since the man-woman relationship is alluded to elsewhere in the Old Testament as analogical to the divine-human relationship (e.g., Ezek. 16). Yet the apparent surplus of language (much of which is never persuasively accounted for by allegorical interpreters) is surprising if this is the case, and certainly nothing else in the Old Testament really prepares us for such an explicitly sexual text about God's relationship to his people—not even Ezekiel 16. One possible way in which to account for this "surplus" is to hypothesize that the person responsible for the book borrowed from elsewhere either pre-existing poems, or at least an existing poetic tradition, with a view to using this already existing material (originally concerning human love) to speak of the divine-human relationship. One cannot discount the possibility, even if we have no direct evidence that this is what actually happened.

If one hesitates in affirming that allegory was the primary intention of the author, however, then at least one must say this: It is impossible to rule out allegory (or at least a second and deeper sense of the text) as one aspect of the text's intentionality. It is here that modern interpreters, in their understandable reaction against the claim that the text is *only* allegory and especially against implausible allegorization at the level of the text's details, have tended to err. They have assumed that if we once demonstrate the unlikelihood that the text was originally meant primarily as allegory, and if we have demonstrated the absurdity of many of the detailed allegorizations that have been offered historically, we have also thereby dismissed allegorization completely as an aspect of the author's likely intentions.

Authors need not have only one aim in writing or only one intention in the words they use. Especially when we consider the language used elsewhere

---

9. I use the term "author" as a shorthand, without claiming any knowledge as to whether there really was one author rather than several. This question is much less important than the question as to whether the Song has any literary coherence as it stands, which I affirm (see below).

in the Old Testament of the God-human relationship, it becomes clear that we cannot rule out the possibility that allegory was at least partly in the mind of the author of this song. If Israel is elsewhere a bride or a vineyard (Isa. 5:1–7; Hos. 1–3); if the whole Bible story begins with a picture of intimacy in a garden, between God and humans and between human and human (Gen. 1–2); and if the individual soul can be said to desire God in much the way that a lovesick lover desires an absent beloved (e.g., Ps. 42:1–2); then it becomes difficult when reading the Song of Songs entirely to dissociate what is said of human love from what might be implied in such speech about divine-human love.

Nor is it clear, once we have remembered these other texts and have recalled in addition the close connection that is generally made throughout the Bible between our relationship with God and our relationships with each other, why we should feel compelled to make any attempt at dissociation. Why can the text not be assumed in its original intention to be both about human love and about divine-human love? Why we should believe that we have to choose, in assessing the original intention of the author of this book, between literal and allegorical interpretation?

It is fairly clear why Christians of earlier times felt that *they* had to choose, for they lived in a culture that made it difficult for them to recognize a song about human love and sexual intimacy as being *at the same time* a spiritual song. Whether we think of the environment of the earliest Christians within a Roman empire so heavily influenced by Greek thought, or of the later Christians who inhabited the Holy Roman Empire and the Europe of the Renaissance, both of which were powerfully shaped by the earlier Greco-Roman culture, we are thinking of cultures that had difficulty in accepting that what was *natural* could also in the end be *good*.

This was particularly true of sexual expression, which was routinely associated with the unholy and the impure; conversely, holiness and purity were associated with sexual renunciation. The Christianity that was birthed in a Greco-Roman culture and was marked by the binding together of celibacy and spirituality proved sadly unable to offer any sustained critique of this culture; in due course, in fact, Christianity came to offer this renunciation of the sexual powerful legitimization, as a heavily ascetic Christianity became the official religion of early and medieval Europe. Such a Christian tradition, dominated by celibate theologians who posited a great gulf between the earthly and the heavenly, the fleshly and the spiritual, and many of whom were clearly frightened by sexuality, was bound to see in the literal reading of this song a profound threat to the whole order of things—a text that could not be reconciled to the dominant ideology.

Allegorization became the powerful means of ensuring that earth and heaven, flesh and spirit, remained separated by some distance and that the terrors of the sexual nature were kept at bay. Origen himself provides us with some of the best insights into the worldview that we are describing here—the man who so resolutely insisted that the prerequisite to acquiring spiritual love was the despising of all bodily things and who allegedly castrated himself in order to deal decisively (as he presumably thought) with his sexual desires.

Thus, we can understand why Christians of earlier times believed that they had to choose between literal and allegorical interpretation of the Song of Songs, but we can equally understand just how seriously misguided they were in this belief. In retrospect it is obvious, in fact, how much more they were influenced by Plato's opposition of the earthly/physical and the heavenly/spiritual and by gnostic thinking, which understood the body as a prison from which the soul must escape, than they were by biblical thinking about the nature of the human being and of human sexuality, as well as biblical teaching on creation and redemption.

The Bible teaches us of a creation that is good and of a sexuality that is a hallowed aspect of what is good (Gen. 1). It knows that sexuality is touched by sin and damaged, as are all aspects of creation; but redemption, biblically, is not about escape from createdness. It is about the restoration of the image of God in human beings (as well as the renewal of all creation); such restoration involves, at least on this side of eternity, the restoration of sexuality and sexual expression as it should be under God. Biblical thinking about redemption thus involves no great dichotomy between creation and redemption or between body and soul. It does not know of any future life with God, in fact, that does not entail the resurrection of the *body*.

There is no justification, then, for thinking that Christian living must necessarily be ascetic living or that ascetic living is somehow more spiritual than living that is not ascetic. God made everything good—and it remains good, even though marred by sin. Sexual expression remains good in itself, even though touched by sin (whether committed by us or upon us). It is indeed one of the wonderful things about the biblical perspective on the world that it honors what is ordinary and human, in itself and for its own sake. The Christian life is the ordinary human life, redeemed and sanctified in all its ordinariness and lived out before the God who created it.[10] The fact that

---

10. The great distance between a properly Christian and a gnostic view of the world is demonstrated clearly by texts such as *The Acts of Thomas*, 12–14, which announces the incompatibility of marriage with the bridegroom Jesus and ordinary, earthly marriage, which leads to sexual intercourse (considered dirty), the cares of life and children, and ultimately eternal damnation. Something close to the gnostic view of the world unfortunately

individual Christians or even whole sections of the church have failed, tragically, to grasp this truth historically and down to the present, and have been particularly confused about sex, does not alter its status as biblical truth.

We do not need to choose between literal and allegorical interpretation of the Song of Songs, as earlier generations of Christian readers felt they had to. There is no good reason to see erotic, earthly love as problematic either in itself or in its ability to speak by analogy of the divine-human relationship. Even if *we* had a problem here, of course, we should still have to ask whether we had good grounds for thinking that the original *author* found any difficulty in this area—and there is in truth no good reason to think that he or she did.

All this is not to claim that we have somehow proved what the original intentions of the author really were—certainty on that point is beyond us. Yet certainty is not necessary for interpretation to proceed. Our sections headed Original Meaning in the commentary that follows will simply adopt a fairly indeterminate, descriptive approach to the text, avoiding any question of what it is that the text is "referring" to outside of the drama of the male-female relationship that is being enacted within the text itself. We will address questions of reference in the Bridging Contexts and Contemporary Significance sections that ensue, exploring in these sections the extent to which we might profitably understand the text as speaking of our relationship with other human beings and the extent to which we might profitably understand it as speaking of our relationship with God.

I have used the term *drama* in the preceding paragraph to describe the Song of Songs, and this term itself requires some explanation and justification. I use it first of all to claim that there is no reason to think of this book as a haphazard collection of shorter poems cast together simply because of their common theme of love. There is every indication, rather, that it is intended to cohere as a unity at a deeper level (even though its unity is not a straightforward one). The heading to the work itself invites us to read it in this way (it is "the song," in the singular), and our ability to accept this invitation becomes all the greater as we proceed in our reading and find frequent repetition of theme and language and consistent characterization throughout the book.

It may well be the case (for all we know) that the author of the book used preexisting poetic material in composing it, but if so, then he or she gives

---

continues to surface in the Christian mystical theology of medieval and modern times that speaks (like the Gnostics) of a mystical marriage of the soul with God. Witness the words of P. P. Parente, "The Canticle of Canticles in Mystical Theology," *CBQ* 6 (1944): 142–58: "Man's spirit in an animal body is capable, with the help of divine grace, of emancipating itself from sensual love and affections to such an extent that it can love God with a purity and ardour that resemble the love of the heavenly spirits" (143).

every impression of having used it carefully and thoughtfully to produce a unified work. The commentary that follows tries to demonstrate the ways in which this is so.[11] I do not use the term *drama* necessarily to imply that the text was written for enactment by actors, whether in the royal court or in worship. We do not know anything, in fact, about its earliest reading and use.[12] I use it, rather, because the Song of Songs has a clearly dramatic form—something recognized already by Origen in the third century and by the Greek translators of Codex Sinaiticus (fourth century) and Codex Alexandrinus (fifth century), who added marginal notes to the text intended to indicate the speakers and the persons addressed.

The Hebrew text of the Song of Songs does not explicitly help us in these ways, although it is usually clear to one who reads the Hebrew text cumulatively from beginning to end which of its various characters or groups of characters is speaking at any given point. We need only pay careful attention to such phenomena as changes of gender in the verbal and noun suffixes in the book. The main characters are a male and a female speaker,[13] who address each other employing the language of love and intimacy. They have a supporting cast of female and male companions, to whom reference is sometimes made (e.g., 1:7) and speech is sometimes directed (e.g., 2:7), and who even on occasion themselves speak (e.g., 5:9; 6:1).

The question as to whether Solomon himself is a member of the supporting cast or is to be identified as the male speaker has been a vexing question in the history of the interpretation of this book. The mainstream of interpretation throughout the ages, where it has paused to consider the human aspects of the drama, has followed Origen's view that we find only two main characters in it—King Solomon and his bride. A second line of

---

11. See further the discussion of literary integrity in Pope, *Song*, 40–54. I find in the Song neither the rigid orderliness nor the charming confusion that many other commentators have found. I find, rather, an overall coherence that is marked by the kind of sudden shifts in perspective that occur in dreams or fantasies, or indeed in some forms of drama, where scene succeeds scene in a manner that is not necessarily entirely linear.

12. The similarities between the Song and various other literature of Palestine and the ancient Near East have from time to time led to suggestions about the original use of the Song (e.g., as poetry performed at a wedding festival or as liturgy performed in syncretistic ancient Israelite worship; see Pope, *Song*, 141–53). Literary similarity cannot be taken necessarily to imply similarity of original social setting, however, especially since similar language and images, whatever their precise origins, can be intended to be read entirely differently in different texts. We remain entirely in the dark about how, where, and when the Song was read in pre-Christian times.

13. There has been much speculation over the centuries as to the identity of the female speaker, and yet hardly anything is told us about her that enables firm conclusions to be drawn. She is called a "Shulammite" in 6:13, which some have taken to indicate a town of origin, but the term is obscure (see comment at 6:13).

interpretation derives ultimately from the medieval Spanish exegete Ibn Ezra, who distinguished the "king" from the "shepherd," suggesting that there were therefore two main male characters to be found. This led in time to an interpretation of the song that understood Solomon as a dark force in the drama, threatening the love relationship between the woman and her shepherd-lover.[14]

The commentary that follows adopts this second understanding of the book. The king, who only ever appears explicitly in the third person, is understood as a third party to the couple who are in dialogue with each other and express their love for each other. It is to my mind particularly clear in 3:6–11 and 8:10–12 that Solomon is not viewed at all positively, in contrast to the woman's lover. He is merely a famous collector of women, of whom the woman in the Song of Songs is certainly one, but he has no true relationship with her. Her heart (and body) is given over wholly to another.

I understand the movement of the drama in the Song of Songs, therefore, in the following way. The woman, already a member of the king's harem, expresses her continuing love for her lover (and, implicitly, her disdain for the king), and her lover reciprocates (chs. 1–2). The contrast between king and lover is forcibly underlined in chapter 3, where both the woman's determination to overcome threats to her relationship with the man and her negative view of the royal bed and its owner are clear. Both the threats to and the depths of the relationship are in evidence in chapters 4–5, where the language and the imagery speak of a committed, marital-like relationship between the man and the woman. Chapters 6–7 portray for us in yet further graphic detail the nature of this relationship. Chapter 8 provides us with a strong closing statement of the woman's passion for the man and her resistance to those other males who claim possession of her, whether her brothers or the king. It is a stirring tale of fidelity to first love in the face of power, coercion, and all the temptations of the royal court.

In summary, what we appear to have in the Song of Songs is a dramatic composition of uncertain date and authorship that sets before us for our consideration two different kinds of male-female relationship. The first, which occupies most of the attention of this song, is that manner of relationship in which a woman and a man enter freely into love and sexual intimacy, binding themselves in lasting commitment to each other and giving themselves to each other, physically and emotionally, in joyful abandonment that knows no reservation or shame. The second kind of relationship, which lurks in the background of the Song of Songs and occasionally has the spotlight

---

14. So, e.g., C. Rabin, "The Song of Songs and Tamil Poetry," *SR* 3 (1973): 205–19, who correctly understands, in my view, that Solomon is presented in the Song as a ridiculous figure whose view of the world is to be rejected.

shone on it, places the male in a dominant and powerful position over the female, such that she does not enter the relationship by choice but is only the pawn in a male game that has to do with legal contracts, money, and the collection of objects of pleasure.

It is the first kind of relationship that the Song of Songs exalts—something underlined by the fact that the woman does most of the speaking in it and takes by far the greater part of the initiative in her relationship with the man. It is the second kind of relationship, however, in which many women have found themselves historically and down to the present day and which the Bible itself has often been used to legitimate as God-ordained. The Song of Songs, whether we understand it literally or allegorically, undermines this hierarchical view of reality, for a God who woos his people and takes their freedom seriously cannot be invoked in support of male power over and coercion of women. Human beings who are made, both male and female, in the image of such a God must not understand God's intentions for their relationships in terms of power and coercion.

This book reminds us, through its story of love portrayed in the imagery of fertile gardens and vineyards, of a time before sin touched all relationships in the universe, when men and women were "naked, and . . . felt no shame" before God and before each other (Gen. 2:25). It recalls the creation of male and female in partnership to multiply and to govern the earth (1:26–28), their very beings as "man" (*ʾiš*) and "woman" (*ʾiššâ*) corresponding to and complementing each other. In reminding us of all this, it invites us to reach for a vision of the male-female relationship that transcends what has been the all-too-common reality of human experience in general as it is described in Genesis 3:16 ("he will rule over you") and which is inevitably also the all-too-common experience of God's people both in the Bible and in subsequent history.

The Song of Songs, in this sense, presents us with a story of love redeemed, which contrasts with the more common human tale of love gone awry.[15] In presenting us with this story, it calls us to shape our own story in its light. The extent to which men in particular have been unwilling to do this, historically, is itself reflected in their reluctance to see the Song of Songs as anything other than a problematic book at the literal level, for without the literal sense of the text as an anchor, it has always been too easy for men to sail the good ship allegory wherever they wished, avoiding those things in the ocean that they did not wish to comprehend.

A text that otherwise might have challenged a typical male way of living through helping men throughout history to see how resolutely this song

---

15. See P. Trible, *God and the Rhetoric of Sexuality* (Philadelphia: Fortress, 1978), 144–65.

undermines all culture in which men relate to women as Solomon and the brothers relate to the heroine of our drama was happily (for them) neutered and rendered impotent. To them, it spoke instead of the love of God in a way that did not require them too greatly to alter their perception of what it meant to love the female neighbor as themselves.

The Song of Songs in the Contemporary Context

IF IT CAN ALREADY be questioned at the level of original intentionality whether we should seek to drive a wedge between literal and allegorical readings of the Song of Songs, then it is certainly true that when we set the Song of Songs within its broader canonical context in the Christian Bible we will find still less reason to do so, for the Bible as a whole holds in closest analogical connection the love that exists between God and humans and between humans and humans. Thus John tells his readers: "Anyone who does not love his brother, whom he has seen, cannot love God, whom he has not seen" (1 John 4:20). The apostle Paul connects the marriage relationship in particular to Christ's relationship with the church, in a famous passage in Ephesians 5:22–33:

> Wives, submit to your husbands as to the Lord. For the husband is the head of the wife as Christ is the head of the church, his body, of which he is the Savior. Now as the church submits to Christ, so also wives should submit to their husbands in everything.
>
> Husbands, love your wives, just as Christ loved the church and gave himself up for her to make her holy, cleansing her by the washing with water through the word, and to present her to himself as a radiant church, without stain or wrinkle or any other blemish, but holy and blameless. In this same way, husbands ought to love their wives as their own bodies. He who loves his wife loves himself. After all, no one ever hated his own body, but he feeds and cares for it, just as Christ does the church—for we are members of his body. "For this reason a man will leave his father and mother and be united to his wife, and the two will become one flesh." This is a profound mystery—but I am talking about Christ and the church. However, each one of you also must love his wife as he loves himself, and the wife must respect her husband.

The human relationship, including its obviously sexual aspects, is analogous to the divine-human relationship as Christ is united with the church. There can be no question but that Christian readers of the Song of Songs thus have canonical warrant for reading it both at the literal and at the allegorical level, drawing conclusions from it for both faith and life that touch on the entirety of who we are as people created and redeemed by God. What are the most important of these conclusions?

As to human relationships, we should begin by frankly acknowledging that we inhabit a world in which relationships between men and women are still significantly distorted, usually to the woman's disadvantage and often to her hurt. This reality manifests itself in many different ways and in many different cultural and religious contexts. Women are still widely regarded in some of these contexts as being the property of males, to be bought and sold as the males desire. They are valued, not as equal persons, but for their usefulness as servants, childbearers, or sexual playthings.

Where they are theoretically equal with males under the laws of a country (as they have generally become in Western countries in relatively recent times), they are nevertheless often treated unequally in practice (e.g., in the financial rewards they receive for work). In the privacy of the home or in the darkness of the streets they are often still regarded as inferior to men and derivative of them and are subject to emotional and physical abuse and exploitation as male power and coercion are brought to bear on them there.

In some countries of the world, such power and coercion have no need even to hide away indoors or in darkness, for coercion, violence, and abuse are tolerated or even approved by society at large. As we consider the reality of this distorted world, it is difficult not to conclude that there is among men a widespread fear of and contempt for women and even a hatred of them, which leads males to attempt to suppress females even while they find that they deeply desire their company, affection, and sexual favor. Many women appear to hold an equally ambiguous attitude toward men, although the damage that consequently ensues for men is minimal in comparison to the damage that men inflict on women, mainly as a result of the unequal nature of the power that is available to each gender.

Bound up with all this dysfunctionality of relationship in the modern (as in the ancient) world is sexual activity. Sexual activity is a blessing from God that is supposed to symbolize in a profound way self-giving in the male-female relationship. It has come instead to symbolize all that is cursed about that relationship. It is commonly bought and sold as a commodity and is practiced as an expression of power, manipulation, and control. Where it is not directly expressive of these realities, it has come to be widely viewed as dirty on the one hand and as quasi-holy on the other—the leisure activity of the "liberated" who are incapable of commitment and who seek in serial sexual relationships some meaning and significance in the midst of the chaos and meaninglessness that characterize their lives.

All of this is a horrendous reality, which only seems "normal" because we have become so accustomed to it. Yet the Christian church has itself found difficulty in being entirely countercultural with respect to male-female relationships throughout its history. It continues to struggle with this challenge as it addresses the modern culture, even though it knows in one part of its brain that there is neither male nor female in Christ (Gal. 3:28).

Modern Christian pastors might hesitate to assert the rights of a husband to beat his wife, as medieval canon law allowed. If they live in Britain, for example, they might well be reluctant to advocate a return to an earlier historical period in which British women had no legal status of their own, independent of their husbands, had no say in the political process, and had little independent access to economic power. To that extent the gospel has made progress in the transformation of society.

Yet significant sections of the church, particularly those that have resisted social change in the past on the grounds that Bible and long Christian practice speak against such change (e.g., those who opposed the abolition of slavery in the nineteenth century), continue to behave as if the calling of the church is to legitimate the fallen world rather than to usher in the kingdom of God. They bring theology and the Bible to bear on social issues only insofar as they tend to provide support for the status quo or for some previous status quo to which they wish society at large to return. For Christian men are still men, and the social world as it has generally been constituted historically suits at least some men very well and certainly favors them over women.

It is still possible to find men who are confessing Christians, therefore, who regard women as being in essence the property of males and who value their wives not as sisters and equals in Christ, but as servants, childbearers, or sexual playthings in respect of whom they have conjugal "rights." It is not uncommon, still, to find churches structured as its men would prefer (but cannot realistically demand) that society should be structured, with the women in an entirely dependent and subordinate position vis-à-vis the men. This is not infrequently connected with convictions about female inferiority that remain deeply rooted in the heart even though they cannot easily any longer be confessed with the mouth in a politically correct modern society.

That fear of and contempt for women, and even a hatred of them, which were mentioned above, have not entirely been exorcised from male Christian hearts, it seems. The responses of Christian women vary from outright rejection of this attempt to define them only in reference to men, through a measured tolerance of a social reality from which they cannot in any case easily escape (albeit a tolerance often combined with a quiet but seething resentment), to a ready and submissive acceptance of a world that is to them God-ordained and may be the only world that they have ever known.

Bound up with all this dysfunctionality of relationship in the church, as in society at large, is sexual activity. A truly countercultural church would at this point confront with balanced biblical teaching on sexual expression both the modern society that idolizes it and the Christian tradition that essentially demonizes it and would seek to proclaim and to live the truth that *God* made the world as a *good* place and redeemed this same world in Christ. The reality is all too often different. The ancient belief (or even just the feeling) that sex is perhaps unclean and certainly not entirely spiritual is still to be found among Christian men and women at the dawn of a new millennium, leading to a view of the Christian life that is instinctually ascetic.

Such people simply do not believe, deep in their hearts, that Christ took on our humanity so as to redeem it in every aspect and to enable us as we are justified and sanctified in Christ to live it out as God intends. They cannot see that the gospel is about *expression* of our humanity. They have come instead to think of it as being about *repression* of significant aspects of our humanity. The collateral damage that the attempt to use Christian faith to repress important aspects of our humanity causes, however, is huge, for if faith and humanness are set in conflict with each other, sooner or later a human being will find the attempt to manage the conflict intolerable and will choose humanness.

Perhaps this is one reason why modern preaching about the Christian life continues to be so frequently and spectacularly undermined by the actual living of Christians, particularly in the matter of sexual activity, both in secret and then later (and inevitably) as it becomes public. They have embraced a false view of the Christian life that has at its heart repression, whether of the self or of others. Unable to live this life consistently, but unable to say so publicly, they develop a secret life in which repression of the self is no longer necessary. In due course their double life is exposed, with discredit then falling on their message and discouragement on those who previously heard it and believed it.

Along the way such dysfunctional Christians have been found to be preaching control to others but exercising little over themselves. Their need for power and authoritarian control over other people (including their own wives) has been found, in fact, to coincide far too directly with their need for a similar degree of sexual control over and manipulation of others—whether through pornography, prostitution, or other avenues open to fractured souls who are at peace neither with their whole selves in Christ nor with the idea that maleness by no means represents the whole of humanness.

In the midst of all the distortions of our lives respecting our relationships with each other, male and female, God speaks his Word to us in the Song of Songs, inviting us to reason with him and to change our thinking and our living so that it reflects what is true and good. He calls into question any assumptions we may have (whether we are men or women) about the status of women in a male-dominated world, making clear to us that a woman, as much as a man, should be able freely to make choices about her life. Insisting that male-female relationships are two-way situations in which each party initiates and responds, God critiques the view that a good woman is one who is always and only passive and receptive in respect of the initiating male. He clarifies for us that sexual intercourse and all that precedes and follows it in the making of love are good things and that frank speech about such matters is simply part of this love-making and nothing to be ashamed of.

Both word and action, whether they come from male or female, are blessed by God. He makes it impossible for us, if we are intent on listening to and registering his words, to understand the spiritual life as something distinct from our ordinary human life. He insists, through the providential presence of the Song of Songs in the Christian canon, that the Christian life is the human life, in all its aspects, redeemed and lived out before God and neighbor. He insists, thereby, that however much the sexual excesses of the culture around us disenchant, anger, and sicken us, we cannot respond to this culture with a gnostic escapism that pretends that Christian redemption is about leaving the body behind and floating off with our soul into a mystical never-never land. The journey is impossible, for there is no gnostic dichotomy between soul and body, as that great nontheologian Oscar Wilde saw (although typically overstating his objection): "Those who see any difference between soul and body have neither."[16]

The only appropriate Christian response to the culture is to go on with our initial vocation—to live out fully the life God has given us, offering it all to him in joyous celebration of his goodness to us. It is only while walking such a path that we will be able to speak persuasively to the culture about what God's kingdom means in respect of our entire lives.

Christians are called, therefore, to proclaim a resounding "yes" to sexual expression, in the context of a resounding "yes" to God. It is in this proclamation, rather than in our repression of humanness and in our preaching of negative rules, that the goodness of God will be seen by others. One of the sad features of church history is that Christians have sometimes managed all too successfully to promote the agenda of the serpent in the Garden of Eden rather than to advertise the kingdom of God. That is, we have presented God to the world, whether consciously or not, as a God of unreasonable prohibition (Gen. 3:1) rather than as a God who blesses us with freedom (2:16).

16. O. Wilde, "Phrases and Philosophies for the Use of the Young," *Chameleon* (December 1894). More sober is John Updike in his foreword to L. Boadt, ed., *The Song of Solomon: Love Poetry of the Spirit* (CBS; New York: St. Martin's, 1999), 10: "Judaism recognized that the body is the person, a recognition extended in the strenuous Christian doctrine of the bodily resurrection."

In truth, however, the negatives of the Christian life generally only make sense in the context of the positives; this is clearly true also in respect of biblical negatives concerning sexuality. Christians stand *against* certain forms of sexual activity because of what we think sexual activity is *for*. It is *for* the building of a lifelong, committed, and intimate relationship between one man and one woman, in which complete self-giving is possible. It is *not* for casual or time-limited relationships, in which people often engage in modern Western culture in particular and which are often focused around entirely selfish needs and desires (even if two sets of selfish needs and desires are temporarily met in the encounter). Nor is it designed for the expression of power and control by one party in respect of another or for the expression of intimacy between people of the same gender.

Sexual activity at the wrong time and with the wrong persons is, in fact— as the Song of Songs itself recognizes—destructive rather than good. The Christian "yes" to sex, as joyous as it should be, is thus always a "yes" in a context, defined by the good God who made all things and knows what is best for his creatures. The Song of Songs is thus seen to be a critique not only of the church but also of the culture, which has invested sexual acts in themselves and outside of any God-ordained context with a mystique and a religious aura that defies rational explanation. If the fact that we have *at least one* biblical book devoted explicitly to love and sex speaks a rebuke to Christians who find no place for love and sex in their Christian thinking and living, then by the same token the fact that we have *only one* biblical book devoted explicitly to love and sex speaks a rebuke to those who have invested love and sex with such ultimate significance. Repression and license are simply two sides of the same nonbiblical coin.

This last point leads directly on to a brief reflection on the Song of Songs as a book that can be read, in the context of the Christian canon, as concerning not only the male-female relationship but also the divine-human relationship. The very point about all created things, when they are divorced from God, is that they can all too easily become idolatrous. They can become "gods" of their own—things we worship and strive after, investing ultimate meaning and significance in them.

There can be no question but that the male-female relationship, particularly in its sexual aspects, has become the focus of idolatrous worship for many people in the modern (as it was for many in the ancient) world. It is widely believed, in the face of much evidence to the contrary, that the key to all existence is meeting "the right person," who will then be able to satisfy all one's needs and desires, especially in the area of sex. The catastrophic consequences in terms of human happiness and contentment that have followed especially in the Western world from this elevation of the "ideal male" or "ideal female" to the status of a god are plain to see, not least in the decision of subsequent generations of young people not even to commence the search but simply to "have a good time" enjoying the mere experience of sex with as many semianonymous partners as the brief span of youth will allow. One is reminded of C. S. Lewis's wise words about what happens to human beings when they invest too much in any created thing and fail to understand that it cannot, because it is created, be a god:

> The books or the music in which we thought the beauty was located will betray us if we trust them; it was not *in* them, it only came *through* them, and what came through them was longing. These things—the beauty, the memory of our own past—are good images of what we really desire; but if they are mistaken for the thing itself they turn into dumb idols, breaking the hearts of their worshippers. For they are not the thing itself; they are only the scent of a flower we have not found, the echo of a tune which we have not heard, news from a country we have not visited.[17]

It is, in the end, "longing" that drives the modern obsession with sex—a longing for intimacy and fulfillment that is far too deep and fundamental to be met by any other human creature and which can only destroy that creature and its lover if the obsession is not faced and understood. For it is a longing that speaks to us of who we are—people made in the image of God and designed to live in fellowship with him. Human love, including erotic love, always points beyond ourselves to the Love that undergirds all of reality and in whose Presence alone all longing can be satisfied. It is a sacred thing, but it points always not to itself, but to the Sacred that lies beyond it.

That is why the Song of Songs can speak to us today, in describing love of man for woman and of woman for man, of the love of God for us all and of the appropriate human response in love toward God. That is why, in the commentary that follows, we will reflect not only on what this song has to say about male-female relationships but also about the God-human relationship in the contemporary world. To speak of one without the other would be, inevitably, to speak falsely and unhelpfully.

Yet we will resist the temptation to which many medieval commentators succumbed when they pressed the many details of the Song of Songs into the service of allegorical reading. It is, for example, an unconvincing reading of 1:13, entirely unconnected to any literal sense, that takes the woman's breasts to be the Old and New Testaments, and the lover who lies between them to be Christ. It is possible, however, to see, in the intimacy of this picture of human love and those others that chapter 1 gives us, the intimacy that should

---

17. C. S. Lewis, *Screwtape Proposes a Toast* (London: Collins, 1971), 97–98.

exist between God and the church, which holds God close to the heart. It is not necessary, for this song to speak *truly* of the divine-human relationship as well as of human relationships, that its every word should be found to have an allegorical as well as a literal sense.

We shall pursue a broadly based "allegorical" approach, therefore, rather than a narrowly focused one. Our approach might better be described as parabolic rather than as allegorical, following the lead of R. E. Murphy:

> The individual verses are not to be taken singly. From this point of view, the Canticle can be compared to the Parable of the Prodigal Son. We accept, for example, that here Almighty God is symbolized under the figure of the father; but we do not apply each pertinent verse to Him. Rather, the whole story is an imaginative description whose sole purpose is to convey the mercy and forgiveness of God. Similarly, the purpose of the Canticle is to express the beauty and fidelity which will characterize the People of God in its Messianic betrothal. The individual scenes are described solely to highlight this aspect.[18]

It is in my view not the *sole* purpose of the Song of Songs to speak of God and the people of God (and Murphy indicates more clearly elsewhere in his writings that he, too, does not believe this). Yet I agree with Murphy's emphasis on the whole in distinction to the details, insofar as the Song *does* speak of God and his people. It is with this in mind that I will be asking as we read through the book what this drama about good human relationships and bad ones has to say about the love of God for the church, and about the true love of the church for God in the midst of the temptations that face her in the world. For the struggle of the woman for fidelity to her lover when confronted with the king does have something to say about this larger struggle of God's people for fidelity to him while being wooed by others—a struggle for faithfulness to their first Love that has continued, the Bible suggests, from ancient history and down to the present day. The balance for which I am striving here is nicely captured by E. J. Young:

> The Song does celebrate the dignity and purity of human love ... it reminds us, in particularly beautiful fashion, how pure and noble true love is. This, however, does not exhaust the purpose of the book. Not only does it speak of the purity of human love, but, by its very inclusion in the Canon, it reminds us of a love that is purer than our own.[19]

---

18. R. E. Murphy, "The Canticle of Canticles and the Virgin Mary," *Carmelus* 1 (1954): 18–28 (quote on p. 27). Ibn Ezra had already, many centuries before, referred to the Song as a parable; others have followed his lead.

19. E. J. Young, *An Introduction to the Old Testament* (London: Tyndale, 1949), 327.

Outline of Song of Songs

AN OUTLINE OF the Song of Songs is already implied in those printed versions of the NIV that place italicized headings in the text referring to *Beloved, Lover,* and *Friends.* Although I often agree with the interpretations of the text implicit in the insertions as they relate to changes in speaker, I have not allowed them to determine how I have broken the text up for discussion in the commentary (which is dictated, in the context of widespread disagreement among scholars as to how best divide the Song up into sections, as much by the need to have passages broadly similar in length to comment on as by anything else). I am, in fact, in general unhappy to find such interpretative glosses standing in what is supposed to be primarily a translation of the Bible. I am unhappy in particular about the choice of *Lover* and *Beloved* to represent the male and female protagonists respectively, since it implies male initiative and female passivity—quite against the grain of the text of Song of Songs itself.

The Lovers Presented (1:1–17)
Springtime in Palestine (2:1–17)
The Terrors of the Night (3:1–11)
A Man Enraptured (4:1–5:1)
The Lovers Entranced (5:2–6:10)
The Dance of Delights (6:11–7:13)
Love Strong As Death (8:1–14)

Select Bibliography
on Song of Songs

A VERY FULL and helpful bibliography, arranged broadly chronologically to run from the early Christian centuries until the present, is to be found in Pope's commentary on Song of Songs (cited below).

Allender, D. B., and T. Longman III. *Intimate Allies*. Wheaton, Ill.: Tyndale, 1995.

Alster, B. "Sumerian Love Songs." *RA* 79 (1985): 127–59.

Astell, A. W. *The Song of Songs in the Middle Ages*. Ithaca, N.Y.: Cornell Univ. Press, 1990.

Ayo, N. *Sacred Marriage: The Wisdom of the Song of Songs*. New York: Continuum, 1997.

Bergant, D. "'My Beloved Is Mine and I Am His' (Song 2:16): The Song of Songs and Honor and Shame." *Semeia* 68 (1994): 23–40.

_____. *Song of Songs: The Love Poetry of Scripture*. Spiritual Commentaries. Hyde Park, N.Y.: New City Press, 1998.

Bernard of Clairvaux. *The Song of Songs: Selections from the Sermons of St. Bernard of Clairvaux*. Ed. H. C. Backhouse. Hodder & Stoughton Christian Classics. London: Hodder & Stoughton, 1990.

Bloch, A., and C. Bloch, *Song of Songs*. New York: Random House, 1995.

Boadt, L., ed. *The Song of Solomon: Love Poetry of the Spirit*. CBS. New York: St. Martin's, 1999.

Brenner, A. "Aromatics and Perfumes in the Song of Songs." *JSOT* 25 (1983): 75–81.

_____. *The Song of Songs*. OTG. Sheffield: JSOT Press, 1989.

_____. "Come Back, Come Back the Shulammite (Song of Songs 7:1–10): A Parody of the *wasf* Genre." Pp. 251–75 in *On Humour and the Comic in the Hebrew Bible*. Ed. Y. Radday. BL 23. Sheffield: Almond, 1990.

_____. "A Note on *bat-rabbim* (Song of Songs 7:5)." *VT* 42 (1992): 113–15.

_____, ed. *A Feminist Companion to the Song of Songs*. Sheffield: Sheffield Academic Press, 1993.

Brenner, A., and F. van Dijk-Hemmes. *On Gendering Texts: Female and Male Voices in the Hebrew Bible*. BibIntS 1. Leiden: Brill, 1993.

Carnes, P. *Contrary to Love: Helping the Sexual Addict*. Minneapolis: CompCare, 1989.

_____. *Don't Call It Love: Recovery from Sexual Addiction.* New York: Bantam, 1991.

Carr, G. L. "The Old Testament Love Songs and Their Use in the New Testament." *JETS* 24 (1981): 97–105.

_____. *The Song of Solomon.* TOTC 17. Downers Grove, Ill.: InterVarsity, 1984.

Casey, M. *Athirst for God: Spiritual Desire in Bernard of Clairvaux's Sermons on the Song of Songs.* CSS 77. Kalamazoo, Mich.: Cistercian Publications, 1988.

Cooper, J. S. "New Cuneiform Parallels to the Song of Songs." *JBL* 90 (1971): 157–62.

Davidson, J. M. "Theology of Sexuality in the Song of Songs: Return to Eden." *AUSS* 27 (1989): 1–19.

Davidson, R. *Ecclesiastes and the Song of Solomon.* DSBOT. Philadelphia: Westminster, 1986.

Dirksen, P. B. "Song of Songs 3:6–7." *VT* 39 (1989): 219–25.

Dorsey, D. A. "Literary Structuring in the Song of Songs." *JSOT* 46 (1990): 81–96.

Elder, D. *The Song of Songs and Enlightenment: A Metaphysical Interpretation.* Marina del Rey, Calif.: DeVorss, 1988.

Elliott, M. T. *The Literary Unity of the Canticle.* New York: Peter Lang, 1989.

Emerton, J. A. "Lice or a Veil in the Song of Songs 1:7?" Pp. 127–40 in *Understanding Poets and Prophets: Essays in Honour of George Wishart Anderson.* Ed. A. G. Auld. JSOTS 152. Sheffield: JSOT Press, 1993.

Exum, C. "A Literary and Structural Analysis of the Song of Songs." *ZAW* 85 (1973): 47–79.

Falk, M. *Love Lyrics from the Bible: A Translation and Literary Study of the Song of Songs.* BL 4. Sheffield: Almond, 1982.

_____. *The Song of Songs.* San Francisco: Harper & Row, 1990.

Fox, M. V. *The Song of Songs and the Ancient Egyptian Love Songs.* Madison, Wis: Univ. of Wisconsin Press, 1985.

Fuerst, W. J. *Ruth, Esther, Ecclesiastes, the Song of Songs, Lamentations.* CBC. Cambridge: Cambridge Univ. Press, 1975.

Garrett, D. A. *Proverbs, Ecclesiastes, Song of Songs.* NAC 14. Nashville: Broadman, 1993.

Giles of Rome. *Commentary on the Song of Songs and Other Writings.* Ed. J. E. Rotelle. The Augustinian Series 10. Villanova, Pa.: Augustinian Press, 1998.

Ginsburg, C. D. *The Song of Songs and Coheleth (Commonly Called the Book of Ecclesiastes).* The Library of Biblical Studies. New York: Ktav, 1970.

Gledhill, T. *The Message of the Song of Songs: The Lyrics of Love.* BST. Downers Grove, Ill.: InterVarsity Press, 1994.

Glickman, S. C. *A Song for Lovers*. Downers Grove, Ill.: InterVarsity, 1976.

Gollwitzer, H. *Song of Love: A Biblical Understanding of Sex*. Philadelphia: Fortress, 1979.

Gordis, R. *The Song of Songs and Lamentations*. Rev. ed. New York: Ktav, 1974.

Goulder, M. D. *The Song of Fourteen Songs*. JSOTS 36. Sheffield: JSOT Press, 1986.

Gregory of Nyssa. *From Glory to Glory: Texts from Gregory of Nyssa's Mystical Writings*. Trans. and ed. H. Musurillo. New York: St. Vladimir's Seminary, 1979.

Grober, S. F. "The Hospitable Lotus: A Cluster of Metaphors: An Inquiry into the Problem of Textual Unity in the Song of Songs." *Semitics* 9 (1984): 86–112.

Grossberg, D. "Two Kinds of Sexual Relationship in the Hebrew Bible." *Hebrew Studies* 35 (1994): 1–25.

Ibn Ezra, A. ben Meir, and R. A. Block. *Ibn Ezra's Commentary on the Song of Songs (Perush Ibn 'Ezra 'Al Shir Ha-Shirim)*. Cincinnati: Hebrew Union College-Jewish Institute of Religion, 1982.

Jinbachian, M. "The Genre of Love Poetry in the Song of Songs and the Pre-Islamic Arabian Odes." *BT* 48 (1997): 123–37.

Kallas, E. "Martin Luther As Expositor of the Song of Songs." *LQ* 2 (1988): 323–41.

Keel, O. *The Song of Songs*. Continental Commentaries. Trans. F. J. Gaiser. Minneapolis: Fortress, 1994.

Knight, G. A. F., and F. W. Golka. *Revelation of God: A Commentary on the Books of the Song of Songs and Jonah*. ITC. Grand Rapids: Eerdmans, 1988.

Lacocque, A. *Romance, She Wrote: A Hermeneutical Essay on Song of Songs*. Harrisburg, Pa.: Trinity Press International, 1998.

Landy, F. *Paradoxes of Paradise: Identity and Difference in the Song of Songs*. BL 7. Sheffield: Sheffield Academic Press, 1983.

_____. "The Song of Songs and the Garden of Eden." *JBL* 98 (1979): 513–28.

Laurin, R. B. "The Song of Songs and Its Modern Message." *CT* 6 (1961–1962): 1062–63.

Leahy, F. S. "The Song of Songs in Pastoral Teaching." *EvQ* 27 (1955): 205–13.

Levine, M. H. "The Song of Solomon: A Dream Ballet." *Dor Le Dor* 14 (1986): 166–74.

Lewis, C. S. *The Four Loves*. London: Fontana Books, 1976.

Luther, M. "Lectures on the Song of Solomon." Pp. 191–264 in *Luther's Works*, vol. 15. Ed. J. Pelikan. St. Louis: Concordia, 1972.

Maloney, G. A. *Singers of the New Song: A Mystical Interpretation of the Song of Songs*. Notre Dame, Ind.: Ave Maria, 1985.

Mason, M. *The Mystery of Marriage*. Portland: Multnomah, 1985.

Mazor, Y. "The Song of Songs or the Story of Stories? The Song of Songs': Between Genre and Unity." *SJOT* 1 (1990): 1–29.

Meyers, C. "Gender Imagery in the Song of Songs." *HAR* 10 (1986): 209–23.

Mulder, M. J. "Does Canticles 6,12 Make Sense?" Pp. 104–13 in *The Scriptures and the Scrolls*. FS A. S. van der Woude. Ed. F. García Martínez, A. Hilhorst, and C. J. Labuschagne. VTS 49. Leiden: Brill, 1992.

Munro, J. L. *Spikenard and Saffron: A Study in the Poetic Language of the Song of Songs*. JSOTSup 203. Sheffield: Sheffield Academic Press, 1995.

Murphy, R. E. "The Biblical Model of Human Intimacy: The Song of Songs." Pp. 61–66 in *The Family in Crisis or in Transition: A Sociological and Theological Perspective*. Ed. A. Greeley. New York: Seabury, 1979.

_____. *The Song of Songs*. Hermeneia. Minneapolis: Fortress, 1990.

Murphy, R. E., and E. Huwiler. *Proverbs, Ecclesiastes, Song of Songs*. NIBC 12. Peabody, Mass.: Hendrickson, 1999.

Neusner, J. *Israel's Love Affair with God: Song of Songs*. BJL. Valley Forge, Pa.: Trinity Press International, 1993.

Origen. *The Song of Songs: Commentary and Homilies*. Ancient Christian Writers 26. Trans. and annotated by R. P. Lawson. New York: Newman, 1957.

Parente, P. P. "The Canticle of Canticles in Mystical Theology." *CBQ* 6 (1944): 142–58.

Pope, M. H. *Song of Songs*. AB 7C. Garden City, N.Y.: Doubleday, 1977.

Rabin, C. "The Song of Songs and Tamil Poetry." *SR* 3 (1973): 205–19.

Ratzhabi, Y. "Biblical Euphemisms for Human Genitals." *Beth Mikra* 34 (1990): 192–96.

Richardson, J. P. "Preaching from the *Song of Songs*? Allegory Revisited." *Churchman* 108 (1994): 135–42.

Sadgrove, M. "The Song of Songs As Wisdom Literature." Pp. 245–48 in *Studia Biblica 1978 I: Papers on Old Testament and Related Themes*. Ed. E. A. Livingstone. JSOTSup 11. Sheffield: JSOT Press, 1979.

Scruton, R. *Sexual Desire: A Philosophical Investigation*. London: Weidenfeld and Nicholson, 1986.

Segal, B. "The Themes of the Song of Songs." *Dor Le Dor* 15 (1986–87): 106–13.

Smedes, L. B. *Sex for Christians*. Grand Rapids: Eerdmans, 1994.

Snaith, J. G. *The Song of Songs*. NCB. London: Marshall Pickering, 1993.

Stadelmann, L. I. J. *Love and Politics: A New Commentary on the Song of Songs*. New York: Paulist, 1992.

Tanner, J. P. "The Message of the Song of Songs." *BSac* 154 (1997): 142–61.

Teresa of Avila, "Meditation on the Song of Songs." *The Collected Works of St. Teresa of Avila*, vol. 2. Trans. K. Kavanaugh and O. Rodriguez. Washington D.C.: ICS Publications, 1980.

Trible, P. *God and the Rhetoric of Sexuality*. Philadelphia: Fortress, 1978.

Turner, D. *Eros and Allegory: Medieval Exegesis of the Song of Songs*. CSS 156. Kalamazoo, Mich.: Cistercian Publications, 1995.

Watson, W. G. E. "Love and Death Once More (Song of Songs 8:6)." *VT* 47 (1997): 385–86.

Webb, B. G. "The Song of Songs: A Love Poem and Holy Scripture." *RTR* 49 (1990): 91–99.

Webster, E. C. "Pattern in the Song of Songs." Pp. 154–72 in *The Poetical Books*. Ed. D. J. A. Clines. BSem 41. Sheffield: Sheffield Academic Press, 1997.

Weems, R. J. "The Song of Songs" Pp. 361–434 in vol. 5 of *The New Interpreter's Bible*. Nashville: Abingdon, 1997.

William of St. Thierry. *Exposition on the Song of Songs*. The Works of William of St. Thierry. CFS 6. Shannon: Irish Univ. Press, 1969.

Winsor, A. R. *A King Is Bound in the Tresses: Allusions to the Song of Songs in the Fourth Gospel*. StudBL 6. New York: Peter Lang, 1998.

Song of Songs 1:1–17

SOLOMON'S SONG OF Songs.

² Let him kiss me with the kisses of his mouth—
for your love is more delightful than wine.
³ Pleasing is the fragrance of your perfumes;
your name is like perfume poured out.
No wonder the maidens love you!
⁴ Take me away with you—let us hurry!
Let the king bring me into his chambers.

We rejoice and delight in you;
we will praise your love more than wine.

How right they are to adore you!

⁵ Dark am I, yet lovely,
O daughters of Jerusalem,
dark like the tents of Kedar,
like the tent curtains of Solomon.
⁶ Do not stare at me because I am dark,
because I am darkened by the sun.
My mother's sons were angry with me
and made me take care of the vineyards;
my own vineyard I have neglected.
⁷ Tell me, you whom I love, where you graze your flock
and where you rest your sheep at midday.
Why should I be like a veiled woman
beside the flocks of your friends?

⁸ If you do not know, most beautiful of women,
follow the tracks of the sheep
and graze your young goats
by the tents of the shepherds.

⁹ I liken you, my darling, to a mare
harnessed to one of the chariots of Pharaoh.
¹⁰ Your cheeks are beautiful with earrings,
your neck with strings of jewels.
¹¹ We will make you earrings of gold,
studded with silver.

¹²While the king was at his table,
   my perfume spread its fragrance.
¹³My lover is to me a sachet of myrrh
   resting between my breasts.
¹⁴My lover is to me a cluster of henna blossoms
   from the vineyards of En Gedi.

¹⁵How beautiful you are, my darling!
   Oh, how beautiful!
   Your eyes are doves.

¹⁶How handsome you are, my lover!
   Oh, how charming!
   And our bed is verdant.

¹⁷The beams of our house are cedars;
   our rafters are firs.

THE BEST OF biblical songs (see the Introduction for discussion of the meaning of the title and the significance of the mention of Solomon) opens with the words of the female protagonist, who will reappear throughout the song as one of its main characters. She gets right to the matter in hand (vv. 2–4), expressing a passionate desire for her lover first in the third person (v. 2a) and then immediately in the second person (v. 2b)—a kind of change of person that is common in Hebrew poetry as the speaker moves in turn to address the self, other persons, and third parties. One finds frequent change of person, for example, in a book like Lamentations,[1] which is, like the Song of Songs, a dramatic composition in which different voices speak.

Since we are dealing with a well-established phenomenon (sometimes referred to as *enallage*), it is unwise upon encountering a puzzling variation of this kind either immediately to emend the Hebrew text to render it more "logical" (a common strategy among translators and commentators, both ancient and modern, in respect of all kinds of biblical texts) or to assume too quickly that a "real" change of speaker in the text is being indicated—a particular mistake of some commentators on Song of Songs. It is entirely likely, in fact, that all of verses 2–4 is spoken by this same female individual, the plurals of two

---

1. Shift in person is also common in literature from the wider ancient Near Eastern context, which has some connection with Song of Songs; see Pope, *Song*, 304, for some detail in respect of sacred marriage songs.

of the lines in verse 4 notwithstanding (although these plurals, as we will see, do intend to draw others into the picture along with the woman). Note how the male lover himself apparently speaks in the plural in verse 11. It is possible that in verse 2 we are supposed to understand the first line as an unexpressed private thought and the second line as the beginning of the woman's speech to her beloved (note the similar transition from thought to speech in vv. 12–17).

The woman wants nothing other than that her lover should kiss her "with the kisses of his mouth," for she considers his "love" (*dod*, referring here to acts of lovemaking, as in Prov. 7:18; Ezek. 16:8; and [negatively] in Ezek. 23:17) to be far better than wine. It intoxicates her and gives her more pleasure and delight than wine could ever provide (Song 1:2).

The recurrence in verse 3 of *ṭobim* ("better," translated in NIV as "delightful" in v. 2 and as "pleasing" in v. 3), when considered in conjunction with the puzzling Hebrew *lᵉ*, which is prefixed to *reaḥ*, "fragrance," perhaps indicates that the man's lovemaking is also to be considered as "better" than the fragrance of his perfumes (lit., "oils," referring to perfumed oils): "Your lovemaking is more delightful than wine, more pleasant than the fragrance of your perfumed oils."[2] Another fine thing that fills up the senses is not to be compared to what this man brings to the woman when he brings himself. His very "name"—in Hebrew thinking closely connected with the essence of a person—is indeed "like perfume poured out."[3] It is no wonder that he is desirable to maidens other than our speaker (v. 3), or at least is *imagined* to be universally desirable by our speaker.

In verse 4 the woman seems in part to identify herself with this wider group of female admirers, while in part distinguishing herself from them. Only thus is it possible to understand the strange mixture of first-person singulars and plurals in the verse, which the NIV partially disguises by choosing to ignore the Masoretic accentuation in the first line of the verse. This accentuation indicates the translation: "Draw me, let us hurry after you." All maidens love (*ʾhb*, v. 3) this man, and they are right to love him (*ʾhb*, v. 4; NIV "adore") and pursue him. Our speaker speaks as one of this wider group, who are all thought of as rejoicing and delighting in the man and are said to join her in praising his lovemaking more highly than wine (cf. v. 2).

---

2. See Murphy, *Song*, 125, for a brief discussion.

3. The NIV's "poured out" takes Heb. *turaq* to be a Hophal from *ryq*, "empty," which is certainly possible (even though the feminine verb does not agree with the masculine subject "oil"), since perfumed oil poured out would spread a pleasant aroma. There is some justification to be found in the tradition and in the cognate languages, nonetheless, for understanding *turaq* simply as a type of cosmetic oil (the Syriac translation renders the phrase as "myrrh"). See further Pope, *Song*, 300.

It is not clear whether their knowledge of the man's lovemaking is real or imagined and whether it is firsthand or secondhand knowledge. To some extent the answer we give to this question depends on our understanding of the second line of verse 4, which the NIV translates, "Let the king bring me into his chambers" (thus paralleling v. 2 in English, even though the verbal tenses are not in fact identical in the Heb.). The NIV translation already suggests that the lover and the king are one and the same person; if this is the case, then the way is opened up to understand the sentiments attributed to the females as a group as rooted in real, firsthand sexual experience of the king as members of the royal harem. The speaker then becomes only one of many women at the royal court (the "daughters of Jerusalem" of v. 5), who are anxious to share the king's intimate company, albeit that she is clearly unusual (vv. 5–6) and obviously focuses for most of the time on her own desires rather than on the desires of others in the group.

The problem with this interpretation, however, is that the second line of verse 4 is actually better understood not as expressing a desire but as referring to a past action: "The king brought me into his chambers" (i.e., into the innermost, most private, and secret parts of a dwelling; cf., e.g., 1 Kings 20:30; 22:25). It is by no means clear, thus understood, that the king and the lover *are* the same person. We could just as easily interpret the line as a report to the male lover by the woman about what the king has already done, perhaps designed to spur him on to similar amorous action—action that is implicitly carried through in 1:13–17. On the second occasion in which the king is mentioned in the chapter, in fact (v. 12), we have reason to think that a *distinction* is being made between the lover and the king (see further below).

It is certainly the case, then, that the female speaker is a member of the royal harem as the book opens, and we are justified in assuming that the other women whom she draws into her praise of the lover include her companions in this harem.[4] There is no clear evidence, however, that it is the *king's* lovemaking that is being praised by this woman or by those she imagines to be in solidarity with her. Evidence will accumulate as we move through this song, in fact, that the king and the lover are certainly *not* to be identified.

Leaving the king aside for the moment, then, we are confronted by a woman captivated by a man. She identifies in part with a wider group of women, who validate her perceptions of this amazing person ("we," v. 4),

---

4. It is not that the phrase "daughters of Jerusalem" of itself at all implies this. It is not necessarily the case that those conceived of as "daughters" in relation to a city, which is their "mother," are even to be understood as living in that city. Yet the woman addresses the "daughters" in the context of a clear reference to the king's "chambers," leading to the natural assumption that the particular "daughters" in mind are her companions in the harem. As the Song progresses it becomes even clearer that this is so (see comments on 3:10).

but she also differentiates herself from them ("me" and "they," vv. 2–4). This differentiation continues in verses 5–6, where it turns out that the speaker is *physically* distinguishable from the "daughters of Jerusalem," who look on her, and that these observers are apt to stare at her because of this. Of the two striking characteristics mentioned in verse 5—her dark skin and her beauty[5]—it is on the former that the emphasis falls in verse 6, implying that it is her dark skin *rather than* her beauty in general that truly marks her out and makes her the focus of attention.

The passage itself makes clear, however, that this darkness (lit., "blackness") of skin is not something with which she has been born, but a coloring that has come about as a result of exposure to the sun. The situation is somewhat like that in Job 30:30, where Job's skin *grows* black (*šḥr*, as in Song 1:5–6) as a result of the heat of a fever. We should also note Job 30:28, where it is said that Job goes about "blackened" (*qdr*), but *not* by the sun (implying that "blackening" by the sun is a fairly normal phenomenon). The verbal root *qdr* is also echoed in the proper name "Kedar" in Song of Songs 1:5—"dark like the tents of Kedar."[6]

There is no evidence in the text, then, that the female speaker is *racially* distinguishable from those who observe her. It is simply that her life has been lived outdoors, and she has consequently been scorched by the sun, which has "gazed" at her (Heb. *šzp*, as in Job 20:9; 28:7) long before humans ever stared at her. This is why she is dissimilar from these other women who have lived (we deduce) a more secluded life.

The life outdoors has, moreover, been imposed on her (v. 6). She fell victim to the anger of the men in her family, whether her own full brothers or

---

5. It is not easy to understand why the NIV translates the first line of v. 5 as "dark am I, *yet* lovely," unless it is simply that the translators were simply so burdened by the weight of tradition or their own assumptions that they could not find any alternative plausible (see Pope, *Song*, 307–10, for a discussion of the history of interpretation, although I do not agree with him on the precise meaning of Heb. *šḥr*). There is nothing in the passage itself that implies that the "staring" of v. 6 is the result of anything other than interest and fascination, and there is therefore no reason to assume that anyone in the speaker's (or author's) mind would doubt that darkness and beauty were perfectly compatible. We should translate the line: "I am dark *and* lovely."

6. The reference is to a tribe in northern Arabia, known from such biblical passages as Gen. 25:13; Ps. 120:5; and Isa. 21:16, as well as from Assyrian and other records. Some have wondered whether the Masoretic text's "Solomon" in Song 1:5 provides a sufficiently neat parallel to "Kedar" and have suggested repointing the text so as to produce "Salma(h)" (cf. NIV note) or "Shalmah" (NEB)—another ancient Arabian tribe. Whether we can demand that biblical authors think and write as neatly as we might prefer is, of course, open to serious question. It would certainly be a curious coincidence to find this tribe mentioned only four verses distant from another occurrence of the same set of Heb. consonants where the name "Solomon" is clearly intended (Song 1:1).

not—"mother's sons" is an ambiguous phrase.[7] These brothers seem to be the dominant males, in the absence of any father (cf. 8:8–9). No father is in fact mentioned anywhere in the song. It is the brothers who have put her to work in the vineyards to "take care" (*ntr*) of them. Her statement that, by contrast, she has "neglected" (lit., "she has not taken care of [*ntr*]") her own "vineyard" (a recurring metaphor throughout the Song for her own person) could in principle be taken as meaning that her neglect was consequent on being given her new task. She has been working outside and *therefore* has been unable to look after her appearance.

It seems more likely, however—since it would be a little curious to hear of the brothers' anger without also hearing of any reason for it—that we are being given a hint here of the event(s) that led to her presence in the vineyards. She has not maintained or protected her own vineyard in a more intimate, sexual sense, but has known the love of a man. This was the cause of the outdoor work, which in turn means that her beauty is not "classical" according to the norms of the society in which she now moves, for it has not been cultivated in the way that is normal in that society. She is bronzed and beautiful but still an object of curiosity to those who have been kept within the home and away from public exposure (or perhaps, within the royal court and away from the countryside).

Our speaker's attention has moved from her beloved man (vv. 2–3) to a wider circle of women, who also admire *him* while finding *her* unusual (vv. 4–6) and then back once again at the end of verse 6 (implicitly) to her beloved. In verse 7 she returns to address him. He is characterized as a shepherd, out in the countryside with his sheep and sought by his beloved in a manner similar to that of Joseph seeking his brothers in Genesis 37:16 (note the similarity of the question), although evidently not for the same purpose. She wishes to know where she can find him when he stops for his siesta at noon.[8] It is important that she should have this information, so that she can go directly to the spot, for she fears otherwise that she will be mistaken by his shepherd-colleagues for a prostitute, lingering among them in the hope of business.

That is the implication of the reference to the "veiled woman" in verse 7, as the story of Judah and Tamar in Genesis 38 makes clear. In this story

---

7. The reference could be to half-brothers. More likely, however, the phrase reflects an emotional distance between the woman and these men who have been so angry with her and who exercise such dominating power over her. See further on 8:8–12 below, where the mutual relationship between lover and beloved stands in stark contrast to the other male-female relationships described. It is, in fact, only the lover who is referred to by the woman in the Song (in aspiration) as "brother." It is a term of intimacy that she refrains from using, for whatever reason, of these other men in her family.

8. See Pope, *Song*, 329, for some relevant information on siestas in warm climates.

Tamar lingers on the road to Timnah during the sheep-shearing season. Judah, seeing her sitting by the roadside with her face covered by a veil, assumes she is a prostitute (38:13–16). Whether we are to think of our speaker as similarly veiled—because this is her normal attire or because she does not wish others to know who she is (cf. Song 4:1)—or whether she only risks being treated "like" a veiled woman because of her behavior is not clear.

The vulnerability of the woman who lingers alone in the company of men is in any case also implied in the man's response to the woman in 1:9. As he is attractive to many women and draws them after him (vv. 3–4), so she is like "a mare harnessed to one of the chariots of Pharaoh." In common with chariots throughout the ancient Near East, Pharaoh's chariots were typically drawn by stallions hitched in pairs; a mare placed among them would have caused great disruption and distraction, as her scent or mere presence was detected.[9]

Both the woman and the man in Song of Songs 1, therefore, are aware of the likely consequences in terms of unwanted male attention, should this "most beautiful of women" wander aimlessly through the countryside. Thus, he gives her some directions (v. 8). The directions are so vague, however, that one detects a sense of playfulness rather than of real threat in verses 7–9 overall. She is to "follow the tracks of the sheep" and, likened to a shepherdess herself, to graze her young goats "by the tents of the shepherds" (v. 8—presumably the place where the shepherds as a group, and thus the lover, have their siesta).

It is unclear whether any of this bucolic language is meant literally. That the lover is a "shepherd" and she is a "shepherdess" may speak as much of their compatibility and of their destiny to be together as of anything else.[10] Whatever the case, his initial acknowledgment of her beauty in verses 8–9 continues in verses 10–11. Here we find both the recognition that she is already adorned with jewelry and the commitment to add to these adornments. The commitment is perhaps shared with the other admirers alluded to in verse 9 and now referred to in the "we" of verse 11. She is as widely admired as he is (cf. v. 3).

The interpretation of the whole chapter turns on precisely how we understand verses 12–14, in particular on whether we think that verses 13–14 are intended in contrast to verse 12. On balance the view taken here is that a contrast is indeed intended between the "king" and the "lover." The woman

---

9. See ibid., 338–40, for a helpful discussion and some historical examples.

10. Although I do not believe that the king and the lover in the Song are the same person, it should be noted that the mere fact that the lover is characterized as a "shepherd" by no means, of itself, proves that he is not also a "king." The king in the ancient Near East was often described as a shepherd of his "flock" (note biblical examples in, e.g., 2 Sam. 5:2; Ezek. 37:24).

reports that while the king was "at his table," her "perfume spread its fragrance" (v. 12). The Hebrew word behind the NIV's "perfume" is *nerd*—the English "nard," an expensive aromatic oil deriving from a plant that grows in northern and eastern India and was widely believed to possess aphrodisiac qualities (cf. Mark 14:3).

This report, however, which does not especially suggest any ongoing intimacy between the woman and the king (it is an isolated incident in the past), immediately gives way to two affirmations about what the *lover* means to the woman, which taken together do imply ongoing intimacy.[11] The lover is like "a sachet of myrrh resting between my breasts" (v. 13). Myrrh is an equally precious substance that is also associated with physical love (e.g., Prov. 7:14–20, but there of illicit sex), yet one whose fragrance does not simply *go out* from the woman to the king but actually *draws* the lover into the most intimate and ongoing embrace. He "lodges" between her breasts—the Hebrew verb is *lyn*, which usually means "to spend the night" (e.g., Gen. 28:11; Job 24:7). He takes up residence in this intimate place, in which a woman might have secreted a sachet or pouch of perfume.

He is, moreover, like "a cluster of henna blossoms," which, in addition to producing their famous reddish dye, also give out a strong, pleasant fragrance. We deduce that women of the time may also have secreted clusters of these blossoms about their person.[12] It is perhaps also significant that a cluster of henna blossoms is shaped somewhat like the male sexual organ. The blossoms in question are said to derive from "the vineyards of En Gedi"—a famously fertile oasis on the western shore of the Dead Sea. The name of the place means literally "kid-fountain," which is interesting in the light of the reference to "young goats" or kids in verse 8. Its presence underlines the extent to which the imagery of the passage carries with it overtones of both eroticism and fertility (cf. Gen. 38:17, where a kid is thought an appropriate payment to the apparent prostitute, Tamar; also Judg. 15:1).

What is particularly noticeable about verses 7–17 as a whole, in fact, is the extent of the outdoor imagery in contrast with the indoor imagery of verse 12. This does not seem unconnected with the fact that the woman herself is said to have come most recently from the outside into the indoor

---

11. The contrast would be still greater if Heb. *bimsibbo* ("at his table") were rendered in the light of the occurrence of the noun in 1 Kings 6:29; 2 Kings 23:5; and Job 37:12 as "round about himself, in his vicinity," rather than understood as referring to a round table or a low couch beside a dining table. The line would make perfect sense (*pace* Snaith, *Song*, 22–23) as emphasizing the distance of the king from the woman (he occupied his own space), in contrast to the intimate closeness of the lover.

12. See Pope, *Song*, 348–49, 350, 352–53, for details on nard, myrrh, and henna (cypress).

world, represented by the king and his chambers (v. 4) and by the staring daughters of Jerusalem (vv. 5–6). She now returns, as it were—when love is the focus of the passage—to the place where she has most recently spent her time. She is a vineyard-keeper (v. 6), and it is with vineyards that she most naturally associates her lover in verse 14.

The conversation between the lovers, suspended in verses 12–14, is picked up once again as the chapter closes (vv. 15–17). The woman is, to the man, "my darling" or "my friend" (ra'yati), and the man is, to the woman, "my lover" or "my love" (dodi)—terms found throughout the song (ra'yati in 1:9; 2:2, 10, 13; 4:1, 7; 5:2; 6:4; dodi on twenty-six occasions, including 1:13–14; 2:3; note that the woman also calls the *man* "my friend" [re'i] in 5:16).

He is struck in particular by her eyes, which he likens to "doves," perhaps referring to their brightness and quickness, to the fact that they flutter, or to their partial concealment behind a veil (like doves that hide away in dark recesses [2:14; 4:1]). She is struck more generally by his beauty and by the luxuriant (NIV "verdant") nature of the bed they share. They are evidently to be found lying together on lush foliage, out in the forest where the only roof-beams are the cedar trees and the only rafters are the firs. They have found their own chambers (cf. v. 4) and their own bed, located in their own forest "palace" (cf. the superfluity of cedar in Solomon's palace in 1 Kings 7:1–12, to which a contrast may be intended here).

As we reflect on the passage as a whole, then, it seems that we have three main characters rather than simply two. (1) There is the woman, who has come (at least in the recent past[13]) from the outside world to the world of the royal court, yet longs to return to the outside, where her special friend is to be found. (2) There is the king, who inhabits the inside world of the court (represented by his chambers and his dining table) and knows the woman (perhaps sexually, although this is not explicit) as a member of his royal harem. It is most natural to assume, in view of verses 1 and 5, that the king is Solomon; it is difficult to understand the presence of the name in verse 5 if this is not so. (3) There is, finally, the man who is to be found (if he does not actually reside[14]) in the outside world, represented by grazing lands, vineyards, and forests. He is certainly romantically and sexually (although this is still only implicit) involved with the woman.

---

13. It is far from clear, however, that her original *home* is outside the city: Both the dreams of 3:1–4 and 5:2–7 and the associated passage in 8:1–2 imply otherwise.

14. That the lover is *associated* with the countryside in the Song does not necessarily mean, of course, that his *residence* is to be found there. If the shepherd imagery of ch. 1 is any indication, we may well imagine that he is not a city dweller, although we must weigh against this the implication of the dreams of 3:1–4 and 5:2–7, which imply that he can (at least in a dream) be found in the city.

As the Song of Songs unfolds, we will discover more of these three and of the ties that bind them. We will also discover in the remainder of the book, as here, that the individuals are always bound up with wider circles of people who are drawn into their story and are involved in it. In a sense we, as readers, are also members of these circles, absorbed into the world of the text as its realities are described to us in such graphic terms and its intimacies become our own.

IF WE ARE fully to understand both the Song of Songs and its history of interpretation down to the present day, one of the first things we must do is to ensure that we understand something of what it meant to be a woman in ancient Israel, as we have access to that reality through the lens with which the Old Testament provides us. Both the laws and the narratives of the Old Testament suggest that the reality was often bleak.

Legally, women were regarded in the first instance as the possessions of males. The Ten Commandments as they appear in Exodus 20:1–17 already suggest this when they include a man's wife in the midst of a list of his possessions (20:17), and other texts presuppose it. Deuteronomy 22:13–21 describes, for example, the case of a man acquiring a woman as wife and subsequently hating her and slandering her by claiming he did not find proof of virginity (22:13–14). The woman does have some protection under the law, but the implication throughout the passage is that she is not a legal person in her own right. She is defended by her previous "owners" (her father and mother); the father, being the one who gave her to the husband in the first place (v. 16), is also the one to whom any fine for slander must be paid (v. 19). It is essentially a business or property dispute between men (did the father sell damaged goods to the other man?). The interest of the passage is resolutely male, the background issue being whether husbands can assure themselves that their children are really theirs. There is no escape for the woman from this situation of hatred and suspicion—she is either put to death, if guilty of not being a virgin, or condemned to live with a man who hates her and has publicly humiliated her, if innocent. Indeed, the penalty for the woman, if guilty, is death; but the penalty for the man, if guilty (and even though he threatened the life of his wife), is only a monetary fine.

The secondary status of women vis-à-vis men before the law is seen again in a passage such as Leviticus 27:1–8, where females are worth roughly half as much as males in financial terms. According to Deuteronomy 22:28–29, moreover, the rape of an unbetrothed, unmarried woman elicits only a fine of fifty shekels of silver from the man, paid to the father to compensate *him* for the damage to *his* property, while the woman, who has no say in the matter, suffers not only the trauma of rape but the further trauma of being forced to live with the man who raped her. It is clear from such examples, along with others, that the legal position of women in ancient Israel seems to have differed little from the legal position of slaves. The law provided them with some protection, but it was protection of a limited kind in a world dominated by men, whose decisions were at all points decisive for their fate.

As we turn to the narratives of the Old Testament, the nature of this world is graphically portrayed. It is not that individual women are by any means always treated badly by individual men, for there are many biblical stories to be found in which men behave virtuously toward women (e.g., the story of Ruth). Yet it is the men who have the overt power, whether they choose to use it for good or ill. The story of Ruth itself displays this reality, even while presenting Boaz to us in a good light.

In the Old Testament world female choices are usually limited and female power is rigorously curtailed, especially when it comes to matters of love and marriage. It is often a dark place, in which male power wreaks havoc on the female world. One of the most striking examples is the story of Jephthah the Gileadite and his daughter in Judges 11:29—40. Jephthah makes a vow that applies to any of his possessions. His daughter, tragically, is the first of his possessions to greet him and is killed as a sacrifice to God. Jephthah does not blame himself for the evil he has brought on her but blames her instead for the evil she has brought on *him* (v. 35); nor does he offer himself in her place or refuse to fulfill the vow and suffer the consequences. The daughter simply serves the needs of the father, having no way of avoiding doing his will and finding solace in a male-ordered world only among her female friends, who weep with her (v. 38)—and even then, permission for this mourning has to be given by the father.

This story of Jephthah is a terrifying tale of the extent to which females, as possessions, could be victimized in the world of male power,[15] and it is by no means the only such tale in the Old Testament. This is what it means that, in our fallen world, men have come to "rule over" women (Heb. *mšl*, Gen. 3:16), regarding them as part of the creation over which governance must be exercised (cf. Heb. *mšl*, also in Ps. 8:6) rather than as partners in that government (Gen. 1:26—28).

The Song of Songs must certainly be understood against this background, as the opening chapter already makes clear. The woman to whom

15. See further P. Trible, *Texts of Terror: Literary-Feminist Readings of Biblical Narratives* (OBT; Philadelphia: Fortress, 1984), 93—116.

we are introduced had previously been subject to the power of the males in her family (the brothers, in the absence of any father). She now finds herself, along with other women, in the royal harem. It is to be doubted, to put it mildly, that she had much choice in the matter, which was probably settled by all the men (see comments on 8:8–12, where we gain some insight into the attitude of both the brothers and Solomon in respect of women).

The story of Esther gives ample evidence of just how little interest was shown by another king (and perhaps even by the author of the book) in the feelings or thoughts of young women whose presence in the royal harem was commanded. That entire tale underlines, in fact, just how man-centered the ancient world was. Queen Vashti is summoned to appear before King Xerxes and his drunken nobles and officials for no other reason than that he wishes to show off her beauty to them and thus to have his ego stroked (Est. 1). Her refusal to oblige creates a moment of crisis in the Persian empire, for the fear is expressed that other women will follow her example and that male power over women will be undermined. Vashti is therefore punished, and the search for a new queen ensues (ch. 2).

The king simply casts his net over his kingdom and trawls in as many beautiful women as he can find. Ridiculous efforts are then made to make these women as appealing as possible to the king (Est. 2:12), and he tests them out sexually, one by one, until he finds a competition winner. The whole exercise emphasizes the absolute power of men over women, the scant regard for the female person or future life they often display in exercising it, and the enormous effort they expend in retaining it. It is to be especially noted in the Esther story that the possibility that Esther herself might refuse to enter the harem or to sleep with the king is never for a moment considered. It is not, apparently, a realistic option.

While it is theoretically conceivable that the woman of the Song of Songs herself did not actually, in entering the royal chambers in 1:4, have sexual intercourse with the king, it is probably a somewhat romantic notion (though sometimes found in commentaries) to think that she would have been given any more say in the matter than Esther apparently was. We cannot be certain since the Song of Songs is not explicit on the matter, but general considerations, combined with the emphasis in 3:6–11 on the royal bed as a place of power and coercion from which sacrificial victims arise, suggest that when this song speaks of fidelity between the woman and her beloved man, it is not necessarily implying that she has never engaged (albeit unwillingly) in the physical act of sexual intercourse with anyone else. It is claiming, rather, that she has not abandoned her first love when faced with all the seductive pomp and glory of Solomon and his royal court.

It is just this fierce self-determination, however, that makes the Song of Songs such a remarkable piece of literature when set in the context of ancient Israelite culture. The world that is dominated by men certainly lies in the background of the book, but in the foreground stands a woman who will not be dominated and who exercises her freedom in extraordinary ways. She initiates love with her man of choice, announcing her intention right at the beginning of chapter 1 (1:2) and pursuing her lover (1:7) even while resident in the contexts that society has successively forced on her (vineyards and court).

She undoubtedly takes risks in doing so, for society will look askance at her course of action (1:7; the theme returns in 5:7 and 8:1); yet she persists. There is in *this* relationship with a man, at least, no male domination or ownership, but only the meeting of equal persons in dialogue with each other, verbally and physically. It is as if the curse of the Fall has been nullified, and we are now back in the Garden of Eden, where it is accepted that male and female are indeed created equally in the image of God (Gen. 1:27) and stand together in partnership as they relate to the rest of creation (Gen. 1:26, 28). It is as if, in the fertile, outdoor space where the lovers meet, they have once again captured the democratic intimacy of the first Garden, where woman is "woman" who corresponds to "man" (Gen. 2:23)—one flesh, naked, and never ashamed—and not simply "Eve," who is defined by her role as mother (Gen. 3:20) and destined to relate to her man only as powerful superior.

It is striking, indeed, that female initiative in Song of Songs 1 *results* in restored intimacy and joy. Female initiative in Genesis 3:6 (at the invitation of the serpent) results only in guilt and alienation—the first instance in the human story of men and women blaming each other for reality, as Adam accuses Eve, Eve the serpent, and the serpent (as it has been well said) finds himself without a leg to stand on.

The Song of Songs thus reminds readers of the Old Testament of something that we ought to have realized without its help, especially as Christian readers of these Scriptures, but have frequently missed. It reminds us that we are called not simply to live in the fallen world and accept its constraints, injustices, and horrors but rather to live out the kingdom of God in its midst. It reminds us of God's creation purposes as they are so wonderfully described in Genesis 1–2, and it rebukes us for forgetting so often throughout church history to keep these chapters in mind as we read Genesis 3 and the rest of the Bible.

When the legal and narrative sections of the Old Testament are read in the context of these opening chapters of Genesis (as Jesus himself invites us to do, Matt. 19:3–8), they are clearly seen only to tell us, first, of the realities of the fallen world and, second, of the ways in which God has provided laws that might mitigate only the worst effects of human wickedness. They do not provide us with any excuse for living contentedly with the world as we find it rather than seeking to live out God's rule in our lives, and they certainly do not provide us with texts that can be used to legitimate the world order as we currently find it in its fallen state.

Law and narrative, and indeed prophecy and other forms of Old Testament literature, must be read in the context of the whole of God's plans for the world in creation and redemption as they are revealed throughout the Bible, if they are not to be misunderstood in their particularity. The Song of Songs helps us to see this by presenting us with a male-female relationship that evokes Genesis 1–2 rather than Genesis 3 and many other parts of the Bible. Christian readers are helped further by texts such as Galatians 3:28: "There is neither Jew nor Greek, slave nor free, male nor female, for you are all one in Christ Jesus." The redeemed community of the church, which is the firstfruits of the redeemed creation, is a community that no longer knows of hierarchical distinctives and divisions. It is a community in which it is only one's identity as a human being in a relationship of love with God and neighbor that is important. It took the early church some time to understand what this really meant for Jews and Gentiles. It took the church that followed the early church a much longer time to understand what it really meant for slaves and masters. It has only very slowly been dawning on the church much more recently what it means for males and females.

The figure of the nonsubmissive woman who actively courts her man, seeking mutuality with him while refusing to give herself to another whose language is that of power, naturally invites reflection, in the context of the canon of Scripture, on the relationship of God to God's people. It has perhaps been one of the more obvious consequences of the fact that biblical interpretation has largely been carried out historically by men who lived in male-dominated societies in which women had little power and were widely regarded as passive, dependent characters, that the understanding of God has often reflected in an unbalanced way the self-understanding of the men who articulated it.

God has frequently been conceived of among Christians, for example, as a distant, emotionally uninvolved person, albeit all-powerful and sovereign over human affairs. If God is the only initiator of all that happens in the universe, human beings only respond fairly passively to his plans and advances. He has been conceived of, in other words, as "male," and "male" has been interpreted in terms of what it means to be male in societies that have been highly patriarchal and hierarchical and to some extent emotionally dysfunctional. The way in which women have often been regarded in Christendom is not unrelated to this fact since, as feminist theologians have pointed out, when God is male, the male tends to be god.

The Bible does, of course, teach us about a God who is all-powerful and sovereign over human affairs and whose will in the end shall be done. It does not teach us that God is any more male than female, however (Gen. 1:27 explicitly suggests otherwise), even though it encourages us to call God "Father," and it does not know of a God who is emotionally uninvolved with his creatures, nor does he coerce them through force of will, expecting only a passive and somewhat fatalistic response.

The Song of Songs, when read in the larger canonical frame, reminds us of what Jesus should already have taught us: that God enters human space vulnerably and quietly, wooing us and intriguing us rather than overwhelming us with power, and he is certainly joyous rather than offended when we take the initiative in pursuing his embrace. It was the Pharisee (as well as the disciples), we recall, who were offended by the woman who came to Jesus in Bethany with perfume, not between her breasts but in an alabaster jar, depositing both perfume and kisses on his head and feet (Luke 7:36–50, with parallels in Matt. 26:6–13; Mark 14:3–9). It is those whose love likewise drives them to seek Jesus who will find him.

No man ... would think to compliment his fair one by writing of her ... as if she had lost her retiring modesty, her female dignity, and degraded herself by doing that for which every man would despise her. The very first word of this Song, then, stands as witness against the notion of its being a human love-song.... Till fishes mount to sing with larks on the shady boughs, and nightingales dive to ocean's depths to court the whales, no man, of any age, of any clime, of any rank, can be supposed to write ordinary love-songs in such a style.[16]

One wonders if the nineteenth-century clergyman who spoke such words had ever for one second considered that Scripture might wish to critique his culture rather than simply to legitimate it. He is only one in a long line of Christian men throughout the centuries, however, who have found themselves unable to look the Song of Songs straight in the eye, as it were, and deal with its implications for a Christian worldview. The description of the strong, self-determined female character presents an obvious challenge to all cultures (and not just Christian Victorian culture) that have sought to disempower

---

16. Dr. James Bennett, 1838, cited in Pope, *Song*, 135.

and to pacify women, not least through caricature, and have considered them (whether legally or simply intellectually) to be second-class human beings.

The roots of caricature and discrimination in Christendom lie in the Old Testament itself, for as we have seen, the biblical legal tradition in particular can be read by those who wish to do so as justifying both bad male attitudes towards women and also all those laws in countries influenced by the Judeo-Christian heritage, which for so long throughout history have denied women the same legal status and rights as men.[17] Jewish law as found in the Mishnah (*m. Qid.*) already builds on biblical law in this way:

> By three means is the woman acquired and by two means she acquires her freedom. She is acquired by money or by writ or by intercourse . . . she acquires her freedom by a bill of divorce or by the death of her husband.

In terms of Jewish *attitudes*, we need only recall the well-known Jewish morning prayer, "Blessed art thou, O Lord our God, King of the Universe, who has not made me a woman." A spectacular exemplar of Christian attitudes is provided by Augustine:

> If it were not the case that the woman was created to be man's helper specifically for the production of children, then why would she have been created as a "helper"? Was it so that she might work the land with him? No . . . a male would have made a better assistant. One can also posit that the reason for her creation as a helper had to do with the companionship she could provide for the man. . . . Yet for company and conversation, how much more agreeable it is for two male friends to dwell together than for a man and a woman! . . . I cannot think of any reason for woman's being made as a man's helper, if we dismiss the reason of procreation.[18]

One might wish that this were the only example of such sentiment that could be found in the history of the church, but it is far from being so. If the strength and self-determination of the woman in the Song of Songs has not been easy to accommodate within a pathologically male and Christian intellectual universe, however, then the fact that she is an overtly *sexual* being has proved still more difficult. Celibate Christian monks like Bernard of Clairvaux, who first became monks partly through fear of female sexual power,

---

17. It is to be fervently hoped that the reader will not seek to defend Western culture at this point by noting that such laws also discriminate against multitudes of men (e.g., slaves, Catholics, Jews)—as if this were truly any defense at all.

18. Cited from C. C. Kroeger and J. R. Beck, eds., *Women, Abuse and the Bible: How Scripture Can Be Used to Hurt or Heal* (Grand Rapids: Baker, 1996), 33.

were hardly likely to welcome the entrance of this sexually powerful literary woman into their intellectual and emotional inner chamber.

We are, after all, thinking of a postapostolic and medieval world, in which the church father Jerome could advise an inquirer not to allow her daughter to bathe because of the danger of exciting her sexual desire. It is intriguing to note that Jewish tradition, even though it has just as routinely allegorized the Song of Songs, has not proved nearly as neurotic as Christian tradition regarding this matter of sexuality. The reason is that it possesses a much more robust creation theology than Christian thinkers have usually managed to articulate. Thus:

> We … believe that God, blessed be He, created everything as His wisdom dictated, and He created nothing containing obscenity or ugliness. For if we were to say that intercourse is obscene, it would follow that the sexual organs are obscene…. And how could God, blessed be He, create something containing a blemish or obscenity, or a defect?

Robert Gordis, who cites this text in his commentary, also reminds us of the story of the rabbinic student found hiding in his rabbi's bedroom, observing his lovemaking. Challenged about his presence there, he declared: "This, too, is Torah, and I wish to learn."[19]

The fact of the matter is that we find in the Song of Songs, and specifically here in chapter 1, a text that challenges all worldviews that insist that women are not fully persons in their own right, that women must not take initiatives and make free choices about their lives and their loves, and in particular that they should not display sexual desire and pursue a beloved man with a view to sexual consummation with him. We have a text that insists that male-female relationships, when lived out in fulfillment of God's creation purposes, are about mutuality and not about dominance/submission. We have a text that absolutely challenges any idea that our humanness in any aspect is incompatible with our spiritual calling. It not only sanctifies sexual intimacy but also sanctifies frank speech about sexual intimacy.

Song of Songs 1 is a text that has a significant amount to say, therefore, to modern Christians who hold the Old Testament to be Scripture and yet find themselves unable, as many Christians historically have been, to bring their attitudes and their behavior into line with this song's vision of the world—unable to affirm that women are truly made in the image of God as equals with men, that they should rightly be confident in their nature as

19. Gordis, *Song*, xi.

women rather than deferential and submissive toward men, that sexual intimacy is a good thing, and that an overtly sexual woman is not thereby a bad person. There is no question but that the embrace of this vision would bring widespread and deep healing both to fractured lives and to fractured relationships within the Christian church, as both men and women understand their humanity more fully in relationship with the good God who created it for integration and for blessing.

The challenge and the healing of the Song of Songs is offered, however, not only to the church, but also to the world at large. For it is by no means only in the church that we find fractured selves and fractured relationships. In many ways, in fact, the sexual revolution in the West, which was in part a reaction to a false and repressive view of sexuality, has resulted in a far worse state of affairs than what preceded it; for sexual expression, when it is not rooted in a committed, lifelong relationship, wreaks destruction. The mantra of the revolution is "sexual freedom," but slavery rather than freedom has resulted, and entire new empires (e.g., Internet pornography) have surfaced in which abusive male power has again reasserted itself over women.

The Song of Songs does not speak in favor of sexual repression or the denial of woman's humanity and rights. But neither does it speak in favor of sexual license and the kind of pursuit of "rights" (by men or women) that in the end destroys all humanity. The sexual intimacy of this song is intimacy in the context of commitment—the kind of commitment that in actuality and in mutuality gives up "rights" in pursuit of relationship.

The self-sacrifice that is thus involved in true love is above all displayed, for the Christian reader of the Song of Songs, in the events of the life of Jesus. This is the model of committed love for human beings, whose erotic moments are thus bound up with a much larger framework of commitment and, beyond that, with the Love that lies at the heart of all things. The freedom of women, although it must be defended against male desires to curtail it (since men are not gods), is in the end not to be understood as different from the freedom of men. It is a God-given freedom, which is only in the end exercised to mutual human benefit when it is embraced as such and offered joyfully and faithfully back to God.

To the extent that the Song of Songs reminds us of that, when read as part of Scripture, it challenges a culture that has lost its bearings and its sense of purpose and has come to look for things in sexual expression itself, as a phenomenon, that it can never find. The challenge to the culture is no greater than the challenge to the church, however; for it is possible that people might not have had such difficulty in understanding how to be sexual beings and godly beings at the same time if Christians had done a better job, historically, of modeling how it can be done.

The man said,

"This is now bone of my bones
  and flesh of my flesh;
she shall be called 'woman,'
  for she was taken out of man."

For this reason a man will leave his father and mother and be united
to his wife, and they will become one flesh.

The man and his wife were both naked, and they felt no shame.
(Gen. 2:23–25)

Song of Songs 2:1–17

¹ I am a rose of Sharon,
   a lily of the valleys.

² Like a lily among thorns
   is my darling among the maidens.

³ Like an apple tree among the trees of the forest
   is my lover among the young men.
 I delight to sit in his shade,
   and his fruit is sweet to my taste.
⁴ He has taken me to the banquet hall,
   and his banner over me is love.
⁵ Strengthen me with raisins,
   refresh me with apples,
   for I am faint with love.
⁶ His left arm is under my head,
   and his right arm embraces me.
⁷ Daughters of Jerusalem, I charge you
   by the gazelles and by the does of the field:
 Do not arouse or awaken love
   until it so desires.

⁸ Listen! My lover!
   Look! Here he comes,
 leaping across the mountains,
   bounding over the hills.
⁹ My lover is like a gazelle or a young stag.
   Look! There he stands behind our wall,
 gazing through the windows,
   peering through the lattice.
¹⁰ My lover spoke and said to me,
   "Arise, my darling,
   my beautiful one, and come with me.
¹¹ See! The winter is past;
   the rains are over and gone.
¹² Flowers appear on the earth;
   the season of singing has come,
 the cooing of doves
   is heard in our land.

¹³The fig tree forms its early fruit;
  the blossoming vines spread their fragrance.
Arise, come, my darling;
  my beautiful one, come with me."

¹⁴My dove in the clefts of the rock,
  in the hiding places on the mountainside,
show me your face,
  let me hear your voice;
for your voice is sweet,
  and your face is lovely.
¹⁵Catch for us the foxes,
  the little foxes
that ruin the vineyards,
  our vineyards that are in bloom.

¹⁶My lover is mine and I am his;
  he browses among the lilies.
¹⁷Until the day breaks
  and the shadows flee,
turn, my lover,
  and be like a gazelle
or like a young stag
  on the rugged hills.

THE DIALOGUE BETWEEN the lovers continues in chapter 2, although with frequent third person references and an occasional aside. The opening verses are best taken as representative of this dialogue (even though it is not absolutely clear from the grammar that v. 1 is indeed spoken by the woman). She compares herself in verse 1 to two flowers, and her lover responds in verse 2 by agreeing with her self-description in at least the second case, and possibly even praising her more highly than she herself does.

Our uncertainty as to what *exactly* is being claimed by each speaker stems from uncertainty as to the precise nature of the flowers mentioned in verses 1–2, with their roots in the fertile soil of the plain of Sharon (extending from the borderlands in the region of Egypt up to the promontory of Carmel on Israel's western side) or in the equally fertile river valleys. If we are indeed dealing with a "rose," then as far as we can tell we are dealing with a flower that would have been unusual in Palestine before the third century B.C. The imagery would in this case suggest the rarity of the woman's beauty (in line with 1:5–6). Isaiah 35:1, however (the only other occurrence of Heb. *ḥᵃbaṣṣelet*), may be taken to imply a more freely blooming and common Palestinian flower that carpets the ground, such as the crocus, hyacinth, or narcissus.

The ancient versions are already uncertain, as their renderings of both Song of Songs 2:1 and Isaiah 35:1 illustrate. A looser translation might be preferable, following the lead provided by LXX: "I am a wild flower." We are unable to decide on the basis of the specific evidence, however, whether the sense is "I am a particularly beautiful wild flower" or "I am only a common wild flower." All that can be said is that the confident tone of 1:5–6 perhaps favors the former understanding.

We are not helped much in our determination here by the reference to the "lily," for we cannot be certain that the Hebrew word *šôšanna* refers to the same plant as Egyptian *sššn*, "water lily," nor whether the *šôšanna* was considered a plant of especially rare beauty.[1] It is only with the man's response in comparative terms that we gain a definite sense that he, at least, regards the woman's beauty as unparalleled: She is a lily among thorns (the unprofitable plant of Job 31:40). If there is any hint of concern in her statement in 2:1, then, that she is only one among many and therefore that her beloved might fall for one of the others who are pursuing him (cf. 1:3–4), he is quick to reassure her. This woman is the only one he thinks of as a beautiful flower (2:2). The others are a bramble patch, which only serves to highlight her uniqueness.

This affirmation from her beloved now leads the woman into an extended reflection on her love for this man who chases after her, woos her, and delights—but exhausts—her (vv. 3–13). As she is to him a flower among thorns, so he is to her a fruit tree among other, nondescript trees of the forest (v. 3). The precise nature of the fruit tree (which reappears in 8:5) is, again, uncertain. It has variously been identified as a tree bearing apples (NIV), apricots, oranges, lemons, and quinces, with the first of these attracting most attention and already being found in the LXX. Yet one wonders whether the suggestion of strong fragrance in both the verbal root *npḥ* ("breathe, flow upon") and the allusion found in 7:8 best fits the apple.

More important than identifying the tree, however, is to understand the imagery, which speaks of both protection and pleasure. This is a tree that offers "shade" (*ṣel*) from the harsh sun (which an apple tree in truth does not)—protection from the outside world analogous to that provided in political terms by those with power, including God (cf., e.g., Heb. *ṣel* in Judg. 9:15; Ps. 17:8; Lam. 4:20). This tree, while it provides shade, also provides delightful sustenance. Its fruit is not only nourishing but also sweet to

---

1. See Pope, *Song*, 367–68, for an extensive discussion of the flowers.

the taste. The woman thus feeds from the man, while sitting in the safety of the orchard.

The imagery of verses 4–6 also suggests both protection and consumption. The beloved man provides the woman not only with food but also with wine. He takes her into a "house of wine" (lit. trans.; NIV " banquet hall"; cf. similar expressions in Est. 7:8; Eccl. 7:2); the NIV translation conjures up in our minds an urban context that does not sit well with the resolutely pastoral imagery throughout the passage. A more rural "drinking spot" is perhaps intended or even just a vineyard.

If the correct translation of Hebrew *diglo* is indeed "his banner," then the allusion is perhaps to a sign hung at a "drinking spot" to indicate the nature of the activities there, rather in the manner of the painted and pictorial signs that hang outside traditional English public houses. The "sign" that the man hangs over his metaphorical drinking house is "love," indicating that love is the defining activity in which the man and the woman engage.

It is stretching the meaning of Hebrew *degel* somewhat, however, to translate it simply as "banner," particularly in this nonmilitary sense. In fact, the primary meaning of the word in the book of Numbers (the only other book in the Bible in which the word occurs) seems to be not "military standard," but "military unit." The associated verbal root *dgl* is found in Psalm 20:5, also in a military context, where any reference to banners is likewise dubious, but a reference to fighting in the name of the Lord makes sense.[2] The root *dgl* is further found in Song of Songs 5:10; 6:4, 10, where warrior imagery can plausibly be accounted for (see below).[3]

Our interpretation should be guided by these other occurrences as well as by the material in chapter 1 that makes it clear that other men find this beautiful woman attractive and by the language of protection in 2:3. The man sustains the woman with wine, as he has in 2:3 with food, but he also offers her military protection, as in 2:3 he offered her "shade." The "military force" that looks after her is his love. His protection of her is attentive, committed, and prepared for trouble, in the manner of a royal bodyguard looking after a well-loved king or queen.

The beloved thus experiences overwhelming, overpowering love and finds herself faint or ill when confronted by it (v. 5). She seeks sustenance—more food to give her strength to meet this power and to heal her lovesickness. She

---

2. The context of plea in Ps. 20:1–5 seems to me to require that the "shout" in v. 5 should not be one of joy after victory but one of entreaty and supplication in pursuit of victory: "We shall cry out for your victory, and fight in the name of our God" (pers. trans.).

3. These latter references make it difficult to accept Gordis's view that the *degel* of 2:4 is to be understood on the basis of Akkadian *dagalu*, "to see, look," as referring to a look or a glance (*Song*, 81–82)—an interpretation followed with different nuances by later commentators such as Murphy, *Song*, 132; Pope, *Song*, 375–77.

may be seeking this food from bystanders (note the masc. pl. form of the verbs in v. 5, which can conceivably refer to the daughters of Jerusalem mentioned in v. 7, where there is also a surprising *masc.* suffix on Heb. *ʾetkem*), or perhaps she addresses the man himself using a plural verb.

Certainly it is more of *his fruit* that she asks for (NIV "apples" in v. 5). This suggests, of course, that although she is overwhelmed, she has no desire that his attentions should cease. There is some evidence, in fact, that the "raisins" or raisin cakes (cf. NIV in 2 Sam. 6:19) she requests were associated with ancient Near Eastern fertility cults (e.g., Isa. 16:7; Hos. 3:1; cf. also Jer. 7:18; 44:19, for "cakes" offered to the Queen of Heaven) and may more generally have been considered to possess aphrodisiac qualities. We note the association of "apples" with love and fertility in Song of Songs 8:5. If so, she asks for food that, while strengthening her, will also heighten her experience of love. Verse 6 finds her lying still in her lover's arms, his left supporting her head and his right embracing her (note the same phrase in 8:3; Heb. *ḥbq* refers to sexual embrace also in Prov. 5:20).

As the lovers embrace, the woman (or possibly the man)[4] addresses the puzzling aside in verse 7 to the "daughters of Jerusalem" (cf. also 3:5; 8:4). They are asked to swear an oath that they will not "arouse or awaken love until it so desires." If "love" is taken to refer to one of the lovers themselves, this is then a request from either the man or the woman that their beloved should not be disturbed as he or she sleeps and should be left in peace until eager to arise. But if love is understood more abstractly as the power that has just been described in verses 3—6, the request becomes more of a warning to these other girls. Because of the devastating and overpowering results of love, they should ensure that it is awakened only when the timing and circumstances are right. There is, in effect, "a time to embrace and a time to refrain" (Eccl. 3:5), and it is as dangerous to awaken love when it does not desire to be woken as it is to rouse the sleeping animal of modern proverbial tradition (e.g., the English dog or the Korean lion).

The terrible power of love is indeed well expressed in Song of Songs 8:6—7, which follows closely on a similar aside to the daughters of Jerusalem in 8:4; this latter passage above all tips the balance in favor of interpreting the aside as a warning. The oath laid on the Jerusalem girls refers, appropriately, to "gazelles" (*ṣᵉbaʾot*) and "does" (*ʾayyalot*; see also 3:5). The man himself is portrayed as a gazelle (*ṣᵉbi*) or young stag (*ʾayyal*) in 2:8—9, 17; 8:14, while 4:5 and 7:3 compare the woman's breasts to two fawns of a gazelle (*ṣᵉbiyya*; cf. Prov.

---

4. It is conceivable that the man speaks here, yet the same aside appears in 3:5, where the context certainly favors the female voice, which has spoken of the (silent) man in the third person throughout vv. 1—4; an abbreviated version of it in 8:4 is also best taken as spoken by the woman, whose words are found in 7:9b—8:3.

5:18–19, where the woman is "a loving doe, a graceful deer"). The emphasis of the imagery falls, among others things, on grace and beauty (underlined by the fact that *ṣᵉbi* also means "beauty," cf. Ezek. 7:20; 26:20).

The oath, in shifting the focus from the singular "gazelle" and "doe" to the plural, thus appears to set the particular relationship described in verses 3–6 in the context of all other relationships of the same kind. The daughters of Jerusalem are to think of the "gazelles and ... does" generally (i.e., all lovers) as they consider whether to "arouse or awaken love." Whether the speaker makes a request or delivers a warning, the verse thus has a "love your neighbor as yourself" aspect to it, for these daughters of Jerusalem are themselves some of the "does" who might in the future be found embracing their "gazelles." They swear as those who have common cause with our speaker and his or her beloved.

The scene now changes as the imagery of the gazelle is developed in 2:8–17. We find ourselves no longer hearing of embrace, but of wooing. The gazelle is swift and athletic as well as beautiful, and he speeds across the mountains and hills toward the woman who waits for him (vv. 8–9). As he arrives at her home, he tries to catch a glimpse of her through the windows[5] and to strike up a conversation with her. She is indoors, along with unspecified others; she addresses a broader group, probably female (cf. esp. v. 15, "our vineyards"), with whom she has solidarity and with whom she shares her life (note *our wall* in v. 9). He seeks to draw her out from this shared and protected space into the beautiful springtime countryside (in the same way that in ch. 1 she has moved from indoors to outdoors to find him).

The winter rains are past, and we have arrived at a season in Palestine when the flowers are blooming, the vines and figs have begun to ripen (cf. Mark 13:28), and migrant birds have begun to appear (Song 2:11–13; note the migratory dove in Jer. 8:7, which knows and keeps its times). The silence of the wet winter has given way to the joyful sounds of spring—"the season of singing" (*zmr*, v. 12), whether of birds or humans.[6] Yet while these

---

5. The NIV's "peering through the lattice" (v. 9) is an intelligent guess at the meaning of some unusual Heb. on the basis of the preceding "gazing through the windows." There is no other case in the Old Testament, however, of Heb. *ṣwṣ* meaning "to peer," and its normal meaning of "to blossom" fits well the general context of spring and new growth (cf. Heb. *niṣṣan*, "blossom," in v. 12, comparing also the verbal *nṣṣ* in 6:11; 7:12). It seems better to understand the line as indicating how the man appears to the woman as she returns his gaze through the window. He is the herald of spring, "blossoming" in front of her eyes.

6. There may also be an allusion to pruning in Heb. *zmr*, which can also mean "to cut." The objection to the idea rests on the allegedly later date of pruning in July–August, whereas the remainder of the imagery suggests that we are in March–June. Whether we can truly press such a pedantic point in a poem of this nature is unclear, however, and it is not entirely clear in any case that pruning was indeed restricted to the later summer (cf. Isa. 18:5 and the discussion in Pope, *Song*, 395–96).

doves sing, enjoying the springtime air, the beloved woman, who is also the lover's "dove" (v. 14), is to be found hidden away inside the house, as inaccessible as if she were lodged in the rocky crevice of a high mountain, where not even a gazelle can go (cf. Jer. 48:28). She is, to him, a divinity (the dove being a symbol of the goddess of love in various ancient cultures),[7] but she is beyond his reach, hiding her face from his gaze. He desires her to come out and be seen.

To this plea that the woman should emerge from the shadows and the safety of her home and fly away with her lover (vv. 10, 13–14), the words in verse 15 are best understood as a female response. The man has suggested to her that her present location is a limiting one defined by fear, and he has spoken of the outside world only in glowing terms, designed to make it attractive to her. Her response is to remind him, however, that the outside world is in fact a dangerous place for herself and other women (the "us" of v. 15).Their reluctance to come outside is justified. It is a world in which there are "foxes" determined to ruin "vineyards"—something for which foxes were well known in the ancient world, as the famous lines from Theocritus (*Idylls*, 1.49) illustrate:

> I hate the brush-tail foxes, that soon as day declines
> Come creeping to their vintaging mid goodman Micon's vines.[8]

The "vineyards" in question in 2:15 are the very women whom men would like to persuade to come outside (cf. 1:6), and the "foxes" are presumably those men intent on sexual conquest. If the woman's lover and his friends really do wish women to come out into the countryside, then, they are invited first to ensure their safety: "Catch [pl. masc. imper.] for us the foxes." As in 1:7 it is difficult to know whether the threat is considered to be a real one or whether the tone is more lighthearted and teasing.

The woman herself has shown no true reluctance to meet her lover in 2:3–6. As the chapter ends she is found once more in his arms (vv. 16–17). The couple are entirely given over to each other ("my lover is mine and I am his," v. 16; cf. 6:3; 7:10) and lie together, safe from all "foxes." As they do so, he "browses among the lilies"; in the light of 4:5, where the woman's breasts also browse among the lilies, implying that the lily field is the female body on which the breasts move and have their being, this phrase may suggest that he covers her body with kisses. The woman has already been described in 2:2 as a lily.

---

7. See Pope, *Song*, 399–400.

8. Cited from Pope, *Song*, 403. I had occasion in 1976 to speak with a vineyard owner near Bordeaux who knew his Bible well, and he claimed some immediate modern knowledge of the same kind of activity.

The final verse draws the whole section from verses 8–17 together by explicitly returning to the imagery of gazelle/young stag, but now probably with a different sense. In verses 8–9 the gazelle/stag bounded across the hills in the hope of persuading his beloved to come out to him. In verses 16–17 his hopes have been realized, and he is invited in all his athletic beauty to bestride "the rugged hills" (Heb. *bare bater*)—hills cut by a deep valley. These are most naturally understood in the context as referring to the beloved's breasts, especially when compared with 4:5–6 and 8:14. In 4:5–6 the description of woman's breasts, which are like twin fawns of a gazelle browsing among the lilies (4:5), is also followed by a reference to the day "breaking" and the shadows fleeing (4:6, paralleling 2:17) and then by a statement of the man's intention of going "to the mountain of myrrh and to the hill of incense" (4:6).

Myrrh has already been associated with the woman's breasts and the presence of the lover there in 1:13, and 8:14, which is similar to 2:17, replaces *bare bater* ("rugged hills") with *bare bᵉśamim* ("spice-laden mountains"). The "gazelle" begins his quest on mountains and ends it there also—but on mountains of a different kind, divided by their own kind of "valley."[9] Whether the lovers are lying together during the night or the day is unclear. The breaking or breathing (*pwḥ*) of the day can refer to daybreak (the fresh breeze of morning) or to the day's end (when the day grows cool and it is possible to breathe freely). Likewise the fleeing of shadows can be caused by the sun rising or going down. In any case, the lovers are together for an extended period and revel in each other's company.

Song of Songs 2 plays with similar ideas to chapter 1. The lovers know both separation, in that he lives in the outside world and she (currently) in the inside world, and intimate communion, in that it is possible to overcome the disjunction at least for a while and enjoy the freedom and joy of the springtime countryside. They are both in solidarity with broader communities, and the woman in particular looks to her broader community for support in her love for the man.

Yet the broader communities also threaten their relationship in various ways, offering places to hide from the lover and presenting certain dangers (rivals for the woman's affection; "foxes"). Strength and protection, as well as passionate love, are therefore themes of the poem. This love is itself a powerful and dangerous force, which must be treated with respect. One of the implied threats to their relationship, the king, is not mentioned in this chapter, but he will return in chapter 3.

---

9. Pope, *Song*, 410, cites an interesting if indirect ancient Near Eastern parallel, in which a goddess invites a king to prance on her bosom like a calf.

Bridging Contexts

THE STORY OF creation in Genesis 1–2 is the story of emergent beauty. God speaks into being the wondrous world we inhabit, and it is in every respect "good" (Gen. 1:4, 10, 12, 18, 21, 25, 31). The trees in this glorious garden, in particular, remind us that the goodness of the world is not simply a matter of practicalities but also of aesthetics, for they are "trees ... pleasing to the eye and good for food" (Gen. 2:9). Human beings were never intended to live by bread alone, starved of beauty.

We ourselves are described as the pinnacle of divine creation, fashioned in the image of God and reflecting, therefore, divine beauty and glory—the beauty that the psalmist so desires to behold as he visits the Jerusalem temple (Ps. 27:4). There is therefore no embarrassment among Old Testament authors in drawing attention to human beauty, which they do frequently (e.g., Gen. 12:11–14; 24:16; 29:17; 1 Sam. 25:3; 2 Sam. 11:2; 14:25, 27). It is only one aspect of the amazing goodness and wonder of creation on which the psalmist in Psalm 8 reflects, remembering above all the position of great dignity and responsibility in which human beings have been placed by God (Ps. 8:3–9):

> When I consider your heavens,
>   the work of your fingers,
> the moon and the stars,
>   which you have set in place,
> what is man that you are mindful of him,
>   the son of man that you care for him?
> You made him a little lower than the heavenly beings
>   and crowned him with glory and honor.
> You made him ruler over the works of your hands;
>   you put everything under his feet:
> all flocks and herds,
>   and the beasts of the field,
> the birds of the air,
>   and the fish of the sea,
>   all that swim the paths of the seas.
> O LORD, our Lord,
>   how majestic is your name in all the earth!

It is important to place Song of Songs 2 first of all in the context of this wider biblical embrace of beauty in part because significant numbers of Christians throughout the ages have been either hostile to beauty or dismissive of it, as if it were something trivial or even dangerous in respect of

Christian faith and life. This unease with beauty has often been bound up with a theology that focuses in an unbalanced way on what is wrong with the world and with human beings at the expense of what is right and good. This theology has often in turn been bound up with a low sense of self-esteem.

We might best refer to this theology as "worm theology," taking as our text Psalm 22:6, "But I am a worm and not a man, scorned by men and despised by the people." The point about the psalmist here, however, is precisely that he has been dehumanized by suffering and oppression. He is not really a worm; he simply feels he is. He is truly a man—a precious creature made in God's image with a view to enjoying God and God's creation to the fullest extent. His true calling is not to crawl into a hole in the ground, that is, to escape the world that is currently causing him so much pain. His true calling is to live, as he is able, in joyous affirmation of God, his own humanness, and the rest of God's creation, thus glorifying God even among those who will not acknowledge him as God. It is this vocation that he is able to own once again later in Psalm 22:22–31, as lament over great pain gives way to extravagant praise.

Worm theology, as a principled stance rather than as a temporary aberration, is not truly Christian theology. It denies the truth that the cosmos is good, even though it is touched in every way also by sin; that human beings are invested with dignity and glory by God, even though they are also touched in every way by sin; and that it is this same creation, human and nonhuman, that has been redeemed in Christ, so that it may reflect once again the undiminished glory of God. We are not summoned to hate ourselves and to despise the rest of creation, as if these attitudes somehow honor the Creator. We are summoned to understand ourselves as precious creatures loved by God and thus to love ourselves and the rest of creation (even while lamenting the dark side of reality as it spoils and corrupts what is good). Such perfect love casts out not only fear (1 John 4:18) but also self-loathing and all contempt for the rest of the universe.

It is the beauty of creation that is the driving theme of Song of Songs 2, as it has also been a focus of chapter 1 (e.g., 1:5, 8, 15–16). The glory of springtime provides the backdrop, as life bursts anew from the earth and all creatures stir and renew their activity. We are invited to picture flowers and fruit trees, mountains and hills, deer and doves, and to marvel at it all. The lovers identify themselves with this wider creation, merging with it and embracing it as they affirm each other with images drawn from the flora and fauna that they see around them, each competing with the other as they try to find ways of extolling the other's beauty. He is to her an apple tree, strong and sweet, and a graceful and athletic stag. She is to him a lovely flower and a beautiful dove.

There is no darkness in all of this. There is only joyous, mutual affirmation and a glorying in what is good. If Genesis 2:23 cites the male cry of delight when confronted by the woman ("bone of my bones and flesh of my flesh"), then Song of Songs 2:16 provides us with the reciprocal female cry ("my lover is mine and I am his"). The warning of 2:7, it should be understood, is not a warning about love as such. It is only a warning about the importance of always placing love in the right context.

There is a broader *biblical* context in which our thinking about beauty must be set, of course, once we have grasped that it is an intrinsically good thing. We need to remember that it is transient and vulnerable to destruction, as is everything created (Isa. 28:1; 40:6–8). Beauty should not blind us to our mortality and thus lead us to live foolishly. It is indeed capable, like every aspect of creation, of leading us astray from God and into damaging relationships with other people (Prov. 6:25–26).

It is entirely possible, of course, to be beautiful but to lack important qualities of character and perhaps even to neglect the development of these through attachment only to the outward appearance of things (Prov. 11:22; cf. also Matt. 23:27). Most centrally, beauty is not to be compared in value to godliness (Prov. 31:30; 1 Peter 3:1–6), and it is no more important than those many other attributes or gifts that make up the human person (note, e.g., the emphases in Prov. 31:10–31). We remember that the suffering servant of Isaiah 53:2–3 is said to lack notable physical beauty and yet to be central to God's redemptive plans for the world.

From all this material we learn not to despise beauty or to trivialize it, but at the same time not to divinize it or to allow it to become more important to us than it should. It is one thing (and an important thing) for two lovers to affirm each other for their beauty, and even for a man to speak of his beloved in terms that compare her to divinity (see comments on 2:14). When he does so, he has precedents in the poetry of the ancient Near East (e.g., in King Keret's description of the beauty of his bride in terms of the divine ideal represented by the goddesses Anat and Ashtarte).[10] It is quite another thing, however, for beauty to become the lens through which all reality is filtered and in the light of which all human worth is judged, and thus to become essentially a false god.

Biblical literature stands apart from its ancient Near Eastern context precisely in its insistence that what is created cannot itself be truly divine, and particularly in its teaching that what is human, although reflecting divinity, is not itself truly divine. Biblical authors are acutely aware that when created things become the objects of worship, they cause great human damage.

---

10. See ibid., 75.

Insofar as beauty becomes to us an idol, it too causes great human damage—to those who have it or desire it or lack it. Insofar as it is received as a gift of God and set in the context of all that is good in God's creation, it enhances our lives and becomes itself a pointer to God, whose own person it reflects.

Since God Almighty has sealed me with the stamp of beauty, I desire that men should behold it and recognize His grace towards me, and I will not veil it.[11]

It is strange that those who believe in a God who has created all things should have been found so frequently throughout history trying to "veil" beauty in various ways. It seems that we human beings, in our fallen state, have a deep and insistent urge toward repression. The physical veiling of women as they participate in public life, extending sometimes to the covering of the whole body, is still insisted upon in some (mainly Islamic) cultures to this day, lest the exposure of feminine charms should lead on to male lust and perhaps even to something worse. The idea that it is perhaps men who have a problem here, if they cannot look on beauty without exhibiting a perverse response to it, does not seem to be on the table for discussion.

The same is true of some modern Christian books on male-female relationships, which do not demand of their female readers any literal veiling but do tend to suggest that the main responsibility for improper male attitudes and actions toward females lies with women and not with men and to urge all kinds of semi-veiling as part of a package that might prevent the Christian brother from stumbling. It is all too often the same books that also place the main burden of responsibility on the woman for the prevention of extramarital sexual intimacy with a man.

Christians are the heirs at this point of a long-standing tradition that has characterized (and caricatured) the female as a calculating temptress and the male as the beleaguered victim of temptation and has sought to repress both beauty and sexuality in the cause (as men thought) of a purer spirituality—a spirituality that indeed eschewed all that was sensual and that set faith over against all normal appetites. The Reformation reflected this same understanding of the world in its sometimes deliberately destructive assault on beauty as it came to expression in medieval churches and in its advocacy of worship in barren spaces where nothing could "distract" the worshipers.

A spiritual person comes to be regarded, in the tradition of Christian asceticism (whether Protestant or Catholic) of which we are thinking here,

---

11. Ayesha, wife of the prophet Muhammad, cited in *CDRSQ*, 136.

as a person who disguises and or trivializes his or her own beauty, and perhaps even comes to deny it or hate it. Such a person in general pronounces himself or herself much more interested in heavenly, internal things than in what is merely external, earthly, and transient, whether in creation generally or in human beings especially. One cannot be spiritual, in fact, if one does not "veil" beauty, whether in oneself, in others, or in creation at large.

The issue is still a live one in the modern church. The Song of Songs is therefore of great contemporary significance for the modern church. It is not at all uncommon to meet Christians whose faith, as it has been taught to them or has simply been "caught" as they have grown up, has left them with extraordinarily low self-esteem and an inability to affirm the world as a good and beautiful place. They have, in one way or another, imbibed "worm theology," in which it is crucially important that one at all times and in all ways affirms how sinful and dark the world and the self truly is and denies that apparent goodness, truth, and beauty is anything other than a cover for deep depravity. It is a theology that always sees the world as a glass of water half empty rather than a glass of water half full.

One test of the extent to which worm theology has laid its clammy hands on our souls would be to discover whether we ourselves feel comfortable as Christian people taking the words of the woman in Song of Songs 1:5 or 2:1 (or even the words cited at the head of this section) on our own lips or would regard someone else badly for taking them on his or her lips. If we have grown up in a family where our ordinary humanity has been constantly diminished and set in conflict with what is spiritual, and where criticism for falling short of an ideal has been more common than affirmation of who we are, or if we have been adopted later in life into a Christian community that has emphasized how sinful we are much more often than it has told us how wonderfully we are made and how marvelously our whole beings have been redeemed, then it is unlikely that these words, as Christian words, will leave us untroubled.

This is even more likely to be the case if we have had to endure at some point in our lives the trauma of physical or sexual abuse, for such experiences make it still more difficult to believe that the real material world in which we live is either beautiful or good. They create all sorts of obstacles to the acceptance of either ourselves or others in all our human physicality. The "veiling of beauty" often becomes, in this case, a necessary means of emotional survival.

Whether for this reason or for others, Christian people often seem deeply ill at ease with their humanness, most specifically their bodies, and find it difficult to accept their entire humanity as a divine creation, whatever their theology may theoretically tell them. A repression of the self that may have begun as an external force has now become a driving, internal force, to such an extent that even long-married couples do not attain to a state of "naked but not ashamed" (Gen. 2:25) but are haunted by the ghosts of times past (as well as sometimes being oppressed by the words of preachers present).

The Song of Songs, especially chapter 2, offers the church both challenge and healing. It challenges false dichotomies between the earthly and the heavenly, demanding that we give up all notions that beauty is somehow incompatible with godliness and even with God. It undermines our false belief that beauty should be veiled because it can be dangerous and that a strong sense of the self and its beauty are undesirable in those (specifically women) who walk the Christian path. It legitimates, rather, the enjoyment of and the mutual embrace of beauty as an aspect of the enjoyment and the embrace of God, and it encourages the affirmation of each other in our beauty and "very goodness" (cf. Gen. 1:31).

This mutual affirmation is itself a direct means by which our healing begins, whether in general community terms or in the unique intimacy of the one-to-one committed relationship of marriage. None of us can ever receive too much affirmation from others of the reality that we are beautiful and beloved. No husband and no wife can ever offer the spouse too much affirmation of this kind, in the midst of the intimacy of lovemaking, or be too frank in their language in doing so. It is one of the most direct ways in which the repression in our lives, along with the causes bound up with it and the consequences that flow from it, begins to be addressed and resolved. It is one of the means by which redemption and healing come to us. As two Christian authors have recently well said:

> God ... calls husbands and wives to use our words to push back the chaos and shape our lives into order and beauty. He calls us to use our words to bring life to those who hear them.[12]

Affirmation of beauty is one way in which this is achieved, for as we understand deep in our being that we are affirmed and loved by God and by others, we will find ourselves able to affirm beauty elsewhere. Only as the church thus reintegrates beauty and godliness in its thinking, in fact, will it be able to act as salt and light in a Western culture that is obsessed with physical human beauty but has lost all sense of perspective about it. Human beauty has indeed become, for the culture, an idol. It is something to be worshiped and adored. It is the provider of all earthly blessings, comfort, and financial security. It is devotion to its cause that leads to such widespread and neurotic attempts artificially to cultivate and prolong it.

---

12. D. B. Allender and T. Longman III, *Intimate Allies* (Wheaton, Ill.: Tyndale, 1995), 97.

The damage to the souls and to the physical and emotional well-being of those who are beautiful is obvious, as is the damage to those who exploit them for profit or pleasure and those who measure themselves by their standard and feel they fall far short. The Christian response to this idolatry should not, however, be that beauty should be repented of (as if this were possible or desirable). It should be that beauty is *God-given* and not a god.

It is already implicit that in speaking such words, whether to those who worship God or those who do not, Christians are following God's example, who called beauty out of nothing with his words and yet also set it in order. The affirmations of beauty that flow between the lovers in Song of Songs 2 are in fact not dissimilar to those that flow from God to Israel in Ezekiel 16:7—13, which also employs typically frank biblical language:

> You grew up and developed and became the most beautiful of jewels. Your breasts were formed and your hair grew, you who were naked and bare.
>
> Later I passed by, and when I looked at you and saw that you were old enough for love, I spread the corner of my garment over you and covered your nakedness. . . . I clothed you with an embroidered dress and put leather sandals on you. I dressed you in fine linen and covered you with costly garments. I adorned you with jewelry: I put bracelets on your arms and a necklace around your neck, and I put a ring on your nose, earrings on your ears and a beautiful crown on your head. So you were adorned with gold and silver; your clothes were of fine linen and costly fabric and embroidered cloth. Your food was fine flour, honey and olive oil. You became very beautiful and rose to be a queen.

The story of Ezekiel 16 has an unhappy ending, of course, for Israel trusted in her own beauty and betrayed her lover. That God looks for an "intimate ally" in his people, however—that he may make her beautiful and affirm her as his own—is clear enough. Human love at its best reflects this divine pursuit of the beloved, for our love for one another reflects (albeit imperfectly) God's love for us. It actually helps us (even enables us), in fact, to believe that God does love us and is pursuing us. It is a means of grace, pointing us toward the end of all things as it is pictured in Revelation 19:7:

> Let us rejoice and be glad
> and give him glory!
> For the wedding of the Lamb has come,
> and his bride has made herself ready.

Song of Songs 3:1–11

¹ All night long on my bed
    I looked for the one my heart loves;
    I looked for him but did not find him.
² I will get up now and go about the city,
    through its streets and squares;
  I will search for the one my heart loves.
    So I looked for him but did not find him.
³ The watchmen found me
    as they made their rounds in the city.
    "Have you seen the one my heart loves?"
⁴ Scarcely had I passed them
    when I found the one my heart loves.
  I held him and would not let him go
    till I had brought him to my mother's house,
    to the room of the one who conceived me.
⁵ Daughters of Jerusalem, I charge you
    by the gazelles and by the does of the field:
  Do not arouse or awaken love
    until it so desires.

⁶ Who is this coming up from the desert
    like a column of smoke,
  perfumed with myrrh and incense
    made from all the spices of the merchant?
⁷ Look! It is Solomon's carriage,
    escorted by sixty warriors,
    the noblest of Israel,
⁸ all of them wearing the sword,
    all experienced in battle,
  each with his sword at his side,
    prepared for the terrors of the night.
⁹ King Solomon made for himself the carriage;
    he made it of wood from Lebanon.
¹⁰ Its posts he made of silver,
    its base of gold.
  Its seat was upholstered with purple,
    its interior lovingly inlaid
    by the daughters of Jerusalem.

¹¹ Come out, you daughters of Zion,
>   and look at King Solomon wearing the crown,
>   the crown with which his mother crowned him
> on the day of his wedding,
>   the day his heart rejoiced.

IF SONG OF Songs 1–2 are characterized by intimate and carefree dialogue between the two lovers, even where there is a physical separation between them that must be (and is) overcome, chapter 3 has a very different character. The longing of the woman for the man that is expressed in the 3:1–4 is communicated not to the man himself, who is entirely absent and "lost," but to unannounced bystanders (the daughters of Jerusalem perhaps, mentioned in v. 5, and through them the readers of the chapter). Moreover, there is a much more anxious tone to the speech, which concerns a frantic search. Verses 6–11 do not explicitly concern the man and the woman at all. They apparently deal with (as translated by NIV, but see further below) a procession associated with King Solomon. The emphasis of this passage falls on possessions rather than on people and their relationships, on opulence rather than simplicity, and (I will argue) on coercion rather than intimacy. *Observation* is invited and indeed commended (v. 11) rather than *engagement*—in line with the third-party and somewhat distanced references to the king in chapter 1.

The major interpretative question concerns the precise relationship between the two parts of the chapter, which both tell us of things that happen during the night (note the unusual Heb. plural *ballelot* in vv. 1, 8), involving a bed (Heb. *miškab* in v. 1 and *miṭṭa* in v. 7, NIV "carriage"), and which both place a "mother" in a prominent position (*ʾem*, vv. 4, 11).

The first bed is the one on which the woman is lying as the chapter opens and on which she seeks "the one my heart loves" (v. 1)—a phrase repeated in verses 2, 3, and 4 (such repetition communicates the intensity of the longing). The phrasing implies that we are reading of a dream (cf. also 5:2–8; Dan. 2:28–29). Thus, 3:2 is intended not so much to tell us what happens next (as the NIV's "I will get up now" implies) as to describe what the woman says to herself and does during the dream. That is, she does not look for the man while in the bed, only later attempting the different strategy of looking for him in the city. She looks for the man only while in the bed, saying to herself in her dream, "Let me arise . . . search" (v. 2).

The identical report of failure at the end of each of verses 1 and 2 refers to the same dreamt search; the first part of verse 2 simply expands on the first part of verse 1. The city in which the search takes place is not identified, and it is perhaps not sensible to pursue this question, given that we are in dreamland. But if a location is sought, then Jerusalem is the obvious candidate.

The watchmen who "find" her (*mṣ³*, v. 3) as they "make their rounds" (*sbb*) of the city—in the midst of her own frantic "rounds" of the city (*sbb*, v. 2; NIV "go about the city") and of her failure to "find" (*mṣ³*, vv. 1, 2) her beloved— are likewise the shadowy figures of dreams. They neither challenge the woman about her unusual presence at nighttime in the city (cf. 5:7), nor do they answer her question. It is not clear how they would have *known* the answer to the question, given that the lover has hitherto been identified as someone from "outside" and has apparently only met his beloved there (chs. 1–2). The shadows of the night simply flit past, as our desperate female moves through the streets; suddenly, without details provided, she finds her man (v. 4).

Her anxiety is communicated in what happens next. She grasps hold of him (*³ḥz*) and refuses to let him go (*rph*, "to leave alone, forsake"), escorting him to her mother's house and, within the home, to her mother's bedroom (*ḥeder*, as in Song 1:4). Now they are reunited in intimacy once again. Whether the dream bed is the same as the real bed of 3:1 is not made clear, but the previous reference to the king's chambers in 1:4 and the following material concerning the royal bed in 3:6–11 suggest not. She does not in reality live with her mother any longer. The maternal home (which is presumably real enough in itself, 8:1–2) is simply symbolic in the dream-world of the security and safety for which the woman yearns—the security and safety of much younger days.

Thus, the mother embraces both her daughter and her lover and hides them away in her inner chamber, with all its associations with the womb ("the room of the one who conceived me," v. 4). A frightening separation has been overcome, and the lovers lie together under parental protection and blessing. The terrifying power of love has once again been demonstrated, however—a love that can invade even the realm of the unconscious and bring with it unsettling thoughts. It is no surprise that the warning that follows the embrace in 2:6–7 and 8:3–4 should therefore also be found following the implied embrace in 3:5. The daughters of Jerusalem, we hear, should be wary of stirring up love until the time is right. It is a power far beyond their control, which drives one to dream crazy dreams, if not to enact them.

Turning now to the adjacent passage in 3:6–11, we need to acknowledge first of all that many commentators have not found any connection between these verses and verses 1–5. Roland Murphy presents the common view (although he does not, like some, believe that the name "Solomon" is literally meant of the ancient Judean king): "These verses describe a procession of 'Solomon,' which has nothing to do with the episode of the woman's search in vv 1–5."[1]

Yet it is far from clear that there is any real procession—usually thought of as a wedding procession (3:11)—in this passage, and once the idea of the wedding procession is banished from the mind and we resist all the questionable interpretations of individual verses that follow on from this false premise, the two parts of chapter 3 have more in common than one might at first think. For the text does not concern, as some commentators seriously seem to believe, the pilgrimage of a princess across the desert from Egypt (or some other distant land) in a heavily defended and expensive sedan chair. It concerns the heavily defended bed of the wealthy Solomon, who has all things at his disposal (including women) and possesses no neurotic fear of losing a unique beloved (in contrast to 3:1–4), yet knows nothing of either intimacy or fulfillment.

We begin with the ʾappiryon that Solomon made (v. 9), which, in spite of the highly misleading definite article in the NIV ("*the* carriage"), is not to be presumed in advance to be identical with the "carriage" (representing a different Heb. word, miṭṭa) of verse 7. That identity remains to be seen.

The word ʾappiryon is unique in the Old Testament and is problematic as to its precise derivation.[2] But the description of it that follows in verses 9–10 clearly suggests a stationary structure (or part of one) rather than a portable structure. Its "interior" or middle (toko) is said to be "paved with love" (NIV "lovingly inlaid," v. 10). The verb rṣp does not otherwise appear in the Old Testament, but the noun riṣpa does, and it always refers to the paved floor of a temple or palace (2 Chron. 7:3; Est. 1:6; Ezek. 40:17–18). The associated noun marṣepet appears in 2 Kings 16:17 of a stone pavement in the temple in Jerusalem (cf. also riṣpa, "glowing stone," NIV "hot coals," in 1 Kings 19:6; Isa. 6:6). These words never appear of the inlaid interiors of movable objects, which would not in truth move far if encumbered by many stones. Therefore, even if (as I will argue below) the "paving" is metaphorical rather than literal, the associations of the word are clearly with large, permanent structures rather than smaller, movable ones.

The Heb. word ʿammud (NIV "posts," v. 10), where it does not refer to a column of smoke, always refers to large pillars of a size and strength sufficient to support a building. It is used, for example, of the pillars in Solomon's palace (1 Kings 7:2–6) and in Ezekiel's temple (Ezek. 42:6), as well as of the prominent bronze pillars Jakin and Boaz that stood before the Jerusalem

---

1. Murphy, *Song*, 151.
2. See Pope, *Song*, 441–42, for a discussion.

temple (1 Kings 7:15–22). It is also used of the pillars of the movable tabernacle (e.g., Ex. 27:10–11), but this structure was also large and could not simply be lifted up *in toto* and carried across the desert. The point is that the
word *ʿammud* never refers to smaller "posts" such as those that might be found
on an allegedly movable *ʾappiryon*. If such hypothetical posts were indeed
fashioned out of silver, they would also add considerable weight to such a
structure.

The same is true of the gold mentioned in verse 10, whatever the unique
Hebrew noun *rᵉpida* (NIV "base") refers to. The verb *rpd* has already appeared
in 2:5 of the refreshment or support that fruit gives. It seems natural, therefore, to understand the *rᵉpida* as something that supports the pillars (cf. Job
17:13; 41:30, where the verb refers to something spread out on the ground)
and thus as the floor or foundation/base of the structure.

As we add all this detail together, we see that the overall impression is not
of a "carriage" at all, but of a large, fixed structure constructed (at least to a
significant extent) of wood and having silver supporting pillars and a gold
base or floor. The associations are, in fact, above all with Solomon's major
building works as described in 1 Kings 5–10, often with the use of the same
verb *ʿśh* ("do, make") that we find in Song 3:9 (cf. 1 Kings 6:31, 33; 7:6, 7,
51; 10:18). Two of the main building materials mentioned in 1 Kings are
indeed wood from Lebanon (5:6–10; 7:1–12) and gold (6:19–22, 30–35;
10:16–21), which can even be used for flooring (6:30).

It is not surprising, then, that some commentators have understood the
passage as alluding to Solomon's throne hall (1 Kings 7:7; cf. 10:18–20 for
the impressive throne), taking the "seat" of Song of Songs 3:10, upholstered
with expensive purple cloth, as the throne. It is certainly possible to read the
description of verses 9–10 as indicating movement, visually, from a vast hall
dominated by wood, presumably including a wooden ceiling, down the great
silver pillars to a golden floor, at last arriving at the centerpiece of the whole
scene—the throne that sits on a specially paved area (a mosaic of other precious stones, perhaps?) in the middle of the hall (cf. the analogous setting of
the great Sea in the temple on a paved area, 2 Kings 16:17). At least one of
the suggested derivations for the Hebrew word *ʾappiryon*, that it is from the
Egyptian word for "house, great house," fits this scenario.

I agree that *ʾappiryon* likely refers to a room within Solomon's palace,
known as the Palace of the Forest of Lebanon because of the heavy use of
wood from Lebanon in its construction. It is important to note, however,
the highly metaphorical language that is used in the second part of verse
10. The centerpiece is not a regular throne (*kisseʾ*, as in 1 Kings 7:7; 10:18–
20), but literally "a chariot" (*merkab*, cf. Lev. 15:9; 1 Kings 4:26); moreover,
the "middle" is not paved in the normal way with stone but with love. In the

context of the Song of Songs, this last reference to "love" (*ʾabᵃba*, as in Song 2:4, 5, 7), with which commentators who take a too literal approach to our chapter have had great difficulty, is much more likely to refer to acts of physical love than to the loving construction of a pavement or mosaic.

The "chariot" is, therefore, in my view best thought of as a bed, not a throne. It is the finely upholstered "vehicle" on which the king travels, as it were, on his journey of sexual delight. The "daughters of Jerusalem" (the king's many wives and concubines, plus other women; cf. 1 Kings 11:3; Song 6:8) pave his way, as it were, by lying with the king in the center of his *ʾappiryon*—his bedchamber. These are the people who provide the "stones" that enable the ongoing royal journey. There is, therefore, "movement" in 3:9–10. It is the movement, however, not of a sedan chair or carriage but of the "chariot" on which the king rides to meet the dawn.

It is now clear that it is this "chariot" within the *ʾappiryon*, and not the *ʾappiryon* itself, that is the *miṭṭa* of verse 7. The word *miṭṭa* is a regular word for a bed or couch, a common item of furniture in the Old Testament found, among other places, in a bedroom (e.g., Ex. 8:3, where the *miṭṭa* is in Pharaoh's *ḥᵃdar miškab*, cf. Song 3:1, 4 above). Beds can sometimes be lifted up and moved, of course (e.g., 1 Sam 19:13–16), depending on their mode of construction, and *miṭṭa* is thus used also of a funeral bier (2 Sam. 3:31). There is no justification in the Old Testament, however, for understanding *miṭṭa* as referring to a "carriage" or sedan chair. It is a bed, and it only "moves" in Song of Songs 3 because it is, metaphorically, a "chariot."

It is not inappropriate in the context of such fictive movement to refer to the sixty warriors associated with the *miṭṭa* as "escorting" it (NIV), so long as it is remembered that they are said in the Hebrew simply to be *sabib lah*, "around it" (v. 7; cf. *sbb* in vv. 2–3). It is the soldiers who are the most striking feature of the scene and thus attract detailed comment from our observer. They are (lit.) "warriors from the warriors of Israel" (v. 7; NIV "warriors, the noblest of Israel")—an elite guard, similar to David's bodyguard (e.g., 2 Sam. 23:8–39) but twice as many in number ("sixty" to David's "Thirty," itself a round number, cf. 2 Sam. 23:24, 39). They are all men who are (lit.) "held fast [*ʾḥz*] by the sword" (NIV "wearing the sword," Song 3:8)—that is, devoted to their profession and possessed by it (cf. *ʾḥz* in v. 4, "I held him")—and battle-hardened, ready for action (note the repetition of "sword" in v. 8, emphasizing military readiness). It is a heavily guarded bed, this "chariot" of Solomon. He goes into "battle" with good men around him to protect him from the "terrors of the night" (v. 8)—if it is indeed Solomon's protection that they are concerned with.

This raises the question, however, of what this section of chapter 3 is really about. It is difficult to read it in the Hebrew, stripped of all the interpretative translation that has confused fictive with real motion, without the thought occurring that we are dealing with satire. Here is the great Solomon driving around in his pretentious chariot-bed. He is the mighty Solomon, but he needs sixty elite warriors to stand around his "chariot" and help get him safely through the night. In truth he cuts a rather pathetic figure, inhabiting a lonely world of materialism and sexual conquest—for it is conquest that is implied by the military overtones of verses 7–8. The charioteer Solomon rides roughshod over the daughters of Jerusalem, on the road paved with sexual acts. It is perhaps *their* terror, rather than his, that is alluded to in verse 8; that is, the guards are stationed as much to keep the women in as to keep intruders out.

It is intriguing in this light that the language of 3:6, which seems partly designed to evoke the picture of clouds of myrrh and incense rising up from the bed, is at the same time very much the language of temple and sacrifice. The NIV's "perfumed" is *qtr* in the Pual, a verb that regularly means in the Piel "to make sacrifices smoke"; "myrrh" can be an ingredient of sacred oil (e.g., Ex. 30:23), and "incense" is heavily associated with sacrifice (e.g., Lev. 2:1– 2; 5:11). The Hebrew feminine noun *ʾabaqa*, "spices," is unique, but a masculine noun from the same root refers figuratively on one occasion to the clouds ("dust") under God's feet (Nah. 1:3). "Smoke" (*ʿašan*) is itself associated with the divine presence in verses like Exodus 19:18 and Isaiah 6:4. Note also Joel 2:30, which gives us the only other occurrence of *timᵃrot ʿašan*, "billows of smoke." The related *timorot* actually designates ornamental palm figures in the Solomonic temple (1 Kings 6:29–35; cf. also Ezekiel's temple in Ezek. 40– 41). Finally, the feminine participle *ʿola* ("coming up") is identical in form to the feminine noun *ʿola* ("burnt offering"), and the verb *ʿlh* is often used of offering up a sacrifice.

A good case can thus be made for taking Song of Songs 3:6 as an allusion to the sacrificial female victim who lies on the "altar," which is Solomon's bed. This is the force of the question, "Who is this coming up from the desert?" with its feminine pronoun *zoʾt*, "this." It is a woman who "comes up," but she is not moving laterally across a (real) desert in the direction of Jerusalem, as has sometimes been argued. She is, rather, arising from the royal bed, in the way that smoke rises up into the sky when sacrifices are burnt. We might translate verse 6 in this way: "Who is this, ascending from the desert like a column of smoke, burned with myrrh and frankincense made from the dust of the merchant?" There is, again, "movement," but it is on this occasion the movement of the sacrificial victim upward and not (at least in the first instance) of the royal "chariot" forward.

It is this initial "movement" in verse 6 that in fact first draws the attention of the observer to the chariot bed in verse 7. Perhaps we are meant to picture in our minds a watchman standing on a city wall, looking out intently into the desert and perceiving in the distance what looks like a column of smoke. As he watches the smoke clear, he sees for the first time ("Look!" in v. 7; *hinneh*, emphasizing the dramatic discovery) the detail of the "chariot." The situation is analogous to that in 2 Kings 9:14–29, where a watchman sees troops approaching in the distance and is gradually able to make out Jehu son of Nimshi driving his chariot. It is thus possible that the "column of smoke" in the end has a double function, suggesting both sacrifice and yet also the dust cloud stirred up by the royal entourage as (in the mind's eye) it approaches the one who is observing it.[3]

The characterization of the royal bed as a "desert" is, of course, a clever touch, for the desert or "steppe" in the Old Testament is uncultivated and unsettled land—an uncivilized place that is often described as harsh and infertile and is thought of as a place of danger, evil, and death (e.g., Ps. 107:33–38; Isa. 32:15; Jer. 4:26). It is the antithesis of the Garden of Eden (Isa. 51:3).[4] To name the royal bed a desert is to offer an understanding of it, we presume, that is very different from Solomon's understanding, in all his wealth and cultured sophistication. It is also to contrast most forcibly the love-making that happens there with the lovemaking that happens elsewhere in this song, which is so routinely associated with fertility and abundant vegetation (e.g., Song 1:13–17; 2:1–13).

If 3:6–11 is thus a dark and bitter satire concerning Solomon and his string of sacrificial female victims, then the point of the juxtaposition of 3:1–5 and 3:6–11, already suggested in the contrast just mentioned between the royal bed and others, becomes clearer. The first part of our chapter concerns an individual woman who is in love with an individual man and initiates an anxious search for him. She is certainly not an unwilling sacrificial victim in *this* relationship (although 1:4, 12 have implied that she has indeed been a victim of the king). She is not, in this relationship, simply a stepping stone on the man's road toward sexual utopia. She is an initiator; she knows no terrors of the night but steps out bravely into the darkness to find her man. Her fear is not that she will be required to spend time with him but that she will *not* be able to spend time.

---

3. The "bed" of v. 7, being a feminine noun, could itself in principle be connected with the pronoun *zo'␣t*, and v. 7 could be the answer to the question in v. 6: "Who is this? . . . the bed!" We might then understand Heb. *mi* (normally "who?") as meaning "what?" following Akkadian usage, or we might simply think of the bed itself as personified. It is by far the most natural reading of v. 6, however, when both normal Heb. grammar and syntax and the similar question in 8:5 are considered, to understand the question as referring to a woman *on* the bed rather than to the bed itself.

4. See L. Ryken et al., eds., *Dictionary of Biblical Imagery* (Downers Grove, Ill.: InterVarsity, 1998), 315–17, 948–51.

Moreover, hers is a vulnerable bed, unguarded by any military force. Her lover can leave it when he wishes. It is not surrounded (*sbb*) by warriors who are "grasped" (*ʾḥz*) by their swords. She herself must therefore "go around" (*sbb*) looking for her lover, risking the encounter with the guards who make their rounds of the city (*sbb*), and she herself must "grasp" him (*ʾḥz*). Yet in the midst of the vulnerability there is intimacy and joy, offered and overseen by the woman's mother, who provides her ordinary bedchamber (with its associations of fertility) for the lovers.

There is, by contrast, no true intimacy experienced in the desert, which is the extraordinary royal bedchamber. It is not even clear that there is Solomonic joy. We do read in 3:11 that Solomon rejoiced on his wedding day when his mother, too, was involved in the proceedings, but that wedding day, for all we know, may have been far in the past. The "crown" may be meant only as a sad reminder of better days—symbolic once of joy but now only of the royal power to command and especially of the unequal terms on which he meets women in his bed.[5] There is certainly no clear evidence elsewhere in 3:6–11 that a wedding is currently being celebrated, nor is there any overall emphasis throughout the passage on joy.

There is one final question that must be asked of 3:6–11: Who is speaking? The most natural conclusion is that it is still the woman who speaks—the one who refers to the king in the third person also in 1:4, 12. Perhaps we are even to think of 3:6–10 as a continuation of the dream in 3:1–4. Whether she dreams or simply conjures up a picture in her imagination, her purpose is to offer a stark contrast between her relationships with the two men already introduced in chapters 1–2, inviting the group of females around her ("daughters of Jerusalem" in v. 5; "daughters of Zion" in v. 11, probably phrased this way in order to avoid immediate repetition of "daughters of Jerusalem" in v. 10) to consider their nature. She is an eager participant in one of these relationships and a reluctant victim in the other, like the woman she observes in verse 6.

The dream of verses 1–4 thus bespeaks her fear of loss, and even a longing to return to the safety and security of her youth when she lived in her mother's house—the natural home of the woman who is not married (cf. Gen. 24:28; Ruth 1:8). The vision of verses 6–10 bespeaks her resentment of royal possession and her longing for release from royal coercion.

---

5. It should be noted that the women in v. 11 are only invited to view the crown, not a wedding. The word *ʿaṭara* is itself ambiguous and could refer to a royal crown or a wedding garland (cf. the picture of the wedding in Isa. 61:10). Given the satirical edge to the passage, it is possible that the intended picture is of Solomon reposing on his ridiculously overstated bed wearing nothing *but* his crown (cf. Amos 6:1–7; also Ezek. 23:40–41, with its interesting association of illicit sexual conduct and misuse of sacrificial incense and oil). The invitation is, in essence, to view a pathetic spectacle.

THE MEMORY OF King Solomon that was kept alive in Israel after his death was far from flattering. True, he was remembered as a wise king, yet also as one whose wisdom was not always used for honorable ends (1 Kings 2:13–46, where he snatches every opportunity presented to him in order to remove threats to his sovereignty over Israel). Toward the end of his reign it had degenerated to a large extent into a self-indulgent playing of games with words (1 Kings 10:1–13).[6] He was remembered as a king who was committed to worshiping and obeying God, yet as one over whom hung, from the start, questions about his integrity. His reign was one of progressive defiance of the Mosaic law concerning kingship (Deut. 17:14–20) as he accumulated horses (1 Kings 4:26, 28), then large amounts of gold (9:10–28), and finally large numbers of women (11:1–3). Eventually his accumulated individual indiscretions turned to outright apostasy (11:4–8). He was in many ways and to a large extent an ideal king ruling over an ideal kingdom; but ideal and reality were always in some degree of tension, and eventually the reality was much less than ideal.

To such an extent was this tension present that Solomon was spoken of among some of the rabbis of a much later time in the same breath as such notorious kings of Israel as Manasseh (2 Kings 21). Already in Ecclesiastes, however, the negative memory of Solomon provides the necessary backdrop against which Qohelet can enact his "Solomonic" quest for "gain" (see comments on Eccl. 1:12–2:26). There "Solomon" is presented as one who first finds wisdom limited in what it can achieve as he strives for profit from his labor, only to discover that pleasure is also a cul-de-sac. He was one who set out in a godlike way to transform his environment and thereby to facilitate his enjoyment of life by building houses, vineyards, gardens, and "parks" (*pardes*, as in Song 4:13) and by filling this earthly paradise with slaves, herds and flocks, hoards of treasure, and women. It did not, however, bring him any advantage. He was not able to burst through the limitations of mortality and frailty and get ahead of the game of life.

It is in the immediate context of 1 Kings 1–11 and Ecclesiastes 1:12–2:26, as they themselves direct us in particular back to the story of Creation and Fall in Genesis 1–3 and the following chapters, that we must understand Song of Songs 3. The biblical story is concerned to teach us that right at the heart of the human problem lies a refusal to live life within the confines that God has ordained for mortal beings, even though this may involve living in a paradise where joy abounds.

---

6. On this and other aspects of the ambiguous presentation of Solomon's reign in 1–2 Kings, see I. W. Provan, *1 and 2 Kings* (NIBC; Peabody, Mass.: Hendrickson, 1995), 23–102.

From the beginning human beings have chosen to transgress these God-given boundaries in search of something more, turning the life that comes to us as a gift to be enjoyed into capital that might fund our own imperial plans for exploitation and expansion. The more power we have, the more we become intent on creating our own paradise to supplant the kingdom of God—which is why it is kings like Solomon, more than any other sort of human being in the Old Testament, who are presented as grasping after godlikeness and seeking to fashion reality after their own liking. They have the resources at their disposal to make a credible attempt at equivalence with the gods.

Yet such human beings only represent in a particularly blatant way what the Bible presents to us as the characteristic set of human choices, and these choices have enormous repercussions for other people as well as for the aspirants to godhood. For if I as a human being grasp after divinity, regarding myself (rather than God) as the center of the universe, I will inevitably not view my fellow human beings any longer as equals made in the image of God toward whom I have a duty of love and respect, but rather as those whose interests must be repressed in favor of my own and whose value will be measured only in terms of their value to me.

The narrative of Genesis 1–6 shows us all too clearly how the progression works, as rebellion against God leads on to alienation between the man and the woman. They were created to be one flesh, naked but not ashamed (2:24–25), but now they are found divided, at odds with each other, concealed from each other (3:7). These humans, at least, stay together and build community, but in 4:1–16 we read of the alienation of brother from brother, with far more serious consequences (death on one side and exile on the other). Here we have the complete breakdown of community. As we move on, the alienation progresses even further outward from the center of the family circle—neighbor and neighbor divided and alienated (4:23–24) and the eventual slide into complete chaos and anarchy (6:5–7, 11–13).

Even humankind's many achievements of culture (4:17–22) cannot disguise this slow but remorseless breakdown of community. Sophistication, we are told, is quite compatible with barbarism. That it depends on some people serving only the interests of others is already suggested in Genesis 5:28–31, where a father welcomes a new son into the world (Noah) not so much as *son* but more as a *worker* who will release him from the toil imposed on all Adam's descendants (5:29).

It is in the context of this breakdown of community that we first hear of someone being married to more than one wife (Gen. 4:19–24); he is not a character whose other exercises in multiplication lead us to think that this development (which is not explicitly commented on) is a good one (note 4:23–24, where Lamech boasts to his two wives of the elevenfold and entirely disproportionate retribution visited on another man). It is a striking departure, in fact, from the creation ideal articulated in Genesis 2:23–24, where the marriage relationship is envisioned as involving one man and one woman. That polygamy became accepted by many Israelites does not mean that it was ever intended by God (any more than was the case with divorce; cf. Mal. 2:16; Mark 10:2–9).

It is in this context that the juxtaposition of Song of Songs 3:1–4 and 3:6–11, separated by the warning about love's dangers in 3:5, may be more fully appreciated. The first passage sets at the center of our attention a woman's desires, hopes, and fears, reminding us that she is not an object to be possessed or a number to be called, but a person to be encountered. In the world of her dreams, at least, she is able to pursue the man of her choice, grasp hold of him, and enjoy the deepest intimacy with him. We, as readers, are exhorted to respect that dream and not to hinder its achievement (as the watchmen do not, on this occasion, hinder its achievement).

The world of love is a dangerous one, however. Thus, in 3:6–11 we are transported to a different location to view its darker side. Here a king who has sought to build a paradise sits in a chariot bed, which is, ironically, a desert. He is the polygamist par excellence, adding ludicrous numbers of female objects to his collection of objects in general; the damage both to these women and to himself is plain. They are victims sacrificed on his altar, and he cuts a pathetic figure, surrounded by his elite troops and his luxurious fitments as he waits for his next offering to present herself. The mutuality of the first garden, so desperately sought by the woman in 3:1–4, is entirely lacking here. There remains only power and objectification.

So it has often been for women throughout history, whether biblical or later. The male lust for divinity has had terrible consequences for them, as the enormous social costs of idolatry have been passed on especially to those who have lacked independence and power. The Song of Songs provides us with a glimpse of what this felt like from the perspective of one of the victims—one of those many women collected by Solomon (and men of his kind) for his pleasure, who were to him (and men like him) merely "a breast or two," to use the casual and offensive words of Ecclesiastes 2:8 (see comments).

If the false gods of the cosmos (whether human or not) are thus apt to regard women only as somewhat anonymous means to their own ends, that is certainly not how the living God regards women (or any creature of his). The Bible teaches us that God made us creatures who possess freedom of will. Each one of us is precious to God as an individual, whom God desires to have in a right and good relationship with him. God has no interest in relating to human beings coercively, therefore (although in the end all mortal beings must reckon with his power if they will not embrace his love). His relating to each of us is highly personal and certainly not anonymous. None of us is merely a means to his ends; we are ends in ourselves.

Thus in the book of Hosea, for example, God speaks of wooing his bride, Israel, back from her sinful ways, restoring that one-to-one relationship she previously had with him (Hos. 2:14–23). When Jesus comes among his people in the Gospels, he likewise invites, rather than forces, those to whom he speaks to pursue a relationship with him. Above all, it is clear that those who yearn for the divine Lover and pursue him will indeed find him, as the woman finds the man in Song of Songs 3:1–4 (e.g., Matt. 7:7–11).

It is striking to note how often throughout the Gospels, in fact, Jesus is found relating to women in particular in ways that would have been considered offensive by many first-century Jewish men but that testify to equivalency of the love and esteem that God has for both women and men.[7] God's relating to us should always set the largest context in which we work out our relationships with each other. Judged in that context, it is clear which of the two kinds of male-female relationships described in Song of Songs 3 we should pursue. By the same token as we pursue relationships of joyful mutuality rather than of oppression and coercion, we will testify truly about who God is.

I was reminded again that our captors' obsessions with God and sex were not about religion or morality. They were ciphers for their own powerlessness: an impotence that they experienced unconsciously at a deeply personal level and also in the world of politics.[8]

Brian Keenan was held hostage along with others for over four years by various Islamic militias in Lebanon in the late 1980s. His account of captivity is a powerful and disturbing one, not least because of its perceptiveness about what happens to human beings when relationships are marked by significant imbalances of power. The captors inhabited a world in which they not only lacked personal and political power but had also embraced a version of Islam that in one sense legitimated their powerlessness and guaranteed its ongoing nature, for it was a religion of repression. As Keenan puts it:

Their submission to God was an act of repression. Their God was a God of judgement and of vengeance and they were afraid of this God. And their own repressed fascination with sexuality hinted at none of

7. R. E. Watts, "Women in the Gospels and Acts," *Crux* 35 (1999): 22–33.
8. B. Keenan, *An Evil Cradling* (London: Hutchinson, 1992), 272.

the liberation that a religion should present to its followers. It held them in bondage. These men existed in their own kind of prison, perhaps more confining than the one that held us.[9]

The consequences for the hostages, however, were not insignificant, for some of the jailers dealt with both their fear of the Westerners and their frustration over their powerlessness by inflicting savage beatings on them. Keenan is frank in drawing attention to the sexual aspect also in these beatings. There is an unholy mixture of God, sex, and violence in the whole environment that the book describes.

It is intriguing, therefore, to read that in the author's own turning to God in the midst of the horror of it all, he not only took comfort in the Psalms as a pathway to the God of love but also delighted in "the gentle eroticism of the Song of Songs."[10] He does not tell us whether he read the Song of Songs as speaking of God's gentle love for him or simply as reminding him powerfully, in an environment of awful human dislocation, of the reality of human intimacy. Perhaps both readings would have been equally comforting. The two loves—of God and of neighbor—are bound up with each other, just as surely as a God of repression is bound up with repression of one human being by another, and first of all with the repression of the self.

Long before God is invoked as the legitimator of self-repression and the repression of others, of course, he has already been abandoned as the bringer of life and of liberation. We need to get sufficient distance from the true God to make our claims about false gods seem plausible. In that abandonment, as we have seen already, we are not only alienated from God but also distanced from each other, as the communal bonds that hold us together are progressively dissolved. We are fractured selves—both damaging other people and being damaged by them, both sinning and sinned against. We find ourselves locked into sets of relationships that at best are flawed and at worst are destructive, marked by significant imbalances of power that lead us either to be oppressors or oppressed.

It is the sad but observable truth that sex is often bound up in this troubled world with power and its abuse, and sexual expression comes to be one of the primary ways in which the fracturedness of our existence is displayed for all to see. That which was gifted to us so that we could witness through it to the Love that governs the universe has thus come to symbolize everything that has gone wrong with human relationships in the world. It is a bitter irony when God is then reintroduced through the world's backdoor as the one who made everything just this way and who desires it to continue just as it is.

---

9. Ibid., 188–89.
10. Ibid., 188.

The conjunction of sex and power is not just seen in King Solomon. It is seen historically in such kings as Ivan the Terrible of Russia who, upon deciding to marry, commanded all the nobles in his realm (on pain of execution) to send their marriageable daughters to Moscow for inspection. Fifteen hundred girls turned up, and he chose one. The girl, naturally, had no choice in the matter, nor did the second wife who followed. A third (compulsory) fiancée in his later years took ill and died when informed of her fate.

The situation has been little different for most women throughout much of history, however. They have been the property of men, often traded between them without the slightest concern for any female opinion and with the shared assumption that the matter was somewhat akin to horse-trading—the money earned, the status gained, and the breeding potential being the main concerns. Outside the realm of law, including marriage law, women have been vulnerable to a deeply rooted male compulsion towards sexual conquest and domination and have frequently been the victims of naked power.

The legal position has altered in much of the modern world, although it remains the case in all sorts of other ways that sex and power are closely bound up with each other. The need that many men appear to have to dominate and to conquer women sexually is still a marked feature of our world, as is revealed by statistics on marital violence, rape, and prostitution (which, it is not well understood, is much more about the need to exert power than the need for sexual intercourse), not to mention child abuse (which itself often leads its victims into prostitution).

The fractured nature of our souls with regard to our sexuality is well illustrated in particular by the veritable explosion of interest in pornography since the Internet began to offer relatively risk-free access to it. The Datamonitor Company released a report[11] in May 1999, noting that in 1998 Internet surfers paid $970 million for access to "adult content sites." It forecast that this amount will rise by more than 25 percent a year to reach $3.12 billion in 2003. The significant thing about these figures is that people are usually unwilling to pay for access to websites. It is only where sex is involved that such massive sums of money change hands.

We are deeply troubled beings indeed. The depths of our trouble and our confusion were exposed in a 1999 movie that examines a woman's sexual exploration and, at times, degradation, and that was by common agreement the most sexually explicit film to play in mainstream movie theaters for some time. The movie, which included graphic scenes of oral sex and anal rape, was (astonishingly) entitled *Romance*.

---

11. My source here is the *Vancouver Sun* (May 21, 1999); the figures are in Canadian dollars.

It is into this twisted world of sex and power, where the power lies mostly in the hands of men and yet to some extent also in the hands of women themselves,[12] that the Song of Songs intrudes with its "gentle eroticism." It acknowledges the all-too-common reality of our male-female relationships, distorted as they are by dark forces that rage within us and without. Yet it rejects that reality as inevitable or normative and looks beyond it to a different way of being, in which persons are taken seriously first of all as persons, whether they are men or women, and joyous mutuality of relationship is the norm. In that context, sexual expression is not a dangerous thing, but outside that context it can indeed lead on to disaster.

The Song of Songs thus lauds romance while reminding us not to be romantic about a world in which coercion and violence all too often mark human affairs. It praises sexual intimacy while reminding us that sexual activity is not itself intimacy and can express the opposite. It also summons us to repentance, however, by presenting us with an ideal we constantly fail to achieve, whether individually or societally. It is almost certain that among the readers of this commentary there will be some who are addicted to pornography, some who have visited prostitutes, and perhaps even some who have raped, inflicted sexual violence on their wives, or sexually abused a child. There will be many who have failed to love their spouses as equals before God and to give themselves wholly and unreservedly to their spouses in loving and sexual intimacy.

The dark side of sexuality affects all of us in one way or another. The Song of Songs calls us to repentance and to a determination to live differently before God and our fellow human beings. It calls us to place the erotic in the context of all that is wholesome and most deeply human and not to allow it to wreak havoc on human life by escaping its proper time and place.

The Song of Songs also calls us, however, beyond repentance to healing— to face the darkness that lies within us (and which was perhaps placed there in the first instance by others who sinned against us, sexually), and in facing it to understand it and have it in due time dispelled by God's light. For the Song of Songs tells us, in telling us of the woman's dream in chapter 3, that God did not make the world the way it is, nor does he ask us to pretend he did or commend us when we do so. It especially tells us not to use him as a means simply of repressing our pain or our fear or of avoiding dealing with our sense of powerlessness.

Repression will never in the end work. Our darkness will always in the end break out. It is just as well, then, that God is in truth no legitimator of self-

---

12. It is evident that some women, at least, would claim to be exercising freedom of choice in participating in prostitution or pornography. The director of *Romance* was indeed a woman, Catherine Breillat.

repression and the repression of others but in reality the bringer of life and of liberation. Only as we present ourselves as we are, in *all* our brokenness, before this God (and before others whom we trust) and only as we seek his healing presence in our lives will we move beyond brokenness to wholeness. Only then for many of us will the words "gentle" and "erotic" come in time to appear well-suited and will the words "sex" and "power" be seen to be deeply incompatible.

This is the message you heard from the beginning: We should love one another. (1 John 3:11)

Light has come into the world, but men loved darkness instead of light because their deeds were evil. Everyone who does evil hates the light, and will not come into the light for fear that his deeds will be exposed. But whoever lives by the truth comes into the light, so that it may be seen plainly that what he has done has been done through God. (John 3:19–21)

¹How beautiful you are, my darling!
　　Oh, how beautiful!
　　Your eyes behind your veil are doves.
　Your hair is like a flock of goats
　　descending from Mount Gilead.
²Your teeth are like a flock of sheep just shorn,
　　coming up from the washing.
　Each has its twin;
　　not one of them is alone.
³Your lips are like a scarlet ribbon;
　　your mouth is lovely.
　Your temples behind your veil
　　are like the halves of a pomegranate.
⁴Your neck is like the tower of David,
　　built with elegance;
　on it hang a thousand shields,
　　all of them shields of warriors.
⁵Your two breasts are like two fawns,
　　like twin fawns of a gazelle
　　that browse among the lilies.
⁶Until the day breaks
　　and the shadows flee,
　I will go to the mountain of myrrh
　　and to the hill of incense.
⁷All beautiful you are, my darling;
　　there is no flaw in you.

⁸Come with me from Lebanon, my bride,
　　come with me from Lebanon.
　Descend from the crest of Amana,
　　from the top of Senir, the summit of Hermon,
　from the lions' dens
　　and the mountain haunts of the leopards.
⁹You have stolen my heart, my sister, my bride;
　　you have stolen my heart
　with one glance of your eyes,
　　with one jewel of your necklace.

¹⁰How delightful is your love, my sister, my bride!
   How much more pleasing is your love than wine,
   and the fragrance of your perfume than any spice!
¹¹Your lips drop sweetness as the honeycomb, my bride;
   milk and honey are under your tongue.
   The fragrance of your garments is like that of Lebanon.
¹²You are a garden locked up, my sister, my bride;
   you are a spring enclosed, a sealed fountain.
¹³Your plants are an orchard of pomegranates
   with choice fruits,
   with henna and nard,
¹⁴   nard and saffron,
   calamus and cinnamon,
   with every kind of incense tree,
   with myrrh and aloes
   and all the finest spices.
¹⁵You are a garden fountain,
   a well of flowing water
   streaming down from Lebanon.

¹⁶Awake, north wind,
   and come, south wind!
 Blow on my garden,
   that its fragrance may spread abroad.
 Let my lover come into his garden
   and taste its choice fruits.

⁵:¹I have come into my garden, my sister, my bride;
   I have gathered my myrrh with my spice.
 I have eaten my honeycomb and my honey;
   I have drunk my wine and my milk.

 Eat, O friends, and drink;
   drink your fill, O lovers.

RESPONSIVE TO THE unsettling dream and distasteful vision of chapter 3, the beloved man now showers the woman with intimate affirmations. She is once again (as in 2:8–15) the inaccessible one who requires to be wooed (4:1–15), but as this chapter closes, she again reveals that she is not resistant to this man who pursues her (4:16 and 5:1; cf. 2:16–17).

The return after the terrors of the night to the quiet normality of the relationship described in chapters 1—2 is signaled immediately by the return to familiar language in 4:1, whose opening words are exactly those of 1:15, albeit now with a slight expansion that mentions the "veil" behind which the woman's eyes hide.[1] It is perhaps significant, after the impersonal sexual activity implied in 3:6—11, that the lover should begin with his beloved's eyes, even though he cannot see them clearly; for to look into the eyes is to encounter a person, not simply a body.

It is the beloved's unique, individual beauty that transfixes him in its totality (note "all" in 4:7), as he considers first her head and neck. Only after he has surveyed this scene does he move on to still-familiar territory (4:5—6), mentioning those breasts that have been alluded to already in 2:17, in the context of a browsing in the lilies and an intimacy that lasts "until the day breaks and the shadows flee." She is not to him merely one woman among many, coveted for sexual charms. She is the one and only woman for him (cf. 2:2), a person to be looked in the eyes.

From her eyes he moves next to her hair (4:1), which is compared to a flock of Transjordanian goats, perhaps in color or in movement as it flows down from her head.[2] From her hair he goes next to her teeth (v. 2), which are shining white (like sheep that have been washed and shorn) and are perfectly matched. The mouth and some part of the side of the face (perhaps the cheeks)[3] comes under consideration next (v. 3). Both have a pleasing redness about them—the color of the inside of a pomegranate when it is halved and lies open to view.

Her neck is like the otherwise unknown "tower of David" (cf. 7:4), heavily decorated with jewelry in the same way that the tower was decorated with warriors' shields and perhaps other weapons (v. 4: the precise meaning of Heb. *šeleṭ* [NIV "shields of warriors"] is uncertain).[4] We assume that the

---

1. Snaith, *Song*, 58, argues that, because she is veiled, she cannot be the same woman of whom we hear in 1:6, who is bronzed by the sun. It is not entirely clear, however, why we must imagine that a woman in ancient Palestine must always have been either veiled or unveiled, rather than varying her dress code according to time and circumstance.

2. The precise meaning of the unique Heb. *glš* (found only in Song 4:1; 6:5) is not known, but the NIV's "descending" is a good guess. For a longer discussion see Pope, *Song*, 458—60.

3. Heb. *raqqa* must presumably refer in Judg. 4:21—22; 5:26, to the higher part of the side of the head, perhaps the temple, although much depends on the angle at which the tent peg was driven into the vital area so as to cause death. It is conceivable that it was driven through the cheek. It is not entirely clear in Song 4:3 why the beloved's temples would be singled out for attention, particularly since the man's eyes seem to be moving downward at this point from the eyes to the area of the mouth. It may be, then, that here at least the reference is to the cheeks.

4. See BDB, 1020.

allusion is to a long and graceful neck, although we are dealing with the unique word *talpiyyot*, which lies behind the NIV's "elegance"; thus, precision eludes us.[5]

What is striking about verses 3–4 taken together, however, is the way in which they echo 3:6–11, not only in the reference to the "warriors" (*gibborim*, 3:7 and 4:4), but also in their use of the unique Hebrew word *midbar* in 4:3 (where it presumably must mean "mouth" in parallel to "lips"), reminding us of the common Hebrew word *midbar*, "desert," in 3:6. It is as if the lover is recontextualizing the traumatic experience of his beloved, placing it once again in a larger and more familiar framework (4:1, 5–6, referring back to 1:13, 15; 2:16–17). The fearsome warriors who guard the king's bed are now denuded of their weapons, which are hung like trophies around the beloved's neck.[6] The thought of the barren desert, which is that same royal bed, is replaced by the thought of the beloved's mouth, described as "lovely" (*na'weh*) but also thereby evoking the image of the pastures (Heb. *n°'ot*, sing. *nawa*) in which sheep and goats graze. Here is a "wilderness" (the beloved's mouth) that is fertile and inviting to one who is a "gazelle" (cf. 2:8–17).[7] The idea of fertility may also be hinted at in the use of Hebrew *s̆patayim*, "lips," which is often used of riverbanks (e.g., Gen. 41:3, 17), and *rimmon*, "pomegranate," a well-known symbol of fertility.

These connections between the chapters only serve to emphasize the contrast between the two relationships described in them. The woman who is to Solomon only one among many daughters of Jerusalem—readily available and coerced to join him in his desert-prison—is to her lover an expansive and fertile landscape, magnificent, flawless (v. 7), and, as we will see, self-possessed. She is to be affirmed and enjoyed rather than controlled. The statement of intent in 4:6, that the man will spend long hours on the two scented mountains (his beloved's breasts) is indeed only a response to an invitation that she has already issued to him to do so (cf. the discussion

---

5. For a full discussion, see Pope, *Song*, 465–68. The allusion is perhaps to multiple necklaces placed one above the other in the way that the stones of a tower may have been built on top of each other, each level of the tower being decorated with weaponry.

6. It is perhaps not a coincidence that one thousand "shields" (Heb. *magen*) are mentioned in 4:4, given the various associations between 1 Kings 1–11 and Song 3:6–11 noted above, for 1 Kings 10 tells us of five hundred gold shields placed in Solomon's palace (1 Kings 10:16–17), in the midst of its general description of the opulence of the place. The doubling in the Song of a number given in the narrative of David and Solomon stands in intriguing parallel to the doubling of the number of warriors in Song 3:7. We might speculate (although it is only speculation) that the "tower" of David was a striking architectural feature of the royal palace, whether external (cf. Neh. 3:25) or internal (and possibly inlaid with ivory, cf. Song 7:4; also Ps. 45:8; Amos 6:4).

7. Snaith, *Song*, 61, says it well: "Her mouth is . . . cleverly portrayed as a fertile oasis."

of 2:16—17). The context of his sojourn there is delight in her whole being (4:7).

The woman's full participation in this relationship and her personal control over this participation is underlined in 4:8—15, as her inaccessibility to the man is also again emphasized (reminding us of 2:8—15). Intimacy cannot be coerced by him. She must freely choose to come with him (v. 8) as he woos her, respecting her integrity and otherness. He woos her even though she is described as his "bride" and is thus already in a marital relationship of sorts with him.

Whether "bride" is being used here literally or only metaphorically to communicate intimacy and closeness of relationship is uncertain. The appearance alongside it of the word "sister" (*ʾaḥot*, v. 10) does not, unfortunately, help us to decide the matter in either direction, for this term could be used metaphorically in the ancient world simply of a beloved one in general (as frequently in Egyptian love poetry) or of a wife in particular (e.g., Tobit 5:21 [NRSV, NAB]; 7:15 [NRSV, NAB]; 1 Cor. 9:5, where the NIV's "believing wife" is lit. "sister-wife"). It was also possible for "sisters," broadly defined, to be wives (e.g., Gen. 20:1—13, where Sarah is Abraham's half-sister but also his wife).

What is significant about the language, however, is that the word "bride" (*kalla*) first appears in the Song of Songs only after the reference to Solomon's wedding in 3:11 and appears *only* in 4:8—5:1. We may at least say, then, that we have portrayed here a true "marital relationship," to be contrasted with what happened in Solomon's bed. Here is a "marriage" that is about the one-to-one intimacy of persons—something clearly communicated by the constant repetition of "bride" throughout the section (4:8, 9, 10, 11, 12; 5:1), in conjunction with all the sensuous imagery employed to describe her.

There is no possession taken for granted here; there is no careless assumption by the man of owning the woman. He woos her, inviting her to come down from Lebanon and its mountain ranges in the north of Palestine (v. 8). These mountains do not signify nearness, as Gilead does (v. 1), but distance. They do not signify accessibility, but inaccessibility (cf. 2:14). They are not harmless places, like the slopes of Gilead where the goats graze, but dangerous places, where lions and leopards (perhaps panthers) prowl. Distance and danger must be overcome if the lovers are to be united as one; yet the man is drawn on because Lebanon is also the fragrant place (4:11, playing on Heb. *lᵉbanon* and *lᵉbona*, "incense"; cf. Hos. 14:6), where his beloved is to be found. He wanders through dangerous land, therefore, calling to her and inviting her to accompany him. She is worth the weariness and risk of the journey. These are the mountains that must be faced if he is indeed to rest on the "mountains," her breasts (Song 4:6).

Various compliments follow, designed to persuade her to "descend," including one that echoes her words to him (4:10; cf. 1:2) and thus reminds her of his identity. The beauty of the eyes and the loveliness of the adorned neck are once again praised in 4:9 (cf. vv. 1, 4),[8] along with the attractiveness of mouth and lips in 4:11 (cf. v. 3), although on this occasion the desire of the man to have his own mouth and lips in contact with hers is more explicit. "Milk" and "honey" are delights to be savored and consumed; they are also items reminding us of the Promised Land, which replaced, in Israelite experience, a wandering in a desert (e.g., Deut. 6:3; 11:9; see comments on Song 4:3). The woman is to her lover a wonderful "landscape" indeed—now described in 4:12–5:1 as a fertile "garden" (*gan*) in which are found choice fruits and spice-producing plants and trees (4:12–14). As a garden she is unparalleled—no ordinary garden in ancient Palestine would have contained such a diversity of plant life, drawn from every corner of the ancient world.[9] At the same time she is also a spring,[10] a fountain, or a well (4:12, 15) that waters the garden.

Both the garden itself and its water supply are described in 4:12, significantly, as "locked up" (*na'ul*), "enclosed" (also *na'ul*), or "sealed" (*ḥatum*). There is no general access to them. Entry can only be attained by those who possess permission or a key. We are powerfully reminded of the imagery of the

---

8. The precise sense of the Heb. verb *lbb*, which is obviously connected with the noun *lebab*, "heart," is unclear. It could be that the woman has *stolen* his heart, but equally it could be that the vision standing before him has *given* him heart (courage) for the dangerous journey among lions and leopards. The conjunction of "eye" and "jewel" suggests a twinkling, attractive preciousness. The light illumines her eyes and neck as it comes into contact with them and draws him on in pursuit of her.

9. For a brief description of the plant life, see Snaith, *Song*, 68–69.

10. The Heb. of the MT is *gal*, lit., "heap (of stones), wave," which is difficult; many have therefore taken their lead from the variant *gan*, "garden," found in various Heb. mss and read by LXX. It is difficult to understand, however, how the readily comprehensible *gan* could have become the difficult *gal*, given that another *gan* sits at the beginning of the line. It is more easily understood how *gal* could have become *gan*. As to the meaning of *gal* in the context, our best lead is perhaps found in Eccl. 12:6, where Heb. *gulla* refers to a vessel that holds water, in much the way that a spring "holds" water within it. Yet it is possible that the imagery of a mound of stones could itself be intended to speak of the vaginal area, in advance of the evident sexual consummation in 5:1 (so Goulder, *Song*, 38). The water imagery probably continues in the difficult Heb. word *šelaḥayik* that follows in 4:13 (NIV "plants," from the verb *šlḥ*, "send," which is used of trees sending forth roots and branches in Ps. 80:11; Jer. 17:8), since Heb. *berekat haššelaḥ* appears in Neh. 3:15. The Nehemiah phrase certainly refers to a pool (Heb. *bereka*), associated, interestingly enough, with a royal garden. The *šelaḥ* in the phrase may simply be a variant for *šiloaḥ* (Siloam, as in NIV), but it has been argued that it refers rather to a conduit that carried water from the Gihon spring to the pool by the royal garden (so, e.g., Goulder, *Song*, 38). If this is so, then we may have a further allusion here in Song 4:13's *šelaḥayik* to the vagina.

Garden of Eden in Genesis 2–3, a place of one-to-one intimacy, where a human couple are to be found naked and unashamed (2:25) before the fracturing of their relationship with God (and with each other) led to their exclusion from this paradise. The Hebrew word behind "orchard" in Song of Songs 4:13 is in fact *pardes*, a word borrowed from the Persian language (meaning "enclosure, park," from which we get our word "paradise").

The memory of Solomon's own construction of gardens and parks lingers in Ecclesiastes 2:1–9, alongside his accumulation of slaves, treasures, and women; it may also linger implicitly here in chapter 4. The emphasis on the inaccessible wonders of the woman is, in this context, significant. Solomon possesses women in his pursuit of paradise. The true love recognizes the sanctity of paradise and respects her boundaries.

The wooing of the man now draws a response from the woman, which may begin in 4:15 (since this can be read in the Heb. as a female exclamation rather than as part of the male description: "a garden fountain . . . !") or even in 4:16a (although this may be spoken by the man), but is certainly found in 4:16b. The hope is expressed, either by the man or the woman, that the wind will blow on the garden, sending its fragrance out into the countryside and thus guiding the lover to find it, as he searches the mountains of Lebanon for his beloved. The fragrance should "spread abroad" (*nzl*, 4:16), just as the waters "stream down" (*nzl*, 4:16) from the mountains. She in turn makes it clear just how willing she is that he should enter the garden and taste its fruit. There is no hesitancy or fear; she welcomes his approach.

Verse 1 of chapter 5 reports the resolution of the whole situation. The man finds the garden and consumes what is within—the myrrh and the spice (4:14), the honeycomb and the honey (perhaps referring to liquid and solid honey, 4:11, although the Heb. word for "honeycomb" is not the same as the word in 4:11), the wine and the milk (4:10–11). As in 2:16–17 the obstacles have been overcome and there is "feasting."

The final part of 5:1 appears to give us the words of some approving bystanders, who encourage the couple to "eat" and "drink" to their hearts' content.

In summation, the man speaks to his beloved in Song of Songs 4 as a husband speaks to his wife, placing the "events" of chapter 3 in the context of their special relationship. He commends her for her beauty while respecting her as one who has her own boundaries and must be wooed (even though they already have a sexual relationship), so that their physical acts of love may be truly mutual. The imagery is once again gentle and pastoral, in contrast to the imagery of the frightening dream and the fortified palace of chapter 3. The man journeys to a far country to find his paradise, and he is welcomed in to taste its fruit.

HITHERTO WE HAVE carefully side-stepped the question of precisely what kind of relationship is assumed in the descriptions of the love match we have read throughout Song of Songs 1–3 and have now found in 4:1–5:1, although we have certainly affirmed that this song has important implications for our understanding of Christian marriage (among others of our relationships). The point has now been reached in our reflections, however, where the question presses itself insistently upon us. Are the lovers married?

It is difficult to imagine that the Song of Songs itself intends to present them to us as legally married. The woman is one of Solomon's wives or concubines; it is not easy to imagine how she could at the same time be married to her lover in any normal and public sense. Song of Songs 8:1 certainly implies that there is no public recognition of any marriage, since a public kiss would allegedly lead to public contempt. Song of Songs 8:8–12 further suggests that the relationship between the man and the woman lies outside the parameters of a normal marriage contract, since their relationship is there implicitly contrasted with such a contract between the woman's brothers and Solomon (see further below).

Yet at the same time, it is undeniable that the language used in this song of the lovers' relationship strongly implies a marriage-like relationship. Nowhere is this more clear than in 4:1–5:1. It is not just that the man calls the woman "bride" and "sister," claiming this marital language for their union over against the claims of Solomon. It is the fact that this language is embedded in poetry that places emphasis on exclusivity in the relationship here and throughout the book (not least in 8:6–7) and does so in a way that reminds us obviously of the story in Genesis 1–2, which certainly has marriage in mind (2:23–25). As has often been noted, another passage with evident connections to Song of Songs 4 is Proverbs 5:15–19, which reads:

> Drink water from your own cistern,
> running water from your own well.
> Should your springs overflow in the streets,
> your streams of water in the public squares?
> Let them be yours alone,
> never to be shared with strangers.
> May your fountain be blessed,
> and may you rejoice in the wife of your youth.
> A loving doe, a graceful deer—
> may her breasts satisfy you always,
> may you ever be captivated by her love.

These passages share the water imagery, specifically the language of "streaming/running down" (*nzl*, Prov. 5:15; Song 4:15—16), "well" (*bᵉʾer*, Prov. 5:15; Song 4:15), and "spring/fountain" (*maʿyan*, Prov. 5:16; Song 4:12, 15), as well as the imagery of the deer in reference to the breasts. The Proverbs passage clearly concerns marital faithfulness and intimacy, even in the face of external sexual threats. It seems that we are more than justified, then, in understanding Song of Songs 4 as an exchange between two lovers who stand in a marital *relationship* to each other and in reading chapters 1—3 in that light as well.

The conclusion to which we are driven by all this interesting but conflicting evidence is this: Although the two lovers *themselves regard* their relationship as a marriage, it is not *recognized* as such by others (beyond those "friends" whom they from time to time address). It is partly for this reason, we imagine, that the relationship is constantly threatened by obstacles (implied in the dreams of 3:1—4 and 5:2—7). It can only truly flourish away from the public gaze—away from the city, in the private spaces of the countryside. For the public world presupposed by the Song of Songs is one of power and coercion, not a world that permits the love relationship between the woman and her lover that is described here.

Commentators who have recognized that we are dealing with three main characters in the Song of Songs have not found it easy to accept that we are thus dealing with a text that in some ways is rather subversive. It undermines a legal marriage and holds up for our approval a "marriage" that society does not recognize. Perhaps some readers of this commentary will themselves find this reality shocking. If so, it will be important to follow shock with reflection on why, precisely, we are shocked. It should not be because a biblical author is thus seen to undermine what is considered legal and even right in a particular society, for any conscientious reader of the Bible knows that its authors frequently undermine what is considered legal and even right in all sorts of societies—and do so unashamedly out of the conviction that God's laws and righteousness are the only proper measure of what we do.

When, for example, Jezebel obtains for Ahab the piece of land that belong to Naboth (1 Kings 21), and does so using due legal process, the action is not for that reason right. There is prophetic resistance. In the New Testament, likewise, the apostles find themselves forbidden by the properly constituted authorities from preaching the good news of Jesus Christ, but they make their position very clear: "We must obey God rather than men" (Acts 5:29). There is prophetic resistance.

All throughout history Christians have rightly resisted societal norms and laws in pursuit of the kingdom of God and have even managed from time to time to change them. It is not the mere fact, then, that the man and woman of the Song of Songs resist legal and societal definitions in pursuing their love that should shock us—although we may find it shocking still, if we have been taught that the main purpose of Christian faith is to undergird social stability and if we have been led to believe that submission to authority is the highest Christian virtue. It is certainly unlikely that many men throughout history would have found such a reading of the Song of Songs anything other than an outrageous assault on their prerogatives to dispose of women as they willed, passing them from one to the other by means of legal contract.

Those who possess power seldom welcome subversion. They always look to phenomena like religion only for legitimization of the way things are at the moment. We may imagine that many men, historically, would therefore have seen in the undermining of Solomon's marriage in this song the undermining of society itself. Personal freedom in general has only recently come to be widely seen as a good thing, as we are reminded by the following words from a famous treatise opposing the abolition of slavery and attacking the abolitionists' manner of interpreting the Bible in support of their cause precisely because of the broader societal upheaval it might produce:

> Significant manifestations of the result of this disposition to consider their own light a surer guide than the word of God, are visible in the anarchic opinions about human government, civil and ecclesiastical, and on the rights of women, which have found appropriate advocates in the abolition publications. Let these principles [of interpretation] be carried out, and there is an end to all social subordination, to all security for life and property, to all guarantee for public or domestic virtue. If our women are to be emancipated from subjection to the law which God has imposed upon them, if they are to quit the retirement of domestic life ... if they are to come forth in the liberty of men, to be our agents, our public lecturers, our committee men, our rulers, if, in studied insult to the authority of God, we are to renounce in the marriage contract all claim to obedience, we shall soon have a country ... from which all order and virtue would speedily be banished ... there is no deformity of human character from which we turn with deeper loathing than from a woman forgetful of her nature, and clamorous for the vocation and rights of men.[11]

We should assuredly be more shocked by these relatively recent words in pursuit of social stability (and using the Bible for support) than by the Song of Song's ancient and biblical words that undermine the status quo in pursuit of personal freedom.

---

11. Arthur Taylor Bledsoe, "Liberty and Slavery: or, Slavery in the Light of Moral and Political Philosophy" (1860), as quoted in W. M. Swartley, *Slavery, Sabbath, War and Women: Case Issues in Biblical Interpretation* (Scottdale, Pa.; Herald, 1983), 49–50.

It is not just any freedom that this song upholds, however. This brings me to a second possible reason why a reader might be shocked. It is possible for the Song of Songs to be perceived as undermining marriage itself, in its juxtaposing of coercive power within marriage and mutual love outside it. We are far from justified in reading the song in this way, however. It does not hold up for our approval a casual relationship between promiscuous people that might one day soon be abandoned by one or both parties out of boredom or the appearance of an alternative lover. Rather, it holds up for our approval a deeply committed, exclusive relationship that is in all but legal reality a marriage (and which indeed began before the woman's marriage to Solomon, 1:6). It does so in a textual (and a historical and social) world in which choices were severely limited and in which what is called marriage was far from the kind of relationship intended by God for his creatures. It is not marriage *as such* that is undermined by this song, then, but marriage as it has often been practiced—an institution that speaks of male power and prerogative and that robs women (and their *chosen* mates) of self-determination.

It is not clear, when we set the Song of Songs in the context of the rest of the Scriptures, how far Christian readers would be justified, if our circumstances were the same as or similar to those of the couple in this song, in behaving in the same way. The Old Testament in particular constantly throws up questions like this to readers who read it as 2 Timothy 3:16 commends for "teaching, rebuking, correcting and training in righteousness" (e.g., if I were in Esther's shoes, should I behave as Esther did?). The Scriptures overall are not so interested in that question as they are in exhorting us to pursue a genuinely Christian marriage in the first place, rather than capitulating to the spirit of the age (which is all too often also the spirit of the church).

As the Scriptures seek to lead us in this direction, they constantly touch on themes already found in the Song of Songs. The woman is to be viewed by the man as someone made equally in the image of God and redeemed to be a sister in Christ; Paul's phrase for a wife in 1 Corinthians 9:5 is indeed the composite Greek *adelphēn gynaika*, "sister-wife." There is to be mutuality in the relationship as each submits to the other out of reverence for Christ (Eph. 5:21–33). There is to be radical commitment to each other (and especially from the male side, Mark 10:2–12) in a one-to-one relationship (1 Tim. 3:2, 12) and constant physical self-giving to one another (1 Cor. 7:3–5). Christian marriage *is* the "marriage" of the lovers in this song and represents the ideal toward which we strive, even if the reality of our marriages often fall short of it in so many different ways.

Marriage will usually also have its legal and public aspects, which are important in providing (among other things) community support, accountability, and protection for those who are married. Those who are able so to marry and yet choose not to do so inevitably invite questions about any claims they may make concerning serious, lifelong commitment. Yet all this should not be allowed to obscure the fundamentally *relational* nature of Christian marriage, beyond and beneath all that is legal and public. Marriages often begin to go wrong, in fact, precisely when one or both of the parties involved in them begin to depend on or take refuge in their legal and public nature, rather than continuing to work daily at a relationship they refuse to take for granted.

Christian marriage itself reflects, however dimly, the relationship we are called to in Christ with God. We are called to worship a God who affirms us and respects our freedom, even as he woos us and desires our intimacy. We are called to love a God who loves us one to one in a radically committed way (although we are always, as Christian *individuals*, also part of the church and the world God also loves), looking for our commitment in response. He is a God whose self-giving is constant and is best exemplified on the cross and who asks us in return to present ourselves as living sacrifices on his altar (Rom. 12:1).

This "marriage" with God is also, above all, not about law but about relationship. This marriage, too, can go wrong when daily attention is not given to its growth because assumptions are made about its formal status. It is the teachers of the law and the Pharisees, we should recall, who in the Gospels take refuge in legality when summoned to relationship. Disciples of Jesus are called to a different way of living.

Now Eros makes a man really want, not a woman, but one particular woman. In some mysterious but quite indisputable fashion the lover desires the Beloved herself, not the pleasure she can give. No lover in the world ever sought the embraces of a woman he loved as the result of a calculation, however unconscious, that they would be more pleasurable than those of any other woman.[12]

The view of erotic love articulated by C. S. Lewis in this passage is precisely that of the Song of Songs. It is widely divergent from the view of the modern world at large, which has reduced eroticism to animal responses to sexual stimuli. It has nothing to do, either, with the ancient world of "Solomon." Any woman (or indeed, any man) will suffice for the mere purposes

---

12. C. S. Lewis, *The Four Loves* (London: Fontana Book, 1976), 88.

of sex, and he or she need not even be particularly physically attractive to the one who seeks it. It is the gender of the other, rather than the person, that is the crucial thing (does this entity have the appropriate equipment?); and the calculation of pleasure, whether conscious or unconscious, is central to the whole transaction. Personhood is in fact an obstacle to the exchange and must ruthlessly be repressed, suspended, and ignored if the exchange is to take place. This is the reality of abuse and pornography, of the harem and the brothel, and even of some marriages. We live in a world saturated by sex while desperate for love. True erotic love is in short supply in it.

Eros focuses on the particular woman, the particular man—the beloved himself or herself. In the midst of the reality of the sexualized and depersonalized world (represented in Song 3:6–11), in which men and women question their unique worth and beauty, experience assaults on their sense of self, and know deep alienation, eros calls us to affirmation, respect, and intimacy—the antidote prescribed in 4:1–5:1.

The duty of affirmation of those whom we love has already been discussed (see comments on ch. 2). It is worth emphasizing again here, however, for 4:1–5:1 provides us with a beautiful example of its practice and of the way in which affirming words function to "push back the chaos and shape our lives into order and beauty."[13] The "chaos" of the Solomonic court is recontextualized and disempowered by the man as he places its harsh reality within the framework of his relationship with the woman. She may be only one of many women to Solomon, but she is the one and only woman for him, and he tells her so at length and in detail.

Whether in our ordinary relationships or specifically in our marriages, we cannot engage in enough such affirmation of the unique worth and beauty of those whom we love. It is itself a major way in which healing comes to our lives (cf. comments on ch. 3) as we seek to recover from the influence of a world that depersonalizes and degrades. The effects of this world on us may initially be so great that we feel deeply embarrassed about affirming our lovers in such direct ways, and we may be reluctant to do so. Many of us have suffered such emotional damage that we have learned to keep all emotion tightly bottled up inside us where (we falsely believe) it can do no damage. We avoid words that might uncork the bottle and spurn them when others use them toward us. We become terrified of direct verbal intercourse, and sexual intercourse thus becomes a silent, awkward affair that does not minister to our emotional and spiritual needs as well as our physical needs. We deprive ourselves and others of a great gift—the gift of affirming words that might, in the context of a loving and trusting relation-

---

13. Allender and Longman, *Intimate Allies*, 97.

ship, bring deep healing to our lives. It is a serious deprivation as we seek to love our spousely neighbors as ourselves.

The Song of Songs leads us along a different path, exhorting the expression of intimacy through thought, imagination, and word as well as action, as lovers take up each other's whole attention. It is in the healing that such things bring, indeed, that the power of activities like pornography is diminished, for that power is bound up closely with deprivation of personal love and affirmation in the first place.

Eros calls us to affirmation, but it also calls us to respect. The most noticeable feature of 4:1—5:1, after the strong implication of female powerlessness in 3:6—11, is the way in which the man goes out of his way to emphasize that the woman is a person in her own right with boundaries that must be respected. He may be her intimate, but he is so only by invitation. He does not own her, nor can he control her. If he is to enjoy her, it must be at her summons. Throughout our passage there is a recognition, in other words, that even though the couple are in a marital relationship, each remains as "other" to the one who loves. There is, consequently, much wooing in the passage. The man accepts that the relationship can only be good if it is mutual, and he pursues his beloved with a passion. He recognizes his beloved as a person before he regards her as a woman.

There is an enduring message here, too, for those who are married. It is an all-too-common root of marital trouble that one or both parties "settle down" in a marriage and begin to take the other person for granted. The legal contracts are signed, and all wooing in due course ceases. Too often there is in fact no ongoing sense of the other as other at all—a separate, unique person with whom it is an enormous privilege to spend one's life. The transgressions of boundaries and the invasions of space become legion, and ownership and control become the governing categories of the marriage. Sexual interaction, which can only ever express what is already there in the relationship, becomes humdrum and predictable and is no longer about the union of two free spirits but about the slow expiration of two souls in bondage.

Eros calls us (back) to the constant recognition of the other—the one who befriends us not because he or she has no choice but out of self-giving and committed love. It calls us to make wooing an ongoing feature of our marriages, not just a prelude to them. Eros thus constantly pushes beyond the legal institution of marriage to the heart of it, insisting that what is respectable is not necessarily good and that what has been accepted as normal is not necessarily to be accepted as what is right.

Eros calls us, finally, to intimacy. The natural and good end of affirmation and wooing is unrestrained and joyous sexual, emotional, and spiritual intimacy. The woman in 4:1–5:1 welcomes her lover with open arms into her garden, and he comes to feast. Here we need to confront a deep-seated difficulty that is connected with, but also goes beyond, our reluctance to affirm and be affirmed as unique and beautiful people. Many people, including Christian married people, have a difficulty with respect to sex. Indeed,

> it is a strange paradox that among those most vociferous about their belief in the Bible "from cover to cover" is often found an attitude that sex is "nasty." The Victorian embarrassment with sexual matters has not disappeared from the contemporary scene.[14]

The problem actually goes much further back, historically, than the Victorians (see the Introduction to this commentary). Many Christians throughout the ages have found it difficult, precisely because of their negative views of sexual expression, to contemplate a literal reading of the Song of Songs without at the same thinking of the book negatively as a "hot carnall pamphlet" (to use the words of the Westminster Confession of Faith). Yet the fact is that it is *both* a "hot carnall pamphlet" *and* a part of Scripture, and this is something with which all of us must come to terms:

> The Bible . . . is, to be sure, fully aware of lust and the misuse of sex; but at the same time it is forthright in approving the wholesomeness of sex. The passionate, physical attraction between man and woman, who find in this the fulfillment of their deepest longings, is seen as a healthy, natural thing . . . the Song of Songs has an important emphasis here.[15]

The Bible approves of the wholesomeness, the wonder, the delight of sex. God confirms his blessing on it, as a wise pastor was known to tell couples during premarital counseling, by placing the Song of Songs at the center of the Bible. If we have a different view, we need to repent of it; and if our married lives reflect in any degree that different view, then this reality also needs to be addressed. It may be that we need help to do this, for a frigid and repressive attitude toward sexual intimacy can have deep roots and can arise from deep hurts. Recognizing that the attitude is problematic, however, is the first and necessary step towards healing and change, as we learn to give up control to a trusted lover and abandon ourselves to him or her. This abandonment is only itself a reflection of the self-abandonment toward God to which each of us is also summoned and which is acted out in the closing

---

14. R. B. Laurin, "The Song of Songs and Its Modern Message," *CT* 6 (1961–1962): 1062–63 (quote on p. 1062).
    15. Ibid., 1062.

sections of the Psalter, where all creation gives itself away in praise of God and in loving wonder of him.

This last comment leads me to a final reflection on the nature of erotic love between a man and a woman. It is perhaps reflective of Christian unease, historically, with eros that there is still a tendency among Christian writers to distinguish too sharply between erotic love and *agape*, the love that Christians are exhorted to have for one another (which older translations call "charity"). C. S. Lewis himself made the distinction in his well-known book, *The Four Loves*.

Clearly agape is a much broader concept than eros; yet we err if we do not see the two as closely related. Biblical Hebrew certainly does not drive a wedge between erotic and "spiritual" love in this way, using the same root ʾbb for love of God (e.g., Deut. 6:5), love for fellow human beings (e.g., Lev. 19:18, 34), and love between a man and a woman (e.g., Song 7:6). A better way of thinking about the matter—one that does not set erotic and other loves in unhelpful tension with each other—is to see *eros* as *agape* directed toward a husband or wife, as we relate to them as sibling-neighbors who are also our most intimate lovers. This helps us to recognize that it is in the *entire* reality of human love that divine love is revealed.

We are not, after all, persons who can be subdivided into different parts, some of which are of interest to God and some not, and only some of which reflect the image of God. We are created as *whole* people in the image of God—our own body, soul, flesh, and spirit being elements that complement and fulfill each other. In the union of husband and wife, likewise, and in the intimate joy they share, there is also complementarity and fulfillment and an expression of transcendent love.

> "For this reason a man will leave his father and mother and be united to his wife, and the two will become one flesh." This is a profound mystery—but I am talking about Christ and the church. (Eph. 5:31–32)

² I slept but my heart was awake.
  Listen! My lover is knocking:
"Open to me, my sister, my darling,
  my dove, my flawless one.
My head is drenched with dew,
  my hair with the dampness of the night."
³ I have taken off my robe—
  must I put it on again?
I have washed my feet—
  must I soil them again?
⁴ My lover thrust his hand through the latch-opening;
  my heart began to pound for him.
⁵ I arose to open for my lover,
  and my hands dripped with myrrh,
my fingers with flowing myrrh,
  on the handles of the lock.
⁶ I opened for my lover,
  but my lover had left; he was gone.
  My heart sank at his departure.
I looked for him but did not find him.
  I called him but he did not answer.
⁷ The watchmen found me
  as they made their rounds in the city.
They beat me, they bruised me;
  they took away my cloak,
  those watchmen of the walls!
⁸ O daughters of Jerusalem, I charge you—
  if you find my lover,
what will you tell him?
  Tell him I am faint with love.

⁹ How is your beloved better than others,
  most beautiful of women?
How is your beloved better than others,
  that you charge us so?

¹⁰ My lover is radiant and ruddy,
  outstanding among ten thousand.

[11] His head is purest gold;
    his hair is wavy
    and black as a raven.
[12] His eyes are like doves
    by the water streams,
  washed in milk,
    mounted like jewels.
[13] His cheeks are like beds of spice
    yielding perfume.
  His lips are like lilies
    dripping with myrrh.
[14] His arms are rods of gold
    set with chrysolite.
  His body is like polished ivory
    decorated with sapphires.
[15] His legs are pillars of marble
    set on bases of pure gold.
  His appearance is like Lebanon,
    choice as its cedars.
[16] His mouth is sweetness itself;
    he is altogether lovely.
  This is my lover, this my friend,
    O daughters of Jerusalem.

[6:1] Where has your lover gone,
    most beautiful of women?
  Which way did your lover turn,
    that we may look for him with you?

[2] My lover has gone down to his garden,
    to the beds of spices,
  to browse in the gardens
    and to gather lilies.
[3] I am my lover's and my lover is mine;
    he browses among the lilies.

[4] You are beautiful, my darling, as Tirzah,
    lovely as Jerusalem,
    majestic as troops with banners.
[5] Turn your eyes from me;
    they overwhelm me.
  Your hair is like a flock of goats
    descending from Gilead.

331

⁶Your teeth are like a flock of sheep
    coming up from the washing.
Each has its twin,
    not one of them is alone.
⁷Your temples behind your veil
    are like the halves of a pomegranate.
⁸Sixty queens there may be,
    and eighty concubines,
    and virgins beyond number;
⁹but my dove, my perfect one, is unique,
    the only daughter of her mother,
    the favorite of the one who bore her.
The maidens saw her and called her blessed;
    the queens and concubines praised her.

¹⁰Who is this that appears like the dawn,
    fair as the moon, bright as the sun,
    majestic as the stars in procession?

THE AUTHOR OF Songs of Songs now reports a second dream, so that the man's long affirmation of the woman in chapter 4 is bracketed between two accounts of loss and desire (3:1–5; 5:2–8). Among the interesting features of the second dream report, however, is the fact that the "vision" that follows it is not focused on the king but on the lover (5:9–16; cf. 3:6–11). That is, whereas 3:6–11 highlights the possessions of the king and has an impersonal atmosphere, 5:9–16 centers resolutely on the person of the beloved. It is a direct response to the man's eulogy on the woman's beauty in chapter 4. He has succeeded, as it were, in reminding her who she is in relationship with him. Thus, a more terrifying dream than the first does not prompt her to think of the *king's bedroom*, but only of her *beloved's body*, which she now anxiously seeks.

As the passage opens (5:2), the woman is asleep, even though her heart is "awake."[1] She hears her lover knocking at her door (as she previously heard him approaching across the mountains, 2:8). He begs her, in familiar language, to let him in (5:2; note "sister," 4:9, 10, 12; 5:1; "darling," 1:9, 15; 2:2, 10, 13; 4:1, 7; "dove," 2:14; the allusion in "flawless one" to 4:7). He has

---

1. There is a double meaning in the use of Heb. ʿwr here, which is the verb that also lies behind "awake" in 4:16, "arouse" and "awaken" in 2:7; 3:5; 8:4, and "rouse" in 8:5. Her heart is "awake" in the sense both that it is dreaming and that it is sexually receptive.

come to her before daybreak, when the sun rises to dispel the dew. In the course of his journey to her he has become soaked through with it (cf. Gideon's fleece in Judg. 6:38).

She seems at first resistant to his pleas, as in 2:15. She has in her dream already removed her everyday clothing and washed her feet and has apparently settled down in bed for the night (v. 3). She is reluctant to get up again and prepare herself to receive him. Her response is a curious one, given the amorous purposes for which the lover has no doubt made his journey (why does she need a robe?), and we detect in it that same playfulness evident in the response of 2:15. As in that earlier chapter, indeed, the woman's resistance does not last long.

It is not entirely clear what happens at the beginning of 5:4, where we are told that the lover (lit.) "sent his hand from the hole";[2] whatever it is, it makes the woman's "heart" pound. The Hebrew behind the NIV's "heart" is *me'im*, which is used in the Old Testament to refer to various aspects (both external and internal) of the lower part of the body in the area of the stomach and the womb and is frequently seen as the abode of deep emotion. The verb *hmh* ("pound") refers elsewhere to such things as groaning in distress, the roaring of the sea, and general commotion and turbulence (e.g., Jer. 4:19; 31:20). A better translation might therefore be, "my insides seethed," understanding that the deep emotion in view here is love. Her passion has been excited by her lover's actions,[3] so she gets up to do what he asked of her—to "open" the locked door (v. 5; cf. v. 2). As she does so, her wetness responds to his; her hands drip with myrrh, either dropping from the hands onto the door or picked up by the hands from the door (where the lover has left it; cf. 5:13).

But she is too late! By the time her hands come into contact with the door and the myrrh "flows" (*'br*, v. 5) over both, he has already "gone" (*'br*, v. 6). She is once again bereft, as in 3:1–3. A new search now ensues, which probably already begins immediately in verse 6b, where we should translate

---

2. The "hole" (Heb. *hor*) is presumably (at least when considered literally, see further below) an aperture in the door, probably a keyhole large enough to accommodate a man's hand (see Pope, *Song*, 518–19). The real difficulty is to know whether the man is at this point persisting in his advances and is thrusting his hand through the hole in a vain attempt to reach his beloved, or whether he is already discouraged by the woman's response and is removing his hand from the hole. Is he sending his hand from the door and into the room (cf. the Heb. preposition *min* in 2:9, where the lover looks "from" the windows/lattice and into the house, with *min* almost having the sense of "through"), or sending his hand away from the door altogether (so Goulder, *Song*, 41–42)? I prefer the latter explanation in the context of his disappearance in v. 6.

3. Many Heb. MSS read at the end of v. 4 "my innards seethed within me" (Heb. *'alay*) for MT's "my innards seethed because of him" (Heb. *'alaw*). The sense of the verse is not much altered by the variant, however.

"I went out when he spoke" (Heb. *nepeš*, NIV "heart," often being best understood simply as a way of referring to the whole self).[4] The thought is that she wastes little time. She goes to the door in response to his words (albeit pausing briefly to make her reply in 5:3), and, finding him already gone, she goes out immediately in search of him.

Her search, however, uncovers no trace of her beloved man. In fact, it produces a similar result to the one in 3:1—5. She does not "find" (*mṣ²*, 5:6) him, but the city watchmen do find (*mṣ²*, v. 7; cf. 3:2—3) her. On this occasion they are not nearly as passive in their response to her. They inflict violence on her and take away her cloak (5:7).[5] Perhaps we are to think that it is this beating and the theft that leaves her exposed to the cold night that bring the search to an end, for whereas in chapter 3 the search continues after the encounter with the watchmen and results in the finding of the man and renewed intimacy with him, there is no such happy ending in chapter 5. In fact, the beating is followed only by a plea that others should help in bringing the lovers back together again (5:8; contrast the "charge" in 3:5).

Here the dream and the reality merge into each other. She has only dreamt of the loss, yet now, in an anxious state, she seeks her absent lover in reality and urges the daughters of Jerusalem to tell the man, should they see him, that his beloved is lovesick (cf. 2:5). It is their response to this request in 5:9—which is essentially to ask her why she is so desperate for this particular man, among all the many men who might admire her beauty—that leads to the woman's description of her beloved in 5:10—16 with its conclusion: "This is my lover, this my friend, O daughters of Jerusalem" (v. 16).

What are we to make of these opening verses of chapter 5? The imagery of verses 2—5 is plainly erotic and speaks to us of sexual intimacy. What is at one level a dream about the opening (or not) of a "door" is in fact at another level a dream about the consummation (or not) of the lovers' physical relationship. This is perhaps most clearly seen in the reference to the man's "hand" that lingers in the region of the "hole" in the door, causing his beloved's insides

---

4. Some commentators prefer, in view of the reference in Gen. 35:18 to the "soul going out" (Heb. *nepeš yṣ²*) from Rachel in her death, to understand the same phrase here in Song 5:6 also to refer to a deathlike distress: e.g., "my soul sank" (Pope, *Song*, 501); "I swooned" (Murphy, *Song*, 164—65). It is not to be doubted that there is indeed an allusion to the woman's severe distress in the phrase, but to understand its primary sense in this way involves reading the following Heb. *bᵉdabbᵉro*, in the light of Akkadian and Arabic, as a verb meaning "turn, flee," which is otherwise unattested in Heb. By far the most natural reference of *bᵉdabbᵉro* in context, however, is to the words that the lover has spoken in v. 2, and by far the most natural understanding in context of Heb. *yṣ²*, "go out," is to the woman's exit from the house and into the city to "look" and to "call."

5. Heb. *rᵉdid* only otherwise appears in Isa. 3:23 (also of female clothing: NIV "shawls") and is of uncertain meaning. "Cloak" is, however, a good guess; "nightdress" is also a possibility.

to seethe (v. 4). The implication of intimacy is already apparent even before one realizes that the Hebrew word *yad* (hand) can also be used as a euphemism for "penis," as in Isaiah 57:8–10 (although obscured there by the NIV in both verse 8, where *yad* is rendered "nakedness," and verse 10, where "renewal of your strength [hand]," *ḥayyat yadek*, probably refers to sexual potency).[6]

The "feet" (*raglayim*) can also be used euphemistically of genitals, as in 2 Samuel 11:8, where Uriah is commanded by David (who hopes to cover up his sin with Bathsheba) to "go down to your house and wash your feet" (his own or Bathsheba's?). There may therefore also be a playful double entendre in Song of Songs 5:3, when the woman "complains" that if she lets her lover in, she will have to wash her "feet" all over again. She lies naked in bed as he, wet with dew (surely an image of sexual arousal here), presses his attentions upon her. She feigns disinterest, and he hesitates, even as she herself is aroused and moves to unbar the door. The moment is lost, however, and consummation never occurs. It is a dream about deep and mutual sexual desire and yet about misunderstanding, loss, and separation.

Even when this is understood, however, the significance of the beating and the theft in verse 7 is still not entirely clear.[7] We may speculate, however (and it would be only that), that it perhaps has something to do with the woman's sense of the overwhelming obstacles that lie in the way of ongoing intimacy with her man. The watchmen are, interestingly, described in the last line of verse 7 as "watchmen of the walls," which may seem redundant after the introduction to them in the first line of the verse. The only other use of Hebrew *ḥoma* (wall) in the Song of Songs is in 8:9–10, where the woman herself is described as a "wall." The function of these watchmen, therefore, may not be so much to keep an eye on the outside world from the city walls as to ensure that the "walls" (i.e., the women) within the city are not "breached." If it was unclear in 3:1–5 that they are actively interested in what occurs in love under their jurisdiction, it is now plain that they represent powers intent on keeping the lovers apart.

The woman's description of the man now follows, as she tries to communicate to her inquisitors and helpers the outstanding beauty of her lover, which marks him out from others. He is "radiant and ruddy," like the princes of Israel described in Lamentations 4:7—a conventional way, apparently, of referring to those of a clear and healthy complexion (cf. David in 1 Sam. 16:12; 17:42).

---

6. See M. Delcor, "Two Special Meanings of the Word *yd* in Biblical Hebrew," *JSS* 12 (1967): 230–40.

7. It is possible, but not entirely certain, that the taking of the garment is supposed to signify that the watchmen regard her as a sexually wayward woman (cf. Ezek. 16:37–39, and the comments below on the significance of Song 8:1).

Yet he is a particularly striking man, one who stands out from the crowd.[8] His head (already mentioned in 5:2) is like that of a precious statue, constructed of "purest gold" (*ketem paz*); he has an imperial, even a godlike visage (cf. Dan. 2:32 with 3:1, where Nebuchadnezzar seems to take his lead from Daniel's words in constructing the image of gold that must be worshiped; note also 10:5, where the figure in Daniel's vision is said to wear a belt of finest gold, *ketem ʾupaz*). His hair (likewise mentioned in 5:2) is the color of a young and healthy man—the black of a raven or crow—rather than the white of an old man, and it is (probably) "wavy."[9]

From the head and the hair the woman turns to her lover's eyes, which are compared (like her own) to doves (cf. 1:15; 4:1). These doves are not hiding away behind a veil, however, but are "by the water streams, washed in milk, mounted like jewels" (v. 12). The final phrase is (lit.) "sitting in fullness," probably rightly interpreted by the NIV as partly evoking inlaid jewels (cf. the Heb. root *mlʾ* also in v. 14a), but it is also an allusion to doves bathing in ample water. The imagery overall suggests glistening, beautiful pupils set in the midst of clear, white eyeballs.

From the eyes attention switches to the cheeks (or the jaw), which are like a bed of spice and (following the vocalization of MT) "towers of ointment."[10] The thought is perhaps of a beard, perfumed with oil as it descends from the area of the face (Ps. 133:2); it could be that the myrrh that drips (Heb. ʿbr, as in 5:5) from the lips is also to be explained in this way. The lips have already been *associated* with lilies on a couple of occasions in this song (2:16; 4:5), and here they are *described* as lilies, perhaps with a red flower in mind (5:13).

The lower part of the body next comes under consideration. Here the statue-like nature of the description is especially evident. The beloved's arms (lit., "hands," which conceivably refer here to fingers) are rods or cylinders of gold, studded with gems of some kind (v. 14).[11] His "body" (according to

---

8. The NIV's "outstanding" probably captures the overall sense, but it is important to note that the Heb. *dagul* probably carries a military connotation (see comments on *dgl* at 2:4), as the LXX translation "picked out of a military unit" correctly understands. He is one among ten thousand warriors.

9. The Heb. is the unique *taltallim*, which is used in later rabbinic literature to refer to curly hair. It is possibly related, however, to Heb. *tel*, "mound, hill" and *talul*, "exalted, lofty," in which case the allusion is perhaps to a full head of hair, sitting majestically on top the head. There is also an Akkadian *taltallu* that refers to part of the date plant that is black, leading some to think that the allusion is to palm branches (cf. LXX, Vulg.).

10. The NIV reads the plural "beds" with a few Heb. MSS and the LXX (cf. 6:2), and also accepts a common repointing of Heb. *migdᵉlot*, "towers," to *mᵉgaddᵉlot*, "yielding" (LXX). Little depends on one's decisions here.

11. The Heb. behind the NIV's "chrysolite" in v. 14 is *taršiš*, which is often in the Old Testament a place rather than a jewel (e.g., Isa. 66:19; Ezek. 27:12, 25)—a port far to the west

the NIV) is like polished ivory (lit., "tooth"), decorated with sapphires. The word "body" is, however, meʿîm (as in v. 4) and is therefore better understood as the lower part of the body below the chest ("belly, loins"; see Dan. 2:32–33, where we progress in the description of the statue from the head of gold to the silver chest and arms, to the bronze thighs [meʿaʾ, the Aram. equivalent of Heb. meʿîm], and finally to the iron legs).

The legs also follow the arms and loins here in 5:15, where we read of "pillars of marble" (ʿammud, cf. 3:10) set on bases or pedestals of gold. His overall appearance is akin to that of majestic Lebanon, with all its mighty cedars. Yet it is to his mouth that the woman returns, once the description is complete and the man's total desirability is affirmed (v. 16)—that locus of "sweetness" (4:11) with which she so much desires to make contact once again, if only she could find her beloved, who is also her "friend" or "neighbor" (reaʿ, as in Ex. 20:17; Lev. 19:18).

As chapter 5 closes, then, the man is still separated from the woman. But the daughters of Jerusalem at least have a description of him and an answer to their question about why the search is so important. As chapter 6 opens, we find the theme of separation briefly continued. The daughters of Jerusalem are all set for the search and require only some hints from the woman as to where the search should be focused (6:1). They want to "look" for her lover in reality as she "looked for him" in her dream (bqš in 5:6; 6:1).

Yet now it transpires that the search is unnecessary and the fears that have come to expression in the dream are groundless. The woman knows where her lover is. He was never really lost to her. He is to be found in his own garden (6:2)[12]—that female "place" where he is accustomed to spend his time (4:12; 5:1) and whose fragrances are complementary to his own (cf. "beds of spice[s]" in 5:13 and 6:2). He has returned to his characteristic activity of "browsing" there, especially among the lilies (6:2–3; cf. 2:16). All is as it was before—the lovers caught up with each other and committed to each other ("I am my lover's and my lover is mine," 6:3; cf. 2:16).

The union of the two now permits yet another direct address by the man to the woman in 6:4–10, as in chapter 4, in contrast to the third-person description by the woman of the man in 5:10–16. This address repeats some

---

that has exotic overtones (and whose geographical location is unknown to us). The identity of the gems mentioned here is likewise unknown to us ("chrysolite" is one guess among many—rubies? topaz?), but they are clearly exotic and precious. The Heb. word sappirim, which lies behind the NIV's "sapphires," in the same line probably refers to the azure blue stone lapis lazuli (see NIV note).

12. The plural "gardens" later in the verse is not intended to refer to other, different locations (pace Goulder, Song, 46, 51), but to the same place. The one garden is simply being thought of in terms of its various parts through which the lover wanders.

of the language and imagery of his previous one (cf. 6:5b–7 with 4:2–4) but also builds on and extends it, especially in respect of the beloved's uniqueness. He begins with general praise of her beauty and loveliness, as in 4:1 (cf. also 1:15), comparing her to two famous Israelite cities, Tirzah and Jerusalem.

The beauty of Jerusalem is lauded elsewhere in the Old Testament (e.g., Jer. 6:2; Lam. 2:15), and the very name Tirzah (Jeroboam's capital city in 1 Kings 14:17) derives from the verb *rṣh*, "to be pleasing" (and was translated in this way in the ancient versions, whose authors did not see a proper name here). To compare female beauty to fortified cities is perhaps itself to imply, of course, a beauty that is awe-inspiring and inaccessible.

The final line of 6:4 draws this facet out explicitly, for the woman is "majestic as troops with banners" (NIV)—or better, as "awe-inspiring as regiments drawn up for battle" (*ᵃyumma kannidgalot*). The Heb. adjective *ᵃyom* appears elsewhere in the Old Testament only in Habakkuk 1:7 of the intimidating Babylonians on the march towards Palestine; the related noun *ᵉyma* means "terror, dread." The participle *nidgalot* comes from the root *dgl* (see comments on Song 2:4; 5:10), which has clear military connotations (even if its precise meaning remains uncertain). The phrase *ᵃyumma kannidgalot* itself reappears in 6:10, in a context that emphasizes its military overtones (although the NIV's "majestic as the stars in procession" somewhat obscures the point); the allusion there is to the heavenly "host" or "army"—the sun, moon, and stars, pictured as part of the divine army that fights under the command of the "LORD of hosts," who is the living God himself (cf., e.g., Deut. 4:19; 1 Kings 22:19).

There is wondrous beauty in all of this, but it is beauty with an edge— an awesome loveliness that induces trembling as well as devotion. It is this aspect of the woman's beauty that is perhaps picked up also at the beginning of 6:5, where her eyes are said to "overwhelm" the man (although what this means precisely is unclear).[13] He can hardly bear to look into them, so unsettling does he find them to be.

---

13. The Heb. verb *rhb* is relatively rare. Thus it is unclear how precisely to translate its Hiphil form here. It is associated in the Qal in Isa. 3:5 and Prov. 6:3 with violent uprising and importunate supplication respectively, giving the impression of strength or force brought to bear upon another. Its only other Hiphil use in Ps. 138:3 is in a context where strength is produced *in* another by God. All of this helps us to see that the woman's eyes are portrayed in Song 6:5 as having an overpowering effect on the man, but none of it in itself helps us to settle definitively which kind of effect that is. Does she overwhelm him with terror, in the manner of an army or even a sea monster (note that the noun *rahab* is the name of a mythical sea monster in verses like Ps. 89:10; Isa. 51:9)? Or does she excite him to passion, so that he is drawn on to desire her (and yet wishes her, not entirely seriously, to refrain from inflaming him)? The history of interpretation points in both directions (see Pope, *Song*, 564–65), and the context does not help, since v. 5a stands at the transition

The lover's attention thus turns from the woman's awesome beauty in general and from her disturbing eyes in particular to more familiar and comforting territory—her hair, teeth, and face (6:5b–7; see comments on 4:1–7). Yet he does not on this occasion linger in his detailed description of her wonderful body—it has all been said before. His main concern on this occasion is to emphasize again his beloved's uniqueness, as she has already emphasized his (5:9–16). The force of the comparison in 6:8–9a, which establishes this, is not captured by the NIV, but by this more literal translation:

> Sixty are they who are queens,
>   and eighty concubines,
>   and girls beyond number.
> One is she who is my dove, my perfect one;
>   one is she to her mother;
>   a shining light[14] to the woman who bore her.

The contrast is between the one precious love of the lover and the many beautiful women of the royal harem[15] and (beyond these) the multitude of young girls in general (ᶜᵃlamot)—those said in 1:3 to love the man speaking here. It is a contrast between one who is intimately known and treasured as an individual, whether by the lover or by her mother, and others known only as members of a group or scarcely at all (they have no identity other than "young girls"). A king may replace one of his harem on a rotation basis and hardly notice, for what matters about the queen or concubine is not that she is a person but that she is a woman. "Girls beyond number" are, by definition, girls without specific identities.

A mother knows her child as *that specific child*, however—one who is irreplaceable and for whom there is no substitute. Likewise, a man who truly loves a woman knows that woman as a specific person, whose identity cannot

---

between the military imagery of v. 4 and the familiar pastoral imagery of vv. 5b–7 (which reminds us of the intimacy of 4:1–5:1). Perhaps *rbb* is deliberately ambiguous, capturing in itself the paradoxical feelings of awe and desire that the man expresses here.

14. The Heb. is *bara*, lit., "pure, clear, clean," a word also used in 6:10 of the sun (cf. Ps. 19:8 of the "commands of the LORD," but with the imagery of the sun in the background in 19:4–6). The language is intended in context to emphasize how special she is to her mother (she is the one sun around whom the mother's world revolves), but the translation "favorite" is unfortunate, since it implies what is not necessarily implied by *bara* in itself, namely, that she is specially favored over other children the mother might have.

15. The numbers differ from those in 1 Kings 11:3, where Solomon is said to have had seven hundred wives and three hundred concubines. In neither case, however, is it clear that the number is intended literally. Both the total of 1000 in Kings and the sequence 60–80–unlimited number in Song 6:8 are probably intended simply to communicate the idea of "endless numbers of women."

simply be collapsed into her gender and is certainly not summed up only in her sexuality and in her sexual relationship with him. She is not simply a woman but *the* woman. This uniqueness, it is claimed in verse 10, has even been grasped by the other women who have been mentioned (since this verse is best taken as representing their words). The man's perspective is attributed to them, no doubt because he cannot think but that it is obviously the only possible perspective.

In the same way, we recall, the woman in the Song of Songs is convinced that her man is universally admired (1:3—4). *Of course* everyone thinks (as the women themselves say in 6:10) that the beloved is "like the dawn, fair as the moon [lit., 'the white one'], bright as the sun [lit., 'the hot one']"—as awesome as the heavenly host, arrayed in all its glory. *Of course* everyone holds her to be a radiant beauty. How could it be otherwise? No other judgment can be contemplated, because she is the only woman for him.

It now appears that this second speech by the lover to his beloved (and its immediate aftermath) has a similar function to the first speech in 4:1—15 (which also followed a dream), for the vision of the royal bedchamber in 3:6—11 still informs it and shapes it. The lover still seeks to assure the beloved of her secure place in his affections, where she is the one and only true love. The queens and concubines are a stark reminder of the very different reality of the royal court, where one man has access to 140 women and can bring each in turn to his opulent bedchamber. It is a potentially overwhelming reality, which might cause the beloved to lose any sense of who she is. The poem here is intended to remind the woman of her identity as far as those who truly love her are concerned; even the royal harem is found to be in agreement with this description.

 DREAMS AND VISIONS are a not uncommon occurrence in the Bible. When Joseph finds himself in prison as a result of the wicked behavior of Potiphar's wife, it is the dreams of Pharaoh (following on the dreams of the cupbearer and the baker) that provide his escape route, as he is able to tell Pharaoh what they mean in terms of the real world of Egypt (Gen. 40—41). Nebuchadnezzar's dreams, likewise, provide the opportunity for Daniel (who is able to describe and interpret them) to ascend the ladder of success in Babylon and to participate at the same time in Nebuchadnezzar's encounter with God (Dan. 2, 4). Daniel himself later has dreams and visions that speak to him of future times (Dan. 7—12). The apostle Paul is summoned to Macedonia in a vision (Acts 16:9—10), and John's account of the end of all things is generated also by a vision (Rev. 1:1—11).

There is throughout the Bible, in other words, a deep conviction that God reveals truth to people through dreams and visions, although it is not always easy to understand what he is saying. The truth is often veiled and requires interpretation, whether by characters in the dream/vision (as in Dan. 8:15–27, where the vision is "beyond understanding," v. 27) or by human beings who possess sufficient insight and wisdom to see through the veil to the truth (as in Gen. 41:39–40, where Joseph's God-given wisdom is acknowledged by Pharaoh). There is a sense in which all dreams are in fact allegories, which require interpretation if their significance for the real, waking world is to be discovered.

The significance of the dream of Song of Songs 5:2–7 is first to be found in what it has to say about the human love of which we have been reading throughout the book. It is, to use the language of Freudian psychiatry, an "anxiety dream," in which there is a pronounced note of frustration and repression (by others) of desire.[16] The desire expressed in the dream is almost tangible and is underlined by the address to the daughters of Jerusalem that follows in 5:10–16, but the dominating notes of the whole section are those of misunderstanding and missed opportunity. It is the fumbling, anxious side of male-female relationships that is in view here as the lovers fail to connect with each other and alienation enters their relationship. Absence, not presence, is the reality with which the dream-passage ends, and longing, not fulfillment, is the governing theme.

The wooing has on this occasion resulted in no consummation. We confront here, then, an aspect of the darker side of love hinted at already in 2:7 and 3:5 (of which the form of 5:8 inevitably reminds us, even while differing in its content). Love, when stirred up, will involve wonderful moments of intimacy and passion. It will also involve moments, however, of vulnerability, insecurity, fear, and loss. As C. S. Lewis puts it (albeit speaking of *agape* rather than *eros*; see Contemporary Significance on 4:1–5:1):

> There is no safe investment. To love at all is to be vulnerable. Love anything, and your heart will certainly be wrung and possibly be broken. If you want to make sure of keeping it intact, you must give your heart to no-one. . . . Lock it up safe in the casket or coffin of your selfishness. But in that casket—safe, dark, motionless, airless—it will change. It will not be broken; it will become unbreakable, impenetrable, irredeemable. The alternative to tragedy, or at least to the risk of tragedy, is damnation.[17]

---

16. See Pope, *Song*, 133–34, for some interesting insights from a practicing psychiatrist.
17. Lewis, *The Four Loves*, 111-12.

The self-giving that human love thus involves is, of course, only a reflection of the self-giving love of God, whose non-coercive, non-controlling wooing of us leads him to the vulnerability, insecurity, fear, and loss of the Incarnation and later of the Cross. The very nature of the universe as a place suited in every respect to human life and fine-tuned so as to enable that life to flourish, often described by scientists as the "anthropic issue" or "anthropic principle," itself speaks powerfully of the divine self-giving in love, as well as underlining our own calling to love in the same way:

> The (apparent) fine-tuning of the cosmological constants to produce a life-bearing universe (the anthropic issue) seems to call for explanation. A *theistic* explanation allows for a more coherent account of reality ... than does a non-theistic account. However, not all accounts of the divine nature are consistent with the patterns of divine action we seem to perceive in the natural world. God appears to work in concert with nature, never overriding or violating the very processes that God has created. This account of the character of divine action as refusal to do violence to creation, whatever the cost to God, has direct implications for human morality; it implies a "kenosis" or self-renunciatory ethic, according to which one must renounce self-interest for the sake of the other, *no matter what the cost to oneself.*[18]

God enters into vulnerable relationship with his creatures. Like the lover who stands at the beloved's door, he too (in another, quite different dream) stands at the door and knocks, desirous of entry (Rev. 3:20). That he knocks is, however, no guarantee of a happy outcome to the visit, whether in the short term or even in the long term, for there must be a hearing and an opening of the door. Love is a risky business, which is often bound up with an agonizing sense of absence (as in Ps. 22, e.g., which represents both the pain of one abandoned by God and the pain of God incarnate, abandoned on the cross: "My God, my God, why have you forsaken me?") and with desperate longing (as in Ps. 42: "As the deer pants for streams of water, so my soul pants for you, O God. My soul thirsts for God, for the living God. When can I go and meet with God?").

Intimate union is not the constant experience of men and women committed to each other in love and marriage; neither is it the constant experience of men and women committed to God, or of God committed to us. The complete union of God and church—and of God and individual creature— is a reality of the future, not of present experience (Rev. 19:7). All human

---

18. N. Murphy and G. F. R. Ellis, *On the Moral Nature of the Universe: Theology, Cosmology and Ethics* (Theology and the Sciences; Minneapolis: Fortress, 1996), xv.

unions, in both their intimacy and their alienation, themselves point us toward that future. The longing for union and the connection between human and divine-human unions are beautifully captured in Song-like language in a poem by Luci Shaw:[19]

> I gave this day to God when I got up, and look,
> look what it birthed! There was the apple tree,
> bronze leaves, its fallen apples spilling richly
> down the slope, the way God spilled his seed
> into Mary, into us. In her the holy promise
> came to rest in generous soil after a long
> fall. How often it ends in gravel, or dry dust.
> Blackberry patches thorny with distraction. Oh,
> I pray my soul will welcome always that small
> seed. That I will hail it when it enters me.
> I don't mind being grit, soil, dirt, mud-brown,
> laced with the rot of old leaves, if only the seed
> can find me, find a home and bear a fruit
> sweet, flushed, full-fleshed—a glory apple.

I love the child. But she is afraid of me. Then how can I come to her, to feed and heal her by my love? Knock on the door? Enter the common way? No. She holds her breath at a gentle tap, pretending that she is not home; she feels unworthy of polite society. And loud imperious bangings would only send her into shivering tears, for police and bill collectors have troubled her in the past. And should I break down the door? Or should I show my face at the window? Oh, what terrors I'd cause then. These have happened before. She's suffered the rapings of kindless men, and therefore she hangs her head. . . . I am none of these, to be sure. But if I came the way that they have come, she would not know me different. She would not receive my love, but might likely die of a failed heart.[20]

We have reflected before on the playfulness of love and sexual intimacy, and we have been confronted directly with the tremendous passion that is

---

19. L. Shaw, "I gave this day to God"—an unpublished poem cited with the gracious permission of the author.

20. W. Wangerin Jr., "An Advent Monologue," in *Ragman, and Other Cries of Faith* (San Francisco: HarperSanFrancisco, 1984), 9–12.

rightly expressed between lovers and intimates. Both are also on display in our current passage (5:2–16; 6:2–3), and we could no doubt spend more time thinking about them in the context of contemporary faith and life. It is to the less satisfactory aspects of relationships that we return instead—whether between mortals, or between mortals and God—and beyond that to the question of redemption and renewal.

It is a fact of human experience that men and women, albeit that they have committed themselves in lifelong relationships to each other, are not thereby immune from problems in these relationships. Some of these have to do with the different ways in which men and women are "wired"—something that all of us are prone to forget or underestimate. We simply assume our spouse thinks and feels more or less as we do, and we fail to remember that "men are from Mars, women are from Venus."[21]

Some of the problems come from previously unhelpful or abusive relationships, whether in families or elsewhere, leaving us with deep scars that make trust and openness in the present difficult. Some of our difficulties are created by our own lack of love and care for a spouse or the spouse's lack of love and care for us. There are multiple reasons why marriage might be or become difficult for us and why sexual intimacy might be or become problematic. Most marriages at some point go through entire periods in which there is a staleness in the air and far too much routine on the ground. Some couples struggle their entire married lives with the consequences of previous sexual abuse, which makes self-giving (esp. physical) love a challenge for one or both parties.

We can all relate to the frustration and anxiety of which Song of Songs 5:2–16 speaks. We all know of misunderstanding, fear, and insecurity, and even of loss—whether the loss of the beloved is more emotional than physical (we pass like ships in the night, even while sharing the same ocean) or whether we have known the tragedy of physical abandonment. We recognize in the ideal relationship that the Song of Songs presents to us the intimacy that we ourselves crave. But we are perhaps glad for the recognition in this song itself that real relationships only approximate at certain times and in some ways to the ideal.

It is no different in our relationship with God. The fact that we may have committed ourselves in a lifelong relationship to him does not make us immune from problems in this relationship too. The problems may, indeed, have the same roots as the problems in our marriages. We forget that God is not like us (which God sometimes feels compelled to remind us of, as in

---

21. J. Gray, *Men Are from Mars, Women Are from Venus: A Practical Guide for Improving Communication and Getting What You Want in Your Relationships* (New York: HarperCollins, 1992).

Hos. 11:9: "For I am God, and not man—the Holy One among you"); we bring the baggage of previous unhelpful or abusive relationships to God, which shapes our understanding of our friendship with God; we act or think selfishly in respect of God and at least perceive a lack of love and care on his part for us. Intimacy becomes problematic.

Historically this problem has been exacerbated among Christians where the transcendence of God has been emphasized and God has become in the process an imperious, holy figure who stands at a great distance from his creatures and with whom intimacy is all but inconceivable. The transcendent God evokes awe and reverence, certainly, but many have found it difficult truly to love such a person. The persistent human craving for intimacy with God has then been met in the creation of all kinds of intermediaries between God and mortal beings, who supply the close relationality that is lacking. In the Christian tradition one such famous intermediary has been Jesus' mother, Mary, who fills with her maternal devotion the void left by the distant and emotionally detached Father.

Even without the exacerbation of the problem, however, it remains the case that the Christian life is not a life of uninterrupted intimacy with God, but it also knows something of the frustration and anxiety of which Song of Songs 5:2–16 speaks, and something of its misunderstanding, fear, and insecurity. We know of divine absence as well as divine presence.

The truth about God, of course, is that he is not only transcendent but also very near; and not only near, but absolutely committed to his creatures; and not only committed, but proactive in wooing them. This is a general truth, but it is also a particular truth, revealed in the Incarnation. It is beautifully and powerfully articulated in Walter Wangerin's "Advent Monologue," a portion of which was cited at the head of this section. Wangerin envisages a beloved child, starving, neglected, and damaged, sitting alone in a room with her knees tucked tight against her breasts, her arms around these and her head down. The narrator wants to rescue her and heal her, but he recognizes that in this case even a knocking at the door will not signify a free choice, but a coercion. The challenge is to find an entrance that will not frighten or kill his beloved:

> By what door can love arrive after all, truly to nurture her, to take the loneliness away, to make her beautiful, as lovely as my moon at night, my sun come morning?[22]

The solution is to have the woman herself become the door, so that the narrator becomes the baby in her womb. In the tender love of mother and

---

22. Wangerin, "Advent Monologue," 10–11.

child she will become transfigured; thus later, when the baby takes his "trumpet voice" again, all fear will have been dispelled. The name of the baby is, of course, Immanuel—God with us. God enters his world in this gentle, healing way at Christmastime and woos us into relationship with himself, helping us to see that his holiness and love are by no means incompatible. There is no need of intermediaries. God is himself the intermediary and the road that leads to himself.

With this God of wonderful grace, who is not like us but becomes like us, it is possible to be intimate. With this God, who is not only with us but *for* us, it is possible to have a love relationship. Learning each day more of this God's true nature and character, we are able gradually to leave behind the baggage of previous unhelpful or abusive relationships, to trust him even when we think we see a lack of love and care on his part for us and to begin to think and act unselfishly in respect of him by offering our worship and very selves to him. Slowly misunderstanding, fear, and insecurity dissipate, even if frustration sometimes remains. Slowly we learn to deal constructively with a sense of divine absence, even as we yearn for a renewed sense of divine presence.

It is this gentle but constant self-giving nature of God, which draws us into relationship with him, that provides us with both the resources and the model for loving our spouses, even when things are not going well in our marriages. For the commitment we make to each other in marriage is not a cold, legal commitment, which can be met simply by staying together and avoiding divorce. It is not the kind of commitment a lawyer holds up before a man looking for a divorce when, having described to him a horrendous, destructive marriage breakdown, he advises his client that he can either risk similar pain or "get up and go home and try to find some shred of what you saw in the sweetheart of your youth."[23] That is marriage as avoidance of something worse.

The commitment we make in marriage, rather, is a warm, passionate commitment, which cannot rest content with anything less than intimacy and which therefore works hard at problems even while recognizing the limitations that all of us face in resolving some of them. The foundation of this hard work must always be self-giving love—the love that drives us to seek to understand this differently gendered and mysterious creature whom God has given us as friend and companion; that constantly desires communication and understanding; that seeks to heal, through patience and kindness, the scars of abuse; that will not allow routine to dominate the relationship and extinguish romance.

The love we have in mind here is well pictured in Song of Songs 5:2—16. It is a love that, when misunderstanding occurs and our friend is lost to us,

---

23. From the movie *The War of the Roses*.

wastes no time in weeping but runs immediately out into the streets and pursues him or her, even at great personal risk. The Gospels give us a different picture—of a shepherd who will not rest until the sheep is safely in his arms (Matt. 18:12–14). True love, whether human or divine, never gives up. It pursues the beloved until the end. It hopes always for the renewal of relationship that is described in Song of Songs 6:1–10, as the lovers know once more the wonder of being unique to the other and lie contentedly in each others arms in their "garden."

If God is for us, who can be against us? (Rom. 8:31)

There is no fear in love. But perfect love drives out fear, because fear has to do with punishment. The one who fears is not made perfect in love. (1 John 4:18)

Song of Songs 6:11–7:13

11 I went down to the grove of nut trees
    to look at the new growth in the valley,
to see if the vines had budded
    or the pomegranates were in bloom.
12 Before I realized it,
    my desire set me among the royal chariots
        of my people.

13 Come back, come back, O Shulammite;
    come back, come back, that we may
        gaze on you!

Why would you gaze on the Shulammite
    as on the dance of Mahanaim?

7:1 How beautiful your sandaled feet,
    O prince's daughter!
Your graceful legs are like jewels,
    the work of a craftsman's hands.
2 Your navel is a rounded goblet
    that never lacks blended wine.
Your waist is a mound of wheat
    encircled by lilies.
3 Your breasts are like two fawns,
    twins of a gazelle.
4 Your neck is like an ivory tower.
Your eyes are the pools of Heshbon
    by the gate of Bath Rabbim.
Your nose is like the tower of Lebanon
    looking toward Damascus.
5 Your head crowns you like Mount Carmel.
    Your hair is like royal tapestry;
    the king is held captive by its tresses.
6 How beautiful you are and how pleasing,
    O love, with your delights!
7 Your stature is like that of the palm,
    and your breasts like clusters of fruit.
8 I said, "I will climb the palm tree;
    I will take hold of its fruit."

> May your breasts be like the clusters of the vine,
>> the fragrance of your breath like apples,
> ⁹ and your mouth like the best wine.
>
> May the wine go straight to my lover,
>> flowing gently over lips and teeth.
> ¹⁰I belong to my lover,
>> and his desire is for me.
> ¹¹Come, my lover, let us go to the countryside,
>> let us spend the night in the villages.
> ¹²Let us go early to the vineyards
>> to see if the vines have budded,
> if their blossoms have opened,
>> and if the pomegranates are in bloom—
> there I will give you my love.
> ¹³The mandrakes send out their fragrance,
>> and at our door is every delicacy,
> both new and old,
>> that I have stored up for you, my lover.

Original Meaning

THE ADMIRING SONG of 6:4–10 has ended, and we find ourselves suddenly in a new section of the text in which it is not at first entirely clear who is speaking (6:11–12). Yet the first-person account of this person who "went down" (*yrd*) to a garden "grove" (*ginna*) corresponds to the third-person description by the woman in 6:2, when she tells her friends that her beloved has "gone down" (*yrd*) to his "garden" (*gan*). In all likelihood, then, the man is speaking in 6:11–12.

The plural speakers who interject in 6:13a are, as we will see, those other men who find the woman desirable. Their words now match the words of the broader community of women who have spoken in 6:10. Song of Songs 7:1–9a is in turn the renewed praise of the lover for his beloved, harking back to passages like 4:1–15 and 6:4–10; thus, 6:13b is also best taken as the words of the lover, introducing the speech of 7:1–9a. His affirmations of the woman lead in turn to her response to him in 7:9b–13, as she invites him (7:13) to accompany her back to the place in which he first lost his senses in her arms (6:11). Chapter 7 thus ends with their one-to-one relationship once again restored, after the brief interlude in which the man found himself only one among a number of men (6:12–13).

The garden the man visits in 6:11 is a fertile area bursting with the new growth of springtime. It is a valley or wadi, responding to the water that rushes in torrents through it in the aftermath of rain by producing lush vegetation. We have heard of vines and pomegranates in this connection before. The "nuts" (*ʾegoz*) are, however, a new feature. The word is unique in the Old Testament but is found in postbiblical Hebrew, referring specifically to the walnut. In modern Arabic, in fact, Jerusalem's Kidron Valley is known as Wadi al-Joz, "Walnut Valley."

It is to a fertile place that the man goes, then—a place that produces fruit in abundance. The woman herself is again clearly in mind, and the imagery may be deliberately chosen (as in 4:12–15) to evoke the intimate parts of her body.[1] Certainly the experience of "going down to the garden" has a profound effect on the man, even if it is a little difficult to be certain as to what exactly that effect is (6:12).

Song of Songs 6:12 is widely considered to be the most difficult verse in the book, and it is definitely challenging. It reads literally (with different possibilities noted, and without punctuation for the moment) "I did not know my soul she set [or 'made'] me chariots of Ammi-Nadib [or 'of my princely/willing people,' or 'of the princely/willing people']." Yet it is not impossible to make sense of it. Our best lead as we make the attempt lies in the mention of "chariots" (*markebot*). This reminds us both of the chariots of Pharaoh in 1:9 (*rekeb*; recall that the woman was compared to a mare among chariots drawn by stallions, with potential for great disruption and distraction as she moved among men) and of the royal bed in 3:10 (*merkab*).

Chariots in the Song of Songs speak of male desire for a woman. In view of this reality, the Hebrew word *nadib* is best taken, not as part of a proper name or as a reference to nobility or royalty, but as a reference to the passion that the woman excites in men. By far the most common use of the root *ndb* in its various forms in the Old Testament is in fact the freewill offering, for service of some kind, of the self or of one's possessions. In passages like Exodus 25:2; 35:21, 29, we are indeed told of the spirit or heart of a person moving or compelling that person to action. There is an interior disposition that results in movement out toward others, whether God or other human beings. The word *nadib* itself often means "willing, generous" (e.g., 35:5, 22).

Thus, in the context of Song of Songs 6:12 we should understand that the lover finds himself "among the chariots of a willing people,"[2] interpreting the

---

1. For a generally interesting discussion of nuts and sexuality in particular, see Pope, *Song*, 574–82, from whom the detail about the Kidron Valley is also drawn. The fertile wadi evokes the area of the vagina (as does the "conduit" of 4:13—see comments in the footnote on 4:13 relating to the NIV's "plants").

2. The preposition behind "among" in this translation is not actually present in the Heb., but is probably to be understood. Words commonly appear in Heb. poetry merely in apposition to each other, inviting the reader to supply the obvious connection. The *yod* in the

"willingness for service" implied here in a sexual sense. By no means for the first time in the song, the lover sets his individual attraction for the woman within a much broader, more general context. All men, when they see his beloved, are ready to offer themselves to her; that is the effect she has on men. With the second part of the verse thus clarified, the remainder falls into place, although its precise sense remains beyond us. There are two possibilities:

- "Before I realized it, my desire [a sense often belonging to Heb. *nepeš*] set me among the chariots of a willing people."
- "I did not know myself [Heb. *nepeš* referring to the whole self, as often in the Old Testament]; she set me among the chariots of a willing people."

In both alternatives the man is pictured as out of control, either caught by surprise by the speed with which he joins the herd of "stallions" straining after the beloved or disconcerted by it and not quite recognizing himself in his own behavior. He begins his journey to the nut grove in possession of himself; he ends it possessed by the object of his desire.

With this interpretation of 6:11–12 in mind, it is now perhaps easier to understand 6:13, which begins with words spoken by a group and ends with a response to this group by the lover. The mere fact that the group is referred to in 6:13b with a masculine plural verb ("Why would you gaze?") does not inevitably mean that it is a male group; the use of gender in the Song of Songs is certainly not sufficiently precise to allow such a conclusion. Yet on this occasion the group is most naturally understood as that same group of males whose presence is implied in verse 12—those many men who wish to "gaze on [the woman]" (6:13a).

The woman has her back turned to them or perhaps is moving away from them to escape their attention. Thus, they plead with her to "come back," or perhaps simply to "turn around" (*šwb*), so that they may view her beauty. The lover, in turn, objects to the attention that his beloved is receiving from this broader group of men, comparing what is happening to what occurs on the occasion of "the dance of Mahanaim." We have no idea which particular dance is being referred to in this phrase,[3] but it is not the particularity of

---

Heb. *ʿammi*, which the NIV takes as a first person suffix, is understood in my translation as an archaic ending indicating a genitival relationship between *ʿammi* and *nadib* (GKC, §90k-m).

3. Heb. *maḥᵃnayim* is a dual form meaning "two camps," and it is also a place name in passages like Gen. 32:1–2, where the location is called "Mahanaim" because Jacob thinks it is "the camp of God." We are perhaps meant to think of the dance's origin (it is a famous type of dance, associated with this town or with a victory in battle and thus with military camps), of its spectacular nature (it is "divine"—the woman herself has sometimes been described in such terms in the Song), or of the manner of its presentation (the people gather in two "camps," male and female, to watch it or even to join in with antiphonal singing and musical

the dance that is important. The main point of the comparison is that these men are looking for the woman to present herself before them for their pleasure and entertainment, in the same way that a woman might dance before an audience. The lover objects to this. He may find himself in the company of these men as they pursue the woman, but he does not accept their right to view his beloved in the same way he has viewed her hitherto in this song.

A further detail touching on the identity of the woman is provided in this exchange—that she is "a Shulammite." This is an opaque term, however. It may refer to the girl's hometown of Shunem, associated with at least one famous beauty in Israel's history (1 Kings 1:3). It could also be an allusion to Sulmanitu, a Mesopotamian goddess of love and war, used here to conjure up the idea of the divinity of the woman's beauty. Or the term might contain an allusion to Solomon, reminding us once more of the way in which kings in particular can command the presence of dancing girls (as well as other girls) for their pleasure. Certainty is beyond us.[4]

It is not the woman's identity as "Shulammite" that is in any case important in what follows in 7:1–9a, but the idea that she is being viewed as a dancer. That is why, as the lover once again launches out in a song of praise to his beloved, he begins with her feet and moves up to her head, in contrast to the movement of his eyes in both 4:1–7 and 6:4–10 (from the head downward). It is the feet of the dancer that first occupy his attention as he leaves behind him the "willing people" (*ᶜammi-nadib*) of 6:12 and contemplates instead the "willing/generous daughter" (*bat-nadib*, 7:1; not "prince's daughter," as in NIV) who is his true love and offers herself to him. It is, after all, *her* desire for *him* that interests him, and not *their* desire for *her*.

He marvels at this woman whose beautiful feet are revealed by her open sandals and whose thighs are so wondrously curved or rounded (v. 1)[5]—the

---

accompaniment). It is also not beyond possibility, given the frequent reference thus far in the Song to the two female breasts, that the "two camps" are breasts here also and that attention is being drawn by the name of the dance to that which is most noticed by the men (the "dancing" of the breasts) during its performance. If the following description of the woman is any guide (and it may not be, since the mind's eye can see things that the eye cannot), it does not appear as if the dancer wears much clothing during the performance; and if breasts are the focus of attention, it may help to explain why the men plead with the woman in 6:13 to "turn round." For a full discussion, see Pope, *Song*, 601–12.

4. See Pope, *Song*, 596–600, for a full discussion.

5. The NIV's "legs" (*yᵉrekayim*) are in reality the upper part of the legs, the thighs (as in 3:8, where each soldier had a sword "at his side"). These are described as "turned" (*ḥmq*, as in 5:6; NIV "graceful") like *ḥᵃlaʾim*. The *ḥᵃlaʾim* (NIV "jewels") are ornaments of some kind (cf. the similar *ḥᵃli* in Prov. 25:12 and *ḥelya* in Hos. 2:13), which we presume to have a rounded quality (since they appear in the Proverbs and Hosea contexts alongside *nezem*, "ring"). Her thighs are rounded, then, like these ornaments.

work of an artist. He is astonished by that most intimate place between her legs, which reminds him of a bowl or cup filled with wine.[6] He is also amazed by her belly,[7] which is "a mound of wheat encircled by lilies" (v. 2)—a reference both to shape and to color. The breasts, which are elsewhere said to browse upon these lilies, come next (v. 3; cf. 4:5), followed by the neck, eyes, and nose (7:4).

The imagery of the "ivory tower" suggests an elegant, long neck with a smooth appearance (cf. 4:4 and comments on the "tower of David"). "The pools of Heshbon" (another famous biblical city, Num. 21:25—30, although "the gate of Bath Rabbim" is unknown) suggest depth and the reflection of light; the lover could, as it were, drown in her eyes. Her nose is also attractive to the man in its length and prominence, although the "tower of Lebanon" to which it is compared is unknown. Some have suggested a mountain (e.g., Mount Hermon, "looking toward Damascus"), just as the head is compared in 7:5 to Mount Carmel in all its glory.

There is possibly a play on words in this last reference between the Hebrew *karmel* and *karmil* (the color purple or crimson), for "purple" (*ʾargaman*)

---

6. It does not seem likely, having viewed the thighs (which already have associations with fertility and procreation, in view of the sexual organs that lie between them; cf. Gen. 46:26; Ex. 1:5; Judg. 8:30) and just prior to viewing the belly (see below), that we should be asked at this point to contemplate the navel (Heb. *šor*). The NIV translation arises from the use of the word *šor* in Ezek. 16:4 of the umbilical cord, which suggests to some that it can be used by extension of the navel; but if this is true, it is presumably also possible that it might be used by extension for other parts of the body with which the umbilical cord is associated, i.e., the womb and every other area through which the cord passes on the way to the baby's navel. In Prov. 3:7—10 the healing of the *šor* (NIV "body") is associated with the liquid refreshment of the bones and with fertility more generally—a reference, perhaps, to the removal of barrenness. The level of usage of the word in the Old Testament makes certainty impossible, but the context in Song of Songs 7 undoubtedly speaks in favor of a translation here, at least, in terms of the vaginal area. It is with this area, after all, that water and fertility have been closely associated already in 4:1—15, and to consider the matter from a biological rather than a literary perspective, it is in respect of this area (rather than the area of the navel) that it makes sense to say that there is ever-present liquid. The metaphorical liquid in question is of uncertain identity, although "blended wine" is a good guess (Heb. *mezeg* being thought of as an Aramaism for Heb. *mešek*, which refers to wine mixed with water or spices). The precise nature and shape of the metaphorical utensil that contains the liquid is also uncertain (but see Pope, *Song*, 618—19, for a more optimistic view).

7. One assumes that the NIV means to refer to the whole front and lower part of the body in using "waist," but it is a strange word to employ. Heb. *beṭen* is the belly or the womb, here nicely rounded like a mound of wheat (the association of flat bellies and beauty is an entirely modern phenomenon, as the history of Western art, among other things, demonstrates). The lilies probably have no function other than to associate the belly with the breasts, which are referred to in v. 3, and to remind us of the lover's previous "browsing" in the field that is his beloved (cf. 2:16; 4:5; 5:13; 6:2—3).

appears later in verse 5 of the woman's hair, which has evidently been dyed.[8] This purple dye was expensive and in early times became an emblem of royalty (cf. 3:10, where it appears in the description of the royal bed). It is no doubt this association that leads on to the comment about the effect of her "tresses"[9] on royalty, although it is not clear that on this occasion a particular king is meant in the first instance (since Heb. *melek* has no definite article, unlike 1:4, 12). It is just that the woman has the kind of hair that would captivate a king.

It is not a king who now addresses her, however, and we are immediately reminded of this in the summary statement by the lover in 7:6 as he takes up language first addressed to him by his beloved and now uses it of her (*yph*, *n°m*, "beautiful . . . pleasing," as in 1:16, where the NIV translates "handsome . . . charming").[10] She is the altogether lovely one, who brings with her "delights" (*ta°ănugim*). It is these delights that the man would like to sample (7:7–8), "climbing" up her tall and slender frame (which is pictured as a "palm" tree) and "taking hold" of her breasts (which are its "fruit"—clusters of date palms). The man's eyes have moved up from his beloved's feet to her head (vv. 1–6); now his body wishes to follow. He hopes that his arrival at his destination will lead him to the enjoyment of the aforementioned fruit (now described as grapes in v. 8, developing the metaphor of the vineyard we

---

8. The NIV's translation of v. 5 is right in understanding Heb. *ʾargaman* as a reference to a purple cloth of some kind ("tapestry"), since to say the hair is "like purple" does not make much sense. To remove the color from the text altogether is, however, unjustified. See Pope, *Song*, 629–30, for ancient evidence touching on the dyeing of hair—a practice that continues to this day, at least in the use of henna to dye the hair red, among women in this area of the Mediterranean (e.g., in southern Tunisia). The "purple" mentioned here could in practice vary in shade. We might paraphrase the first two lines of the verse thus: "Your head sits atop your body like purple Carmel; the threads [Heb. *dalla*, as in Isa. 38:12, where the NIV has 'loom'] which are your hair remind me of purple cloth."

9. Heb. *rehatim* appears in Gen. 30:38, 41; Ex. 2:16 of watering troughs for animals, and we perhaps imagine that its use here is meant to evoke the streams that run down a mountainside, in much the same way that hair is associated with goats coming down a mountainside in Song 4:1; 6:5. It is intriguing nevertheless that the same word appears in 1:17 in what looks like a dialectical variant (with a *bet* for a *he*, as also in the Samaritan Pentateuch at Ex. 2:16), the Qere inviting us to read the word in the same way as in Song 7:5. The imagery in 1:17 is that of housing, and the NIV translates the word as "rafters." It is not impossible, therefore, that Mount Carmel only appears in 7:5 because of the play on "purple" and that the dominating imagery throughout all of vv. 4–5 is architectural—towers, pools, gates, and now a magnificent royal palace with impressive rafters and hangings, in which the king is held captive.

10. Heb. *yph* has frequently appeared by itself in both verbal and adjectival forms in the Song, always otherwise in reference to the woman: 1:8, 15; 2:10, 13; 4:1, 7, 10; 5:9; 6:1, 4, 10; 7:1.

have encountered in verses like 1:6). He also looks forward to tasting the "apples" (cf. 2:3, 5 for the identity of the fruit), which are to be found still higher up this amazing, multifaceted tree, at the site of the beloved's mouth and nose.[11] The man eagerly anticipates drinking the wine that flows there (7:9a; cf. 5:16 for *her* desire for *his* mouth).

The woman's attention has been engaged by this fine speech, so that she is no longer a dancer observed but a lover aroused. No sooner has the man expressed his own wish to taste her wine than she responds with the fervent hope that he will indeed enjoy it (7:9b), that it will in fact flow over the lips of both the lovers as they lie together (cf. NIV note[12]). She willingly gives herself over to him in his "desire" (*tešuqa*, 7:10) of her, in the context of their mutual love for each other (cf. the similar "my lover is mine and I am his" in 2:16; and "I am my lover's and my lover is mine" in 6:3). She invites him (7:11–13) to go with her to those fertile regions of the countryside where

---

11. The "fragrance of your breath" in v. 8 is lit. "the fragrance of your nose" (Heb. *ʾap*). The NIV may be correct in interpreting this as a reference to the beloved's "breath," since the nose is clearly an organ of breathing and is often referred to in the Old Testament, in addition, when both human and divine anger are described (BDB, 60). Breath exits the nose as well as entering it in Heb. thought, esp. in cases where passion is involved, and it is natural that any such breath would be, to the lover, fragrant—as the whole world of love that the Song describes is suffused with "fragrance" (cf. *reaḥ* also in 1:3, 12; 2:13; 4:10–11; 7:13). Yet it is also possible that it is the scented nature of the face itself (including the nose) that is in view here. The nose has already been highlighted in 7:4 as being like "the tower [*migdal*] of Lebanon," and we recall that earlier in the Song the man's cheeks (or jaw) were referred to (lit.) as "towers [*migdᵉlot*] of ointment" (5:13). We cannot allow the fact that *we* might not refer to the female nose in this way to influence us overly in our reading of the Heb., which frequently refers to the human body in ways that are unfamiliar to us. A safer translation is, therefore, "the fragrance of your nose like apples"—or perhaps, recognizing that the part can often stand for the whole in Heb. poetry, "the fragrance of your face like apples" (as the dual form *ʾappayik* in some Heb. MSS at v. 8 explicitly indicates). There is no justification, since the man is moving upward in vv. 8–9a and thinking in the end of kisses on the mouth, and since the normal sense of Heb. *ʾap* fits the overall context, for Pope's speculative "vulva" or his (in principle) more defensible "nipples" (Pope, *Song*, 636–67). This is esp. the case given the fondness in the ancient world for the "nose kiss" (involving nose contact and smell) as well as the "mouth kiss" (involving mouth contact and taste; see Snaith, *Song*, 108).

12. The phrase "flowing gently over lips of sleepers" (NIV note) is a difficult one, and the NIV therefore follows other ancient versions at this point. It is the unique verb *dbb*, however, and not the reference to the "lips," that presents the real difficulty in the verse. We are forced to make an intelligent guess from the context here, mainly on the basis of Heb. *mešarim* (NIV "straight"), which refers in Prov. 23:31 to the passing of wine smoothly down the gullet. The "sleeping lips," clearly, cannot but belong to the lovers. The wine of the woman's mouth is pictured as passing smoothly into his as they lie together (not lit. asleep) in bed. In English, too, we can use "sleep" as a verb indicating activity in a bed that does not literally involve unconsciousness.

---

his own desire for her was first kindled (cf. 6:11 and 7:12, with their references to budding vines and blooming pomegranates), so that they may consummate their love. She wishes for the two of them to "spend the night" (*lyn*) among the henna bushes (NIV note[13]), just as he has previously spent the night (*lyn*, 1:13; NIV "resting") between her scented breasts; she then wishes to rise early in the morning to come together once again in the vineyards ("there I will give you my love," 7:12).

The "mandrakes" of 7:13 are plants with aphrodisiac qualities (note the interesting similarity between Heb. *duda'im*, "mandrakes," and Heb. *dodim*, "love"),[14] which are pictured as growing in this locale where lovemaking will take place. The "locale" is, of course, as much the woman herself as a "place" to which both lovers go, as it was in 6:11 (cf. also 4:12–15). This is particularly clear in the remainder of 7:13, which speaks of a "door" (*petaḥ*) giving access to "every delicacy" that has been stored up for the man—an opening already hinted at in the opening (also *ptḥ*) of the blossoms in 7:12.

We are reminded of 5:6 (see comments) and the double entendres of the dream there as the woman opens (also *ptḥ*) the door to the man. His own desire had been aroused previously by the sight of the vines budding and the pomegranates blooming (6:11); she now speaks to him in 7:12 of an additional reality of spring (the opening of blossoms), as a prelude to inviting him to her "door" to taste her own delicious fruits (cf. *mᵉgadim*; NIV "delicacy," also in 4:13, 16, where it appears with Heb. *pᵉri* and is translated "choice fruits"). It is an invitation to sexual bliss, involving both things familiar to the man and things he has not yet experienced ("new and old," 7:13).

THE BIBLE IS a book in which fertile gardens with their abundant vegetation play a central role.[15] The biblical story begins in the Garden of Eden (Gen. 2)—an original perfection where human beings enjoyed intimacy with God and with each other and all creation worked in harmony together. It ends with the new Jerusalem (Rev. 21)—a city that nevertheless has at its center a river of life lined with trees providing food and healing leaves.

---

13. In spite of the long interpretative tradition that favors the translation "villages" here, it provides an unsatisfactory parallel to "countryside." If it is not a poetic plural or a plural of generalization (GKC, §124 c, e), it also provides an unnecessary enigma for the interpreter, who must then explain how and why the lovers wish to "spend the night" in various locations rather than one. It makes much more sense to understand Heb. *kᵉparim* as the scented "henna bushes" from which derives henna (Heb. *koper*, 1:14; note *kᵉparim* itself in 4:13).

14. See further Pope, *Song*, 648–49.

15. See L. Ryken et al., eds., *Dictionary of Biblical Imagery*, 315–17.

The route from one to the other runs through two other crucially important gardens. One is the Garden of Gethsemane (Mark 14:32), which was the location of a human decision that reversed the course of human history (since it was a decision to obey, rather than to disobey, the Father). The other is the garden that is the site of Jesus' burial and resurrection (John 19:41; 20:15), which means that human beings may die and be buried like a seed in the ground but have the possibility of breaking through the soil once again to new life.

Also located in the wondrous yet risky space between Eden and the new Jerusalem are the gardens of the Song of Songs, which tells us of a blossoming love that recaptures something of Eden and foreshadows something of Jerusalem, even though touched by sin and darkness. These are the gardens of human love—places of seclusion, intimacy, and security, even though the desert may encroach on them and seek to swallow them up (Song 3:6; 8:5), and even though the darkness of fear and loss may threaten to engulf them. The threats are real, and the Song of Songs itself provides us with no certainty that in the end they can be overcome.

It is only the Bible as a whole, which tells us of the gardens of the Passion and Resurrection, that provides us with a firm hope that human passion will endure and find its own fulfillment in resurrection. Indeed, this whole Bible enables us to understand more fully what human love is and how it contributes to the redemptive process in which the God who has created all things is engaged. What we are called to in love is to demonstrate something of God's original purposes for human beings, male and female, and to hint at something of God's future.

We have already noted on numerous occasions in our reflections thus far how the Song of Songs evokes Genesis 1–2 and calls us to refuse to accept the inevitability of living out in our relationships the fallenness of Genesis 3–11 (and indeed the rest of the Old Testament). The woman who in Genesis 3:1–6 took the initiative and introduced alienation into relationships becomes in the Song of Songs the woman who, in taking initiative, draws the man into intimacy. The man and the woman together restore in their love what was fractured in the Fall—a world in which man and woman, made in God's image and jointly commissioned to the task of exercising dominion over the earth, meet face to face as equals, their commonality and harmony stressed in the language of "bone of bones . . . flesh of flesh . . . one flesh" in Genesis 2:23–24 and in their nakedness without shame in 2:25. There is a fervent wooing of the unique other, employing frank language, as here in Song of Songs 6:11–7:13, and there is eager, enthusiastic response to this expression of "desire" (7:10).

The Hebrew word for "desire" (*t̆šuqa*) itself reminds us of the fractured world of Genesis 3 and the following chapters, for we find the same word used in Genesis 3:16 of a female desire for the male. In the Genesis context it does not connote straightforward sexual desire, of course, which is bound up with Creation rather than with Fall; human beings are, after all, sexual beings right from the beginning (Gen. 1:28–30; 2:23–25). In spite of long-standing Christian interpretation of Genesis 1–3 along these lines, therefore, sexual desire itself cannot be understood as an aspect only of the fallen world. More careful exegesis makes clear that what happens in the Fall is that sex is wedded in unholy matrimony to power. This is already suggested by Genesis 3:16, where the female desire is met with male power and control (he "will rule" [*mšl*] over her). Genesis 4:7 confirms this impression, for here the word *tšuqa* is used of sin's desire to possess Cain, to which he must also respond by seeking to "master" (*mšl*) it. This implies that the female "desire" referred to in 3:16 is at least in part a desire for power over the man, to which he responds with his own force.

Insofar as we have had occasion thus far in this commentary to emphasize male power in regard to sex (see, e.g., comments on 3:6–11), then, in reflecting on the way in which sex and power are all too often bound up with each other in the fallen world of our experience, it is important to recognize here that it is not only men who are fallen beings, but also women. A woman, too, can use sex as a means to her private ends (e.g., security, status, wealth) rather than embracing it as an expression of mutual and self-sacrificing love. Sexual expression thus can become, in the hands of women, as manipulative and abusive (and as little liberating and affirming) as it can be in the hands of men.

The woman of the Song of Songs has, however, given up all "desire" of this kind. She only welcomes the desire of her *lover* for *her*. The Genesis 3 reality is thus rejected in favor of the Genesis 1–2 ideal. The abrupt halt that is thus brought to the ever-expanding circle of alienation in Genesis 3–4 is suggested not only by the use of the word *tšuqa* in Song of Songs 7:10 but also by the phrasing of 7:11, as the woman offers an invitation to her lover: "Let us go to the countryside" (*neṣeʾ haśśadeh*). Her purpose in inviting him outside is that they should spend the night (and indeed the morning) in making passionate love to each other. It is intriguing to note, however, that this is the very invitation offered to Abel by Cain at the beginning of Genesis 4:8—an invitation now missing in the Masoretic text but preserved in the Versions. Cain's purpose in issuing the invitation was to get Abel to a quiet spot so that he could murder him. He thus demonstrated that he had not been able to master sin, rather that sin's power had grasped hold of him. The woman's initiative in the Song of Songs, in welcoming her lover's desire and leading him out to the countryside, leads to a very different outcome.

Human love that thus lays down power and looks, rather, to be welcomed into intimacy reflects divine love. It is the love of the God who, having banished his creatures from a garden, quietly entered gardens of suffering and death in order to woo his beloved back to him and have her welcome him eagerly into her arms. It is the love of the God who, like the woman in 7:10 ("I belong to my lover"), binds himself to his people in marriage covenant and promises to be devoted to them: "I will walk among you and be your God, and you will be my people" (Lev. 26:12). The final wedding may be some time coming, but it will assuredly happen (Matt. 25:1–13; Rev. 19:7).

Dear Lord and Father of mankind,
  forgive our foolish ways;
Reclothe us in our rightful mind, in purer
  lives thy service find,
In deeper reverence praise.[16]

It is a fine hymn. It is difficult to suppress a smile, however, when it is chosen by couples as the hymn sung just before they take their marriage vows, for in that context a request for "reclothing in our rightful mind" suggests the recognition of prior insanity, only now (and almost too late) discovered. Perhaps we only hear it that way because many of us inhabit cultures that hold marriage in such low esteem and regard it as having little to do with romance and lasting love. If it could previously be sung that "love and marriage go together like a horse and carriage," it is not something widely believed now, particularly by those multitudes who have experienced the breakdown of their own marriages or who have witnessed such a breakdown from close quarters.

Marriage has become instead the target of bitter humor and the focus of widespread suspicion, even as men and women still crave ongoing and committed intimacy. It is an institution in which we may find ourselves imprisoned, it is felt, if we succumb to the insanity of love long enough to take us to the altar (or its secular equivalents) and beyond. It is a dark pit into which we will certainly fall unless we, like the prodigal son, "come to our senses" in sufficient time (Luke 15:17).

Perhaps the real problem with marriage, however, is not that we come to our senses too late but that we come to our senses at all. Love has drawn us out of ourselves and enabled us for a while and to an extent to behave unselfishly. It has even led us to a place in which we find ourselves making promises to another person about commitment. There is in the idea of "recovery" from the sickness that led us in such directions the idea also of withdrawal. We suffer hurt perhaps, or disappointment, as we give ourselves in

---

16. Part of a hymn written by John Greenleaf Whittier, 1807–1892.

vulnerability to the other. We draw back, ashamed that we were so naïve and trusting in the first place. Now we are being realistic, we claim; now we see the matter clearly. We will not make that mistake again.

Thus, by degrees, a romance that altered our perception of reality and in so doing changed *us* is suffocated by an insistence that reality is truly otherwise and that all claims to the contrary are false. Self-protection becomes the driving concern and is indeed the compelling force in many marriages. Intimacy, a frail plant that requires constant attention from those who tend the garden, cannot survive in such a harsh and self-focused climate.

God never "comes to his senses" in his love affair with us, withdrawing from us out of a desire for self-protection. The wounds that still mark Jesus' hands and side witness to his ongoing vulnerability and indeed to the true nature of "reality," in spite of mortal claims to the contrary. "Reality" is self-giving Love. It is those who insist otherwise who dwell in unreality.

The vision of the ongoing and committed man-woman relationship presented to us in the Song of Songs, likewise, knows of no decision, after due consideration, to conserve the self and gain distance from the other. The man who first lost his senses in pursuing the woman is indeed encouraged by her to return to the place in which it happened and to experience still fresh delights in doing so (6:11–12; 7:11–13). Ongoing unselfconsciousness marks this relationship, in fact, paralleling the unselfconsciousness of the Garden of Eden. The lovers are so caught up in each other that the boundaries around the self are simply not recognized, even if each does understand that there are boundaries around the other. The idea that it might be a good thing that they should each "come to their senses" is nowhere in evidence. Senselessness is positively embraced by these intoxicated lovers.

The real problem with marriage is not that we come to our senses too late but that we come to our senses at all. We give up on the "insanity" of self-giving love and embrace the deadly "common sense" of self-possession. Into the spaces freed up by this "common sense" come all kinds of "little foxes" (2:15), which wreak their own special havoc on our lives. Liberated from their "bondage" to one beloved spouse who takes up our whole horizon, our erotic impulses redirect themselves elsewhere. They play out in our sexual fantasies about other men and women who, we imagine, might better meet our needs, whether these are people genuinely accessible to us or simply those who inhabit TV and movie screens, magazines, or websites.

It is not uncommon in troubled marriages to find that while the physical act of love is with the spouse, the emotional and mental act is with someone else entirely. These impulses may even play out in actual sexual encounters with those who are not our spouses, whether money changes hands or not. The advantage that all these avenues of sexual expression share is that none of them requires any self-giving at all. They are entirely self-focused and bound up with manipulation, abuse, and power. They are all of them, therefore, necessarily destructive to self and to others, but that is a truth that is never fully acknowledged by those who indulge in them. It is an aspect of the lostness of our souls, rather, that we are constantly to be found calling what is right and good "insane" and that which is wicked and destructive "normal."

Jesus, who was himself described as a madman (John 10:20), calls us to a higher vision. He insists that we learn what commitment means, and he defines that commitment as a matter of thought and imagination as well as a matter of action (Matt. 5:27–28, 31–32):

> You have heard that it was said, "Do not commit adultery." But I tell you that anyone who looks at a woman lustfully has already committed adultery with her in his heart. . . .
>
> It has been said, "'Anyone who divorces his wife must give her a certificate of divorce.'" But I tell you that anyone who divorces his wife, except for marital unfaithfulness, causes her to become an adulteress, and anyone who marries the divorced woman commits adultery.

The Song of Songs expands on what this kind of relationship involves and how *good* it is. It involves the filling of the whole horizon of the imagination with the beloved one, so that there is constant meditation on one's uniqueness and beauty and on one's desirability. It involves constant renewal of the springs of our love, as each *reminds* the other of his or her uniqueness and beauty in frank and straightforward terms, and both return to the beginning of infatuation to remember the context in which the relationship first blossomed. Communication, which can also be called intercourse, is centrally important to this renewal.

It involves, finally, generosity—not just in words but also in all our self-giving to each other. Generosity in the giving of our bodies is one aspect of this, as enthusiastic wooing meets its reciprocation in enthusiastic response (see how the lovers in 7:6–13 tell each other how much they want each other!) and in ever-new experiences of sexual bliss. It is in this "senseless" abandonment to one another that we will find it easier to be erotically insensible to others, whether in thought or in deed. It is in the wholehearted focusing of *eros* on our one life-partner and friend that we will find ourselves more able to see clearly just how truly insane is the culture's view of sexual expression. It is herein that the power of the "little foxes" of life to bite and to spoil our vineyard will be diminished.

It turns out, therefore, that it is by no means inappropriate to sing, as we prepare to make our marriage vows (or as we renew them daily), "Forgive our foolish ways; reclothe us in our rightful mind." The reclothing of our mind is precisely what we require as we begin married life and also as we proceed each day on the journey, for to understand and live out Christian marriage is to embrace one of the ways in which we "in purer lives thy service find, in deeper reverence praise." Some of us need to be reclothed so that we understand that radical commitment is good, for we have lived in a world that knows little about commitment. Others need to be reclothed in order to understand what purity of thought and action regarding a husband and wife means, for they have lived too long in a semiadulterous condition, with the loyalty of heart and mind fragmented, an attitude so widely believed to be normal that they have not even noticed.

Others need to be reclothed in their mind, frankly, in order that they can with greater enthusiasm and joy get unclothed in their body, for they have inhabited a world in which sexual expression is not entirely compatible with Christian virtue and where duty has been more important than joy. In resisting what they consider evil and in failing to give themselves wholeheartedly to wife or husband, they do not understand just how wide they are opening the door to temptation and sin. We all need reclothing, every day, in this matter of love, sex, and marriage, for we are all, to some extent, naked and ashamed.

> All of you who were baptized into Christ have clothed yourselves with Christ. (Gal. 3:27)

> Therefore, I urge you, brothers, in view of God's mercy, to offer your bodies as living sacrifices, holy and pleasing to God—this is your spiritual act of worship. Do not conform any longer to the pattern of this world, but be transformed by the renewing of your mind. Then you will be able to test and approve what God's will is—his good, pleasing and perfect will. (Rom. 12:1–2)

Song of Songs 8:1–14

¹ If only you were to me like a brother,
    who was nursed at my mother's breasts!
Then, if I found you outside,
    I would kiss you,
    and no one would despise me.
² I would lead you
    and bring you to my mother's house—
    she who has taught me.
I would give you spiced wine to drink,
    the nectar of my pomegranates.
³ His left arm is under my head
    and his right arm embraces me.
⁴ Daughters of Jerusalem, I charge you:
    Do not arouse or awaken love
    until it so desires.

⁵ Who is this coming up from the desert
    leaning on her lover?

Under the apple tree I roused you;
    there your mother conceived you,
    there she who was in labor gave you birth.
⁶ Place me like a seal over your heart,
    like a seal on your arm;
for love is as strong as death,
    its jealousy unyielding as the grave.
It burns like blazing fire,
    like a mighty flame.
⁷ Many waters cannot quench love;
    rivers cannot wash it away.
If one were to give
    all the wealth of his house for love,
    it would be utterly scorned.

⁸ We have a young sister,
    and her breasts are not yet grown.
What shall we do for our sister
    for the day she is spoken for?

⁹ If she is a wall,
　　we will build towers of silver on her.
If she is a door,
　　we will enclose her with panels of cedar.

¹⁰ I am a wall,
　　and my breasts are like towers.
Thus I have become in his eyes
　　like one bringing contentment.
¹¹ Solomon had a vineyard in Baal Hamon;
　　he let out his vineyard to tenants.
Each was to bring for its fruit
　　a thousand shekels of silver.
¹² But my own vineyard is mine to give;
　　the thousand shekels are for you, O Solomon,
　　and two hundred are for those who tend its fruit.

¹³ You who dwell in the gardens
　　with friends in attendance,
　　let me hear your voice!

¹⁴ Come away, my lover,
　　and be like a gazelle
or like a young stag
　　on the spice-laden mountains.

Original
Meaning

THE OPENING SCENES of the Song of Songs concern a woman whose brothers have previously been angry with her and have made her "take care" (*nṭr*) of the vineyards (1:6). The only possible reason for the anger that could be found in 1:6 lies in her claim that she has not taken care of her own "vineyard." She is in love with a man, who is associated (like the vineyards) with the countryside. She now finds herself at the royal court and at the beck and call of the king—another male figure who interposes himself between the woman and her lover (as in 3:6–11). There are thus significant obstacles to be overcome if the lovers are to continue their relationship—something hinted at in the two dream sequences of 3:1–4 and 5:2–7, in the midst of dialogues of the deepest intimacy and mutuality throughout 1:2–2:17; 4:1–5:1; 6:4–7:13.

　　Chapter 8 draws many of these threads together as the Song of Songs comes to its conclusion. The obstacles to the coveted relationship are implied already in verses 1–5 in the references to those who would "despise" the woman for her kisses (v. 1) and in the allusion to the king's bed (v. 5a). The woman's brothers themselves apparently speak in verses 8–9, drawing a sharp retort from the woman in verses 10–12, which establishes her independence from both the brothers and Solomon. This response returns to the language of vineyards and "keepers" (*noṭᵉrim;* NIV "tenants" in v. 11; "those who tend" in v. 12) already introduced in chapter 1. The passion of the lover's relationship, finally, is powerfully communicated in verses 5b–7, and the song ends with their words to each other as they transcend all obstacles and reaffirm their love (vv. 13–14).

The man has previously and on several occasions referred to his beloved as "sister" (4:9, 10, 12; 5:1–2), which speaks of intimacy and closeness of relationship. She has never before referred to him as "brother," however. When the word is eventually used in 8:1, it expresses a desire that cannot be realized. Only in her dreams is she able to go outside (3:2; 8:1), find (*mṣ²,* 3:4; 8:1) her lover, and bring him to her "mother's house" (*bet ²immi,* 3:4; 8:2). Even in her dreams she has encountered opposition (5:7). It is only in the private world of her relationship with her lover that words like "sister" and "bride," and indeed "brother," have any substance to them and that her deep desire for intimacy with him, first announced in 1:2, can be satisfied.

As the woman looks back on that request in 1:2 for kisses and lovemaking that are better than wine, and as she indeed now lies in her lover's arms (8:3), having just spoken with him about the wine that flows from her mouth to his (7:8–9),[1] she recognizes the gulf that separates the real and public world from the world of dream and private moment. The world in which she must for much of her time live her life does not know her lover as "brother"; it is in fact inhabited by real brothers, who stand in the way of her love. She is not able to kiss him in public, therefore, without risking public contempt,[2] nor is she able to bring him to the family home to taste her "wine" or "nectar of . . . pomegranates"—to join her in sexual union (cf.

---

1. The play on kissing/drinking that is already found in places like 1:2 and 7:9 becomes explicit wordplay in 8:1–2: "I would kiss you [*²eššaqᵉka*] . . . I would give you to drink [*²ašqᵉka*] spiced wine."

2. It is not clear whether this is the reality of public life only in the city (of which the mention of the mother's house reminds us, cf. 3:4) or also out in the countryside. Our lack of certainty here is allied to our lack of certainty as to whether the couple are "husband and wife" only in their own eyes or also in the eyes of at least some other people (see comments on 4:1–5:1). To add uncertainty to uncertainty, we do not know whether it is the *public* nature of the demonstration of affection that is societally problematic (even if they *were* man and wife) or the fact that they would not be regarded by the observers as having sufficiently close family ties with each other. Gen. 26:8; 29:11 do not help us at all here (in spite of some claims to the contrary), since in the first case the caress was certainly not intentionally public and in the second case it was certainly not sexual.

4:13; 6:11; 7:12, for the erotic overtones of "pomegranate").[3] She must rest content with what they have.

In the context, which includes the woman's own description of her "rousing" (ʿwr) the man and of the nature of their love (8:5b—7), the charge of verse 4 not to "arouse or awaken" (ʿwr) love until the right time is particularly clearly heard not only as warning about the dangerous power of love but also as a warning about the complications it brings to life (cf. 2:7; 3:5). Both aspects are developed in 8:5—12.

The speakers who refer in verse 5 to the woman and her lover are not explicitly identified, but they are most naturally taken to be the "daughters of Jerusalem" who have just been addressed in verse 4. This was also the case in 3:6, where the same question is asked: "Who is this coming up from the desert?" The interpretation offered in the comments on 3:6 earlier identified the "this" as the female lover. This same woman is certainly referred to here in 8:5. In our comments on 3:6 we also understood the "desert" as the royal bed. It is interesting, then, to notice the different way in which 3:6 and 8:5 end and are then developed. Song of Songs 3:6 has the woman arising from the royal bed in the way that smoke rises up into the sky when sacrifices are burnt; 3:7—11 then focus on the bed itself rather than the woman who is in it, emphasizing the impersonal nature of what happens between the king and his women. Song of Songs 8:5, by contrast, has the woman arising from the bed, leaning for support on her beloved man;[4] a highly personal and intimate address follows, in which the woman describes their relationship.[5]

There is a stark contrast, then, between these two passages, which implies that this second "ascending from the desert" is a leave-taking of the royal palace to match the arrival of the woman there in chapter 1. As the two

---

3. The mother, it seems, not only provides the accommodation for the union (3:4) but has also been the girl's mentor in preparing her for sexual experience (she has "taught" her daughter).

4. The verb *rpq* is otherwise unknown in Old Testament Heb., but its meaning in postbiblical Heb. fits the context here well. A related later noun *marpiq* means "elbow" (see Pope, *Song*, 662—63).

5. The speaker is not clearly identified in v. 5b, and some have argued that it is the man (whose mother is not otherwise mentioned in the Song). The context certainly favors the woman, however, who clearly speaks in vv. 6—7 (as the gender of the suffixes indicates). She has previously asked the wind to "awake" (ʿwr) in 4:16 and to blow the fragrances of her garden abroad so that her lover may be aroused and come into that garden. Now she claims similarly to have "awoken" *him* to sexual desire in 8:5 (also ʿwr; NIV "roused"). It is because she has done so, indeed, with all the difficulties (as well as the ecstasies) that have ensued, that she knows enough to warn the daughters of Jerusalem *not* to "arouse or awaken" love before its time (ʿwr twice in 8:4 and earlier in 2:7; 3:5). The panic-in-loss of the dream associated with the awakening of her own heart (ʿwr in 5:2) is perhaps still fresh in her mind.

lovers walk away together, she reminds her lover of a previous amorous encounter that took place, not in a "desert," but in an orchard (8:5b; see comments on "apple tree" in 2:3)—a place linked to his own conception and birth, just as the house of the woman's mother was linked with *her* conception (and presumably birth, 3:4). The associations are once again those of intimate family relations. It was in this sacred, fruitful place that she aroused and awakened his love.

Having thus aroused and awakened it, she looks now for reciprocation (8:6). She wants her man to place her "like a seal" over both his heart and his arm. The seal was a valuable possession in the ancient world, both in terms of its manufacture (made of precious and semiprecious metals and stones) and of its use (to mark and protect other possessions). It was commonly kept in close proximity to its owner, whether on a cord around the neck (Gen. 38:18) or as a ring on the hand (Gen. 41:42; Jer. 22:24; Hag. 2:23). The woman desires her lover to clasp her close to him in the same way,[6] in response to her loving movement toward him in Song of Songs 8:5b.

There follows a reflection on the nature of the love they share, which makes clear its powerful and enduring nature.[7] It is "as strong as death" itself— the most powerful of enemies in the Bible and a force that cannot be overcome by mere mortals. Death comes to all. Yet love, we are told, is its equal, and the passion[8] that the lovers share is as stubborn and unrelenting as the underworld (šᵊʾol; NIV "grave"), which pursues all living things to swallow

---

6. The imagery of the "seal" might lead us to expect a reference to the hand rather than the arm in v. 6. "Arm" is, in fact, regularly explained as a poetic synonym for "hand." This may be so, but it is also likely that the imagery is being influenced not only by the idea of the seal but also by the idea of the embrace in which the lover clasps his beloved with his arms to his heart. The general idea of carrying important things around the neck and close to the heart is also found in Prov. 6:20–23, where the young man is to remain in intimate relationship with his parents' advice—advice that concerns, in particular, relationships with women.

7. The sense of the NIV's "for" before "love" in v. 6 is unclear. How, precisely, does the request "place me . . ." lead on to the statement "love is as strong as death . . ."? It might be better to understand Heb. *ki* at this point simply as asseverative: "Surely love is as strong as death . . ."

8. The translation "jealousy" is perhaps not the best, given the almost entirely negative connotations this word has come to have in English usage. Heb. *qinʾa* refers to passionate love that acts in protection of the loved one and of the covenant relationship constituted in the love relationship. It is used, e.g., of God's love for Israel, which leads him to fight on Israel's behalf and to direct his anger against her enemies. It is evidently a good thing in itself, although it can lead mortal beings, touched by sin, to actions that must be judged as wrong in the context of the Bible's ethical teaching as a whole (e.g., Prov. 6:34). A better translation, therefore, is "passion," which does not carry the same baggage in modern English usage as "jealousy" does.

them up. In this respect it is also like "blazing fire," looking for things to consume. It is indeed like "the flame of the LORD,"[9] who is himself a consuming fire (Ex. 24:17; Deut. 4:24; Heb. 12:29), particularly in the respect that "many [better, 'mighty'] waters cannot quench love [and] rivers cannot wash it away" (Song 8:7).

The background echoes here are of the mighty waters (*mayim rabbim*) or rivers (*neharot*) that are the powers of chaos, which only the Lord God can overcome.[10] His flame is by no means extinguished by these waters, nor is the flame of human love. Love is so utterly precious to those who experience it, indeed, that it is regarded as beyond price. No amount of wealth would be exchanged for it if the offer were ever made, and the person offering it would in fact be regarded contemptuously by the lovers: "He would be utterly scorned"[11] (8:7).

True love is thus valued far more highly by those who know it intimately and who "scorn" (*bwz*) those who wish to buy it (8:7) than by people who view it from the outside and are apt to "despise" (*bwz*) those who give expression to it (8:1). Lovers *utterly* scorn those who think they can buy love, indeed (the emphatic Heb. *boz yabuzu*, v. 7), whereas women who kiss lovers in public are only routinely (and less emphatically) despised by society (*yabuzu*, v. 1).

The contrast that is thus set up between those who know love and those who regard it as a commodity to be bought and sold is especially intriguing in view of what follows in 8:8–12, for here we meet various people who seem to view love in precisely the commercial way just alluded to. The speakers in verses 8–9 are not explicitly identified, but the mention of "little sister," the role of brothers elsewhere in the Old Testament in overseeing the arrangements for the marriages of sisters (e.g., Gen. 24:29–60; Judg. 21:22), and the earlier reference to "brothers" in Song of Songs 1:6 lead us most naturally to think of the woman's brothers as the contributors here. These brothers regard her as their possession ("*we have* a young sister") as well as their responsibility ("what shall we do to/for our sister until the day she is spoken for?"—i.e., on the day when her hand is requested in marriage, 1 Sam. 25:39).

---

9. The Heb. is *šalhebetya*, in which the final *ya* appears to be the short form of the divine name "Yahweh," which is known from such passages as Ps. 118:5. Since divine names can sometimes indicate a superlative (e.g., Ps. 36:6, where the NIV renders "mountains of El" as "mighty mountains"), the word can be translated "mighty flame" or "most vehement flame," but the context, with its various allusions to the cosmic forces of death and chaos that Yahweh elsewhere in the Old Testament is regularly described as overcoming, favors the more literal translation.

10. Note, e.g., Gen. 1:1–31; Isa. 43:1–2, 16–17; 51:9–10; also Ps. 69:1–2.

11. It is possible to translate: "it [the wealth] would be utterly scorned." The scorning of the man is a better match for the scorning of the woman in v. 1, however.

Their answer to their own question is given in verse 9. They recognize that the sister is both a "wall" and a "door." The wall speaks of fortification and impregnability, indeed virginity; their task is to ornament as well as to strengthen this "wall" with "towers" (lit., "a tower") of silver, increasing both its impregnability and its beauty and thus its value to a potential suitor.

The "door" (*delet*) is a more ambiguous thing, both preventing people from passing through the opening in a city wall and allowing them, under certain circumstances, to do so. We have already read of the woman's "opening" (*petaḥ*) in 7:13. To the woman as "door" these men apparently respond in a different way: They literally "besiege" (NIV "enclose") her with a "plank" of cedar (a wood famed for strength and durability, 8:9), laying emphasis now on defense rather than on beautification.[12] They see their task, in other words, both as ensuring that men stay away from their sister until the proper time and as making sure that she is a prize catch when that time comes. They themselves are, evidently, the arbiters of what the proper time might be.

Possession is also the focus of verses 11 and 12b. Here it is Solomon himself who owns something—a "vineyard" in Baal Hamon, which is entrusted to others so that they may "tend" its fruit. The NIV refers to these people as "tenants" (v. 11), but this is misleading. The Hebrew is *noṭrim*, which is exactly the same word as "tend" in verse 12; the same verbal root also appears twice in 1:6, where the woman tells the daughters of Jerusalem that her brothers made her "take care" of the vineyards, although she did not "take care" of her own. Elsewhere in the Old Testament this verb is used of maintaining anger over a long period of time (Lev. 19:18; Ps. 103:9; Jer. 3:5, 12; Nah. 1:2). It refers in the Song of Songs simply to the maintenance of the vineyard, and the relevant line in 8:11 is best translated: "He entrusted the vineyard to overseers."

This particular Solomonic vineyard is extraordinarily valuable: "A man would bring for its fruit one thousand silver pieces" (v. 11).[13] It is above all the fantastic price that alerts us to the fact that we are not dealing here with a literal vineyard. The "vineyard" is once again, as characteristically in this

---

12. The NIV seems to be thinking of still further decoration in v. 9b, with its "panels of cedar." If this is indeed what the NIV means, one can only say that, while the beautification of the woman as "wall" is comprehensible, it is not clear why these men would be desirous of making the woman as "door" attractive to others. The imagery is better understood as indicating the boarding up of the "city" rather than the beautifying of it. The contrast is then more clearly seen between the woman-as-fortified (but also beautiful)-city in v. 9 and the woman-as-city-at-peace-with-the-enemy in v. 10 (see below).

13. The NIV appears to be suggesting that it is the keepers of the vineyard who bring the money, but this makes little sense (esp. since they only receive back two hundred silver pieces in v. 12—a poor return on their investment). The keepers only look after the vineyard; it is the visitors who are charged money for access to its fruit.

song, simply a metaphor for a woman—one of the most valuable of Solomon's possessions in "Baal Hamon." The place name is interesting, for it not only means "husband of a multitude" (alluding to Solomon's harem, as the figure of one thousand possibly also does, cf. 1 Kings 11:3) but also evokes through its use of "Baal" (the Canaanite deity so often mentioned in 1–2 Kings and elsewhere in the Old Testament) the story in 1 Kings 11, where Solomon's many wives lead him astray into idolatry. Here is one prized possession among the many possessions of the idolater king (cf. Song 6:8). The truly mutual love of one man and one woman as described in 8:5–7 (cf. 6:9), by contrast, invokes a form of the name of Israel's God, "Yahweh."

Speaking out of the midst of all these men with their prized female possessions we find, in 8:10 and 12a, the woman who has already spoken in 8:5b–7. She, it seems, is both the "young sister" whom the brothers in verses 8–9 regard as living under their domination and protection and the "vineyard" that Solomon regards as his most treasured possession in verse 11. Her words represent a firm statement of independence in respect of both. It seems as if she is looking both to the past and to the present and future as she speaks for herself, rather than being "spoken for." She remembers her brothers' claims and rejoices in having escaped their control.

It may once have been the case that her breasts were not fully developed and that she was simply the object of her brothers' construction plans, with their "towers of silvers" and "planks of cedar." She is now a "wall," however, that has assuredly been breached, as a matter of her own free choice. She has no need any longer of their ornamental "silver towers," for she has towers of her own—her mature breasts; these "towers" are by no means defensive fortifications but themselves draw her lover into her "city." In these towers he finds "contentment" (*šalom* in 8:10, a sense of well-being and peaceful satisfaction).[14]

The mention of contentment or peace, however, reminds us of that other reality of the woman's present and her future. She knows not only a lover who finds in her breasts "peace" (*šalom*) but also a king whose name is "Solomon" (*šᵉlomoh*). In response to Solomon's claim to ownership of her as "vineyard," she responds most forcibly: "My own vineyard is mine to give" (v. 12). The Hebrew is stronger still than this NIV translation suggests; literally it reads: "My vineyard which is mine is my own to dispose of" (cf. 1:6 [lit.]: "my vineyard which is mine I have not maintained"). This is not a vineyard that can be entered simply by the payment of a fee, even if the fee-paying visitor

14. The point is that the brothers prepared for war, fortifying the sister against prospective enemies (lovers), while the sister has offered terms of peace. The "towers" (albeit not the ones built by the brothers) have indeed proved attractive to the conquering army, but the fortification of the door has quietly been dispensed with, so that the wall is not so impregnable as previously.

who brings with him his "thousand pieces of silver" is the mighty Solomon himself, who owns the vineyard.[15]

That the silver and the vineyard can have nothing to do with each other is made clear in the structuring of verse 12: "My vineyard which is mine [Heb. *li*] is my own to dispose of; the thousand pieces of silver are yours [Heb. *lᵉka*], O Solomon; and two hundred belong to those who take care of the fruit [Heb. *lᵉnotᵉrim*]." In other words: "Keep your money, O king—with the exception of what you owe your employees." The "silver" (*kesep*) that symbolizes throughout verses 8–12 the possession of the female by the male (vv. 9, 11, 12b) is thus evidently despised by the woman. Money has nothing to do with true love—a point already made in a different way in verse 7. The woman thus emphatically rejects all these male attempts to "look after" her "fruit," whether the males are the brothers or the *notᵉrim* of verses 11–12 (presumably those who oversee the royal harem).[16] She will not be possessed by any man other than the one she has chosen (v. 6).

This stark reminder of the common realities of life for women in ancient Israel—owned by men and traded as possessions from one to the other in marriage—sets in sharp relief the love poetry of the whole song and the relationship to which we return as chapter 8 closes. The beloved man comes to the boundaries of the "gardens," where the woman and those companions[17] whose voices have often been heard throughout this song are to be found. He longs to hear her voice. Her voice, when it responds, invites his intimacy.

This is not the defiant response to brothers and the king of a woman who is viewed as possession. It is the openhearted and willing response to a lover of a woman who is viewed only as beloved. She invites him to run like a

---

15. Solomon is thus apparently portrayed both as owner of the vineyard and also as prospective, fee-paying consumer of the fruit. It is a complex image, but it is difficult otherwise to know how to make sense of the verse. Nothing in the Song encourages us to adopt the only other plausible interpretation—that Solomon himself did not visit the vineyard but simply allowed others to use it for a fee (cf. 1:4, 12; 3:6–11). In all likelihood the reference to the "fee" is simply a means of emphasizing that the woman was an exceedingly precious possession as far as the king was concerned and at the same time beyond all other men's grasp (who could afford one thousand silver pieces?). This fiction is developed in order to make one main point: that even Solomon, who could afford the fee, was not for that reason allowed access.

16. The question remains in all of this as to what, precisely, the relationship is between Solomon and the brothers. The implication seems to be that it is the brothers who have first intervened to prevent their sister's relationship with her lover and who have then later arranged for her to enter the royal harem.

17. The word is *hᵃberim*, which appeared also of the shepherds in 1:7. In this context in 8:13, however, it presumably refers only to the female companions and confidantes of the woman, rather than also to the broader male group who characteristically appear in the Song associated with the man.

gazelle or a stag over the spice-laden mountains, her breasts—those very places in which he has taken such pleasure throughout the preceding episodes. It is perhaps testimony to the seriousness of the contrast between the relationships of 8:8–12 and that of 8:13–14, however, that whereas a similar request from the man in 2:14 that he should hear her voice was followed by the teasing of 2:15, no such teasing is found in 8:14. Here the request for speech is met straightforwardly by a response similar to that in 2:17—an immediate invitation to sexual consummation. She moves, on this occasion, directly to the point; it is with this point that the Song of Songs, fittingly, ends.

THROUGHOUT THE SONG of Songs, the lovers' relationship has been played out against the background of the often harsh realities of life in the ancient world. Chapter 8 is no exception. This was a world in which it was *not* generally the case that "if one were to give all the wealth of his house for love, it would be utterly scorned" (8:7). Quite the contrary; it was a world in which women were routinely regarded as possessions to be traded from one male (or group of males) to another, and "profit" was central to the exercise—whether the gain was in terms of money, status, or power. Marriage was entirely bound up with economics and politics, and there was only limited room for individual choice or indeed romantic love (unless one was fortunate enough to find such love in marriage after the fact). It was a world in which lovers might occasionally propose, but in which dominant males like the brothers or the king regularly disposed.

The harshest reality of all, however, we do not touch upon in this song before we arrive at this final chapter. It is the reality that threatens every life, whether invested with temporal power or not—the reality of death.

Death, as the book of Ecclesiastes so powerfully reminds us, overshadows all of life. It is a mighty power, as the peoples of the ancient Near East already understood when they characterized Death as a hungry deity, dragging all life down into the deep pit from which there could be no escape—the world of the dead, from which no return was possible. The god in question was known in the Canaanite pantheon—evoked by the allusion to the deity "Baal" in 8:11—as "Mot." Death was thus one aspect of the dark and disorderly side of existence that stood in ongoing tension with creative life and order and was routinely associated with images like the sea and sea monsters. The Old Testament itself reflects this worldview in various passages, as when it speaks, for example, of the world of the dead as a place that even righteous Job will experience as darkness and chaos and from which even he will not return (Job 7:9–10; 10:20–22). It is a place in which a person is separated from God

(Ps. 6:5; 30:9; 115:17). It is a ravenous beast that waits to devour its victims (Isa. 5:14; Hab. 2:5). Song of Songs 8:6–7 itself reflects this general perspective in alluding to death in terms of unrelenting power and watery chaos.

In what sense is love as strong as this great power of death (8:6)? It seems a ridiculous statement—a piece of human bravado in the face of crushing, overwhelming reality.[18] It is very much the kind of statement that Qohelet in the book of Ecclesiastes would savagely attack. Death clearly comes to all—whether to those who seek to make some "profit" out of life and love or to those whose love has been pure and undefiled. Love can certainly be enjoyed while we live, but it must be enjoyed while we live precisely because it cannot be enjoyed when we die (Eccl. 9:7–10). Death, Qohelet would say, is much stronger than love, and nowhere is love as unyielding as the grave. Even if love for the departed continues for a short time after death in the hearts of the survivors, death soon obliterates that as well. The flame is extinguished, despite Song of Songs 8:6. It is, in the end, no match for the rivers of death that deluge it, despite 8:7. Thus would Qohelet speak; and common sense must lead us, as astute observers of the world, to agree. Death is much stronger than love—despite the ludicrous De Beers TV ad inviting men, as 1999 closed, to show their women (by purchasing a diamond) that they would love them for another thousand years.[19]

We require a context beyond observable reality, therefore, if we are to regard 8:6–7 as anything other than desperate hyperbole. We require, in fact, the canonical context in which the Song of Songs is set. We need to recognize, first, a crucial difference between the Old Testament view of the nature of death and the view typically found in the literature of the surrounding cultures. Simply put, reality in Old Testament thinking is not in the end dualistic. Good and evil are not two equally matched powers locked in an endless struggle that has an uncertain outcome. There is one God; there are not two, and there certainly are not many. Death in Old Testament thought is, therefore, although a formidable enemy, not a god. It is a power that is, like other powers and principalities in the cosmos, subject to the sovereignty and power of God.

---

18. W. G. E. Watson, "Love and Death Once More (Song of Songs 8:6)," *VT* 47 (1997): 385–86, makes the act of love itself "a defiant act against death because, in effect, the possible product of such a union is life."

19. It is for this reason impossible to agree with M. Sadgrove, "The Song of Songs as Wisdom Literature," *Studia Biblica 1978 I: Papers on Old Testament and Related Themes*, E. A. Livingstone, ed. (JSOTS 11; Sheffield: JSOT Press, 1979), 245–48, on p. 248, when he says: "In this exploration of the complex psychology of erotic love . . . and in the climactic conclusion that 'love is strong as death,' wisdom is indeed to be found." It is not at all clear within the frame of the Song taken by itself that there is any wisdom to be found here at all.

God can, indeed, deliver mortal beings from this power (e.g., Ps. 18:4–19). Perhaps the best narrative example of this reality in the Old Testament, because of the way in which the story consciously addresses the question of whether gods like Baal and Mot are stronger than the living Lord, is found in 1 Kings 17.[20] Here Elijah first challenges, in God's name, the assumption that Baal is the god of fertility. He is not the god of fertility, it turns out, even in the very heartland of Baal worship in Sidon and its environs. It is the living God who brings drought and sustains both Elijah and the widow with her son in the midst of the drought. It is the living God who, faced by "Mot's" claims over the boy, is able even to storm the world of the dead and bring him back to life. There is only one true God, and no other power is able to withstand him.

God can redeem mortal beings from death's power, and beyond that, God will one day destroy the power of death altogether, as Isaiah testifies in Isaiah 25:7–9:

> On this mountain he will destroy
>   the shroud that enfolds all peoples,
> the sheet that covers all nations;
>   he will swallow up death forever.
> The Sovereign LORD will wipe away the tears
>   from all faces;
> he will remove the disgrace of his people
>   from all the earth.
>   The LORD has spoken.
> In that day they will say,
> "Surely this is our God;
>   we trusted in him, and he saved us.
> This is the LORD, we trusted in him;
>   let us rejoice and be glad in his salvation."

It is this vision that is picked up in the New Testament, of course, and interpreted in terms of Jesus' own death and resurrection and their consequences for all humanity. God's self-giving love brings Jesus to the cross and to the tomb and to the apparent defeat of love that has been rejected and trampled upon. Jesus' descent into the world of the dead is only a temporary one, however. He rises again, love victorious over the grave, and the ultimate consequence of this will be the destruction of death itself (1 Cor. 15:12–28, 50–55; Rev. 21:4). It is important to note that the announcement of death's demise in Revelation 21:1–4 is accompanied both by the observation that

---

20. See Provan, *1 and 2 Kings*, 132–35.

---

there is no longer any sea (v. 1—all chaos has been dispelled, all sea monsters destroyed, as in Isa. 27:1) and by the proclamation of the ongoing wedding between God and his faithful people. Love has proved as strong as death indeed. It has, in fact, proved stronger.

It is only the whole biblical story, then, as it moves from the creation of the world (where the loving God first imposes order on chaos and brings forth a good world, Gen. 1:2), through the account of human rebellion against God and the first appearance of death (Gen. 3; cf. 2:17), and on toward redemption and renewal, that makes sense of the apparently hopelessly optimistic statement in Song of Songs 8:6 that "love is as strong as death." It even helps us to see that this statement is not quite optimistic enough. The power of God's love is vastly greater than the power of death, outlasting it by the distance of eternity.

In the light of this great truth we ourselves can be assured that our own love for others, although only a pale reflection of the divine love, will also pass through the valley of the shadow of death and endure. There will be no marriage in life beyond death, it is true (Matt. 22:30), but we may be sure that all that is best about our marriages as we give ourselves to our wives and husbands in love and intimacy will be found there:

> Heaven will be all marriage. Indeed, in earthly marriage we may detect the sign and promise that in eternity everyone is to be married to everyone else in some transcendent and unimaginable union, and everyone will love everyone else with an intensity akin to that which now is called "being in love," and which impels individual couples to spend their whole lives together. In this way Christian marital love is (or should be) as close as we are likely to experience to being "a piece of Heaven on earth," for it is a true leftover from Paradise.[21]

Even if in the end profit is indeed futile, love most certainly is not. Love lasts. Its fire is eternal (Song 8:6). The whole Bible story allows us to say so and not sound foolish. It allows us to speak to our lovers thus, without reservation:

> How do I love thee? Let me count the ways.
> I love thee to the depth and breadth and height
> My soul can reach, when feeling out of sight
> For the ends of Being and ideal Grace.
> I love thee to the level of every day's
> Most quiet need, by sun and candle-light.
> I love thee freely, as men strive for right;
> I love thee purely, as they turn from praise.

---

21. M. Mason, *The Mystery of Marriage* (Portland: Multnomah, 1985), 68.

I love thee with the passion put to use
In my old griefs, and with my childhood's faith.
I love thee with a love I seemed to lose
With my lost saints—I love thee with the breath,
Smiles, tears, of all my life!—and, if God choose,
I shall but love thee better after death.[22]

Death cannot stop true love. All it can do
is delay it for a while.[23]

The Princess Bride is a wonderful movie. The committed love of two young lovers, Wesley and Buttercup, survives separation and all the threats introduced by a wicked king who pursues the woman for purposes of his own. It eventually survives even death. Wesley is discovered only to be "mostly dead" and, revived by a miracle worker, he is able to rescue his beloved just in time from the clutches of the horrible monarch. Justice is thoroughly done, and all the good characters (including Wesley and Buttercup) ride off into the sunset.

This is not how life truly is, of course. Good does not always triumph over evil in the world of our experience, and justice often falls victim to injustice. Powers intervene in our lives to restrict and deny our choices, and they overwhelm us rather than in the end being overwhelmed. The course of true love does not usually run smooth, and if we find love, it is all too quickly snatched away, as committed to the other as we may be. Chaos all too often marks our lives, and death follows in its train, ensuring that we are entirely rather than "mostly" dead and that happy endings are beyond us. We ride, not into the sunset, but into the darkness. That is how life truly is, as far as it can be observed.

Yet the myth that "death cannot stop true love" is a powerful one, which continues to captivate our souls. We have an insatiable desire to have it told to us again and again. Hollywood regularly obliges, knowing that the myth will always sell. Against all sense, it seems, many human beings are incurable romantics and optimists. They will not accept that fairy stories are only fairy stories. They have a deep need to believe them to be true, even as they have ceased to believe in any God who might reveal to them what Truth is.

Perhaps it is just as well, for those who look observable reality straight in the eyes are often unbalanced by the experience; in recognizing death as

---

22. A sonnet of Elizabeth Barrett Browning (1806–1861).
23. Wesley in the movie *The Princess Bride*.

the ultimate power in the universe—because they do not recognize God—they come to promote (whether consciously or unconsciously) a culture of death as a fitting response to it. Where God himself is dead, as Friedrich Nietzsche so famously proclaimed him to be in his book *The Gay Science* (1882), death must evidently be victorious in the end, and it even begins to consume life in the present. For the death of God means there is no longer any truth that can claim absoluteness, universality, and eternity. There is no Truth, only many truths; there is no Right, only self-created moralities.

Nietzsche himself challenged, for example, the idea that such things as exploitation, domination, and injury to the weak are universally objectionable behaviors. Who is to say? God cannot, and when it dawns on people that God cannot because he is dead, what follows is first widespread nihilism (a pervasive sense of purposelessness and meaninglessness) and then widespread idolatry (as people embrace alternative absolutes to God as a way of investing life with meaning). Idolatry leads in turn (as always) to inhumanity to others, as the false gods require their sacrifices.

This is Nietzsche's world, and we currently live in it. It is a culture of death, and romantic escapism is in truth a fairly innocuous response to it when compared with those other responses evoked from human beings as the twentieth century has passed. It has been a century marked at one and the same time both by unparalleled progress in technology and by unparalleled despair and brutality as the value of human beings, set loose from the valuation of God, has plummeted in the world markets.

The cultural passion for romance and fairy story can be seen as an emotional and moral refusal to accept that God is dead even while there has been a widespread intellectual capitulation to the idea. It is a sign of transcendence—an indication that we are indeed created in the image of God and cannot escape that reality even if part of us wishes to. The larger story that makes sense of these fairy stories—the biblical story—has long since been abandoned, yet the culture cannot give up on its hope that *somehow* it *is* true that "death cannot stop true love. All it can do is delay it for a while."

In other words, our culture refuses to accept that what it intuitively knows to be good—self-sacrificing love, commitment, intimacy—has no lasting place in the universe. It insists, against all the evidence, that good, in the end, defeats evil. It does so because the truth of God has not yet been fully suppressed in human hearts or in society and because nihilism has not yet, therefore, become a contagion. We will be in a pitiable state if it ever becomes the normal way of looking at the world, and it may yet, if the youth culture of the present moment is any guide.

Romance is thus seen to be the great leap of faith that modern secular people (and too many unthinking Christians) make in order to escape the realm of death, dimly perceiving that love is indeed stronger than death but lacking any reason to think so. The sexual promiscuity of our culture can itself be understood in a similar way, as a doomed attempt to push away the chaotic darkness of the cosmos through the pursuit of serial intimate encounters with other lost souls. Since it is at least a faith of some kind, romanticism is in the end much closer to the truth than nihilism, for it recognizes, however imperfectly, that Love lies at the heart of things. Only the gospel supplies the larger framework, however, in which its lacks can be made up and its errors corrected. For it tells us of a wooing God whose love makes sense of ours:

Love bade me welcome; yet my soul drew back,
Guilty of dust and sin.
But quick-eyed Love, observing me grow slack
From my first entrance in,
Drew nearer to me, sweetly questioning
If I lacked anything.
"A guest," I answered, "worthy to be here."
Love said, "You shall be he."
"I, the unkind, the ungrateful? Ah, my dear, I cannot look on Thee."
Love took my hand, and smiling, did reply,
"Who made the eyes but I?"[24]

It is the same gospel that proclaims God's love that tells us that we do not need to leap blindly from death to love in the vague hope that love will prevail. It shows us how Love has already prevailed by conquering death. It thus enables us to look forward with confidence and with our eyes open to the future, while enjoying such good things as come our way in the life in the present. It is wonderful Good News, which makes sense even of our fairy stories. It should enable those of us who believe it to live our lives fully in response to our Creator, who made us as physical, sexual, emotional, and spiritual beings to enjoy our lives and thus witness to his glory; and to our Redeemer, who will take us beyond death to share in that glory.

Death has been swallowed up in victory. Where, O death, is your victory? Where, O death, is your sting? (1 Cor. 15:54–55)

For I am convinced that neither death nor life, neither angels nor demons, neither the present nor the future, nor any powers, neither height nor depth, nor anything else in all creation, will be able to separate us from the love of God that is in Christ Jesus our Lord. (Rom. 8:38–39)

---

24. Poem by George Herbert (1593–1633).

Scripture Index

Subject Index

Jerome, 25, 237, 279

Jerusalem, 26, 29, 50, 67, 157, 170, 192, 198, 299, 338; as new Jerusalem, 356, 357

Jesus, 26, 57, 60, 78–80, 95, 100, 108, 111, 113, 118, 120, 123, 136, 144, 158, 160, 174, 184–86, 202, 207–8, 210, 219, 230, 243n, 275–77, 280, 309, 322, 356, 360–61, 374

Jew, 23–24, 32, 34, 57, 170, 235, 237, 239, 240, 276, 278

Jewish law, 278

Jezebel, 322

Job, 93, 131, 156, 184, 267; Job's comforters, 34, 36,

Joseph, 172, 268, 340

Jovinian, 238

joy, 23, 39, 41–42, 67, 71, 73–74, 77–80, 85, 91, 94, 96, 101, 107, 128, 139, 144, 147, 182, 186, 197, 210, 212–13, 219, 221, 224, 228, 274, 277, 280, 292, 305–6, 327, 362

Judah, 170, 198

Judaism, 111, 239, 252n; rabbinic, 238

Judeo-Christian tradition, 109, 278

judgment, 37, 69, 78, 89, 92, 95, 97, 110, 143, 166, 168, 172, 192, 195, 212, 216, 228

justice, 42, 78, 92, 103, 126, 165, 168, 376

Kedar, 267, 267n

Keenan, Brian, 309–10

Khmer Rouge, 111n

Kidron Valley, 350, 350n

King Asa, 194

King David, 26, 29, 67, 317, 335; bodyguard of, 302

King Jeroboam, 338

King Keret, 292

King Manasseh, 306

King Rehoboam, 200

king, 26–27, 29, 50, 67–68, 71–74, 75n, 80–82, 95, 107–8, 126, 148, 163, 164–65, 165n, 166, 167, 169–71, 192, 196, 197, 235, 246, 255, 266, 266n, 269, 269n, 270, 270n, 271, 274, 285, 302, 305–6,

308, 317, 332, 339, 354, 364, 370–72, 376

kingdom, 80, 95, 169, 170, 174, 274, 306; of God, 61, 64, 95, 169, 170–71, 175, 232–33, 250, 252, 307, 322

knowledge, 39, 71, 79, 82–83, 95, 139, 150, 153–54, 156, 158, 180, 182, 198, 205, 226–27, 229

Lamech, 109–10, 307

law, 110, 118, 143, 156, 220, 230, 272, 325; of God, 143, 224, 276, 322–23

letter to the Galatians, 157

Lewis, C. S., 64, 84–85, 254, 325, 329, 341

life, 88, 89; as brief or fleeting, 51, 52, 55, 56, 57, 60, 67, 212, 219; as Christian, 60–61, 99, 111, 122, 233, 243, 251, 253, 291, 345; as fragile, 58; as gift from God, 74, 80, 184, 209–10, 212, 217; as joyful, 221, 224; as meaningless or futile, 76, 91, 106, 130, 218; as mortal, 80; as precious, 60, 139; as serious, 143–44, 221, 224; as unpredictable, 183; control of, 156; earthly, 210; eternal, 145; legalistic approach to, 100; life beyond death, 85, 98; lived before God, 78, 131, 224, 313; lived well, 168; lived wisely, 204; mortal, 151; to be embraced, 96, 142, 206–7; trials in, 181–82; *see also* eternal

light, 75, 130, 172, 199, 312

Lion King, The, 61, 62

Loneliness of the Long Distance Runner, The, 114

literal reading, 237–38, 240n, 241, 244, 247–48, 255

Locke, John, 224

Lord, 27, 39, 41, 95–96, 109, 118–19, 143, 156, 169, 172, 175, 184, 368, 374; of Hosts, 338

love, 89, 96, 120, 134, 145, 179, 180–82, 185, 188, 198, 209–10, 219, 223, 225, 235, 237, 239n, 240–46, 248, 253–55, 265, 273, 277, 284–86, 289–91, 292, 296,

We want to hear from you. Please send your comments about this book to us in care of zreview@zondervan.com. Thank you.

ZONDERVAN.com/
AUTHORTRACKER
follow your favorite authors